365 Homemade Chocolate Cake Recipes

(365 Homemade Chocolate Cake Recipes - Volume 1)

Lori Tyson

Copyright: Published in the United States by Lori Tyson/ © LORI TYSON

Published on October, 12 2020

All rights reserved. No part of this publication may be reproduced, stored in retrieval system, copied in any form or by any means, electronic, mechanical, photocopying, recording or otherwise transmitted without written permission from the publisher. Please do not participate in or encourage piracy of this material in any way. You must not circulate this book in any format. LORI TYSON does not control or direct users' actions and is not responsible for the information or content shared, harm and/or actions of the book readers.

In accordance with the U.S. Copyright Act of 1976, the scanning, uploading and electronic sharing of any part of this book without the permission of the publisher constitute unlawful piracy and theft of the author's intellectual property. If you would like to use material from the book (other than just simply for reviewing the book), prior permission must be obtained by contacting the author at author@bisquerecipes.com

Thank you for your support of the author's rights.

Content

365 AWESOME CHOCOLATE CAKE RECIPES 9

1. 10 Minute Chocolate Pudding Cake Recipe 9
2. 3 Layers Chocolate Ganache Cake Recipe . 9
3. 5 Minute Chocolate Mug Cake Recipe 10
4. 5 Minute Chocolate Mug Cake Recipe 11
5. 5 Layers Chocolate Meringue Cake Recipe 11
6. A Tunnel Runs Through It Chocolate Glazed Chocolate Cake Recipe 12
7. Age Of Ice 4: Scrat On The Floating Island Recipe 13
8. Allergy And Vegan Friendly Chocolate Cake Recipe 14
9. Almond Praline Chocolate Cake Recipe ... 14
10. Amazing Chocolate Cake Recipe 15
11. Aunt Georgies Chocolate Cake Recipe 16
12. Autumn Chocolate Spice Cake Recipe 16
13. BARCARDI RUM CHOCOLATE CAKE Recipe 16
14. BEETROOT CHOCOLATE CAKE Recipe 17
15. Banana Cake With Chocolate Ganache Recipe 17
16. Banana Chocolate Caramel Cake Recipe .. 18
17. Banana Chocolate Turtle Cake Recipe 18
18. Banana Coffee Cake With Chocolate Chip Streusel Recipe 19
19. Banana Coffee Cake With Chocolate Chip Streusel Recipe 19
20. Banana And White Chocolate Mud Cake Recipe 20
21. Beet Chocolate Cake Recipe 20
22. Best Ever Chocolate Cake Recipe 21
23. Bird Nest Chocolate Cake Recipe 21
24. Black Forest Cake With Chocolate Ganache Recipe 22
25. Black Rum Chocolate Cake Recipe 23
26. Bob Sykes Bar B Qs Hersheys Perfectly Chocolate Chocolate Cake Recipe 23
27. Buttermilk Chocolate Cake Recipe 24
28. Butterscotch Chocolate Cake Recipe 24
29. CHOCOLATE CHUNK CAKE Recipe . 25
30. CHOCOLATE COCONUT CAKE Recipe 25
31. CHOCOLATE IRISH TIPSY CAKE Recipe 26
32. CHOCOLATE ORANGE CHEESE CAKE Recipe 26
33. CHOCOLATE PEANUT BUTTER CHEESE CAKE Recipe 27
34. CHOCOLATE SNACK CAKE For HUNGRY KIDS Recipe 27
35. COUSIN Anns Chocolate Chip Brownie Cake Recipe 28
36. CRUNCHY CHOCOLATE PEANUT BUTTER CAKE Recipe 28
37. Carrot Cake With Chocolate Icing Recipe 29
38. Castle Chocolate Cake Recipe 30
39. Celebration Chocolate Raspberry Cake Recipe 31
40. Cheesecake Stuffed Dark Chocolate Cake Recipe 32
41. Cherry Chocolate Cake Recipe 32
42. Cherry Chocolate Chipper Cake Recipe 33
43. Chewy Chocolate Raspberry Cake Recipe 33
44. Chocolate Peppermint Ice Cream Cake Recipe 34
45. Chocolate Almond Crunch Cake Recipe .. 35
46. Chocolate Almond Marble Pound Cake Recipe 35
47. Chocolate And Cherry Polenta Cake Recipe 35
48. Chocolate And Orange Bundt Cake Recipe 36
49. Chocolate Angel Cake Recipe 36
50. Chocolate Angel Food Cake Recipe 37
51. Chocolate Apple Cake Recipe 37
52. Chocolate Applesauce Cake Recipe 38
53. Chocolate Applesauce Cake With Glaze Recipe 38
54. Chocolate Banana Cake Recipe................... 39
55. Chocolate Banana Loaf Cake Recipe 39
56. Chocolate Beet Cake Recipe 40
57. Chocolate Birthday Cake Recipe 40
58. Chocolate Butter Pound Cake Recipe 41
59. Chocolate Butterfinger Cake Recipe 42
60. Chocolate Cake Low In Cholesterol Recipe 42
61. Chocolate Cake Pudding Recipe 42

62. Chocolate Cake Recipe 43
63. Chocolate Cake Without The Box Recipe 43
64. Chocolate Cake In A MUG Recipe 44
65. Chocolate Cake With Four Chocolates Recipe 44
66. Chocolate Cannoli Cake Recipe 45
67. Chocolate Caramel Cake Recipe 45
68. Chocolate Carrot Cake Recipe 46
69. Chocolate Carrot Cake With Cream Cheese Frosting Recipe 47
70. Chocolate Carrot Cake With Chocolate Frosting Recipe 47
71. Chocolate Celebration Cake Recipe 48
72. Chocolate Cherry Beer Cake Recipe 49
73. Chocolate Cherry Bomb Cake Recipe 50
74. Chocolate Cherry Cake Recipe 50
75. Chocolate Cherry Magic Cake Recipe 51
76. Chocolate Cherry Magic Cake Recipe Recipe 51
77. Chocolate Chip Cake Recipe 51
78. Chocolate Chip Cherry Cake Recipe 52
79. Chocolate Chip Cookie Surprise Cake Recipe 52
80. Chocolate Chip Ice Cream Cake Recipe ... 53
81. Chocolate Chip Pound Cake Recipe 54
82. Chocolate Chip Sour Cream Cake Recipe 54
83. Chocolate Coconut Rum Cake Recipe 54
84. Chocolate Coffee Fudge Cake Recipe 55
85. Chocolate Cornflake Cakes Recipe 55
86. Chocolate Covered Cherry Cake Recipe ... 56
87. Chocolate Cream Cake Recipe 56
88. Chocolate Decadence Flourless Cake Recipe 57
89. Chocolate Dobash Cake Recipe 57
90. Chocolate Eclair Cake Recipe 58
91. Chocolate Flan Cake Recipe 58
92. Chocolate Fudge Cake Recipe 58
93. Chocolate Fudge Pecan Cake And Icing Recipe 59
94. Chocolate Fudge Pound Cake Recipe 60
95. Chocolate Glazed Banana Cake Recipe 60
96. Chocolate Glazed Carrot Cake Recipe 61
97. Chocolate Guinness Cake Recipe 61
98. Chocolate HoHo Cake Recipe 62
99. Chocolate Irish Cream Cake Recipe 62
100. Chocolate Italian Cream Cake Recipe 63
101. Chocolate Kahlua Cake Recipe 64

102. Chocolate Lava Cake With Warm Liquid Center Recipe 64
103. Chocolate Layer Cake Recipe 65
104. Chocolate Lovers Dream Cake Recipe 65
105. Chocolate Macaroon Filled Cake Recipe .. 66
106. Chocolate Meringue Cake Recipe 67
107. Chocolate Meringue Surprise Cake Recipe 67
108. Chocolate Mint Layer Cake 1 Recipe 68
109. Chocolate Mocha Mud Cake Recipe 69
110. Chocolate Moist Cake Recipe 70
111. Chocolate Mousse Cake Recipe 70
112. Chocolate Oatmeal Cake Recipe 70
113. Chocolate Oatmeal Cake Mix Cookies Recipe 71
114. Chocolate Orange Cake Recipe 71
115. Chocolate Orange Carrot Cake Recipe 72
116. Chocolate Passion Cake Recipe 73
117. Chocolate Peach Cake Recipe 73
118. Chocolate Peanut Butter Swirl Cake Recipe 73
119. Chocolate Peanut Ripple Cake Recipe 74
120. Chocolate Pistachio Nut Marble Cake Recipe 74
121. Chocolate Polenta Cake Recipe 75
122. Chocolate Potato Cake Recipe 75
123. Chocolate Pound Cake Recipe 76
124. Chocolate Praline Cake Recipe 76
125. Chocolate Praline Mousse Cake Recipe 77
126. Chocolate Prune Cake 1 Recipe 78
127. Chocolate Pudding Cake And Hazelnut Sauce Recipe 79
128. Chocolate Pudding Cake Recipe 79
129. Chocolate Raspberry Ice Cream Cake Recipe 80
130. Chocolate Ribbon Cake Recipe 80
131. Chocolate Sandwich Cake Triggers Passion Recipe 81
132. Chocolate Sandwich Cake Recipe 81
133. Chocolate Sheath Cake With Chocolate Frosting Recipe 82
134. Chocolate Snickerdoodle Cake With Cinnamon Chocolate Cream Cheese Frosting Recipe 82
135. Chocolate Soda Pop Cake Recipe 83
136. Chocolate Sour Cream Cake Recipe 83
137. Chocolate Sourkrout Cake Recipe 84

138. Chocolate Sponge Cake Recipe 84
139. Chocolate Sponge Cake With Fresh Fruit Recipe 85
140. Chocolate Strawberry Cake The Ultimate Combination Recipe 86
141. Chocolate Supreme Layer Cake Recipe 87
142. Chocolate Syrup Bundt Cake Recipe 87
143. Chocolate Syrup Cake Recipe 88
144. Chocolate Toffee Cake Recipe 88
145. Chocolate Triple Layer Cake With Fluffy Chocolate Frosting Recipe 89
146. Chocolate Turtle Cake Recipe 90
147. Chocolate Upside Down Cake Recipe 90
148. Chocolate Valentines Day Cake Recipe 91
149. Chocolate Voodoo Drunken Zombie Cake Recipe 92
150. Chocolate Walnut Apple Cake Recipe 94
151. Chocolate Walnut Cake Recipe 95
152. Chocolate Wave Cake Recipe 95
153. Chocolate Zucchini Cake Recipe 96
154. Chocolate And Raspberry Cake Recipe 97
155. Chocolate Banana Mousse Cake Recipe ... 97
156. Chocolate Cake Vegen Recipe 98
157. Chocolate Cake Wit Blueberry Topping Recipe 98
158. Chocolate Cherry Bavarian Cake Recipe .. 99
159. Chocolate Coconut Cake Recipe 100
160. Chocolate Moist Bundt Cake Recipe 100
161. Chocolate N Cheese Tunnel Cake Recipe 100
162. Chocolate Peppermint Truffle Cake Recipe 101
163. Chocolate Profiteroles Cake Recipe 101
164. Chocolate Truffle Cake With White Chocolate Truffles Recipe 102
165. Chocolate Covered OREO Cookie Cake Recipe 103
166. Chocolate Espresso Layer Cake With Mocha Marscapone Frosting Recipe 104
167. Chocolate Malt Ice Cream Cake Recipe .. 105
168. Chocolate Peanut Butter Cake With Cream Cheese And Butterfinger Frosting Recipe 105
169. Chocolate Peanut Butter Refrigerator Cake Recipe 106
170. Chocolate Raspberry Cake Recipe 106
171. Chocolate Glazed Hazelnut Mousse Cake Recipe 107
172. Chocolate Peanut Butter Cake With Cream Cheese And Butterfinger Frosting Recipe 108
173. Chocolate Peanut Ice Cream Cake Recipe 109
174. Coconut Cake With Chocolate Chunks And Coconut Drizzle Recipe 110
175. Coffee Cake With Chocolate Recipe 110
176. Coffee Chocolate Layer Cake With Mocha Mascarpone Frosting Recipe 111
177. Crazy Chocolate Lava Cake Recipe 112
178. Crazy Green Watercress Sponge Cake And Chocolate Sauce Recipe 112
179. DUNCAN HINES DEEP CHOCOLATE CAKE Recipe 113
180. Dark Chocolate Amaretto Cake Recipe . 113
181. Dark Chocolate Cake With Rich Chocolate Frosting Recipe 114
182. Dark Chocolate Chip Pound Cake Recipe 114
183. Dark Chocolate Chip Whole Wheat Loaf Cake With Chocolate Frosting Recipe 115
184. Death By Chocolate Cake Recipe 115
185. Decadent Lil Chocolate Cheese Cakes Recipe 116
186. Decadent Chocolate Cake Recipe 117
187. Deep Chocolate Cake By Better Homes Amp Gardens Recipe 117
188. Deep Chocolate Triple Layer Cake Recipe 118
189. Deep Dark Chocolate Bundt Cake Recipe 119
190. Deep Dark Chocolate Cake Recipe 119
191. Deep Fried Chocolate Pound Cake Recipe 120
192. Differently Delicious Chocolate Cake Recipe 120
193. Disneys Chocolate Chip Crumb Cakes Recipe 121
194. Double Chocolate Gooey Butter Cake Recipe 121
195. Double Chocolate Lava Cakes Recipe 122
196. Double Chocolate Rum Cake With Rasberry Rum Glaze Recipe 123
197. Double Chocolate Zucchini Cake Recipe 123
198. Double Dark Fudge Brownie Cake With Chocolate Glaze Recipe 124

199. Dr Pepper Chocolate Cake Recipe 124
200. Dr Pepper Chocolate Cake Recipe 124
201. EASY Decadent Chocolate Pudding Cake Recipe 125
202. Earthquake Cake Aka A Quick Version Of German Chocolate Cake Recipe 125
203. Easy Chocolate Mousse Cake Eagle Brand Recipe 125
204. Easy Chocolate Peanut Butter Cake Recipe 126
205. Eggless Chocolate Cake Recipe 126
206. Ever So Moist Chocolate Cake With Chocolate Sour Cream Frosting Recipe 127
207. Extreme Coffee Chocolate Mousse Cake Recipe 128
208. Fabulous Chocolate Flourless Cake Recipe 128
209. Flan Chocolate Cake Recipe 129
210. Flourless Chocolate Cake With Toasted Marshmallows Recipe 129
211. Flourless Chocolate Cake With Chocolate Mousse And Raspberry Sauce Recipe 130
212. Flourless Chocolate Decadence Cake Recipe 131
213. Flourless Chocolate Almond Cake Recipe 132
214. Fondant Chocolate Cake Recipe 132
215. French Chocolate Coffee Cake Recipe ... 133
216. Frozen Chocolate Bar Cookie Cake Recipe 134
217. Fudge Fudge Chocolate Syrup Cake Recipe 134
218. Fudgy Chocolate Layer Cake Recipe 134
219. German Chocolate Cake Recipe 135
220. German Chocolate Pound Cake Recipe .. 136
221. German Chocolate Pound Cake Recipe Recipe 136
222. German Chocolate Upside Down Cake Recipe 137
223. German Chocolate Upside Down Cake Recipe 137
224. German Chocolate Yum Yum Cake Recipe 137
225. German Chocolate Upside Down Cake Recipe 138
226. Giannas Chocolate Whipped Cream Cake Recipe 138

227. Golden Chocolate Cake Recipe 139
228. Heavenly Chocolate Hazelnut Cake Gluten Free Recipe 139
229. Heavenly Deep Dark Chocolate Cake Recipe 140
230. Hersheys Perfectlatey Chocolate Cake Recipe 140
231. Hersheys Perfectly Chocolate Cake Recipe 141
232. Holy Cow Cake Recipe 141
233. Homemade Candy Bar Cake Recipe 142
234. Homemade Chocolate Cake With Homemade Chocolate Frosting Recipe 143
235. Homemade Yellow Cake With Chocolate Buttercream Frosting Recipe 143
236. Hot Chocolate Pudding Cake A La Mode Recipe 144
237. Hush Chocolate Cake Recipe 144
238. I Love A Nutty German Chocolate Cake Recipe 145
239. Individual Chocolate Melting Cakes Recipe 146
240. Irish Cream Chocolate Cake Recipe 146
241. Italian Chocolate Cake Recipe.................. 147
242. Its A Chocolate Wonder Cake With Chocolate Cream Cheese Frosting Recipe 147
243. Jack Daniels Chocolate Cake Recipe....... 148
244. Jetts Chocolate Peanut Butter Cake Recipe 148
245. Jubilee Chocolate Cake Recipe................ 149
246. Killer Chocolate Marshmallow Cake Recipe 149
247. Layered Chocolate Tortilla Cake Recipe 150
248. Liezels Chocolate Cake Recipe................ 150
249. Mango Chocolate Mousse Cake Recipe . 151
250. Maroon Chocolate Cake Recipe 151
251. Mary Starrs Chocolate Wet Cake Recipe 152
252. Mayo Chocolate Syrup Cake Recipe 152
253. Merry Cherry Dense Chocolate Black Forest Easy Cake Recipe 153
254. Mexican Chocolate Icebox Cake Recipe 153
255. Microwave Chocolate Cake Recipe 154
256. Milk Chocolate Bar Cake Recipe 154
257. Mini Chocolate Bundt Cakes With Peanut Butter Filling And Chocolate Glaze Recipe 155
258. Mini Chocolate Christmas Cakes Recipe 155
259. Miracle Orange Chocolate Mini Cakes

Recipe 156
260. Mississippi Chocolate And Coffee Cake Recipe 156
261. Mocha Layer Cake With Chocolate Rum Filling Recipe 157
262. Moist Red Beet Chocolate Cake With Chocolate Cream Cheese Frosting Recipe 158
263. Molten Chocolate Cake Recipe 158
264. Molten Chocolate Cake With Peanut Butter Filling Recipe 159
265. Molten Chocolate Cakes Recipe 159
266. Moms Chocolate Souffle Cake Recipe 160
267. Moosewoods Six Minute Vegan Chocolate Cake Recipe 162
268. Most Dangerous Chocolate Cake In The World Minute Chocolate Mug Cake Recipe 162
269. Mothers Day Chocolate Peanut Ice Cream Cake Recipe 163
270. My Chocolate Fudge Layer Cake Recipe 163
271. My Favorite Chocolate Cake Recipe 164
272. My Moms Chocolate Mayo Cake Recipe 164
273. Non Butter Chocolate Cake Recipe 165
274. Nougat Chocolate Cake Recipe 165
275. Old Fashioned Chocolate Cake And Frosting Recipe 166
276. Omas Chocolate Pudding Cake Recipe... 166
277. Ooey Gooey Double Chocolate Butter Cake 1 Recipe 167
278. Ooh La La Adult Chocolate Cake Recipe 167
279. Orange And Chunksa Dark Chocolate Pound Cake Recipe 168
280. Orange Cola Chocolate Cake Recipe 168
281. Oreo Buttermilk Bundt Cake With Chocolate Glaze Recipe 169
282. Organic Chocolate Fudge Brownie Cake Recipe 170
283. Original German Chocolate Cake With Coconut Pecan Frosting Recipe 170
284. PISTACHIO CHOCOLATE CAKE Recipe 171
285. Party Size One Bowl Chocolate Cake Recipe 171
286. Paul Neumans Chocolate Cake Recipe ... 172
287. Peanut Butter Bundt Cake With Chocolate Peanut Butter Ganache Recipe 172
288. Peanut Buttery Chocolate Cake Recipe ... 173

289. Peppermint Chocolate Pound Cake Recipe 174
290. Peteys Birthday Cherry Chocolate Bundt Cake Recipe 174
291. Pistachio Chocolate Cake Recipe 175
292. Praline Chocolate Jar Cakes Recipe 175
293. REAL And I Mean REAL German Chocolate Cake Recipe 176
294. Raspberry White Chocolate Mousse Cake Recipe 177
295. Rich Beet Chocolate Cake Recipe 178
296. Rich Chocolate Chip Honey Cake Recipe 179
297. Rich Chocolate Pound Cake Recipe 179
298. Run The Extra Mile PB And Chocolate Cake Recipe 180
299. Russian Chocolate Strawberry Cake Recipe 181
300. Shirleyomas Fabulous Chocolate Flourless Cake Recipe 182
301. Shortcut Chocolate Malted Cake Recipe 182
302. Silky Chocolate Truffle Cake Recipe 183
303. Sinful Chocolate Cake Recipe 183
304. Slow Cooker Chocolate Brownie Cake Recipe 184
305. Slow Cooker Chocolate Cake Recipe 184
306. Slow Cooker Chocolate Peanut Butter Spoon Cake Recipe 184
307. Slowbake Buttermilk Chocolate Cake Recipe 185
308. Souffle Chocolate Cake 2 Recipe 185
309. Sour Cream Chocolate Cake Recipe 186
310. Strawberry Chocolate Farm Cake Recipe 187
311. Stumps Chocolate Angels Food Cake Recipe 188
312. Super Chocolatey Zucchini Bread Recipe 188
313. Susans Chocolate Cake Recipe 189
314. Sweet Chocolate Pound Cake Recipe 189
315. Sweet Potato Chocolate Nut Cake Recipe 189
316. TRIPLE CHOCOLATE MARSHMALLOW CAKE Recipe 190
317. TWISTED GERMAN CHOCOLATE CAKE Recipe 190
318. The Devil Made Me Do It Chocolate Cake Recipe 191

319. The Millionaire Chocolate Chip Pound Cake Recipe 191
320. The Mother Of All Chocolate Cakes Recipe 191
321. The Official Killer Chocolate Cake Recipe 192
322. The Perfect Chocolate Cake Recipe 192
323. The Best Chocolate Lovers Cake Recipe 193
324. Three Chocolate Mousse Cake Recipe 194
325. To Die For Chocolate Cake Recipe 195
326. Triple Chocolate Cake Recipe 195
327. Triple Chocolate Coffee Cake Recipe 195
328. Triple Chocolate Pudding Cake With Raspberry Sauce Recipe 196
329. Triple Nut Chocolate Upside Down Cake Recipe 196
330. Triple Layer Chocolate Mousse Cake Recipe 197
331. Twisted German Chocolate Cake Recipe 197
332. Upside Down Chocolate Chip Cake Recipe 198
333. Valentine Chocolate Cake Recipe 198
334. Vegan Chocolate Cake Recipe 199
335. Vegan Chocolate Snack Cake Recipe 199
336. Very Rich Chocolate Fudge Cake Recipe 200
337. White Chocolate Cake With Raspberry Filling Recipe 200
338. White Chocolate Cake With White Chocolate Frosting Recipe 201
339. White Chocolate Coconut Cake Recipe .. 202
340. White Chocolate Fruit Cake Recipe 202
341. White Chocolate Mousse Cake Recipe 203
342. White Chocolate Mousse Sweet Potato Cake Recipe 203
343. White Chocolate Mud Cake Recipe 204
344. White Chocolate Sweet Potato Cake Recipe 205
345. White Chocolate Truffle And Chocolate Fudge Layer Cake Recipe 206
346. White Chocolate OPERA Cake Recipe .. 207
347. White Chocolate Mousse Cake 2 Recipe 209
348. White Chocolate Strawberry Mousse Cake Recipe 210
349. White Chocolate Truffle Cake And Mango Pana Cotta Recipe 210
350. Worlds Most Dangerous Chocolate Cake Recipe 211

351. Xtra Moist Chocolate Cake Recipe 212
352. YIN YANG CHOCOLATE CAKE WITH MARZIPAN DECORATIONS Recipe 212
353. Yammy Chocolate Marble Cake Recipe . 213
354. Yummy Chocolate Cake Recipe 214
355. Zucchini Chocolate Cake Recipe............. 214
356. Zucchini Fudge Cashew Cake Recipe..... 215
357. Chocolate Covered Cinnamon Apple Cake Recipe 215
358. Chocolate And Apricot Tortilla Cake Recipe 216
359. Chocolate Bar Cake Recipe....................... 216
360. Chocolate Cinnamon Flan Cake Recipe . 216
361. Chocolate Eclair Cake Recipe 217
362. Gooey Chocolate Cake Recipe................. 217
363. Leebears Quick Chocolate Banana Cake Recipe 218
364. Vanilla Chocolate Pound Cake Recipe ... 219
365. White Chocolate Hazelnut Creamy Cake Recipe 220

INDEX 221
CONCLUSION 224

365 Awesome Chocolate Cake Recipes

***

1. 10 Minute Chocolate Pudding Cake Recipe

Serving: 8 | Prep: | Cook: 5mins | Ready in:

Ingredients

- 1 cup granulated sugar
- 2/3 cup unbleached all-purpose flour
- 2/3 cup Dutch-process cocoa
- heaping 1/4 teaspoon salt
- 1 teaspoon baking powder
- 1 teaspoon espresso powder (optional)
- 3 large eggs
- 2 tablespoons butter, melted
- 1 teaspoon vanilla
- 1/2 cup boiling water

Direction

- In a medium-sized mixing bowl, whisk together the sugar, flour, cocoa, salt, baking powder, and espresso powder.
- Add the eggs, melted butter, and vanilla, beating until smooth.
- Scoop the batter into a lightly greased 9-inch microwave-safe pie pan (glass or ceramic), or a microwave-safe 9-inch round or 8-inch square cake pan.
- Pour the boiling water very gently over the top of the cake; don't stir it in.
- Cover the pan with a dinner plate, glass lid, or whatever you usually cover pans with in the microwave.
- Microwave the cake for 5 minutes at regular power.
- Remove the cover, and poke a spoon into the center of the cake.
- It should be set, but have a layer of chocolate "sauce" at the bottom. If it's done, remove it from the oven, and wait 5 minutes before serving.
- If it seems way too moist, put it back into the microwave, without a cover, and cook for another minute or so.
- Sprinkle with confectioners' sugar, if desired, before serving.

2. 3 Layers Chocolate Ganache Cake Recipe

Serving: 10 | Prep: | Cook: 40mins | Ready in:

Ingredients

- caramelized hazelnuts:
- 1 cup sugar
- ¼ cup water
- ½ cup hazelnuts
- Dissolve the sugar in the water in a saucepan over a medium heat, boil without stirring till caramelized (8minutes).Stir in the hazelnuts till all combined and spread on an oiled baking sheet. Leave to cool.
- chocolate Cake:
- 4 ounces (120 grams) unsweetened chocolate, chopped
- 1/3 cup (28 grams) unsweetened cocoa powder (not Dutch-processed)
- 1 cup (240 ml) boiling water
- 2 1/4 cups (315 grams) all purpose flour
- 2 teaspoons baking powder
- 1 teaspoon baking soda
- 1/4 teaspoon salt
- 1 cup (226 grams) unsalted butter, room temperature

- 2 cups (400 grams) granulated white sugar
- 3 large eggs
- 2 teaspoons pure vanilla extract
- 1 cup (240 ml) milk
- For the chocolate filling
- 1 cup heavy cream
- 12 ounces (340 gram) semi-sweet chocolate, diced
- 2 ounces (60 gram) butter, at room temperature
- For the finishing and the glaze
- ¾ cup heavy cream
- 6 ounces (180 gram) semi-sweet chocolate, diced
- 1 tsp clear honey.

Direction

- Preheat oven to 350 degrees. Butter and line with parchment paper, a 23 x 5 cm loose bottomed baking pan. Set aside.
- In a stainless steel or heatproof bowl place the chopped chocolate and cocoa powder. Pour the boiling water over the chocolate and cocoa powder and stir until they have melted. Set aside to cool while you make the batter.
- In a separate bowl, whisk to combine, the flour, baking powder, baking soda, and salt. Set aside.
- In the bowl of your electric mixer, cream the butter. Gradually add the sugar and continue beating until the mixture is fluffy (this will take about 3-5 minutes). Add the eggs, one at a time, mixing well after each addition. Add the vanilla extract and melted chocolate mixture and beat to combine.
- Add the milk and flour mixtures in three additions, beginning and ending with the flour mixture. Beat only until the ingredients are incorporated.
- Pour the batter in the prepared pan and smooth the top. Bake for about 35 - 40 minutes or until a toothpick inserted in the center comes out clean. Remove from oven and place on a wire rack to cool for about 10 minutes.
- When completely cooled, split the cake into 3 layers; place one layer in the same baking pan after you have washed it.
- Chocolate filling:
- Put the cream in a saucepan and turn the heat to medium. Remove the pan from the heat immediately before the cream starts boiling. Add the diced chocolate, and stir until dissolved.
- In a small bowl, using a spatula or a fork beat the butter until soft. Stir the butter into the cream and let it cool at room temperature for about 2 hours. Spread 1/3 of the filling over the cake half and sprinkle some caramelized hazelnuts over. Place a second layer on top and repeat layering using same amount of the filling and hazelnuts. Finish with the last layer and spread the rest of the filling overt the top and sides of the cake. Place the cake in the refrigerator.
- Make the glaze:
- Get the cream to a simmer over a medium heat in a heavy saucepan, add the diced chocolate and stir till smoothed. Leave to cool for 5 minutes and then add the honey. The honey gives a shiny look to the glaze but you can omit it if you don't want that much of sweet taste. Whisk till smoothed and mixture begins to thicken. Pour
- The mixture immediately over the cake and tilt the rack or use a spatula to cover all the surface and sides. Refrigerate at least for 2 hours.
- ENJOY!!

3. 5 Minute Chocolate Mug Cake Recipe

Serving: 2 | Prep: | Cook: 3mins | Ready in:

Ingredients

- 1 coffee Mug

- 4 tablespoons flour(that's plain flour, not self-rising)
- 4 tablespoons sugar
- 2 tablespoons baking cocoa
- 1 egg
- 3 tablespoons milk
- 3 tablespoons oil
- 3 tablespoons chocolate chips (optional) some nuts (optional)
- Small splash of vanilla

Direction

- Add dry ingredients to mug, and mix well.
- Add the egg and mix thoroughly.
- Pour in the milk and oil and mix well.
- Add the chocolate chips (if using) and vanilla, and mix again.
- Put your mug in the microwave and cook for 3 minutes on high.
- The cake will rise over the top of the mug, but don't be alarmed!
- Allow to cool a little, and tip out onto a plate if desired.
- EAT! (This can serve 2 if you want to share!)
- And why is this the most dangerous cake recipe in the world?
- Because now we are all only 5 minutes away from chocolate cake any time of the day or night

4. 5 Minute Chocolate Mug Cake Recipe

Serving: 2 | Prep: | Cook: 3mins | Ready in:

Ingredients

- 4 tablespoons cake flour or all purpose (plain, no self-rising)
- 4 tablespoons sugar
- 2 tablespoons baking cocoa
- 1 egg
- 3 tablespoons milk
- 3 tablespoons oil
- 3 tablespoons chocolate chips(optional)
- A small dash of vanilla flavoring
- 1 coffee mug

Direction

- Add dry ingredients to mug, and mix well
- Add the egg and mix thoroughly.
- Pour in the milk and oil and mix well.
- Add the chocolate chips (if using) and vanilla flavoring, and mix again.
- Put your mug in the microwave and cook for 3 minutes at 1000 watts.
- The cake will rise over the top of the mug, but don't be alarmed!
- Allow to cool a little, and tip out onto a plate if desired. EAT! (This can serve 2 if you want to feel slightly more virtuous).
- And why is this the most dangerous cake recipe in the world? Because now we are all only 5 minutes away from chocolate cake at any time of the day or night.

5. 5 Layers Chocolate Meringue Cake Recipe

Serving: 10 | Prep: | Cook: 45mins | Ready in:

Ingredients

- cake Batter:
- 3 large egg yolks
- 1/2 cup (45 grams) Dutch-processed cocoa powder
- 1 cup (140 grams) all purpose flour
- 1 teaspoon baking powder
- 1/8 teaspoon salt
- 1/2 cup (1 stick) (114 grams) unsalted butter
- 1/2 cup (100 grams) granulated white sugar
- 1 teaspoon pure vanilla extract
- 1/4 cup (60 ml) milk
- Meringue Layer:
- 3 egg whites

- 1/8 teaspoon cream of tartar
- 2/3 cup (130 grams) granulated white sugar
- Topping:
- 1 cup (240 ml) heavy whipping cream
- 1 tablespoon (28 grams) granulated white sugar
- 1/2 teaspoon pure vanilla extract
- 1/4 cup (30 grams) ground almonds
- 1/2 cup (70 grams) finely grated semi-sweet chocolate

Direction

- Preheat oven to 325 degrees F (160 degrees C) and place rack in center of oven. Butter and line the bottoms of two - 8 x 1 1/2 inches (20 x 3.75 cm) round cake pans with parchment paper. Set aside.
- Separate the eggs in separate bowls. Cover and set aside.
- In a large bowl sift the cocoa powder, flour, baking powder, and salt. Set aside.
- Cream the butter until soft. Add the sugar and beat until light and fluffy. Add the egg yolks, one at a time, beating well after each addition. Scrape down the sides of the bowl and then beat in the vanilla extract. With the mixer on low speed, alternately add the flour mixture and milk, in three additions, beginning and ending with the flour. Divide the batter evenly between the two cake pans. Set aside while you make the meringue layer.
- Beat the egg whites until foamy. Add the cream of tartar and continue beating until soft peaks form. Gradually add the sugar and continue to whip until stiff peaks form.
- Evenly divide the meringue and place on top of the cake batter in the two pans, gently smoothing the tops. Bake for approximately 40-45 minutes, or until a toothpick inserted in the center of the cake comes out clean. The meringue layers will be crisp to the touch but soft inside. Place the pans on a wire rack to cool completely.
- For the whipped cream:
- In a large mixing bowl place the whipping cream, vanilla extract, and sugar and stir to combine. Beat the mixture until stiff peaks form. Fold in the ground almonds and chocolate.
- To Assemble Cake:
- Place one of the cake layers, meringue side down, on a serving platter. Spread with the whipping cream. Gently place the second cake layer, cake side down so the meringue layer is facing up, onto the first layer. Garnish as you desire. The original recipe used fresh strawberries and icing sugar, but I used melted chocolate as you see in the picture.
- N.B Chill in the fridge immediately and take it out if the fridge 20 minutes before serving time.

6. A Tunnel Runs Through It Chocolate Glazed Chocolate Cake Recipe

Serving: 12 | Prep: | Cook: 70mins | Ready in:

Ingredients

- 2 cups sugar
- 1 cup vegetable oil
- 2 large eggs
- 3 cups all-purpose flour
- 3/4 cup cocoa
- 2 teaspoons baking soda
- 2 teaspoons baking powder
- 1-1/2 teaspoons salt
- 1 cup brewed coffee
- 1 cup buttermilk
- 1/2 cup chopped pecans
- 1 teaspoon pure vanilla extract
- TUNNEL FILLING
- 1-8 ounce package cream cheese, softened
- 1 egg
- 1/4 cup sugar
- 1 teaspoon pure vanilla extract
- 1 cup semisweet chocolate chips
- chocolate glaze
- 2 tablespoons butter

- 3 tablespoons cocoa
- 1 cup powdered sugar
- 1-3 tablespoons cream
- 2 teaspoons vanilla extract

Direction

- In large mixer bowl, beat 2 cups sugar, oil, and 2 eggs at high speed 1 minute.
- In medium bowl, combine flour and next 4 ingredients, whisk.
- Combine coffee and buttermilk.
- Add flour mixture and coffee mixture alternately to sugar/oil mixture.
- Beat at medium speed 3 minutes.
- Stir in nuts and vanilla.
- Pour half of batter into a greased, floured 12-cup Bundt pan.
- TUNNEL FILLING
- Beat cream cheese at medium speed until fluffy.
- Gradually add 1/2 cup sugar and egg.
- Beat until blended.
- Stir in vanilla and chocolate chips.
- Spoon over batter in pan, leaving a 1/2-inch border around center and edge.
- Top with remaining batter.
- Bake at 350 degrees 1 hour and 10 minutes, test for doneness with pick.
- Cool in pan on wire rack for 15 minutes.
- Remove from pan and cool completely THEN make glaze.
- GLAZE
- Melt butter in a saucepan over low heat, stir in sugar, and remaining ingredients.
- Pour while warm over COOL cake.
- NOTE: May add 1/2 cup flaked coconut to tunnel filling, but reduce sugar to 1/4 cup.

7. Age Of Ice 4: Scrat On The Floating Island Recipe

Serving: 0 | Prep: | Cook: 1hours30mins | Ready in:

Ingredients

- chocolate muffins without butter
- 3 eggs
- ½ cup of sugar
- ½ cup of flour
- 200 grams of chocolate
- 1 packet of vanilla sugar
- ½ packet of yeast
- Custard sauce
- 3 egg yolks
- 30 fl oz milk
- 1 ½ tablespoon of sugar
- 1 teapoon of cornflour
- ½ vanilla bean
- Natural blue food coloring agent
- Egg whites
- 3 white eggs
- 20 grams of sugar
- 1 pinch of salt
- Character SCRAT and a tree in sugar paste
- 50 grammes of sugar paste
- Natural food colouring agent - differents colors
- 1 nut

Direction

- Chocolate muffins without butter.
- Start by preheating your oven to 350° F (Gas mark 4 or 180° C). In a pan, melt the chocolate with a little water over low heat. In a bowl, beat eggs, sugar and vanilla sugar. Finally, add the molten chocolate, flour and yeast. Blend together with electric beater. This is ready, pour the preparation into the muffin tin and bake 15 minutes at 350° F (Gas mark 4 or 180° C) in the oven. Let cool the chocolate muffins, then unmold them.
- Custard sauce
- In a bowl, whip egg yolks and sugar. Then, take the vanilla bean, split it into two lengthwise and collect the seeds with tip of knife. In a pan, mix the cornflour with the milk, then add the vanilla seeds. Heat for 5 minutes over low heat without boiling. Take the preparation egg / sugar and pour into

milk. Mix them together using a whisk. Cook in bain-marie during 10 minutes. Add the blue food colouring agent and mix.

- Egg whites
- Beat 3 white eggs until stiff with a pinch of salt. Add gradually the sugar and beat. The stiff egg whites should be firm. To make sure of it, you must be able to return the bowl with stiff egg whites without they fall. Then heat up a pan of water. Put large spoonfuls of white snow in the water and make poach 1 minute per side. With a slotted spoon, get back the floating islands and drop them on paper towels.
- Character SCRAT and a tree in sugar paste
- Take white sugar paste. Knead it and then mix it with food coloring agent. Then assemble the body parts of Scrat.
- Training of the plate Scrat on the floating island
- In a plate, pour the custard sauce. Place the floating islands on the custard sauce. Put down the character Scrat and his nut on the floating islands. Finally, place the continent "earth" (chocolate muffin) and a tree in sugar paste.
- Your plate is ready!

8. Allergy And Vegan Friendly Chocolate Cake Recipe

Serving: 12 | Prep: | Cook: 25mins |Ready in:

Ingredients

- 1 3/4 c. white spelt flour (you could use regular flour if you weren't avoiding wheat)
- 2 t. baking powder
- 1 t. baking soda
- 1/2 t. salt
- 1/2 t. xanthan gum
- 1 c. plain soy milk
- 3/4 c. cocoa powder
- 1/2 c. canola oil
- 1 1/2 c. pure maple syrup
- 1 t. apple cider vinegar
- 2 t. vanilla

Direction

- Preheat oven to 350 F. Spray 9-inch springform pan or lightly grease and flour two 8-inch tins.
- Stir together flour, baking powder, baking soda, salt and xanthan gum in a large bowl; set aside.
- In a saucepan, heat the soy milk over medium low heat. When it is slightly bubbling, add the cocoa powder and whisk well until it is smooth. Remove from heat.
- Combine the other liquid ingredients in a bowl and whisk well. Add the cocoa mixture and combine. Add the wet ingredients to the dry and stir.
- Pour batter into prepared pan(s) and bake for 25 minutes or until tester comes out clean. Cool completely.

9. Almond Praline Chocolate Cake Recipe

Serving: 10 | Prep: | Cook: 30mins |Ready in:

Ingredients

- Cake:
- 225 grams good quality plain chocolate (I use Lindt)
- 175 grams butter, softened
- 225 grams caster sugar
- 65ml flour
- 6 eggs separated
- Topping:
- 225 good plain chocolate
- 225 grams heavy cream
- 1 tsp orange extract or rum flavor (optional)
- Garnish and additions:
- 1/3 cup roasted almonds or hazelnuts
- 1/3 cup sugar

Direction

- Preheat oven to 375 F and grease a 20cm cake pan with butter, line
- The base with parchment paper and grease the paper.
- Make the garnish and additions first:
- On a cookie sheet, arrange the almonds or hazelnuts evenly.
- Melt the sugar in a saucepan over low heat till all is dissolved and
- You reach a deep brown colour. Pour the melted hot sugar over
- The almonds coating all evenly. Leave to cool completely.
- Once cooled, break it into small pieces, put in the food processor
- And grind it finely. Set aside.
- Cake:
- Melt the chocolate in a bowl over a pan of simmering water, add the
- Butter and stir till all butter is melted. Add the flour, sugar and the beaten egg yolk.
- In a stainless bowl with clean beaters, whisk the egg whites till stiff. Fold 2 tbsp. of the egg whites to the chocolate mixture and then add the rest of the whites folding slowly and carefully. Pour the batter mixture in the cake pan and bake for 40 minutes. The cake should have a crust on the top and muddy inside. Cool completely.
- Topping:
- In a heavy saucepan over medium heat, mix the cream and the chocolate stirring till all chocolate melts. Cool slightly and add the flavor if using, stir. Leave 1 hour in room temperature. Whisk till thickened slightly
- Assembling:
- Sprinkle 1 tbsp. of the grinded almonds over the cake in pan. Top with half of the Chocolate and cream mixture. Add 1 tbsp. to the rest of the chocolate and cream mixture, stir till combined and pour over the cake .Sprinkle the rest of the grinded almonds over the top.
- Chill for 4 hours. As Charlie states in his direction the cake should be served out of the fridge 30 minutes before serving so that the chocolate topping would be tender and I agree the advice was just great.

10. Amazing Chocolate Cake Recipe

Serving: 12 | Prep: | Cook: 25mins | Ready in:

Ingredients

- 8½ ounces (2 sticks plus 1 tablespoon) unsalted butter, more for greasing pan
- 7 ounces bittersweet chocolate (50 percent or higher cocoa), chopped
- 5 large eggs, separated
- 1 cup sugar
- ½ cup all-purpose flour
- Pinch of salt
- whipped cream for serving

Direction

- Place rack in top third of oven and heat to 400 degrees. (For best results, use a separate oven thermometer.)
- Butter a 9-inch springform pan and set aside. Original recipe calls for a loaf pan
- In a double boiler or microwave oven, melt together 8½ ounces butter and the chocolate.
- Stir to blend.
- In a medium bowl, stir together egg yolks and sugar.
- Stir in flour.
- Add chocolate mixture and stir until smooth.
- Using an electric mixer, whisk egg whites and salt until stiff but not dry.
- Fold whites into chocolate mixture just until blended. Pour into cake pan.
- Bake for 25 minutes.
- Remove cake from oven and allow to cool for 1 hour.
- Wrap with foil and refrigerate until cake is firm and cold, at least 2 hours.
- Two hours before serving, remove cake from refrigerator and bring to room temperature.

- Slice (center of cake will be fudgy) and serve, if desired, with whipped cream and strawberries or raspberries (optional)
- Optional: ganache on top.

11. Aunt Georgies Chocolate Cake Recipe

Serving: 6 | Prep: | Cook: 20mins | Ready in:

Ingredients

- 1 1/2 cups (150 g) sifted flour
- 1 cup (200 g) sugar
- 3 Tbsp (50 ml) baking cocoa
- 1 tsp (5 ml) baking soda
- 1/2 tsp (2.5 ml) salt
- 1 egg
- 1/4 cup (60 g) butter, melted
- 1 cup (250 ml) sour milk (see note below in Directions, Tip #1)
- 1/4 cup (60 ml) hot strong coffee (or hot water)
- 1 Tbsp (15 ml) vanilla

Direction

- Preheat oven to 350F or 175C Sift together flour, sugar, cocoa, baking soda and salt into mixing bowl.
- Add egg, butter, sour milk, hot water and vanilla.
- Beat (preferably with an electric mixer) at medium speed for 2 minutes.
- Pour batter into a greased 13 x 9 x 2-inch (33 x 22 x 5-cm) baking pan.
- Bake at 350F or 175C for 20 minutes or until it tests done (a toothpick or fork comes out clean). Cool in pan.
- Tip #1: To sour sweet milk, place 1 Tbsp. (15 ml) vinegar in a measuring cup and add enough milk to make 1 cup (250 ml)
- Tip #2: I usually double this recipe. It works just fine doubled, but bear in mind that the baking time is roughly doubled when the recipe is doubled.

12. Autumn Chocolate Spice Cake Recipe

Serving: 32 | Prep: | Cook: 30mins | Ready in:

Ingredients

- 1 box yellow cake mix
- 1 cup all-purpous flour
- 8 oz sour cream
- 4 eggs
- 1 cup sugar
- 5 Tbsp melted butter
- 1 tsp vanilla
- 1 1/2 Tbsp cinnamon
- 2 tsp allspice
- 1/2 bag milk chocolate chips (I've used semi sweet too)
- 1-2 Tbsp flour

Direction

- Preheat oven to 350.
- Put chips in your chopper and let them rip w/ 1-2 tbsp. flour to prevent clumping.
- Sift cake mix and flour.
- In a separate bowl, mix sour cream and one egg until smooth. Add remaining eggs one at a time, mixing well after each.
- Add sugar and mix to combine.
- Add butter and mix well.
- Stir in spices, vanilla, and chocolate chips.
- Bake for about 30 minutes. Do not over bake!

13. BARCARDI RUM CHOCOLATE CAKE Recipe

Serving: 10 | Prep: | Cook: 30mins | Ready in:

Ingredients

- cake
- 1 pk chocolate cake mix
- 1 pk chocolate instant pudding 4-serving size
- 4 x eggs
- 1/2 c Barcardi dark rum
- 1/4 c Cold water
- 1/2 c oil
- 1/2 c slivered almonds or nuts
- FILLING
- 1 1/2 c Cold milk
- 1/4 c Barcardi dark rum
- 1 pk chocolate instant pudding
- 1 Envelope Dream whip topping

Direction

- Preheat oven to 350F. Grease and flour two 9-in layer cake pans. Combine all cake ingredients together in large bowl. Blend well, then beat at medium mixer speed for 2 minutes. Turn into prepared pans. Bake for 30 minutes or until cake tests done. Do not underbake. Cool in pans for 10 minutes. Remove from pans, finish cooling on racks.
- Split layers in half horizontally. Spread 1 cup filling between each layer and over top of cake. Stack. Keep cake chilled. Serve cold. Optional: Garnish with chocolate curls.
- Filling: Combine milk, rum, pudding mix and topping mix in deep narrow-bottom bowl. Blend well at high speed for 4 minutes, until light and fluffy. Makes 4 cups.

14. BEETROOT CHOCOLATE CAKE Recipe

Serving: 8 | Prep: | Cook: 50mins | Ready in:

Ingredients

- 8oz SR flour
- 1oz cocoa powder
- 1 tsp baking powder
- 4oz caster sugar
- Pinch of salt
- 3oz dark chocolate melted
- 3oz butter melted
- 4oz raw grated beetroot peeled weight
- 2 eggs beaten

Direction

- Heat the oven to GM4/180'C/350'F. Grease and line a 2lb-loaf tin or cake tin.
- Sift together the flour, cocoa powder, salt and baking powder.
- Stir in the sugar, beetroot, melted chocolate and butter and the eggs.
- Turn into the tin and bake for 50 minutes or until firm on top and an inserted skewer comes out clean.

15. Banana Cake With Chocolate Ganache Recipe

Serving: 10 | Prep: | Cook: 45mins | Ready in:

Ingredients

- 3 cups light spelt flour
- 1 cup raw sugar
- 2 teaspoons baking soda
- 1 teaspoon baking powder
- 1 teaspoon sea salt
- 3 ripe bananas pureed
- 2/3 cup vanilla soy milk
- 1/2 cup sunflower oil
- 1/3 cup water
- 1/4 cup apple cider vinegar
- 2 teaspoon vanilla
- Ganache:
- 1 cup semisweet chocolate chips
- 1/3 cup vanilla soy milk

Direction

- Preheat oven to 350.
- Grease 10-inch Bundt pan.

- In large bowl whisk together flour, sugar, baking soda, baking powder and salt.
- Make a well in center of dry ingredients.
- Add bananas, soy milk, oil, water, vinegar and vanilla then whisk until just mixed.
- Immediately pour into prepared pan and place on baking tray.
- Bake on middle rack of oven 45 minutes.
- Cool 30 minutes and invert onto serving plate.
- In stainless steel bowl set over pan of hot but not boiling water melt chocolate chips. Remove from heat then with wooden spoon stir in soy milk and pour over cake.

16. Banana Chocolate Caramel Cake Recipe

Serving: 12 | Prep: | Cook: 20mins | Ready in:

Ingredients

- 1 Round Ready-Baked angel food cake (8-9 inch)
- 1 Cups (4 oz. each) refrigerated chocolate pudding snacks (from 24-oz package0
- 3 Medium bananas
- 1/2 Cup caramel Icecream Topping, room temperature
- 1 Aerosol Can (7 oz.) whipped cream
- 2Tablespoons chocolate candy sprinkles
- 12 cherries

Direction

- Cut angel food cake in half horizontally; separate layers.
- Spread 1 pudding snack on top of bottom cake layer.
- Slice 2 of the bananas into 1/8-inch-thick slices; arrange slices on top of pudding.
- Place top layer on bottom layer, cut side down.
- Top with second pudding snack.
- Refrigerate at least 2 hours or overnight before serving.
- To serve, cut the cake into 12 slices; place on individual dessert plates. Drizzle with whipped cream and banana slices. Sprinkle each with 1/2 teaspoon candy sprinkles and top with a cherry. Enjoy!

17. Banana Chocolate Turtle Cake Recipe

Serving: 1 | Prep: | Cook: 25mins | Ready in:

Ingredients

- 1 (18.25 ounce) box super moist devil's food cake mix
- 1 1/3 cups water
- 1/2 cup plus 2 teaspoons vegetable oil, divided
- 3 eggs
- 2 medium bananas, finely chopped
- 1 (14 ounce) bag caramels, unwrapped
- 1/2 cup evaporated milk
- 1 1/3 cups semisweet chocolate chips, divided
- 1 cup chopped pecans

Direction

- Preheat oven to 350 degrees F. Lightly spray the bottom only of a 13 x 9-inch baking pan with non-stick cooking spray.
- Beat cake mix, water 1/2 cup oil and eggs in large bowl on low speed.
- 1 minute, scraping bowl as needed. Pour half the batter into the pan.
- Bake 25 minutes.
- Heat caramels and evaporated milk in saucepan over medium heat, stir frequently, until melted and smooth. Stir in pecans.
- Sprinkle warm cake evenly with bananas. Pour caramel mixture over bananas. Sprinkle with 1 cup chocolate chips. Carefully spread remaining batter over top.
- Bake an additional 30 minutes.
- Melt over low heat, 1/3 cup chocolate chips and 2 teaspoons oil in small saucepan. Stir

constantly until smooth. Drizzle over cake. Cool 20 minutes.

18. Banana Coffee Cake With Chocolate Chip Streusel Recipe

Serving: 12 | Prep: | Cook: 45mins | Ready in:

Ingredients

- 1 1/4c   semi sweet chocolate chips
- 2/3c   packed brown sugar
- 1/2c   chopped pecans or walnuts
- 1Tbsp   cinnamon
- 1 1/2c   all purpose flour
- 3/4tsp   baking soda
- 3/4tsp   baking powder
- 1/4tsp   salt
- 3/4c   granulated sugar
- 1/2c   soft butter, unsalted
- 1   egg
- 1 1/3c   mashed ripe bananas, about 3 large
- 3Tbsp   buttermilk

Direction

- Preheat oven to 350F.
- Butter and flour 8x8x2 metal baking pan
- Mix chocolate chips, nuts, brown sugar and cinnamon together in a small bowl. Set aside.
- Sift flour, baking soda, baking powder and salt into a medium bowl.
- Beat butter and sugar until fluffy, add egg. Beat until well mixed.
- Mix in flour mixture alternately with the bananas and buttermilk, starting with the dry ingredients.
- Spread half the batter evenly into prepared pan. Sprinkle evenly with chocolate mixture. Repeat with last of the batter and topping.
- Bake for about 45 minutes.

19. Banana Coffee Cake With Chocolate Chip Streusel Recipe

Serving: 12 | Prep: | Cook: 45mins | Ready in:

Ingredients

- 1 1/4 cups semisweet chocolate chips (about 8 ounce)
- 2/3 cup packed golden brown sugar
- 1/2 cup chopped walnuts
- 1 tablespoon ground cinnamon
- 1 1/2 cups all-purpose flour
- 3/4 teaspoon baking soda
- 3/4 teaspoon baking powder
- 1/4 teaspoon salt
- 3/4 cup granulated sugar
- 1/2 cup (1 stick) unsalted butter, room temperature
- 1 large egg
- 1 1/3 cups mashed very ripe bananas (about 3 large)
- 3 tablespoons buttermilk

Direction

- Preheat oven to 350 degrees F. Butter and flour an 8-inch square baking pan.
- Stir chocolate chips, brown sugar, walnuts and cinnamon in small bowl until well blended; set streusel aside.
- Sift flour, baking soda, baking powder and salt into medium bowl.
- Using electric mixer, beat sugar, room temperature butter and egg in large bowl until fluffy. Beat in mashed bananas and buttermilk. Add dry ingredients and blend well.
- Spread half of batter (about 2 cups) in prepared baking pan. Sprinkle with half of streusel. Repeat with remaining batter and streusel.
- Bake coffee cake until tester inserted into center comes out clean, about 45 minutes. Cool coffee cake in pan on rack.

20. Banana And White Chocolate Mud Cake Recipe

Serving: 8 | Prep: | Cook: 60mins | Ready in:

Ingredients

- 250g margarine or butter
- 250g white chocolate melts
- 150ml hot water
- 1 cup caster sugar
- 1 3/4 cups plain flour
- 1 cup self - raising flour
- 1 teaspoon vanilla essence
- 2 eggs
- 3-4 mashed bananas

Direction

- Preheat oven to 150 d C.
- Melt chocolate and margarine in microwave or 1-2 minutes.
- Add water and sugar, stir and put in microwave until sugar has dissolved. Set aside to cool.
- Line and grease the base and sides of a cake tin.
- Mash bananas, eggs and vanilla together in a separate bowl until it has a paste-like consistency.
- When cool add sifted flours to the chocolate mixture. Add the egg and banana and mix well, using a whisk.
- Pour into prepared tin and cook for approximately 45 minutes to 1 hour, depending on size of tin using.
- Cake is cooked when skewer comes out clean and the sides should be a light golden colour.
- NOTES: Always check cake after 45 minutes and leave longer if needed; Ice with white chocolate icing or cream cheese icing. Nestle White Choc Melts were used for this recipe; but you can use whatever you prefer.

21. Beet Chocolate Cake Recipe

Serving: 12 | Prep: | Cook: 35mins | Ready in:

Ingredients

- 398 mL can sliced beets, drained
- unsweetened apple sauce
- 2 tbsp. water
- 2 tsp. vanilla extract
- 1 tsp. white vinegar
- 1 cup whole wheat flour
- 1/2 cup white flour
- 1/2 cup cocoa
- 1/4 cup sugar
- 3/4 cup Splenda
- 1 tbsp. cornstarch
- 2 tsp. baking soda
- 1/2 tsp. salt
- 1/2 tsp. ground cloves

Direction

- Preheat the oven to 325 degrees. Oil or spray two 8- or 9-inch cake pans.
- Put the drained beets into the food processor with 1/4 cup (clear) water, and process until pureed.
- Put the pureed beets into a 2-cup measure. Add enough apple sauce to reach the 2-cup line.
- Add the 2 tablespoons water, vanilla extract, and vinegar to the beets and mix well.
- Mix the dry ingredients together, add the beet mixture and stir until well-combined.
- Bake for 35 minutes Test by inserting a toothpick into the center; it's done when the toothpick comes out clean.
- Allow to cool completely before cutting and serving.

22. Best Ever Chocolate Cake Recipe

Serving: 12 | Prep: | Cook: 25mins | Ready in:

Ingredients

- cake
- 1 cup Unsifted unsweetened cocoa
- 2 cup boiling water
- 2 3/4 cup Sifted all-purpose flour
- 2 tsp. baking soda
- 1/2 tsp. salt
- 1/2 tsp. baking powder
- 1 cup butter Or margarine
- Softened
- 2 1/2 cup sugar
- 4 eggs
- 1 1/2 tsp. vanilla
- Frosting:
- 6 oz. semisweet chocolate pieces
- 1/2 cup light cream
- 1 cup butter Or Regular margarine
- 2 1/2 cup Unsifted confectioners'
- sugar
- -----FILLING-----
- 1 cup heavy cream, chilled
- 1/4 cup Unsifted confectioners'
- sugar
- 1 tsp. vanilla extract

Direction

- In medium bowl, combine cocoa with boiling water, mixing with wire whisk until smooth.
- Cool completely.
- Sift flour with soda, salt and baking powder.
- Preheat oven to 350F.
- Grease well and lightly flour three 9 by 1 1/2 inch layer-cake pans.
- In large bowl of electric mixer, at high speed, beat butter, sugar, eggs, and vanilla, scraping bowl occasionally until light-about 5 mins.
- At low speed, beat in flour mixture (in fourths), alternately with cocoa mixture (in thirds), beginning and ending with flour mixture.
- Do not overbeat.
- Divide evenly into pans; smooth top. Bake 25 to 30 mins. or until surface springs back when gently pressed with fingertip.
- Cool in pans 10 mins.
- Carefully loosen sides with spatula; 4. Remove from pans; cool on racks.
- Frosting: In medium saucepan, combine chocolate pieces, cream, butter; stir over medium heat until smooth.
- Remove from heat.
- With whisk, blend in 2 1/2 cups confectioners' sugar.
- In bowl set over ice (I use ice cubes) beat until it holds shape.
- Filling: whip cream with sugar and vanilla; refrigerate.
- To assemble cake: On plate place a layer, top side down; spread with half of cream.
- Place second layer, top side down; spread with rest of cream.
- Place third layer, top side up. To frost: With spatula, frost sides first, covering whipped cream; use rest of frosting on top, swirling decoratively.
- Refrigerate at least 1 hour before serving.

23. Bird Nest Chocolate Cake Recipe

Serving: 8 | Prep: | Cook: 45mins | Ready in:

Ingredients

- 1 23cm chocolate butter cake
- chocolate butter cream filling:
- 1 cup butter, softened
- ¾ cup powder sugar
- 5 oz plain chocolate, melted
- chocolate ganache filling:
- 16 oz plain chocolate, chopped
- 1 ¾ cup heavy cream
- ¼ cup butter
- 1/3 cup hazelnuts, chopped

- caramel bird nest:
- 1 cup granulated sugar
- 2 tbsp water

Direction

- Split the chocolate cake into three layers and set aside.
- In a large bowl, beat the butter and powder sugar together until fluffy and then add the melted chocolate and beat again. Set aside
- Heat the heavy cream until simmering in a heavy sauce pan over low heat and pour over the chopped chocolate. Stir until chocolate melts, add the butter and stir again. Set aside to cool and thickens stirring it occasionally.
- Set the first chocolate cake layer over your work surface. Top with 2 tbsp. of the butter cream mixture, spread with a spatula. Carefully add 2 tbsp. of the Chocolate ganache, spread carefully and sprinkle half of the chopped hazelnuts. Repeat the process with the second layer and third layer and the sides too. Chill
- For 2 -3 hours.
- Measure the rounded side of the cake with a parchment stripe and make two marks making them your guide for the caramel stripes.
- In a heavy saucepan, melt the sugar with the water over a low heat until sugar turns to deep brown color.
- Remove from heat, dip a brush inside the pan and drizzle caramel sauce over the space between the two marks working quickly. Leave to set. Meanwhile and before the caramel sauce gets dry, dip the brush again in the saucepan , and make sure to set your hand 1 feet over the cake To make a thin stripes and drizzle over the top of the cake. Gather the set stripes on the parchment and use on the sides of the cake pressing lightly. Chill!!!

24. Black Forest Cake With Chocolate Ganache Recipe

Serving: 810 | Prep: | Cook: 60mins | Ready in:

Ingredients

- For Cake:
- 150g dark cooking chocolate
- 150g butter, soft
- 150g castor sugar
- 6 eggs, separated
- 150g self-raising flour
- pinch of salt
- 250ml cream
- 1 tbsp extra castor sugar
- For Cherries:
- 2 1/2 tbsp cornflour
- 750g jar of sour cherries
- 75g-100g sugar (depends on how sour the cherries are. Add to taste)
- 30ml cherry puree/juice
- For Ganache:
- 375g dark chocolate, roughly chopped (this can be done in the food processor)
- 250ml cream

Direction

- For Cake:
- Preheat oven to 170C.
- Gently melt the chocolate in a microwave or over a double boiler. In a bowl, combine the melted chocolate with the soft butter and beat until creamy.
- Slowly and gradually beat in the sugar and egg yolks (adding one at a time). Fold in the sifted flour. Beat the whites until stiff with a pinch of salt and very gently fold through the mixture.
- Pour into a lined and greased 26cm springform tin. Bake for 40-50 minutes or until a skewer comes out clean. Remove from the oven and allow to cool.
- For Cherries:
- In a separate bowl mix the cornflour with enough cherry juice to make a paste.

- Combine the rest of the juice with the cornflour paste and put into a saucepan with the desired amount of sugar. Cook, stirring, until it boils and thickens. Add the cherries and puree, remove from heat and allow to cool.
- For Ganache:
- Separately, gently heat the chocolate and cream in a saucepan, stirring constantly until the chocolate has melted and the mixture is smooth. Do not let it boil.
- Pour into a bowl and allow the ganache to cool until you have the right consistency, i.e. thin enough to pour but thick enough so it stays on the cake. It's about right at room temperature.
- Pour over the top of the cake and wait until it is set.
- To Assemble:
- Whip the 250ml cream with the 1 tablespoon extra castor sugar until thick. Cut the cake in half horizontally.
- Sprinkle the bottom layer with a little extra juice/puree and spread over the cherry mixture.
- Top with the cream then place the other half of the cake on the top. Pour over the ganache and allow to set before cutting.

25. Black Rum Chocolate Cake Recipe

Serving: 10 | Prep: | Cook: 60mins | Ready in:

Ingredients

- 1 package chocolate cake mix
- 12 ounces semisweet chocolate chips
- 1 small chocolate instant pudding divided
- 1 cup black rum
- 1 cup raspberry preserves
- 3/4 cup water
- 2 tablespoons shortening
- 1/2 cup oil
- 1 ounce vanilla baking bar square
- 4 eggs

Direction

- Preheat oven to 350.
- Combine cake mix, pudding, egg 1/2 cup rum, water and oil in a large mixing bowl.
- Using an electric mixer beat at low speed until moistened then at medium speed 2 minutes.
- Stir in 1 cup of the chocolate pieces then pour batter into greased rube pan and bake 50 minutes.
- Cool in pan 15 minutes then remove from pan and cool on wire rack.
- Heat raspberry preserves and place cake on a serving platter.
- Prick surface of cake with a fork several times then brush glaze over top in several batches.
- Combine remaining 1 cup chocolate then microwave on high for 1 minute until melted.
- Stir until smooth then spoon chocolate icing over cake and allow to stand 10 minutes.
- Combine vanilla baking bar and 1 teaspoon water then microwave on high 30 seconds.
- Drizzle over top of icing.

26. Bob Sykes Bar B Qs Hersheys Perfectly Chocolate Chocolate Cake Recipe

Serving: 12 | Prep: | Cook: 45mins | Ready in:

Ingredients

- 2 cups sugar
- 1 3/4 cups all-purpose flour
- 3/4 cup Hershey's cocoa
- 1 1/2 teaspoons baking powder
- 1 1/2 teaspoons baking soda
- 1 teaspoon salt
- 2 eggs
- 1 cup milk
- 1/2 cup vegetable oil
- 2 teaspoons vanilla extract

- 1 cup boiling water
- ---
- "PERFECTLY CHOCOLATE" chocolate frosting
- ---
- 1 stick (1/2 cup) butter or margarine
- 2/3 cup Hershey's cocoa
- 3 cups powdered sugar
- 1/3 cup milk
- 1 teaspoon vanilla extract

Direction

- CAKE

- In a saucepan, bring butter, water and cocoa to a boil.
- In a mixing bowl, combine the flour, sugar, baking powder, baking soda and salt.
- Add cocoa mixture; mix well.
- Combine buttermilk and vanilla; add to batter and mix well.
- Beat in eggs.
- Pour into a greased 13-in. x 9-in. x 2-in. baking pan.
- Bake at 350° for 23-27 minutes or until a toothpick comes out clean. Cool on a wire rack.
- FROSTING:
- In a small saucepan over medium heat, cook and stir butter and cocoa until smooth.
- Remove from the heat.
- In a small mixing bowl, combine confectioners' sugar, vanilla and salt.
- Add cocoa mixture and enough milk until frosting reaches desired consistency.
- Frost cake.

27. Buttermilk Chocolate Cake Recipe

Serving: 16 | Prep: | Cook: 25mins | Ready in:

Ingredients

- CAKE:
- 1 c butter
- 1 c water
- 2 T baking cocoa
- 2 c all-purpose flour
- 2 c sugar
- 1 t baking powder
- 1 t baking soda
- 1/2 t salt
- 1/2 c buttermilk
- 1 t vanilla extract
- 2 eggs
- FROSTING:
- 3 T butter
- 2 T baking cocoa
- 3 c confectioners' sugar
- 1 t vanilla extract
- 1/8 t salt
- 3 to 4 T milk or whipping cream

Direction

28. Butterscotch Chocolate Cake Recipe

Serving: 15 | Prep: | Cook: 10mins | Ready in:

Ingredients

- 1 pkg. chocolate cake mix for 9x13 pan
- 1 - 17 oz. jar butterscotch ice cream topping
- 1 - 8oz. frozen whipped topping, thawed
- 3 - 2.1 oz. butterfinger candy bars, coarsely crushed

Direction

- Prep cake according to pkg. directions.
- Cool for 30 mins. on a wire rack (or like me, throw it in the freezer or fridge in the pan for a shorter time if you're in a huge hurry! Although this is not the best method.)
- With handle of wooden spoon, poke at least 12 holes in cake.

- Pour topping over cake.
- _____
- Be sure cake is completely cool for this part:
- Spread with whipped topping. (I dollop blobs all over, then spread out evenly)
- Sprinkle with crushed candy bars.
- Refrigerate at least 2 hours before serving (or not.)

29. CHOCOLATE CHUNK CAKE Recipe

Serving: 12 | Prep: | Cook: 60mins | Ready in:

Ingredients

- Topping: 10 ozs. semi-sweet chocolate, coursely chopped
- 3/4 cup chopped walnuts (or pecans)
- 2/3 cup granulated sugar
- Cake:
- 3/4 cup butter or margarine, softened
- 1 1/4 cups granulated sugar
- 3 eggs
- 1 1/2 cups sour cream
- 2 tsp. vanilla
- 2 1/2 cups all-purpose flour
- 2 1/2 tsps. baking powder
- 1 tsp. baking soda
- 1/2 tsp. salt

Direction

- Preheat oven to 350%F. Grease 10 in. tube pan.
- In small bowl, combine topping ingredients; set aside. Beat butter and sugar in large bowl until light and fluffy.
- Beat in eggs, sour cream, and vanilla until well mixed. Combine flour, baking powder, baking soda and salt in bowl. On low speed, add flour mixture to batter, beating until smooth.
- Spoon 1/3 (about 2 cups) of the batter into prepared pan, spreading evenly. Sprinkle with 1/3 of the topping (scant 1 cup). Repeat layering 2 more times. Bake 55 to 65 min. or until a wooden pick inserted in center comes out clean. Cool in pan on wire rack for 20 min. Remove from pan. Makes 12 servings.
- Note: For better mixing results, have all ingredients at room temperature.

30. CHOCOLATE COCONUT CAKE Recipe

Serving: 12 | Prep: | Cook: 50mins | Ready in:

Ingredients

- 4 eggs
- 3/4 c. oil
- 3/4 c. water
- 1 t. vanilla
- 1 pkg. (18 1/4 oz.) chocolate cake mix
- 1 pkg. (3.9 oz.) instant chocolate pudding
- FILLING:
- 2 c. flaked coconut
- 1/3 c. swt. condensed milk
- 1/4 t. almond extract
- TOPPING:
- 1 can (16 oz.) chocolate frosting

Direction

- In mixing bowl, beat the eggs, oil, water and vanilla. Add the cake and pudding mixes; beat for 5 minutes. Pour 3 cups into a greased and floured 10 inch fluted tube pan.
- Combine the coconut, milk and extract; mix well. Drop by spoonfuls onto the batter. Cover with remaining batter. Bake at 350 degrees for 50 - 60 minutes or until a toothpick inserted near the center comes out clean. Cool for 10 minutes before removing from pan to a wire rack to cool completely.
- Frost with chocolate frosting.

31. CHOCOLATE IRISH TIPSY CAKE Recipe

Serving: 12 | Prep: | Cook: 45mins | Ready in:

Ingredients

- 1 package chocolate cake mix
- 1 (3-4-ounce) package instant chocolate pudding mix
- 3/4 cup Irish whiskey or bourbon, divided
- 1/2 cup cooking oil
- 4 jumbo or extra large eggs, at room temperature
- 3/4 cup sugar
- 1/4 cup butter or margarine
- 1/4 cup water
- 1 teaspoon lemon juice
- whipped cream for garnish

Direction

- In a large bowl, combine cake mix, pudding mix, 1/2 cup Irish whiskey, and oil, add eggs and beat at medium speed of an electric mixer for 4 minutes, scraping down sides of bowl as necessary.
- Spoon into a greased and floured 10-inch Bundt or tube pan.
- Bake in a preheated moderate oven (350 degrees) for 45 minutes, or until a cake tester inserted into the cake comes out clean.
- When cake is almost done, prepare syrup.
- Combine sugar, butter, water, and lemon juice in a small heavy saucepan.
- Bring to a boil slowly, stirring until sugar is dissolved.
- Remove from heat and stir in remaining 1/4 cup Irish whiskey or bourbon.
- Turn cake out onto two large sheets of aluminum foil placed together to form the shape of a cross.
- Let cake cool for 10 minutes, top side up for tube cake and upside down for Bundt cake.
- Using a skewer or long bamboo pick, make holes all over top and sides of hot cake.
- Drizzle syrup very slowly over cake, being careful that too much does not run into any cracks on top of cake.
- Bring foil up around cake and wrap securely.
- Cake may be served when completely cool, or store in an airtight container overnight.
- Cake may be wrapped securely in foil and stored in the refrigerator for several weeks or in a freezer for up to six months.
- Serve with whipped cream.

32. CHOCOLATE ORANGE CHEESE CAKE Recipe

Serving: 9 | Prep: | Cook: 45mins | Ready in:

Ingredients

- butter for greasing
- 1 large ready-made sponge flan case
- 3 tbsp orange liqueur
- 200g/7oz caster sugar
- 2 large oranges, zest of both and juice of 1 orange
- 4 tbsp cornflour
- 850g/1and half lb full-fat soft cream cheese
- 3 medium eggs
- 1 vanilla pod, seeds scraped out
- 375ml/13fl oz double cream, plus extra to serve
- 345g/12oz dark chocolate pieces

Direction

- Preheat oven to 180c / 350f / gas 4.
- Grease a 23cm / 9in spring-form cake tin.
- Cut a circle from the sponge flan case to fit the base of the tin, then slice this circle in half across the middle to make two thin sliced discs. Use one of these to line the cake tin-the other disc can be used in another dish.
- Drizzle the sponge with one tablespoon of the orange liqueur.

- Mix together the sugar, orange zest and juice and cornflour in a bowl using a wooden spoon,
- Use an electric hand whisk to beat in the cream cheese.
- Crack in the eggs one by one, beating constantly until all the eggs are well incorporated.
- Add the vanilla seeds and the remaining two tablespoons of orange liqueur to the mixture and mix well.
- Add the cream and beat well until the mixture is smooth.
- Pour a third of the mixture over the sponge base in the cake tin.
- Sprinkle over a third of the chocolate pieces and smooth over with a palette knife. Repeat twice more with the remaining cheese cake mixture and chocolate pieces.
- Place the tin into a baking tray with 2-3mm of warm water-this helps to create steam during cooking. Transfer to the oven and bake for 50 minutes, or until the top is lightly golden.
- Remove from the oven and leave to cool and set completely before moving from the tin.
- To serve cut into wedges and serve with a drizzle of cream

33. CHOCOLATE PEANUT BUTTER CHEESE CAKE Recipe

Serving: 12 | Prep: | Cook: 80mins | Ready in:

Ingredients

- 1 (12 oz.) box vanilla wafers
- 1/2 c. sugar
- 2 tbsp. (1/4 c.) butter, melted
- FILLING:
- 1 lb. cream cheese, room temp.
- 1 1/2 c. sugar
- 1 (6 oz.) jar creamy peanut butter (2/3 c.)
- 5 eggs
- 1/2 c. sour cream
- 2 tsp. fresh lemon juice
- 3/4 - 1 c. semi-sweet chocolate chips
- TOPPING:
- 1 c. sour cream
- 3/4 c. semi-sweet chocolate chips, melted
- 1/2 c. sugar

Direction

- For crust:
- Preheat oven to 350 degrees.
- Butter bottom and sides of 9 inch springform pan.
- Combine all ingredients in food processor and process to uniform crumbs.
- Press mix onto bottom and sides of pan.
- Bake for 10 minutes. Cool slightly.
- For filling:
- Combine all ingredients except chocolate chips in processor and blend until smooth. Add chips and mix 10 seconds using on/off turns.
- Spread filling in crust.
- Bake until center of filling is firm, about 70-80 minutes.
- Let stand at room temperature for 15 minutes before adding topping.
- Keep oven on at 350 degrees.
- Meanwhile, prepare topping.
- Blend all ingredients.
- Spread over cheesecake. Bake 10 minutes. Let cake cool, then refrigerate at least 3 hours before serving.

34. CHOCOLATE SNACK CAKE For HUNGRY KIDS Recipe

Serving: 18 | Prep: | Cook: 60mins | Ready in:

Ingredients

- butter – ½ cup/100gms
- eggs – 3
- sugar – 1 ¼ cups

- flour – 1 1/4 cups
- cocoa – ½ cup
- baking powder – 1 tsp
- baking soda – ¼ tsp
- salt – ¼ tsp
- yogurt – 4 tbsp / thick
- Cream – 2 tbsp / 25 % fat
- vanilla essence – 1 tsp

Direction

- Preheat oven to 180 deg C. Grease well and line bottom of 8" ring tin
- Sift the dry ingredients together. Keep aside
- Mix the yogurt + cream in a small bowl. Keep aside
- Beat the butter + sugar well until light and fluffy.
- Beat in the eggs 1 by 1, scraping the sides down after each addition.
- Beat in the vanilla essence
- On low speed, beat in the dry ingredients alternatively with yogurt and cream mix…in 3 goes.
- If you like, you can add chocolate chips and/or chopped walnuts.
- Put the batter into the tin and level out. Sprinkle with coloured/chocolate sprinkles if desired.
- Bake for approximately 60 mins, or till the tester comes out clean.
- Cool in tin on rack for 10 mins
- Turn it out on rack, handling gently while warm, as it's quite delicate while warm.
- This cake is delicious and moist when fresh out of the oven!!

35. COUSIN Anns Chocolate Chip Brownie Cake Recipe

Serving: 0 | Prep: | Cook: 25mins | Ready in:

Ingredients

- 2 stick butter melted
- 2 eggs slightly beaten
- 2 cups light brown sugar
- 2 tsp. vanilla flavor
- 2 cups self rising flour
- 1-2 cups pecans to your liking
- 1 bag of semi sweet chocolate chips

Direction

- Mix together all ingredients
- Place in 9x13 pan or glass dish sprayed with Bakers Joy, Pam, etc. your choice.
- Top with 1 small bag of semi-sweet chocolate chips.
- Bake in preheated oven at 350 degrees for 20 to 30 minutes depending on the oven.
- Do not over bake. Should be extra moist in the middle like brownies.
- WHEN YOU BITE INTO IT, IT SHOULD ALMOST LOOK LIKE COOKIE DOUGH.
- CUT INTO SMALL PIECES (SQUARES).
- RECIPE SERVINGS DEPENDS ON WHAT SIZE YOU CUT IT.

36. CRUNCHY CHOCOLATE PEANUT BUTTER CAKE Recipe

Serving: 16 | Prep: | Cook: 105mins | Ready in:

Ingredients

- Cake:
- 2 cups plus 2 tblsp. sugar
- 1-3/4 cups flour
- 3/4 cup plus 2 tblsp. unsweetened cocoa powder
- 1-1/2 tsp. baking powder
- 1-1/2 tsp. baking soda
- 1-1/2 tsp. salt
- 2 large eggs
- 1 cup milk or buttermilk
- 1/2 cup vegetable oil
- 1 tblsp. vanilla extract

- 3/4 cup plus 2 tblsp. boiling water
- Filling:
- 1/3 cup sliced almonds
- 1/2 cup powdered sugar
- 2 large egg whites
- 1 tblsp. granulated sugar
- 1/2 cup salted roasted peanuts, coarsely chopped
- 1 cup creamy peanut butter
- 2 tblsp. butter, softened
- 3 ounces chocolate, chopped (milk or dark)
- 1 cup Rice Krispies
- Ganache:
- 1-1/4 pounds of chocolate (milk or dark), chopped
- 1-3/4 cups plus 2 tblsp. heavy cream, warmed

Direction

- Make the cake:
- Preheat oven to 350 degrees
- Butter and flour a 9 x 13 cake pan.
- In a large bowl, whisk the sugar, flour, cocoa, baking powder, baking soda and salt.
- In a medium bowl, whisk the eggs, milk, oil and vanilla.
- Whisk the wet ingredients into the dry ingredients. Whisk in the boiling water.
- Pour the batter (it will be thin) into the prepared pan and bake for about 50 minutes, until a toothpick inserted in the center comes out clean. Let cool in pan.
- Reduce oven temperature to 325 degrees.
- Invert the cake onto a work surface. Working carefully, slice the cake horizontally.
- Make the filling:
- Trace a 9 x 13 rectangle onto a sheet of parchment paper and lay it on a large baking sheet.
- In a food processor, pulse the almonds with the powdered sugar until the almonds are finely ground.
- In a bowl, using an electric mixer, beat the egg whites at medium speed until soft peaks form. Add the granulated sugar and beat until the whites are stiff and glossy, about 2 minutes more.
- Using a rubber spatula, fold the almond mixture into the egg whites.
- Spread the meringue onto the parchment to fill the rectangle. Sprinkle the chopped peanuts on top.
- Bake for about 20 minutes, until lightly browned and firm. Let cool.
- In a medium bowl, set in a saucepan of simmering water, heat the peanut butter with the butter and chocolate, stirring constantly until smooth and melted.
- Remove chocolate mixture from heat and fold in the Rice Krispies.
- Spread the chocolate mixture over the meringue rectangle.
- Transfer to the freezer and let cool completely.
- Make the ganache:
- In a medium bowl set in a saucepan of simmering water, melt the chocolate.
- Whisk in the cream until smooth.
- Remove from the heat and refrigerate for 1 hour, whisking occasionally, until thick enough to spread.
- Assemble the cake:
- Place the bottom cake layer, cut side up, on a large board. Spread 1/3 of the ganache over the cake.
- Invert the filling onto the cake and peel off the paper.
- Spread half the remaining ganache over the filling, then top with the remaining cake layer, cut side down.
- Refrigerate until firm, at least one hour.
- Using a serrated knife, trim the edges.
- Spread the remaining ganache over the top and sides.
- Refrigerate to set.

37. Carrot Cake With Chocolate Icing Recipe

Serving: 10 | Prep: | Cook: 15mins | Ready in:

Ingredients

- Cake:
- 4 medium carrots
- 3 eggs
- 1 tea cup of corn oil
- 2 cups of flour
- 1 1/2 cups of sugar
- 1 tablespoon of baking powder
- butter and flour to grease
- Icing:
- 1 tea cup of sugar
- 1/2 tea cup of nesquik or similar
- 3 tablespoons of milk

Direction

- Mix in the blender the carrots, eggs, oil and sugar
- Put this mix in a bowl add the flour and mix it vigorously using a whisk
- Add the baking powder and stir it delicately
- Pour it in a greased and floured baking pan
- Take to pre heated oven at 180C (medium temperature)
- Bake it until it's slightly golden (around 15 mins)
- Icing:
- Mix all the ingredients, it should have a thick paste consistency
- Spread it over the cake while it is still hot

38. Castle Chocolate Cake Recipe

Serving: 8 | Prep: | Cook: 20mins | Ready in:

Ingredients

- Cake:
- Nonstick vegetable oil spray
- 4 ounces bittersweet chocolate, chopped
- 3 tablespoons unsweetened cocoa powder
- 1/2 cup hot coffee
- 1/2 cup hot water
- 1 cup plus 1 tablespoon all purpose flour
- 1 teaspoon baking powder
- 1/2 teaspoon baking soda
- 1/8 teaspoon salt
- 1/3 cup vegetable oil
- 1/2 cup sugar
- 1/2 cup (packed) golden brown sugar
- 3 large eggs
- 1/2 cup yogurt
- Panna Cotta:
- 1/2 cup water
- 5 teaspoons unflavored gelatin
- 7 1/2 ounces bittersweet chocolate, chopped
- 5 ounces high-quality milk chocolate, such as Lindt or Perugina, chopped
- 2 1/2 cups heavy whipping cream
- 2 1/2 cups whole milk
- 1/2 cup plus 2 tablespoons sugar
- 1 1/4 teaspoons vanilla extract
- 1 1/4 vanilla beans, split lengthwise
- chocolate Band:
- 16x3-inch strip waxed paper
- 5 ounces bittersweet chocolate, chopped

Direction

- For cake:
- Preheat oven to 350°F. Spray two 10-inch-diameter springform pans with 2 1/2-inch-high sides with non-stick spray. Place chocolate and cocoa in medium bowl. Pour hot coffee and hot water over; whisk until smooth. Whisk flour, baking powder, baking soda, and salt in another medium bowl. Using electric mixer, beat oil and both sugars in large bowl 1 minute (mixture will be crumbly). Add eggs 1 at a time, beating to blend after each addition. Beat in yogurt. Mix in half of dry ingredients. Beat in chocolate mixture. Add remaining dry ingredients; beat on low speed just to blend (batter will be thin). Divide batter between pans (layers will be shallow).
- Bake cakes until tester inserted into centers comes out clean, about 20 minutes. Cool in pans on rack.
- For panna cotta:
- Place 1/2 cup water in small bowl. Sprinkle gelatine over; let soften 10 minutes. Place both chocolates in large metal bowl. Combine cream, milk, sugar, and vanilla extract in large

saucepan. Scrape in seeds from vanilla beans; add beans. Bring to boil, stirring until sugar dissolves; remove from heat. Add gelatine mixture; whisk to dissolve. Pour cream mixture over chocolates in bowl; whisk until completely melted. Place bowl over a larger bowl of ice water. Stir often until mixture thickens like pudding, draining off water and adding more ice to larger bowl as needed, about 30 minutes. Remove from over water.

- Pour 1/2 of panna cotta over cake in 1 pan (mixture may drip down sides of cake). Freeze 45 minutes. Keep remaining panna cotta at room temperature.
- Remove pan sides from second cake. Using large metal spatula, carefully slide cake off of pan bottom and place atop panna cotta in cake pan. Pour remaining panna cotta over, filling pan completely. Chill overnight. DO AHEAD: Can be covered and frozen for 2 weeks. Defrost overnight in refrigerator before continuing.
- For chocolate band:
- Place waxed paper strip atop a large one on your work surface. Stir chocolate in medium bowl set over pan of simmering water until smooth. Pour half of melted chocolate down center of waxed paper strip. Using small offset spatula, spread chocolate to cover strip evenly, allowing some of chocolate to extend beyond edges of paper strip, making sure strip are completely covered. Set aside until chocolate just begins to set but is still completely flexible, about 2 minutes. Using fingertips, lift strip and Wrap band around cake, waxed-paper side out, lining up 1 long edge with bottom of cake (band will be higher than cake). Gently peel off waxed paper. Chill leftovers…

39. Celebration Chocolate Raspberry Cake Recipe

Serving: 8 | Prep: | Cook: 35mins | Ready in:

Ingredients

- Cake:
- 2 cups sugar
- 1 3/4 cups all-purpose flour
- 3/4 cup cocoa
- 1 1/2 t baking powder
- 1 1/2 t baking soda
- 1 t salt
- 2 eggs
- 1 cup milk
- 1/2 cup vegetable oil
- 2 t vanilla
- 1 cup boiling water
- frosting & Filling:
- 8 T butter, melted
- 2/3 cup cocoa
- 3 cups confectioner's sugar
- 1/3 cup milk
- 1 t vanilla
- 1 jar raspberry All-fruit spread
- Optional:
- fresh raspberries
- candies
- sprinkles

Direction

- Heat oven to 350.
- Grease and flour 2 9-inch round cake pans.
- In large bowl, combine sugar, flour, cocoa, baking powder, baking soda and salt.
- Add eggs, milk, oil and vanilla.
- Beat on medium for 2 minutes.
- Stir in boiling water. (Batter will be thin.)
- Pour into prepared pans.
- Bake until wooden toothpick inserted in middle comes out clean, 30 to 35 minutes.
- Cool for 10 minutes before turning onto wire racks.
- To prepare frosting:
- In a large mixing bowl, combine butter and cocoa.
- Alternately add the confectioner's sugar and milk. Add small amount of additional milk if necessary to adjust consistency.
- Stir in vanilla.

- Prepare bottom layer of cake. Spread raspberry jam evenly on top.
- Spread layer of frosting on top of jam and place second layer.
- Frost.
- Garnish with fresh raspberries, sprinkles, or red or pink round candies (like Strawberry Whoppers.)

40. Cheesecake Stuffed Dark Chocolate Cake Recipe

Serving: 16 | Prep: | Cook: 32mins | Ready in:

Ingredients

- Unsweetned cocoa
- 1 18.25oz package devil's food cake mix
- 1 3.4oz box instant chocolate pudding mix
- 3 large eggs-room temperature
- 1 1/4 cups milk
- 1 cup oil-vegetable, canola, or corn
- 1 tablespoon vanilla extract
- 1 1/2 teaspoon chocolate extract-optional
- 1 teaspoon almond extract
- 3 1.55oz milk chocolate bars(such as Hershey's)
- 3 16oz tubs homestyle cream cheese frosting
- 3 7.75oz boxes frozen cheesecake bites(such as Sara Lee)-chopped.
- 1 12oz jar dulce de leche or caramel sauce
- Double chocolate rolled wafer cookies(such as Pirouline)
- chocolate fudge rolled water cookies(such as Pepperidge Farm)

Direction

- Grease two round 9" cake pans. Dust with cocoa powder.
- Beat cake mix and next 7 ingredients on medium speed for two minutes.
- Fold in milk chocolate. Spread batter into prepared pans.
- Bake at 350 degrees for 30-32 minutes or until cake springs back when touched.
- Cool layers for 10 minutes in pans then transfer to wire racks to cool completely.
- Wrap layers and chill for at least 1 hour or up to 24 hours.
- Using a serrated knife, slice layers in half horizontally to make four layers.
- Place 1 layer cut side up onto cake plate.
- Spread with 1/2 cup frosting.
- Sprinkle one-fourth of chopped cheesecake bites over frosting.
- Repeat process with three remaining layers. Spread frosting only over top layer and then on sides of cake.
- Drizzle Dulce de Leche (caramel sauce) over the top of cake letting it drip down the sides.
- Break rolled wafer cookies into various length pieces and sprinkle over top of cake along with any remaining cheesecake pieces.
- Store in refrigerator until ready to serve.
- Refrigerate leftovers (if there are any).
- Note:
- I once substituted a bag of semisweet mini chocolate chips for the chopped candy bars.
- Decorate with chocolate chips, chopped Oreo cookies, chopped peanut butter cups or whatever you like.

41. Cherry Chocolate Cake Recipe

Serving: 18 | Prep: | Cook: 30mins | Ready in:

Ingredients

- 1 package (18-1/4 ounces) chocolate cake mix
- 3 eggs, lightly beaten
- 1 t almond extract
- 2 cans (20 ounces each) reduced-sugar cherry pie filling, divided
- 3/4 t confectioners' sugar

Direction

- In a large mixing bowl, combine the dry cake mix, eggs and almond extract.
- Stir in one can of pie filling until blended.
- Transfer to a 13-in. x 9-in. x 2-in. baking pan coated with cooking spray.
- Bake at 350° for 30-35 minutes or until a toothpick inserted near the center comes out clean.
- Cool completely on a wire rack.
- Dust with confectioners' sugar.
- Top individual servings with remaining pie filling.

42. Cherry Chocolate Chipper Cake Recipe

Serving: 8 | Prep: | Cook: 40mins | Ready in:

Ingredients

- 1 cup all purpose flour
- 3/4 cup granulated sugar
- 1/2 cup sour cream
- 1/4 cup butter softened
- 1/4 cup water
- 1/2 teaspoon baking soda
- 1/2 teaspoon baking powder
- 1 egg
- 1/2 cup miniature semisweet chocolate chips
- 21 ounce can cherry pie filling

Direction

- Heat oven to 350. Grease and flour round cake pan. Beat all ingredients except chocolate chips and pie filling in large bowl with electric mixer on low speed for 30 seconds scraping bowl occasionally. Beat on high speed for 2 minutes. Stir in chocolate chips with spoon just until mixed then pour into pan. Bake 40 minutes then cool 10 minutes remove from pan to wire rack then cool completely. Top cake with pie filling.

43. Chewy Chocolate Raspberry Cake Recipe

Serving: 0 | Prep: | Cook: 105mins | Ready in:

Ingredients

- • 2 1/2 cups all-purpose flour
- • 1/2 cup NESTLÉ® TOLL HOUSE® baking cocoa
- • 1/2 teaspoon salt
- • 3 cups granulated sugar
- • 1 1/2 cups (3 sticks) butter, melted
- • 4 large eggs
- • 1 tablespoon vanilla extract
- • 2 to 3 teaspoons almond extract
- • 1/4 cup seedless raspberry jam
- • 1/2 cup NESTLÉ® TOLL HOUSE® Semi-sweet chocolate Mini Morsels
- • 3/4 cup sliced almonds, divided

Direction

- PREHEAT oven to 300° F. Grease 9-inch springform pan. Line bottom of pan with wax paper. Grease wax paper.
- SIFT together flour, cocoa and salt into medium bowl. Combine sugar and butter in large mixer bowl on low until blended. Add eggs, one at a time, beating well after each addition. Add the almond and vanilla extracts; beat until smooth. Pour into prepared pan, reserving about 1/3 of the batter. Carefully smooth a thin layer of the raspberry jam over the batter in pan. Top with morsels and 1/2 cup of the sliced almonds. Carefully cover with the remaining batter. Sprinkle batter with remaining 1/4 cup of almonds.
- BAKE for 1 hour 45 minutes to 2 hours or until wooden pick inserted near center comes out clean. Cool completely in pan on wire rack. Remove side of springform pan.

44. Chocolate Peppermint Ice Cream Cake Recipe

Serving: 12 | Prep: | Cook: |Ready in:

Ingredients

- *************************   CRUST   *********************
- 1/2 CUP (1 STICK) unsalted butter
- 8 OUNCES   bittersweet chocolate ONLY.......(NOT SEMI-SWEET OR UNSWEETENED). CHOPPPED
- 1-1/2 (9 OUNCE PACKAGES)
- chocolate wafer cookies (ABOUT 61)
- **********************   glaze   ****************************
- 1/2 CUP whipping cream 1/4 CUP light corn syrup
- 8 OUNCES BITTERSWEET - chocolate.....CHOPPED
- **************************FILLING ****************************
- 7 CUPS PREMIUM vanilla ice cream, SLIGHTLY SOFTENED
- 1-1/4 CUPS COARSELY CRUSHED RED AND WHITE STRIPED peppermint candies ABOUT (10 OUNCES)
- 2 TEASPOONS peppermint extract

Direction

- **************** FOR CRUST ***********
- MELT BUTTER WITH CHOCOLATE IN A HEAVY SAUCEPAN OVER LOW HEAT.
- FINELY GRIND COOKIES IN FOOD PROCESSOR
- ADD WARM, CHOCOLATE MIXTURE.
- BLEND JUST UNTIL CRUMBS ARE MOISTENED.
- RESERVE 1 CUP OF CRUMB MIXTURE IN A SMALL BOWL.
- PRESS REMAINING CRUMB MIXTURE ONTO SIDES, THEN BOTTOM OF A 9 INCH SPRINGFORM PAN WITH 2 3/4 INCH HIGH SIDES.......FREEZE.
- ***************************GLAZE*******************************
- BRING CREAM AND CORN SYRUP TO A BOIL IN A HEAVY SAUCEPAN.
- REMOVE FROM HEAT, ADD CHOCOLATE, AND WHISK UNTIL MELTED AND SMOOTH.
- LET STAND UNTIL COOL ABOUT 1 HOUR......
- ***************************FILLING*******************************
- WORKING QUICKLY, MIX ICE CREAM, 1 1/4 CUPS CRUSHED PEPPERMINTS, AND EXTRACT INTO A LARGE BOWL JUST UNTIL BLENDED.
- SPOON HALF OF ICE CREAM INTO CRUST; SPREAD EVENLY (PLACE REMAINING ICE CREAM MIXTURE IN BOWL IN FREEZER.
- SPRINKLE RESERVED 1 CUP OF COOKIE CRUMB OVER ICE CREAM IN PAN; PRESS GENTLY.
- POUR 1 CUP OF THE CHOCOLATE GLAZE OVER THE ICE CREAM IN PAN. FREEZE 1 HOUR.
- TOP WITH REMAINING ICE CREAM, SPREAD EVENLY.
- FREEZE UNTIL FIRM ABOUT 4 HOURS.
- STIR REMAING GLAZE OVER LOW HEAT JUST UNTIL POURABLE BUT NOT WARM.
- POUR GLAZE OVER ICE CREAM; SOREAD EVENLY FREEZE OVERNIGHT.
- TO TAKE CAKE OUT RUN SHARP KNIFE BETWEEN CRUST AND PAN SIDES TO LOOSENCAKE, RELEASE PAN SIDES, TRANSFER TO A PLATTER. GARNISH WITH CRUSHED PEPPERMINTS ON TOP AND SERVE.
- I KNOW THIS SOUNDS LIKE ALOT OF WORK BUT WORTH IT IT'S MOSTLY FREEZING TIME.

45. Chocolate Almond Crunch Cake Recipe

Serving: 10 | Prep: | Cook: 65mins | Ready in:

Ingredients

- 2 cups almonds, slivered, slightly toasted
- 12 ounces chocolate chips
- 1 (18.25 ounce) box devil's food cake mix
- 1 (3 1/2 ounce) box instant chocolate pudding
- 4 eggs
- 1 cup sour cream
- 1/2 cup water
- 1/4 cup vegetable oil
- 1 teaspoon vanilla extract
- 1 teaspoon almond extract
- 1/4 teaspoon cinnamon

Direction

- Sprinkle 1/2 cup almonds on bottom of greased 10-inch tube pan. Set aside remaining almonds and all the chocolate chips.
- Place remaining ingredients in mixer bowl.
- Beat 4 minutes. Fold in almonds and chocolate chips, then pour into pan.
- Bake at 350 degrees F for 60 to 70 minutes.
- Cool 15 minutes and remove from pan.
- Top with whipped cream and berries if desired.

46. Chocolate Almond Marble Pound Cake Recipe

Serving: 16 | Prep: | Cook: 65mins | Ready in:

Ingredients

- 1 1/4 cups semi-sweet chocolate chips
- 3 Cups of flour
- 2 tsp. baking powder
- 1/2 tsp salt
- 1 1/2 Cups sugar
- 1 C vegetable oil
- 3/4 tsp almond extract
- 5 eggs
- 1 Cup milk
- confectioners sugar (optional)

Direction

- Preheat oven to 350.
- Melt 1/2 cup of chips over hot, (not boiling) water; stir until smooth and set aside.
- In a medium bowl combine dry ingredients; set aside.
- In a large bowl combine sugar, oil and extract; beat well.
- Add eggs, one at a time, beating well after each addition.
- Gradually beat in flour mixture alternately with milk.
- Divide batter in half.
- Stir melted morsels and remaining unmelted morsels into one half of the batter, mix well.
- Pour half of plain batter into greased and floured 10" tube pan, top with half of chocolate batter and repeat layers with remaining batters.
- Bake approximately 65 - 75 minutes or until toothpick or tester comes out clean.
- Cool 15 minutes; remove from pan.
- Cool completely on wire rack and sprinkle with confectioner's sugar, if desired.

47. Chocolate And Cherry Polenta Cake Recipe

Serving: 10 | Prep: | Cook: 55mins | Ready in:

Ingredients

- 1/3 cup quick-cook polenta, or yellow cornmeal
- 7 oz. semi-sweet chocolate (use sweet chocolate if you prefer a sweeter taste)
- 5 eggs, separated
- 3/4 cup superfine sugar
- 1 cup ground almonds

- 4 tbsp. flour
- grated rind of 1 orange, or 1 tbsp. dried orange rind (availiable in the spice section)
- 1 small jar marachino cherries, drained and halved
- confectioners sugar for dusting

Direction

- Place polenta or yellow cornmeal in a bowl and pour over just enough boiling water to cover it, about 1/2 cup. Stir well, then cover the bowl and let it stand for about 20 minutes, or until polenta has absorbed all the excess moisture.
- Line the base of an 8-1/2 inch round springform pan with a greased parchment paper. Preheat the oven to 375F.
- Break the chocolate into squares and melt it in a heat-proof bowl set over a pan of simmering water (water bath).
- Whisk the egg yolks with sugar in another bowl, until thick and pale. Beat in the melted chocolate, then fold in polenta, ground almonds, flour and orange rind.
- In a clean bowl, whisk the egg whites until stiff. Stir 1 tbsp. of the stiff egg whites into the chocolate mixture, then fold in the rest. Fold in the cherries.
- Spoon the mixture into the prepared pan and bake at 375F for 45-55 minutes, or until firm to the touch. Cool on a wire rack. Remove from pan and dust with powdered sugar. Serve with coffee or tea.

48. Chocolate And Orange Bundt Cake Recipe

Serving: 12 | Prep: | Cook: 65mins | Ready in:

Ingredients

- 3 cups sifted all purpose flour
- 2 tsp. baking powder
- 1/2 tsp. salt
- 1 cup sweet butter
- 2 cups sugar
- 2 large eggs
- 1 1/2 tsp vanilla extract
- 1 cup milk
- 3/4 cup chocolate syrup, stir it well
- 1/4 tsp. baking soda
- 1/4 - 1/2 tsp orange extract

Direction

- Preheat oven to350 and put the rack in the centre of the oven.
- Grease a 10" tube pan or Bundt pan. Dust it with dried bread crumbs.
- Cream the butter and sugar until fluffy.
- Add the eggs, one at a time, mixing after each.
- Add the vanilla to the milk, stir it in.
- Alternately add the dry ingredients with the milk: dry, milk, dry, milk, dry.
- Pour about 2/3 to 3/4 of the batter into another bowl. Mix the orange extract in to that.
- Turn the orange batter in to the prepared pan and level it.
- Mix the chocolate syrup into the remaining batter.
- Pour the chocolate batter over the white one, do not mix it.
- Bake for 65 to 70 minutes, test with a toothpick.
- Do not invert this cake. Let it cool completely in the pan on a rack.
- When you cut the cake the chocolate batter will have sunk into the white part and looks decorative and pretty.
- You can top with chocolate icing. I think it's extraneous and just dust with a bit of confectioner's sugar when presenting.

49. Chocolate Angel Cake Recipe

Serving: 8 | Prep: | Cook: 40mins | Ready in:

Ingredients

- 3/4 cup sifted cake flour
- 1/4 cup cocoa
- 3/4 cup sugar
- 12 egg whites
- 1-1/2 teaspoons cream of tartar
- 1/4 teaspoon salt
- 1-1/2 teaspoons vanilla
- 3/4 cup sugar

Direction

- Sift flour, cocoa and sugar two times then set aside.
- Beat egg whites with cream of tartar, salt and vanilla until soft peaks form.
- Add remaining sugar 2 tablespoons at a time continuing to beat until egg whites hold stiff peaks.
- Sift about 1/4 of flour mixture over whites then fold in.
- Repeat folding in remaining flour by fourths.
- Bake in ungreased tube pan at 375 for 40 minutes.
- Invert cake in pan and cool.

50. Chocolate Angel Food Cake Recipe

Serving: 12 | Prep: | Cook: 50mins | Ready in:

Ingredients

- 3/4 cup flour
- 1/3 cup cocoa
- 1/3 cup sugar
- 1/4 teasp. salt
- 1 1/2 cups egg whites (about 10) at room temperature
- 1 teasp. cream of tartar
- 1 cup sugar
- 1 teasp. vanilla
- 1/2 teasp. almond extract

Direction

- Sift together the flour, cocoa, 1/3 cup sugar, and the salt...
- Sift 3 times
- Beat egg whites with the cream of tartar and the flavouring, slowly at first increase the speed
- When the whites are quite frothy slowly sift in the sugar, beating hard until firm peaks form
- Slowly sift the flour mixture over the whites, folding constantly and gently until it's smooth
- Turn into an ungreased tube pan
- Bake in a preheated oven at 325'F for 50 minutes or until the cake is brown and is slightly resistant to the touch
- Cool in the pan inverted over a rack
- When cool loosen the sides with a thin knife
- Serve at room temperature
- Optional: you can cut the cake into 3 layers and ice between the layers with Two Whiskey Chocolate Mousse or other fillings.

51. Chocolate Apple Cake Recipe

Serving: 12 | Prep: | Cook: 45mins | Ready in:

Ingredients

- 4 cups apples, peeled and sliced
- 2 cups sugar
- 1 cup oil
- 2 eggs
- 3 cups flour
- 2 teaspoons baking soda
- 1 tablespoon cinnamon
- 1/2 teaspoon salt
- 1 cup chocolate chips

Direction

- Stir sugar into apples and let stand 15 minutes. Mix in oil and then eggs. Mix together dry ingredients (no need to sift) and stir into apple mixture. Add chocolate chips and mix.

Mixture will be stiff. Spoon into greased 9x13 pan and bake for 45-55 minutes in a 350 oven. Serve warm.

52. Chocolate Applesauce Cake Recipe

Serving: 0 | Prep: | Cook: 1mins | Ready in:

Ingredients

- 3 c. Gold Medal flour
- 1 1/2 tsp. soda
- 1/2 tsp. salt
- 1/2 tsp. cloves
- 1 tsp. nutmeg
- 1/2 c. cocoa
- 3/4 c. butter
- 1 1/2 c. sugar
- 2 medium eggs
- 2 c. thick applesauce
- 1 1/2 c. raisins
- 1 1/2 c. chopped walnuts

Direction

- Sift dry ingredients and chocolate together.
- Cream butter and sugar.
- Add the eggs one at a time beating well.
- Alternately add dry ingredients, add applesauce, beating until smooth after each addition.
- Add raisins and nuts which have been mixed together.
- Bake at 350 degrees for 1 hour.
- ==
- Note: Recipe does not say what to bake this cake in.

53. Chocolate Applesauce Cake With Glaze Recipe

Serving: 8 | Prep: | Cook: 90mins | Ready in:

Ingredients

- 1 cup (2 sticks) unsalted butter, room temperature, plus more for pan
- 2 ¼ cups superfine sugar
- 2 large eggs
- 2 ½ cups unsweetened applesauce, preferably homemade style
- 1 ¾ cups all-purpose flour
- 1 cup unsweetened cocoa powder
- 2 tsp baking powder
- 1 tsp ground cinnamon
- 1 tsp ground ginger
- ½ tsp ground nutmeg
- Pinch of salt
- 6 oz. bittersweet chocolate, cut into ½-inch pieces
- 1 tsp pure vanilla extract
- 1 Tb confectioners' sugar
- 2 Tb calvados or brandy (optional)
- cider glaze (optional, recipe follows)

Direction

- Preheat oven to 325. Butter a 9 ½-inch Bundt pan. Coat with ¼ cup superfine sugar; tap out excess sugar, and set mold aside.
- In the bowl of an electric mixer fitted with the paddle attachment, beat butter and remaining 2 cups superfine sugar on medium speed, scraping down sides as needed, until mixture is light and fluffy, about 5 minutes. Add eggs, and beat 2-3 minutes more. Fold in applesauce (if you use homemade, make sure to let it cool down first!), being careful not to over mix.
- Into a large bowl, sift together flour, cocoa powder, baking powder, cinnamon, ginger, nutmeg, and salt. Fold mixture into applesauce mixture. Add chocolate pieces, Calvados and vanilla; mix until just combined. Pour batter into prepared pan; smooth top with a rubber spatula.

- Bake until cake pulls away from sides of pan and is springy to the touch, and a cake tester inserted in center comes out clean, about 1 1/2 hours. Transfer to a wire rack to cool slightly before inverting cake onto rack. Re invert; let cool completely.
- Sift confectioners' sugar over cake. Pour cider glaze over top of cake, allowing it to drip down sides.
- **Cider Glaze**
- 2 cups apple cider, plus more as needed
- 4 cups confectioners' sugar, sifted
- 2 lemons
- Combine cider and 1 cup sugar in a small saucepan; bring to a boil over medium heat. Skim surface, removing any cider sediment that rises to top. Reduce heat; simmer until liquid begins to thicken into a glaze, about 30 minutes.
- Remove cider glaze from heat; let stand until cool enough to touch.
- Return to low heat and allow to reduce until ¾ cup. Whisk remaining 3 cups confectioners' sugar into glaze. Remove from heat. If glaze is too thin, let it cool slightly. If it is too thick, add a little more cider. Use immediately.

54. Chocolate Banana Cake Recipe

Serving: 15 | Prep: | Cook: 40mins | Ready in:

Ingredients

- 2 cups flour, do not sift
- 2 cups sugar
- 2/3 cups cocoa powder
- 1 1/2 tsp baking soda
- 1/2 tsp salt
- 1/2 tsp ground cinnamon
- 2 eggs
- 1/2 cup vegetable oil
- 1/2 cup water
- 1 tsp vanilla
- 1 cup buttermilk
- 1 cup mashed banana

Direction

- Preheat oven to 350 and grease and flour 13x9 pan.
- Stir together 1st 6 ingredients (dry ingredients) in a medium bowl.
- In large mixer bowl beat eggs with mixer until fluffy.
- Beat in oil, water and vanilla.
- Alternate adding flour mixture with the buttermilk, 4 additions of buttermilk and 3 of flour mixture, beginning and ending with buttermilk.
- Beat in banana until smooth and pour into pan.
- Bake 40 to 45 minutes or until it springs back lightly when touched.
- Cool.

55. Chocolate Banana Loaf Cake Recipe

Serving: 12 | Prep: | Cook: 60mins | Ready in:

Ingredients

- 2c flour
- 3/4tsp baking powder
- 1/2tsp salt
- 1/4tsp baking soda
- 3/4c granulated sugar
- 2Tbs butter, room temperature
- 2 bananas, mashed
- 1/2c vanilla soy milk
- 2 egg whites
- 1oz. Semi-sweet chocolate, melted and cooled
- 1/2c confectioners sugar

Direction

- Preheat oven to 350. Coat 81/2x41/2" loaf pan with cooking spray; coat with flour. Mix flour, baking powder, salt and soda. In med. bowl,

mix granulated sugar and butter till combined. Stir in flour mixture until just blended. Stir in bananas, milk and egg whites; batter will be slightly lumpy.
- Stir 2/3 batter into chocolate. Pour plain batter into pan. Spoon chocolate batter over; swirl slightly.
- Bake 55-60 mins or till pick inserted comes out clean. Cool 5 mins. Remove from pan; cool completely on rack. Mix confectioners' sugar with 1 1/2 tsp water; drizzle over cake.

56. Chocolate Beet Cake Recipe

Serving: 24 | Prep: | Cook: 35mins | Ready in:

Ingredients

- 1-3/4 cups all-purpose flour
- 1-1/2 teaspoon baking soda
- 1/4 teaspoon salt
- 1 can (15 oz.) whole or quartered beets, drained (reserve liquid)
- 1-1/4 cups granulated sugar
- 1 cup vegetable oil
- 1/2 cup juice from beets
- 3 large eggs
- 1 teaspoon vanilla extract
- 4 squares (1 ounce each) unsweetened chocolate, melted
- 1 cup semi-sweet chocolate chips

Direction

- Preheat oven to 350 degrees F.
- Arrange rack in the center of the oven.
- Line a 9 x 13-inch baking pan with non-stick foil.
- In a medium bowl, measure flour, baking soda, and salt. Whisk to combine. Set aside.
- Puree drained beets in a food processor or heavy-duty blender. Scrape into a large bowl.
- Add sugar, vegetable oil, and 1/2 cup reserved beet juice to the pureed beets and mix on medium speed until combined.
- Add eggs and vanilla extract, blending until completely incorporated.
- Add flour mixture to the beet mixture. Using medium speed, mix until combined, at least two minutes, scraping down sides often.
- Add melted unsweetened chocolate and mix until combined.
- Pour into baking pan.
- Distribute chocolate chips evenly over the top of the batter.
- Bake for 30 to 35 minutes or until toothpick inserted in the center comes out clean.
- Do not over-bake or it will become dry.
- Let cool to room temperature.
- This cake is moist and delicious without any topping.
- However, if you would like to dress it up, you may sift powdered sugar over the top or frost with your favorite icing.

57. Chocolate Birthday Cake Recipe

Serving: 8 | Prep: | Cook: 40mins | Ready in:

Ingredients

- CAKE:
- 3/4 cup water
- 4 oz. bittersweet chocolate, finely chopped (about 2/3 cup)
- Note: You must use the best bittersweet chocolate you can find. Make certain it doesn't contain any milk solids.
- 1/2 cup vegetable oil
- 2 tsp. vanilla extract
- 1-1/2 cups all-purpose flour
- 1/3 cup unsweetened cocoa powder, sifted
- 1 cup sugar
- 1 tsp. baking soda
- 1/2 tsp. kosher salt
- 2 Tbsp. balsamic vinegar
- GLAZE:
- 4 oz. bittersweet chocolate, finely chopped (about 2/3 cup)

- 1/4 cup water
- 1 tsp. corn syrup

Direction

- CAKE:
- Preheat the oven to 375 F (190 C).
- Line the base of a 9-inch round spring form pan with parchment paper.
- Place water and chocolate in a small heavy pot over medium-low heat and stir until chocolate is almost fully melted. Remove from heat and continue to stir until chocolate is melted and mixture is well combined. Stir in oil and vanilla and set aside.
- Combine flour, cocoa, sugar, baking soda and salt in a bowl and stir with a fork until uniform. Add liquid mixture to dry ingredients and stir until well combined. Scrape batter into prepared pan.
- Pour vinegar on top of batter and use a fork to incorporate it into the batter as quickly as possible. There will be pale swirls in the batter from the baking soda and vinegar reacting. Stir just until vinegar is evenly distributed. Bake for 35 to 40 minutes or until a cake tester comes out clean.
- Let cake cool fully in pan, then run a knife around the edge to loosen it from the sides. Remove sides of pan, carefully invert cake onto a plate, remove bottom of pan and peel off parchment paper. Use another plate to turn cake right-side up.
- GLAZE:
- Place cake on serving plate and make glaze. Place chocolate, water and corn syrup in a small heavy pot over medium-low heat and stir until chocolate is almost fully melted. Remove from heat and continue to stir until chocolate is melted and mixture is shiny. Allow to cool for 5 minutes or until it has thickened slightly, and then pour glaze evenly over top of cake.

58. Chocolate Butter Pound Cake Recipe

Serving: 16 | Prep: | Cook: 80mins | Ready in:

Ingredients

- chocolate butter Pound cake
- Cream well:
- 2 sticks butter
- 1/2 cup shortening
- 3 cups sugar
- 2 tsp. vanilla
- 2 tsp. brandy (optional)
- 1/4 tsp. salt
- Sift together:
- 3 cups flour
- 1 tsp. baking powder
- 3/4 cup unsweetened cocoa
- Add these dry ingredients to the creamed mixture alternately with:
- 1 1/4 cups milk
- Beat well.
- Fold in:1 cup chopped pecans or walnuts
- Glaze:
- 1 1/2 squares unsweetened baking chocolate
- 2 Tbsp. butter confectioners' sugar 1 tsp. vanilla

Direction

- Pour batter into a well-greased 10-inch tube pan or two 9 x5x 3-inch loaf pans. Bake in a preheated 325° oven for about 1 hour and 20 minutes. Be sure to test for doneness with a cake tester.
- Glaze:
- In a saucepan, melt baking chocolate with butter. Remove from burner; add enough confectioners' sugar and hot water to make glaze thin enough to drizzle on cake, adding 1 tsp. vanilla last.

59. Chocolate Butterfinger Cake Recipe

Serving: 12 | Prep: | Cook: 30mins | Ready in:

Ingredients

- 1 Box of cake mix (I used Betty Crocker Super Moist Hershey's)
- 1 Small Bag of Butterfinger Candy Bar Minatures
- 1 Small Can of Carnation Evaporated Milk
- 1 Jar or Bottle of caramel ice cream topping

Direction

- Bake cake according to directions on the cake mix box.
- After baking, pierce top of cake with fork - numerous times.
- Pour milk slowly over the top of cake.
- Cover with caramel topping.
- Remove Butterfinger candy bars from their wrappings and place in zip lock bag. Crush with a rolling pin into small particles.
- Sprinkle Butterfinger on top of cake.
- Refrigerate after serving.

60. Chocolate Cake Low In Cholesterol Recipe

Serving: 10 | Prep: | Cook: 60mins | Ready in:

Ingredients

- 3 cups of self raising flour
- 6 spoonfuls of cocoa powder
- 1 small spoonful cooking soda
- 2 cups of sugar
- 10 spoonfuls of corn oil
- 2 spoonfuls of wine vinegar
- 2 vanillas
- orange zest
- 2+ cups of water
- powder sugar

Direction

- Put all fluids together and slightly beat (no mixer needed), then add remaining ingredients and beat again
- We oil a baking pan and bake cake for about an hour in a preheated oven at 170o until a toothpick inserted in the center comes out clean. We frost it with powder sugar on top. If we like we can add pieces of dark chocolate (without milk) in the cake before baking.

61. Chocolate Cake Pudding Recipe

Serving: 8 | Prep: | Cook: 45mins | Ready in:

Ingredients

- Cake:
- 3/4 c. sugar
- 1 c. flour
- 1/8 t. salt
- 2 t. baking opwder
- (OR just 1 c SR flour)
- 2 T cocoa
- 1/2 c. milk
- 3 T melted butter
- 1 t vanilla
- Topping:
- 1/2 c white sugar
- 1/2 c brown sugar
- 1/4 c cocoa
- 1 1/2 c. water or coffee

Direction

- Pre-heat oven to 350.
- In a 9" square pan, sift sugar, flour, salt, baking powder and cocoa.
- Stir in milk, melted butter and vanilla.
- Spread across pan.
- Mix topping sugars and cocoa together.
- Sprinkle over batter.
- Pour water or coffee over all.

- Bake 45 minutes, or until top springs back when lightly touched
- **NOTE** Let it cool a little while, even though you will be tempted to cut immediately! THAT FILLING IS hot! Thickens to a more pudding-ish consistency as it cools. A tad heavy-handed on the water/coffee will result in a more liquid filling, like lava-cake. A tad shy will give you a thicker filling.

62. Chocolate Cake Recipe

Serving: 20 | Prep: | Cook: 30mins | Ready in:

Ingredients

- 200 g self raising flour plus 20 gm cocoa pwd
- 200 g sugar
- 220 ml mayo
- 3 L eggs
- 1 tsp vanilla essence
- ....
- ganache :
- 200 g baking chocolate
- 1 tbsp olive margarine
- 1 tbsp cocoa pwd

Direction

- Pre heat oven at 180 deg C and line a 20 cm square pan.
- Beat the sugar and mayo.
- Add the eggs and beat it.
- Add the flour and essence.
- Mix well.
- Pour and bake for 30 mins or until done.
- Cool it.
- ....
- Microwave the ganache for 40 secs.
- Pour over the cake.
- Spread evenly.
- Cool for 30 mins.

63. Chocolate Cake Without The Box Recipe

Serving: 12 | Prep: | Cook: 35mins | Ready in:

Ingredients

- 2 cups flour
- 1¾ cups white sugar
- ½ cup Special dark cocoa, or ¾ cup regular cocoa
- ½ teaspoon salt
- 1 tablespoon baking soda
- 1 teaspoon cinnamon
- 1 egg
- ⅔ cup vegetable oil
- 1 cup buttermilk
- 1 cup strong, hot coffee
- 1 teaspoon vanilla extract
- Frosting:
- 4 to 6 tablespoons butter, melted
- 3 to 4 cups powdered sugar, depending on how much frosting you like on your cake!
- ¼ to ½ cup Special Dark or regular cocoa, depending on how chocolatey you like your frosting
- 1 tablespoon vanilla extract
- enough half-and-half to make the frosting spreadable (about ¼ cup or so) - the half-and-half really makes this frosting creamy and rich

Direction

- For the cake, stir together the first 6 ingredients in a large mixing bowl.
- Add egg, oil, buttermilk; mix on medium speed until blended.
- Add hot coffee and vanilla; mix until smooth.
- Pour batter into a lightly greased 9x11 pan.
- Bake at 350° for about 35 minutes, or until toothpick can be poked into center of cake and it comes out clean.
- Set cake pan on rack and allow it to cool completely before frosting.
- For the frosting, melt butter in glass (microwaveable) mixing bowl. Add powdered sugar, cocoa and vanilla. Slowly begin mixing

on low speed, adding half-and-half until frosting is right consistency. Spread over cooled cake. No need to refrigerate the leftovers - refrigeration tends to pull the moisture from baked goods.

64. Chocolate Cake In A MUG Recipe

Serving: 1 | Prep: | Cook: 5mins | Ready in:

Ingredients

- 4 Tbsp. cake flour (plain, not self-rising)
- 4 Tbsp. sugar
- 2 Tbsp. cocoa
- 1 egg
- 3 Tbsp. milk
- 3 Tbsp. oil
- Small splash of vanilla
- 3 Tbsp. chocolate chips, optional

Direction

- In a microwave safe MUG:
- Add dry ingredients to mug, mix well with a fork.
- Add egg, mix thoroughly.
- Pour in milk and oil and vanilla, mix well.
- Add chips, if using.
- Put mug in microwave, and cook for three minutes on 1000 watts.
- Cake will rise over top of mug--do not be alarmed!
- Allow to cool a little; tip onto a plate if desired.

65. Chocolate Cake With Four Chocolates Recipe

Serving: 12 | Prep: | Cook: 30mins | Ready in:

Ingredients

- cooking spray
- vegetable shortening
- 1/2 (4 ounce) semisweet chocolate baking bar, chopped
- 1/2 (1 ounce) bittersweet chocolate baking bar, chopped
- 1/2 cup butter, softened
- 2 cups firmly packed light brown sugar
- 3 large eggs
- 2 teaspoons vanilla extract
- 2 1/4 cups cake flour
- 2 teaspoons baking soda
- 1/2 teaspoon salt
- 1/4 teaspoon ground cinnamon
- 1/2 cup buttermilk
- 1 cup boiling water
- coffee liqueur Ganache icing (on my page)
- Mocha-chocolate Cream Filling (on my page)
- Garnish: chocolate curls

Direction

- Coat 3 (8-inch) round cake pans with cooking spray. Line bottoms of pans with wax paper; grease wax paper with shortening, and set aside.
- Melt chocolate in a small saucepan over low heat, stirring until smooth; set aside.
- Beat butter at medium speed with an electric mixer until creamy. Gradually add sugar, beating until light and fluffy. Add eggs, 1 at a time, beating just until yellow disappears after each addition. Stir in melted chocolate and vanilla.
- Sift together flour and next 3 ingredients; add to butter mixture alternately with buttermilk, beating at low speed just until blended, beginning and ending with flour mixture. Stir in boiling water. Pour batter evenly into prepared pans.
- Bake at 350° for 28 to 30 minutes or until a wooden pick inserted in center comes out clean. Cool in pans on wire racks 10 minutes; remove from pans, and cool completely on wire racks.
- Place 1 cake layer on a serving plate; spread top with 4 tablespoons Coffee Liqueur

Ganache Icing. Spread half of Mocha-Chocolate Cream Filling evenly over ganache on cake layer. Top with second cake layer; spread top with 4 tablespoons Coffee Liqueur Ganache Icing and remaining Mocha-Chocolate Cream Filling. Top with remaining cake layer. Spread remaining Coffee Liqueur Ganache Icing on top and sides of cake. Garnish, if desired.

- gradually beat into sugar mixture until blended.
- Transfer to a 13x9x2 inch baking dish coated with cooking spray. Top with heaping tablespoons of ricotta mixture; cut through the batter with a knife to swirl.
- Bake at 350 for 25-30 min or until a toothpick inserted near the center comes out clean. Cool on wire rack, refrigerate any left overs.

66. Chocolate Cannoli Cake Recipe

Serving: 15 | Prep: | Cook: 25mins | Ready in:

Ingredients

- Topping:
- 1 egg white, ligtly beaten
- 1 cup ricotta cheese
- 1/4 c sugar
- 1 tbs cold brewed coffee
- 2 tsp grated orange peel
- 1/2 c mini semisweet chocolate chips
- Bater:
- 1 c sugar
- 1/2 c cold brewed coffee
- 1/3 c canola oil
- 1/3 c orange jice
- 1 egg
- 1 egg white
- 1 tbs cider vinegar
- 1 tbs vanilla extract
- 1 cup all purpose flour
- 1/2 c whole wheat flour
- 1/3 c baking cocoa
- 1/2 tsp salt

Direction

- In a small bowl, combine the topping ingredients; set aside
- In a large bowl, combine the first 8 batter ingredients; beat until well blended. Combine the flours, cocoa, baking powder, salt;

67. Chocolate Caramel Cake Recipe

Serving: 10 | Prep: | Cook: 40mins | Ready in:

Ingredients

- cake ingredients:
- 60 grams plain chocolate, chopped
- 15 grams unsweetened cocoa powder (not Dutch-processed)
- ½ cup boiling water
- 160 grams all purpose flour
- 1 teaspoon baking powder
- 1/2 teaspoon baking soda
- Pinch of salt
- 115 grams unsalted butter, room temperature
- 1 cup granulated white sugar
- 2 eggs
- 1 teaspoon pure vanilla extract
- ½ cup milk
- For the caramel sauce:
- 1 cup sugar.
- 60 grams butter.
- 1 cup whipping cream.
- walnut praline:
- 85 grams sugar
- 100 grams walnut halves
- Heat the 85 grams sugar with 4 tbsp water till dissolved, and then boils until It forms a caramel. Stir in the walnut halves, cool on an oiled baking sheet.
- Topping:
- 225 good plain chocolate
- 225 grams heavy cream

Direction

- Cake:
- Preheat oven to 350 degrees. Butter and line with parchment paper, a 23 x 5 cm loose bottomed baking pan. Set aside.
- In a stainless steel or heatproof bowl place the chopped chocolate and cocoa powder. Pour the boiling water over the chocolate and cocoa powder and stir until they have melted. Set aside to cool while you make the batter.
- In a separate bowl, whisk to combine, the flour, baking powder, baking soda, and salt. Set aside.
- In the bowl of your electric mixer, cream the butter. Gradually add the sugar and continue beating until the mixture is fluffy (this will take about 3-5 minutes). Add the eggs, one at a time, mixing well after each addition. Add the vanilla extract and melted chocolate mixture and beat to combine.
- Add the milk and flour mixtures in three additions, beginning and ending with the flour mixture. Beat only until the ingredients are incorporated.
- Pour the batter in the prepared pan and smooth the top. Bake for about 35 - 40 minutes or until a toothpick inserted in the center comes out clean. Remove from oven and place on a wire rack to cool for about 10 minutes. When completely cooled, split the cake in half horizontally; place one half in the same baking pan after you have washed it and save the other half for another use.
- Caramel:
- Heat the sugar over medium heat till it all dissolve and turn golden color, add the butter in small pieces stirring with a wooden spoon, add the cream in a steady stream so slowly while stirring. Pour the caramel in the pan and keep aside till cooled.
- Topping:
- In a heavy saucepan over medium heat, mix the cream and the chocolate stirring till all chocolate melts. Cool slightly. Leave 1 hour in room temperature. Whisk till thickened slightly
- Assembly:
- Put back the cake layer in the same spring form pan after you washed it and pour the cooled caramel over, sprinkle with walnuts praline. Leave to harden in the fridge, covered. Pour chocolate topping over caramel and chill 4 hours. Sprinkle some grated chocolate over top and loosen from pan.

68. Chocolate Carrot Cake Recipe

Serving: 8 | Prep: | Cook: 35mins | Ready in:

Ingredients

- 1 pkg (6 oz) chocolate chips
- 3 cups flour
- 1 tsp baking soda
- 1 tsp baking powder
- 1 tsp salt
- 1 tsp cinnamon
- 1/2 tsp nutmeg
- 1/4 tsp cloves
- 1/2 cup water
- 3/4 cup butter or margarine
- 1 1/4 cup sugar
- 2 eggs
- 1 cup grated carrots
- 1 cup raisins

Direction

- Preheat oven to 350 degrees.
- Grease and place waxed paper in 9 x 13 pan.
- Melt chocolate in top of double boiler. Remove from heat when melted.
- Mix thoroughly flour, powder, soda, salt, cinnamon, nutmeg, and cloves.
- Soften butter or margarine by beating with electric mixer. Add sugar gradually, beat until well blended.
- Beat in eggs, one at a time.
- Stir in melted chocolate alternately with water and flour.
- Stir in carrots and raisins.

- Pour in pan. Bake for about 35 minutes or until cake is done.

69. Chocolate Carrot Cake With Cream Cheese Frosting Recipe

Serving: 12 | Prep: | Cook: 45mins | Ready in:

Ingredients

- 2-1/2 ounces unsweetened chocolate
- 1-1/3 cup unbleached white flour
- 2/3 cup unsweetened coca powder
- 1-1/2 teaspoon baking powder
- 1-1/2 teaspoon baking soda
- 1/2 teaspoon salt
- 1 teaspoon ground cinnamon
- 3 eggs room temperature
- 1-1/4 cup honey
- 2/3 cup unsalted butter
- 2 teaspoons vanilla extract
- Finely grated zest of 1 lemon
- 3/4 cup buttermilk room temperature
- 1-1/2 cups grated carrots
- chocolate Cream Cheese Frosting:
- 1/2 cup butter room temperature
- 1-1/2 cup neufchatel cheese softened
- 3/4 cup maple syrup
- 3/4 cup unsweetened cocoa powder
- 2 tablespoons instant coffee
- 1 tablespoon rum

Direction

- Preheat oven to 350.
- Melt chocolate in a double boiler then set aside to cool.
- In bowl combine flour, cocoa powder, baking powder, baking soda, salt and cinnamon.
- In a separate bowl beat eggs then add honey and beat until light.
- Add butter to eggs and beat well then stir in vanilla and lemon zest.
- Add cooled chocolate and mix well.
- Stir in buttermilk then dry ingredients just until combined then stir in grated carrots.
- Pour batter into two buttered and floured cake pans and bake for 40 minutes.
- Let cool before taking out of pans then cool completely and frost.
- To make frosting beat butter then add cream cheese and beat until creamy.
- Add syrup and beat again then add cocoa, coffee and rum and beat until well combined.

70. Chocolate Carrot Cake With Chocolate Frosting Recipe

Serving: 16 | Prep: | Cook: 60mins | Ready in:

Ingredients

- 1 ¾ cup all-purpose flour
- 1 ½ cup sugar
- 1 cup canola oil
- ½ cup orange juice
- ½ cup cocoa
- 2 teaspoons baking soda
- 1 teaspoon salt
- 1 teaspoon ground cinnamon
- 1 teaspoon vanilla extract
- 4 eggs
- 2 cups shredded carrots (about 3 large carrots)
- 1 1/2 cups shredded coconut

Direction

- A DAY BEFORE SERVING:
- Preheat oven to 350 degrees F. Grease & flour 10-inch Bundt pan. In large bowl, with mixer at low speed, beat first 10 ingredients just until blended, constantly scraping bowl with rubber spatula. Increase speed to high; beat 2 minutes, occasionally scraping bowl. Stir in carrots & coconut. Spoon batter into pan.
- Bake 50 to 55 minutes until toothpick inserted in centre of cake comes out clean. Cool cake in pan on wire rack 10 minutes; remove cake

from pan; cool completely on rack. Makes 16 servings.
- Once the cake is completely cooled, frost with Chocolate Frosting (separate posting).

71. Chocolate Celebration Cake Recipe

Serving: 20 | Prep: | Cook: 40mins | Ready in:

Ingredients

- cake
- 2 3/4 cups cake flour
- 1 cup unsweetened cocoa powder
- 2 teaspoons baking soda
- 3/4 teaspoon salt
- 1/2 teaspoon baking powder
- 2 3/4 cups sugar
- 4 large eggs
- 2 large egg yolks
- 1 cup vegetable oil
- 1 cup sour cream
- 1 tablespoon vanilla extract
- 3/4 cup miniature semisweet chocolate chips
- Ganache
- 3 cups whipping cream
- 1 1/2 pounds bittersweet (not unsweetened) or semisweet chocolate, finely chopped
- Mousse
- 4 1/3 cups chilled heavy whipping cream
- 1/2 cup light corn syrup
- 1 1/4 pounds bittersweet (not unsweetened) or semisweet chocolate, finely chopped
- Assembly and serving
- 2/3 cup seedless raspberry jam
- parchment or wax paper (for cake pans and two 4 1/2-inch-wide by 15 3/4-inch-long strips for chocolate decoration)
- 3/4 pound bittersweet (not unsweetened) or semisweet chocolate, finely chopped
- 3 1/2-pint baskets raspberries
- 1/2 pound cherries
- 1 1-pint basket small strawberries
- 1 1/2-pint basket blueberries
- 1 1/2-pint basket blackberries

Direction

- Make cake:
- Position rack in center of oven and preheat to 350 F. Butter and flour two 10 inch diameter cake pans with 2-inch-high sides; line each with round of parchment paper or waxed paper. Combine first 5 ingredients in medium bowl; whisk to blend well. Using electric mixer, beat sugar, eggs and egg yolks in large bowl until very thick and heavy ribbon falls when beaters are lifted, about 6 minutes. Add oil, sour cream and vanilla, then dry ingredients all at once to egg mixture. Beat at low speed until just blended, about 1 minute. Scrape down sides of bowl. Beat at high speed until well blended, about 3 minutes. Fold in chocolate chips; divide batter between prepared pans (about 3 3/4 cups batter in each).
- Bake cakes until tester inserted into center comes out clean, about 40 minutes. Cool cakes completely in pans on racks. Cover; let cakes stand at room temperature overnight.
- Make ganache:
- Bring cream to simmer in heavy large sauce pan over medium-high heat. Remove from heat. Add chocolate and whisk until melted and smooth. Transfer ganache to glass bowl. Let stand until thick enough to spread, about 4 hours. (Can be made 1 day ahead. Cover; chill.)
- Make mousse:
- Using electric mixer, beat 3 1/3 cups cream in large bowl until peaks form; refrigerate. Combine remaining 1 cup cream and corn syrup in heavy medium saucepan and bring to simmer. Remove from heat. Add chocolate and whisk until melted, smooth, and still warm to touch. Pour warm chocolate mixture directly onto whipped cream and fold in gently. Chill until mousse is set, at least 8 hours. (Can be prepared 1 day ahead. Cover and keep refrigerated.)

- Assemble and serve cake:
- Cut around pan sides; turn out cakes. Peel off paper. Cut each cake horizontally in half. Place 1 cake layer, cut side up, on round 9 inch cake board. Place another layer, cut side up, on clean baking sheet. Spread each with 1/3 cup raspberry jam. Chill until jam sets, about 15 minutes
- If ganache is chilled, microwave on defrost setting in 15-second repetitions until just soft enough to spread, stirring occasionally. Drop 1 cup ganache by rounded teaspoonfuls over each jam layer. Using offset spatula (angled blade), gently spread ganache to cover jam. Drop 3 cups mousse by heaping spoonfuls onto each ganache layer; gently spread to cover. Refrigerate cake layers 30 minutes. Using large metal spatula, place cake layer from baking sheet, mousse side up, atop cake layer on cake board. Place third cake layer, cut side down, on cake (reserve remaining cake layer for another use). Spread 1 cup mousse over top of assembled cake. Using spatula, spread sides of assembled cake with enough ganache (about 1 1/2 cups) to fill gaps and make smooth surface. Transfer cake to platter.
- Turn 1 large baking sheet upside down on work surface. Arrange two 20-inch-long pieces of foil on work surface. Cut two 4 1/2-inch-wide by 15 3/4-inch-long strips from parchment paper. Lay 1 parchment strip, onto each sheet of foil. Place chocolate in medium metal bowl; set bowl over saucepan of simmering water (do not allow bottom of bowl to touch water). Stir until chocolate is smooth and very warm to touch (about 115°F). Remove bowl from over water.
- Pour thick ribbon of melted chocolate (about 2/3 cup) onto 1 parchment strip. Using long offset spatula, spread chocolate evenly over parchment strip, covering completely (chocolate will run over sides of strip). Lift edge of chocolate-coated strip with tip of knife. Slide hands between parchment strip and foil, lift entire parchment strip and place it, chocolate side up, on inverted baking sheet. Refrigerate until chocolate on strip is set and loses gloss but is still flexible (do not let chocolate become too firm), about 1 1/2 minutes. Using fingertips, lift chocolate-coated strip and attach, chocolate side in, to side of cake. Press strip to seal chocolate to side of cake (strip will stand about 1 inch above top edge of cake).
- Coat remaining parchment strip with chocolate, transfer to inverted baking sheet; chill until set but still flexible. Arrange 1 end of second strip against (but not overlapping) 1 end of first strip. Press second strip to seal chocolate to side of cake (both strips will just encircle cake). Refrigerate cake until chocolate strips are firm, about 30 minutes.
- Carefully peel parchment paper off chocolate strips. Chill cake at least 3 hours and up to 1 day.
- Mound fruit atop cake. Refrigerate until ready to serve. (Cake can be assembled up to 8 hours ahead.)

72. Chocolate Cherry Beer Cake Recipe

Serving: 24 | Prep: | Cook: 50mins | Ready in:

Ingredients

- 2/3 C. butter
- 2 eggs
- 3 C. all-purpose flour
- 1 tsp. salt
- 3/4 C. buttermilk
- 8 oz. cherries, pitted and halved
- 2 C. white sugar
- 2 1 oz. squares unsweetened chocolate, melted
- 2 tsp. baking soda
- 1 C. beer
- 1/4 C. cherry juice
- 1 C. chopped walnuts, pecans or mixed nuts
- 2/3 C. butter
- 1 egg
- 4 1 oz. squares unsweetened chocolate, melted

- 4 C. sifted confectioners' sugar
- 3 Tbs. milk

Direction

- Preheat oven to 350 degrees.
- Grease and flour a 9x13 inch pan.
- Sift flour, baking soda and salt. Set aside. In a large bowl, cream 2/3 C. butter and white sugar until light and fluffy.
- Add 2 eggs and 2 squares melted chocolate.
- Add flour mixture alternately with beer, buttermilk and cherry juice.
- Mix until smooth, then fold in cherries and chopped nuts.
- Pour batter into a 9x13 inch pan. Bake at 350 degrees for 45-60 minutes, or until a toothpick inserted into the center of cake comes out clean.
- **To make frosting: in a large bowl, combine 2/3 C. butter, 1 egg, 4 squares melted chocolate, confectioners' sugar and milk. Beat until smooth. Spread on top of cooled cake.**

73. Chocolate Cherry Bomb Cake Recipe

Serving: 20 | Prep: | Cook: 45mins | Ready in:

Ingredients

- 1 box chocolate cake mix
- 1 pkg. instant chocolate pudding
- 4 eggs
- 3/4 C. vegetable oil
- 1 can cherry Coke
- 1 can cherry pie filling
- chocolate frosting

Direction

- Preheat oven to 350.
- In large mixing bowl, mix together first 5 ingredients.
- Fold in cherry pie filling. (If you want, reserve some to put on top of finished cake)
- Pour batter into a 9x13 greased and floured cake pan.
- Bake at 350 for 45 minutes, or until toothpick inserted into cake comes out clean.
- Cool to room temperature and frost with chocolate frosting.
- Serve.

74. Chocolate Cherry Cake Recipe

Serving: 10 | Prep: | Cook: 30mins | Ready in:

Ingredients

- 1 3/4 c flour
- 2 c sugar
- 3/4 c unsweetened cocoa powder
- 2 tsp baking soda
- 1 tsp baking powder
- 1 tsp salt
- 2 eggs
- 1 c strong black coffee
- 1 c buttermilk or sour milk by adding 1 tbls vinegar to 1 c milk
- 1/2 c vegetable oil
- 1 tsp vanilla
- For the Cherry topping:
- 1 22 oz can of cherry pie filling (approx. 2 1/2 cups)
- 2 tbls sugar
- 2 tbls cherry Kirscher liquor
- whipped cream

Direction

- Combine first 6 ingredients in a bowl.
- Add ingredients 7 - 12 while stirring.
- Batter will be thin.
- Add batter to two greased round floured cake pans.
- Bake at 350 degrees for 25 - 30 minutes.
- Let cakes cool.

- To make the cherry filling, combine the pie filling, sugar, and liquor in a bowl.
- When the cakes are cool, take them out of pans.
- Cut the top off of one cake so it has a flat top to stack easier.
- Put cherry filling and a ring of whipped cream between the cakes so that the stick together.
- Put the cherry filling in the center of the top of the cake and ring with whipped cream.
- Spread whipped cream on the sides of the cake.

75. Chocolate Cherry Magic Cake Recipe

Serving: 16 | Prep: | Cook: 75mins | Ready in:

Ingredients

- 1 pkg chocolate cake mix
- 1 can (21 oz) cherry pie filling
- 10 oz. marshmallows
- 3 oz. pkg. cherry jello
- 1 cup cold water

Direction

- Put marshmallows in the bottom of a greased 9x13" pan.
- Mix cake mix as directed on box, and pour over marshmallows. Sprinkle with dry Jell-O. Top with cherry pie filling. Pour the water over filling and do not mix.
- Carefully place in 350° oven, and bake for 75-80 min. Cool at least 30 min.

76. Chocolate Cherry Magic Cake Recipe Recipe

Serving: 1 | Prep: | Cook: 75mins | Ready in:

Ingredients

- 1 pkg chocolate cake mix
- 1 can (21 oz) cherry pie filling
- 10 oz. marshmallows
- 3 oz. pkg. cherry jello
- 1 cup cold water

Direction

- Put marshmallows in the bottom of a greased 9x13" pan.
- Mix cake mix as directed on box, and pour over marshmallows. Sprinkle with dry Jell-O. Top with cherry pie filling. Pour the water over filling and do not mix.
- Carefully place in 350° oven, and bake for 75-80 min. Cool at least 30 min.

77. Chocolate Chip Cake Recipe

Serving: 1216 | Prep: | Cook: 30mins | Ready in:

Ingredients

- Pie:
- 2 3/4 cups all-purpose flour
- 1 1/2 teaspoons salt
- 1 1/4 teaspoons baking soda
- 1 teaspoon baking powder
- 1 cup (2 sticks) unsalted butter, softened
- 1 1/2 cups packed light brown sugar
- 1/2 cup granulated sugar
- 3 large eggs
- 1 tablespoon vanilla
- 3 cups chocolate chips
- 2 cups chopped walnuts (optional)
- Whipped Cream:
- 2 pints (4 cups) heavy cream
- 1/4 cup confectioners' (powdered) sugar
- 1/2 cup miniature semisweet chocolate chips

Direction

- Preheat oven to 350o F. Grease two 9-inch pie plates; set aside.
- In a large bowl, sift together the flour, salt, baking soda, and powder. In the bowl of an electric mixer, cream together butter, brown sugar, and granulated sugar. Add the eggs, one at a time, beating until incorporated. Beat in the vanilla. Add flour mixture, a little at a time, and mix until fully combined. Fold in the 3 cups chocolate chips and, if desired, the walnuts. Divide the dough between the prepared pie plates and smooth the tops with a spatula.
- Bake about 30 minutes or until pies are golden and slightly firm to the touch but still soft. If the pies begin to darken too much before they are baked through, cover with foil and continue baking. Let pies completely on a wire rack.
- While the pies cool, whip the cream until soft peaks form (tips curl). Add the confections' sugar and whip until just combined. Fold in the chocolate chips. Refrigerate whipped cream until ready to use. Spread the whipped cream over the pies and serve.
- Makes 12 to 16 servings

78. Chocolate Chip Cherry Cake Recipe

Serving: 12 | Prep: | Cook: 60mins | Ready in:

Ingredients

- 1 pkg. of yellow or white cake mix
- 1/2 c. Crisco oil
- 3 eggs
- 1 (8 oz.) pkg. cream cheese
- 1 cup of canned cherries for pie mix
- 1 cup semi-sweet chocolate chips
- 1/2 c. chopped pecans or walnuts

Direction

- Preheat your oven to 325 degrees

- Mix all ingredients except for the chips, cherries and nuts in a large bowl. When mixed well, gently fold in the cherries, chips and nuts.
- Bake in a greased and floured Bundt pan or tube for 45 minutes at 325 degrees.
- *Optional: Sprinkle lightly with powdered sugar after the cake has cooled completely.
- *For a Black Forest-style of cake, use a chocolate cake mix.

79. Chocolate Chip Cookie Surprise Cake Recipe

Serving: 15 | Prep: | Cook: 20mins | Ready in:

Ingredients

- 1 box Betty Crocker® SuperMoist® yellow cake mix
- 1 cup milk
- 1/2 cup butter or margarine, melted
- 3 eggs
- 1 pouch (1 lb 1.5 oz) Betty Crocker® chocolate chip cookie mix
- 1/2 cup butter or margarine, softened
- 1 egg
- 1 container Betty Crocker® Rich & Creamy chocolate frosting

Direction

- 1. Heat oven to 350°F (325°F for dark or non-stick pan). Generously grease and lightly flour, or spray with baking spray with flour, bottom only of 13x9-inch pan.
- 2. In large bowl, beat dry cake mix, milk, melted butter and 3 eggs with electric mixer on low speed 30 seconds; beat with electric mixer on medium speed 2 minutes. Pour into pan.
- 3. Make cookie mix as directed on pouch using softened butter and 1 egg. Drop dough by teaspoonfuls evenly over batter in pan.

- 4. Bake 60 to 63 minutes (58 to 62 minutes for dark or non-stick pan) or until toothpick inserted in center comes out clean. Run knife around sides of pan to loosen cake. Cool completely, about 1 hour. Spread frosting over top of cake. Store loosely covered at room temperature.

80. Chocolate Chip Ice Cream Cake Recipe

Serving: 12 | Prep: | Cook: 22mins | Ready in:

Ingredients

- For chocolate Chip cookie Layers
- 3/4 cup unsalted butter at room temperature
- 1/2 cup light brown sugar, packed
- 1/4 cup + 3 Tbsp sugar
- 2 tbsp golden corn syrup
- 1 x whole large egg
- 1 x large egg yolk
- 2 tsp vanilla extract
- 1 1/2 cups all purpose flour
- 2 tbsp cornstarch
- 1 tsp baking soda
- 1 tsp salt
- 1 cup miniature chocolate chips
- For chocolate Chip ice cream Layer
- 4 x large egg yolks
- 6 tbsp sugar
- 1 tsp cornstarch
- 1 1/4 cups half and half cream
- 1 tsp vanilla extract
- 1 1/4 cups whipping cream
- 1 1/2 cups miniature chocolate chips

Direction

- To Assemble
- For chocolate chip cookie layers, preheat oven to 325 °F and grease 2 9-inch cake pans, lining the bottoms with parchment paper.
- Cream butter, both sugars and corn syrup until smooth. Add eggs and vanilla extract and combine well. In a separate bowl, stir flour with cornstarch, baking soda and salt to blend. Add flour to butter mixture and stir until dough just comes together. Stir in chocolate chips. Divide dough evenly between the two cake pans and spread to level the dough. Bake for 20 to 25 minutes, until cookie turns a light golden brown. Allow to cool completely.
- For chocolate chip ice cream, whisk egg yolks, sugar and cornstarch in a saucepot to combine. Whisk in half & half cream and stir mixture over medium-low heat until it thickens and become just a little glossy, about 8 minutes. Remove from heat and strain. Stir in vanilla and let mixture cool to room temperature, stirring occasionally, then chill completely. Whip cream to soft peaks and whisk into chilled ice cream. Pour mixture into an ice cream maker following manufacturer's instructions. Just before removing ice cream, pour in chocolate chips. Scrape ice cream into a container and freeze while preparing cookies for assembly (if ice cream is still quite fluid, freeze for about 40 minutes to firm up – this will prevent chocolate chips from sinking).
- For assembly, turn cookies out of pan and peel off parchment. Line the side of a 9-inch springform pan with plastic wrap and place one cookie layer, nice side down into lined pan. Remove ice cream from freezer and spread over cookie. Lay remaining cookie layer on top of ice cream, pressing only lightly. Wrap cake and freeze until ready to serve.
- To serve, let cake temper (soften) at room temperature for at least 15 minutes. Remove springform pan and peel away plastic wrap. Slice into wedges and serve.

81. Chocolate Chip Pound Cake Recipe

Serving: 12 | Prep: | Cook: 60mins | Ready in:

Ingredients

- 1(18.25 oz) yellow cake mix with pudding
- 1(3.9oz) pkg. chocolate instant pudding
- 1/2c sugar
- 3/4c veg oil
- 3/4c water
- 4 lg eggs
- 1(8oz.) carton sour cream
- 1c(6oz)semi-sweet chocolate morsels
- sifted powdered sugar

Direction

- Combine first 3 ingredients in a large mixing bowl, stirring with a wire whisk to remove large lumps. Add oil and next 3 ingredients, stirring until smooth. Stir in chocolate morsels. Pour batter into greased and floured 12c Bundt pan.
- Bake at 350 for 1 hour or till wooden pick inserted in center comes out clean.
- Cool cake in pan on wire rack 10 mins; remove from pan, and let cool completely on wire rack.
- Sprinkle with sifted powdered sugar.

82. Chocolate Chip Sour Cream Cake Recipe

Serving: 12 | Prep: | Cook: 45mins | Ready in:

Ingredients

- One stick of butter, room temp
- Two cups sugar
- Three eggs, separated
- 16 ounces sour cream
- 1 1/2 teaspoons vanilla
- Three cups all purpose flour
- 1 1/2 teaspoon baking soda
- 1 teaspoon baking powder
- 1/2 teaspoon salt
- 1 teaspoon cinnamon
- 12 ounces chocolate chips

Direction

- Grease a 9X13 baking pan; set oven at 350 degrees;
- In large bowl, cream butter and 1 1/2 cups sugar; mix in egg yolks, sour cream and vanilla;
- In medium bowl, sift together flour, baking powder, baking soda, and salt; stir into butter mixture;
- Beat egg whites until they hold stiff peaks; fold into batter;
- In small bowl, mix cinnamon with remaining sugar and chocolate chips;
- Pout half the batter into the greased pan;
- Sprinkle with half the cinnamon-sugar-choco chip mixture;
- Pour remaining batter on top;
- Sprinkle with remaining cinnamon-sugar-choco chip mixture;
- Make 40 to 50 minutes or until toothpick comes out clean.

83. Chocolate Coconut Rum Cake Recipe

Serving: 16 | Prep: | Cook: 30mins | Ready in:

Ingredients

- 4 oz. semi-sweet chocolate, roughly cut
- 1/4 cup coffee
- 3/4 lb. (3 sticks) unsalted butter, cut into small pieces
- 2 cups sugar
- 3 lg. eggs
- 1/4 cup coconut rum
- 2 cups all-purpose flour
- 1 tsp. baking powder

- 1 tsp. vanilla
- 1 tsp. ground cinnamon
- 1/2 tsp. baking soda
- 1/2 cup buttermilk
- 1/8 tsp. ground cloves
- cinnamon Whipped Cream: 1/4 cup confectioner's powder sugar
- 1 cup heavy cream
- 1 tsp. vanilla
- 1 tsp. ground cinnamon
- 2 tbsp. coconut rum

Direction

- Preheat oven to 350 degrees F. Grease and flour 2-8 inch cake pans.
- In a double boiler combine, chocolate and butter until melted, stirring frequently.
- Remove chocolate and butter mix from heat. Stir in coconut rum, coffee, and sugar until sugar dissolves.
- Transfer to a lg. bowl, beat in eggs. Then stir in flour, cloves, cinnamon, baking soda, and baking powder.
- Add buttermilk and vanilla and mix well. Transfer to pans.
- Bake until toothpick inserted into cake comes out clean or about 30 min. Remove and cool about 2 hrs. Serve with cinnamon whipped cream or butter cream icing.

84. Chocolate Coffee Fudge Cake Recipe

Serving: 6 | Prep: | Cook: 50mins | Ready in:

Ingredients

- 150 gm Soft cheese Light
- 1/2 tsp vanilla extract
- 1 c caster sugar
- 200g self raising flour
- 3 heaped tsp Van Houten pure cocoa pwd
- 2 eggs
- 1/2 c demerara sugar .
- 1/2 cup grape seed oil or olive oil
- 2 tsp Nescafe Blend 37 instant coffee pwd
- 3 tbsp Evaporated low fat milk
- icing
- 1 tsp Nescafe Blend 37 instant coffee pwd
- 2 tsp heaped tsp Van Houten pure cocoa pwd
- 100g icing sugar
- 1 tbsp grape seed oil or olive margarine
- 1/2 cup water .
- 1 tbsp Evaporated low fat milk
- 1/4 C beaten cream cheese and condensed milk

Direction

- Whip the Cheese, Vanilla and Caster sugar. Keep inside fridge.
- Preheat oven 180 deg.
- Sift the flour and the Cocoa powder.
- Beat the eggs. Add the demerara sugar. Add the oil, coffee powder and the milk.
- Pour half the batter into greased pan. Pour the cheese mixture. Level it. Pour the remaining batter.
- Bake for 45 to 50 mins.
- Meanwhile gently heat the coffee powder, cocoa powder, and icing sugar.
- Once caramelized, add the oil, water. Let it boil in low flame. Add the milk. Cool it.
- Pour it on top of the cake.
- Drizzle some condensed milk and cream cheese mixture on top with a spoon.

85. Chocolate Cornflake Cakes Recipe

Serving: 8 | Prep: | Cook: 10mins | Ready in:

Ingredients

- The base
- 150 grams (7/8 cup) cornflakes
- 50 grams (1.765 ounces) chopped toasted hazelnuts

- 50 grams (1.765 ounces) raisins soaked in Grand Marnier
- 100 grams (3 1/2 ounces) best quality dark chocolate
- 50 grams (1.765 ounces) ready to eat apricots
- The Topping
- 350g (12.3 ounces) chocolate
- 350ml (11.8 ounce) whipping cream
- 1tsp cinnamon

Direction

- Melt the chocolate - Melt the 100g of chocolate, mix with the hazelnuts raisins, chopped apricots and the cornflakes.
- Spread the mixture - Spread the mixture into the base of a six-inch spring-loaded cake tin, or similar size lined, deep tray.
- Whip the cream - Whip the cream to the ribbon stage, that is, until it leaves the trail of the whisk. Whisk in the cinnamon.
- Fold in the chocolate - Fold in the melted chocolate. Mix to amalgamate leaving a smooth truffle-like consistency. Pour on to the cornflake base.
- Leave to set and serve - Leave to set for at least four hours. Dust with cocoa and serve.

86. Chocolate Covered Cherry Cake Recipe

Serving: 10 | Prep: | Cook: 35mins | Ready in:

Ingredients

- 1 pkg. Devil's Food cake mix
- 1 can(21oz) cherry pie filling
- 2 large eggs
- 1 tsp. almond extract

Direction

- Place rack in center of oven and preheat to 350. Lightly mist a 9x13" baking pan with cooking spray. Set aside
- Place all ingredients into large mixing bowl and beat with mixer on low for 1 min. Stop machine and scrape down bowl with spatula.
- Increase speed to medium, beat 2 mins more. Batter should look thick and well blended.
- Pour into prepared pan and smooth the top with spatula.
- Bake 30-35 mins. Remove from oven, place on wire rack to cool.
- This is delicious with an easy chocolate glaze:
- 1/2c semi-sweet chocolate chips, 2 Tbsp. butter and 1 Tbs. corn syrup.
- Microwave chocolate till melted and blend in other ingredients.

87. Chocolate Cream Cake Recipe

Serving: 1 | Prep: | Cook: | Ready in:

Ingredients

- 1 pkg. (8 oz.) cream cheese, softened
- 1 c. Confectioners' 's sugar
- 1 tsp. vanilla extract
- 1 1/2 c. heavy cream, whipped
- 1 pkg. chocolate chocolate chip cookies
- 1 lg. banana, sliced
- 1 can (8 oz.) pineapple chunks,
- Drained
- 1 c. Halved strawberries
- strawberries for garnish, optional

Direction

- In a mixer bowl, whip cream cheese with sugar until light and fluffy. Blend in vanilla. Fold in whipped cream.
- Arrange cookies around sides and bottom of 9 inch springform pan or cake pan with removable bottom. Spread 1/2 of filling in pan. Arrange fruit on filling. Top with remaining filling. Chill until set. Garnish with whole strawberries if desired. Makes one 9 inch cake.

88. Chocolate Decadence Flourless Cake Recipe

Serving: 16 | Prep: | Cook: 45mins | Ready in:

Ingredients

- 12 oz semi-sweet chocolate chips or good quality semi-sweet chocolate chopped
- 4 oz unsweetened chocolate
- 1½ cups butter, melted
- 1¾ cups Granulated sugar
- ½ cup water
- 7 eggs
- 2 cups whipped cream, for garnish (I like to make cocoa or chantilly whipped cream)

Direction

- Preheat oven to 350 degrees F (175 degrees C). Grease a 10 inch round pan and line bottom with parchment paper.
- Chop chocolate squares and place in a large bowl with chocolate chips. Add melted butter. Heat water and 1 1/2 cups sugar in a saucepan until boiling, then pour over chocolate. Stir until smooth.
- In a separate bowl, whip eggs with remaining 1/4 cup sugar until thick. Fold into chocolate mixture. Pour batter into 10 inch pan.
- Place 10 inch pan on a cookie sheet in the oven and fill the cookie sheet with water.
- Bake at 350 degrees F (175 degrees C) for 40 to 50 minutes. Remove from oven. Cool and refrigerate for several hours. Be extremely careful not to burn yourself on the hot water when removing the sheet pan from the oven.
- Dip the pan in hot water to remove cooled cake. Garnish with whipped cream and serve. I've also topped with ganache for an even more elegant presentation

89. Chocolate Dobash Cake Recipe

Serving: 8 | Prep: | Cook: 30mins | Ready in:

Ingredients

- 3 eggs, separated
- 1-1/2 cups sugar
- 1-1/2 cups cake flour
- 3/4 teaspoon baking soda
- 3/4 teaspoon salt
- 1/3 cup cocoa powder
- 1/3 cup vegetable oil
- 1 cup milk
- » Frosting:
- 1-1/2 cups water
- 1 cup sugar
- 1/4 teaspoon salt
- 1/4 cup butter or margarine
- 1/2 cup cocoa powder
- 1/3 cup cornstarch
- 1/2 cup water

Direction

- Preheat oven to 350 degrees.
- Grease and flour 2 8-inch pans.
- ******
- Beat egg whites until frothy and gradually beat in 1/2 cup sugar until stiff.
- Sift together remaining 1 cup sugar, flour, baking soda, salt and cocoa.
- Make a well in center; add oil and half of milk.
- Beat until well-blended at medium speed.
- Add remaining milk and egg yolks and beat until smooth.
- Fold mixture into egg whites.
- Pour batter into pans and bake 30 to 35 minutes.
- Cool, then slice each layer in half to make 4 layers.
- ******
- To prepare frosting:
- Combine water, sugar, salt and butter in saucepan and bring to boil. Combine cocoa, cornstarch and water; add to boiling mixture and return to boil.

- Cool completely.
- Frost between cooled layers, sides and top.
- Enjoy!

90. Chocolate Eclair Cake Recipe

Serving: 12 | Prep: | Cook: | Ready in:

Ingredients

- 15-20 graham crackers-4 sections per cracker, unbroken
- 2 3oz boxes instant vanilla pudding mix
- 1 8oz package cream cheese-softened
- 3 cups cold milk
- 1 16oz tub chocolate frosting

Direction

- Line the bottom of a 9" x 13" x 2" baking dish with half of the graham crackers. It's okay if they overlap.
- In a large mixing bowl, combine pudding mix, cream cheese, and milk.
- Beat until smooth.
- Pour pudding mixture over graham crackers.
- Top with remaining graham crackers.
- Remove cover and seal from frosting container. Microwave for 45-60 seconds or until runny.
- Pour over graham crackers. Spread evenly.
- Cover loosely with foil and refrigerate for 24 hours before serving.

91. Chocolate Flan Cake Recipe

Serving: 12 | Prep: | Cook: 120mins | Ready in:

Ingredients

- 1 box chocolate cake mix
- Ingredients to make cake as directed on box
- 1 jar of caramel icecream topping
- 1can sweetened condensed milk
- 1can evaporated milk
- 1/2 cup regular milk (use whole milk for this)
- 8 ounces cream cheese, softened
- 1 teaspoon vanilla
- 5 eggs
- hot water

Direction

- Preheat oven to 350 degrees; spray a 12-cup Bundt pan with cooking spray;
- Pour caramel topping into Bundt pan, distributing equally;
- Prepare cake mix according to package directions;
- Pour the prepared cake batter into the cake pan over the caramel topping;
- Pour condensed, evaporated and regular milks into a blender or mixing bowl;
- Add softened cream cheese, vanilla and eggs; blend or mix until smooth;
- Pour the milk (custard) mixture very carefully over the cake batter;
- Spray a sheet of aluminum foil with cooking spray and cover the Bundt pan tightly with the foil;
- Set the Bundt pan into a large baking pan and put it into the oven;
- Carefully pour hot water into the larger pan to a depth of 2 inches;
- Bake two hours; remove cake from water bath and oven;
- Allow cake to cool for 15 minutes;
- Remove aluminum foil;
- Invert cake onto a large plate;
- The caramel topping should flow down the sides!
- Cool cake completely then refrigerate.

92. Chocolate Fudge Cake Recipe

Serving: 8 | Prep: | Cook: 35mins | Ready in:

Ingredients

- 1 box devil's food cake mix
- 1 cup water
- 3 eggs
- 1/3 cup corn oil
- 1/3 cup sour cream
- 2 teaspoons vanilla
- 1/2 teaspoon kosher salt
- 1 cup semisweet chocolate chips
- Icing:
- 2 cups semisweet chocolate chips
- 2 cups sugar
- 2/3 cup milk
- 1 cup unsalted butter cut into pieces
- 1/4 teaspoon kosher salt
- 1 teaspoon vanilla

Direction

- Heat oven to 350.
- Butter 3 non-stick 8" cake pans.
- Combine cake mix, water, eggs, oil, sour cream, vanilla and kosher salt in bowl of mixer.
- Beat on low speed until mixture is well blended.
- Increase speed to medium and beat 2 minutes then stir in chocolate chips.
- Pour batter into pans and bake for 25 minutes.
- When cool put icing between layers and on tops and sides of cake.
- To make icing put chocolate chips in metal bowl of a stand mixer fitted with whisk attachment.
- Combine sugar, milk, butter and kosher salt in a medium saucepan over high heat.
- Bring to a boil stirring occasionally.
- Let boil vigorously for exactly 1 minute.
- Pour the hot sugar mixture over the chocolate then add vanilla.
- Beat on medium speed until mixture begins to thicken to spreading consistency.

93. Chocolate Fudge Pecan Cake And Icing Recipe

Serving: 18 | Prep: | Cook: 35mins | Ready in:

Ingredients

- cake
- 2 cups sugar
- 2 cups plain flour
- dash of salt
- 1 stick butter
- 1/2 cup Crisco
- 6 tablespoons cocoa
- 1 cup water
- 1/2 cup buttermilk
- 1 teaspoon baking soda
- 2 eggs
- 1 teaspoon vanilla
- l teaspoon cinnamon
- chocolate FUDGE pecan ICING:
- 1 stick butter
- 1/3 cup Coke
- 4 tablespoons cocoa
- 1 lb. powdered sugar
- 1 teaspoon vanilla
- 1/2 cup chopped pecans.

Direction

- CAKE
- Grease 9 X 13 cake pan and set oven to 375.
- Sift together: sugar, flour, & salt. In sauce pan, mix butter, Crisco, cocoa and water; boil, pour over flour mixture and mix.
- Add buttermilk, baking soda, eggs, vanilla, & cinnamon.
- Pour in prepared pan and bake for 35 minutes.
- Leave in pan and prepare icing.
- ICING
- In a medium sized saucepan, melt butter; add Coke and 4 tablespoons cocoa.
- Bring to a boil and remove from heat.
- Stir in: powdered sugar and vanilla.
- Beat with mixer until smooth.
- Stir in 1/2 cup chopped pecans.
- Quickly spread on cake.

94. Chocolate Fudge Pound Cake Recipe

Serving: 1 | Prep: | Cook: 60mins | Ready in:

Ingredients

- 3 oz. unsweetened chocolate, chopped
- 1/2 lb. (2 sticks) butter, room temperature
- 2 c. sugar
- 4 eggs
- 2 tsp. vanilla
- 3 tbsp. brandy or water
- 2 1/4 c. all-purpose flour
- 1/2 tsp. salt, or to taste
- 1 tsp. baking soda
- 1 1/4 c. buttermilk
- chocolate glaze, OPTIONAL:
- 4 oz. semi-sweet chocolate, chopped
- 6 tbsp. (3/4 stick) butter
- 2 tsp. light corn syrup
- 1 tsp. water

Direction

- Heavily grease a 12 cup Bundt pan; set aside. Preheat oven to 350 degrees.
- To make the cake, place chocolate in top of a double boiler over simmering water or in a microwave; stir until melted and smooth. Set aside to cool slightly.
- In a large mixing bowl with an electric mixer, cream butter and sugar until light and fluffy. Mix in eggs one at a time, beating after each addition. Mix in chocolate, vanilla and brandy or water. In a small bowl stir together flour, salt and baking soda. With mixer on low speed, alternately add flour in fourths and buttermilk in thirds, beginning and ending with the flour.
- Pour into prepared pan.
- Bake in center of oven for 1 hour or until a toothpick inserted in the center comes out clean. Remove to rack and cool 10 minutes. Invert to remove from pan and cool 20 minutes before frosting.
- Meanwhile make Chocolate Glaze, if desired, by melting chocolate and butter in a small saucepan or microwave.
- Remove from heat and stir in corn syrup and water. If too thin, let sit until it thickens slightly. Pour warm glaze over top of cake, allowing it to drop down the sides. If the glaze is too thick, reheat slightly. Let cake sit several hours before serving.

95. Chocolate Glazed Banana Cake Recipe

Serving: 9 | Prep: | Cook: 35mins | Ready in:

Ingredients

- 1/2 cup soft butter or margarine
- 1 1/4 cups sugar
- 2 eggs
- 1 1/2 cups all-purpose flour
- 1/2 tsp. baking powder
- 1/2 tsp. baking soda
- 1 1/2 tsp. salt
- 3 Tbsp. buttermilk, sour milk or sour cream
- 2 very ripe bananas, mashed (about 3/4 cup)
- 1/2 cup chopped English or black walnuts
- ----Butterscotch-chocolate Glaze----
- 1/3 cup butterscotch chips
- 1/3 cup chocolate chips
- 2 tbsp. whipping cream

Direction

- Preheat oven to 350F.
- Cream butter and sugar until blended. Add eggs and beat until fluffy.
- Stir together flour, baking powder, baking soda and salt. Add to creamed mixture along with buttermilk and mashed bananas. Mix just until batter is smooth and well blended. Stir in 1/4 cup of the nuts.
- Spread in a buttered 9-inch square cake pan.

- Bake for 30 to 35 min. or until cake feels firm to the touch.
- Meanwhile, prepare Butterscotch-Chocolate Glaze. Spread on cake after cake has cooled. Sprinkle with remaining nuts.

96. Chocolate Glazed Carrot Cake Recipe

Serving: 15 | Prep: | Cook: 75mins | Ready in:

Ingredients

- 1 1/2 cups blanched whole almonds
- 3/4 cup all purpose flour
- 2 teaspoons baking powder
- 1/4 teaspoon salt
- 2/3 cup golden raisins
- 3 tablespoons orange juice
- 4 squarkes semi sweet chocolate
- 1 cup sugar
- 1/3 cup butter (2/3 stick)
- 4 eggs
- 1 1/2 cups shredded carrots
- 1 1/2 teaspoons grated orange zest
- 1/2 teaspoon vanilla
- sweet chocolate glaze:
- 9 squares German sweet chocolate
- 2 tablespoons water
- 2 teaspoons butter
- 3/4 cup sifted confectioners sugar

Direction

- Toast almonds and set aside.
- Grease a 13 x 9 inch loaf pan; line bottom with waxed paper and grease again.
- Mix flour with baking powder and salt.
- Combine raisins and orange juice in small bowl; set aside.
- Cut chocolate in chunks; chop coarsely in food processor or blender with almonds and 1/2 cup of the sugar.
- Beat butter in large mixer bowl until soft; beat in remaining sugar.
- Add eggs, one at a time, blending well.
- Stir in flour, nut and raisin mixtures, the carrots, zest and vanilla.
- Pour into pan.
- Bake at 350 degrees for 1 hour and 15 minutes or until top springs back when lightly pressed.
- Cool in pan 10 minutes.
- Remove and cool on rack.
- Top with Sweet Chocolate glaze.
- Sweet Chocolate glaze:
- Melt the German Sweet chocolate with 2 tablespoons water and 2 teaspoons butter in saucepan, stirring constantly.
- Gradually blend into confectioners' sugar and beat until smooth.
- Top cake.

97. Chocolate Guinness Cake Recipe

Serving: 10 | Prep: | Cook: 50mins | Ready in:

Ingredients

- Cake:
- 1 cup Guinness
- 1/2 cup plus 2 tablespoons butter
- 1/2 cup cocoa
- 2 cups superfine sugar
- 3/4 cup sour cream
- 2 eggs
- 1 tablespoon vanilla extract
- 2 cups all-purpose flour
- 2 1/2 teaspoons baking soda
- Frosting:
- 8 ounces cream cheese
- 1 1/4 cups powdered sugar
- 1/2 cup heavy cream

Direction

- Preheat oven to 350° and grease and line with parchment paper a 9-inch springform pan.
- Pour the Guinness into a large saucepan and add the sliced butter. Heat until the butter is melted and remove from the heat. Whisk in the cocoa and sugar. In a separate bowl, beat the sour cream with the eggs and vanilla. Add the sour cream mixture to the Guinness mixture in the saucepan. Finally, beat in the flour and baking soda.
- Pour the batter into the greased and lined springform pan and bake for 45 minutes to an hour. (I baked mine for 53-55 minutes, checking with a toothpick for doneness and it came out well. Your oven may vary.) Cool completely in the pan on a wire rack.
- For the frosting, beat the powdered sugar and cream cheese together until well combined and creamy. Add the cream and beat again until it's a spreadable consistency. I found slowly adding the cream and beating the icing very well gave excellent results. At first there seems like a lot of frosting for just the top of a 9-inch cake but don't skimp! The idea is to frost the top of the cake until it resembles the frothy head of a pint of Guinness. It's quite dramatic and lovely.

98. Chocolate HoHo Cake Recipe

Serving: 16 | Prep: | Cook: 35mins | Ready in:

Ingredients

- 1 package devil's food or chocolate cake mix, any brand, but I prefer Duncan Hines!
- 3/4 cup granulated sugar
- 1 stick butter or margarine, melted
- 2/3 cup shortening
- 2 teaspoons vanilla extract
- 2/3 cup evaporated milk
- pinch of salt
- 1 can ready-to-spread chocolate frosting

Direction

- Preheat oven to 350 degrees,
- Prepare 9 x 13-inch cake pan by spraying with non-stick cooking spray or by greasing and flouring.
- In a large mixing bowl, mix and prepare chocolate cake mix according to package directions.
- Bake according to directions on box, approximately 35 minutes.
- Remove cake from oven when done and let cool completely.
- While cake is cooling, prepare white cream filling:
- In medium mixing bowl with electric mixer at medium-high speed, beat together granulated sugar, melted butter or margarine, shortening, vanilla, evaporated milk, and salt until light and fluffy. (About 5 minutes.)
- Spread cream filling on cooled cake.
- Refrigerate until set (approximately 20 minutes.)
- Remove foil seal on can of ready-to-spread frosting.
- Microwave container of frosting on high for about 60 seconds.
- Stir until smooth.
- Drizzle frosting on top of crème filling on cake.
- Spread carefully with spatula or knife to evenly cover crème filling.
- Refrigerate until set and ready to serve.
- Chocoholics rejoice! :))

99. Chocolate Irish Cream Cake Recipe

Serving: 12 | Prep: | Cook: 20mins | Ready in:

Ingredients

- Cake:
- 1 (18.25-ounce) package chocolate cake mix
- 1 (4-ounce) package chocolate instant pudding mix

- 4 large eggs
- 1/2 cup irish cream liqueur
- 1/2 cup cold water
- 1/2 cup vegetable oil
- 1/2 cup slivered almonds (optional)
- Filling:
- 1 1/2 cups cold milk (see Cook's Note)
- 1/2 cup irish cream liqueur
- 1 (4-ounce) package chocolate instant pudding mix
- 1 (5.2-ounce) package whipped topping mix - (contains 4 envelopes)
- chocolate curls (optional)

Direction

- Preheat oven to 350*F (175*C). Grease and flour two 9-inch round cake pans. Set aside.
- Combine all cake ingredients together in a large bowl. Blend well, then beat at medium mixer speed for 2 minutes. Pour into prepared pans. Bake for 20 to 25 minutes. Do not over bake. Cool in pans 10 minutes on wire rack. Remove from pans and finish cooling on racks.
- For filling, combine milk, liqueur, pudding mix and topping mix (use all 4 envelopes) in a deep narrow bottom bowl. Blend well at high speed for 4 minutes, until lightly and fluffy.
- Split layers in half. Spread one cup filling between each layer and on the top layer. Garnish with chocolate curls, if desired.
- Cook's Note: For more of the Irish cream liqueur flavor in the filling, decrease the amount of cold milk to 1 cup and increase the amount of Irish cream liqueur to 1 cup.

100. Chocolate Italian Cream Cake Recipe

Serving: 10 | Prep: | Cook: 60mins | Ready in:

Ingredients

- 1 (18.25 ounce) box chocolate cake mix
- 3 eggs
- 1/3 cup vegetable oil
- 4 cups ricotta cheese
- 1 cup granulated sugar
- 1 teaspoon vanilla extract
- 1 (3 1/2 ounce) box instant chocolate pudding mix
- 8 ounces non-dairy whipped topping

Direction

- Heat oven to 350 degrees F.
- Grease and flour a 13 x 9 x 2-inch cake pan.
- Prepare cake as per package instructions using 3 eggs and 1/3 cup oil; pour into prepared pan and set aside.
- Combine ricotta cheese, sugar and vanilla extract in a large mixing bowl; mix until thoroughly combined.
- Pour over cake batter.
- Swirl through the batter with a knife.
- Bake for 1 hour or until a toothpick inserted in the center comes out clean.
- Remove from oven; let cool down and transfer to a serving platter.
- Meanwhile, combine chocolate pudding mix and non-dairy whipped topping; beat with an electric mixer on medium speed until smooth about 3 to 4 minutes.
- Refrigerate pudding mixture.
- Cover cake with pudding mixture.
- Serve immediately or keep refrigerated until serving time.
- TIP: For baking purposes, when buying ricotta cheese in a plastic container, it is best to take the following precautions in order to not end up with a soggy cake: In a small skillet over very low heat, add ricotta. Once the cheese has shed its excess liquid, discard liquid. Wrap ricotta in cheesecloth and place over a bowl. Ricotta is ready for baking once it has stopped dripping.

101. Chocolate Kahlua Cake Recipe

Serving: 1 | Prep: | Cook: 60mins | Ready in:

Ingredients

- Box of dark chocolate cake mix
- 1 small box vanilla instant pudding
- 1 pint sour cream
- 1 6 oz bag semi sweet chocolate chips (I use Nestles)
- ~ 4 large eggs
- 1/4 cup canola oil
- 3/4 cup Kahlua

Direction

- Preheat oven to 350
- Spray the bottom of a 12 c Bundt pan with a good baking spray with flour.
- Place all ingredients, except the chips, in to a large mixing bowl and mix by hand until everything is combined. The mixture will be lumpy, but that's ok. If you see any really large lumps break them up. After everything is mixed together, add the chocolate chips and mix to disperse.
- Pour mixture into the Bundt pan and bake for 50-60 minutes. Serve this baby warm with vanilla ice cream and it's heavenly. This is one of those cakes that tastes better the next day and will keep on your counter, covered, for up to 5 days. Never lasts that long though. You can also change the chocolate chips for mint chocolate chips which is also yummy.
- I've tried it with peanut butter chips but didn't care for that. I've experimented with this recipe changing out the cake mix, liqueur and chips. I've made rum cake, used Chambord, different brandies, frozen orange concentrate, lime juice. All were big hits.
- This is a very versatile recipe so you can get really creative with it.
- I made a yellow cake with strawberries and a topping I whipped up that was out of this world good. Here's the topping recipe. It's great on the rum cake too, and works well as a fruit dip for strawberries, apples, etc.
- Quick Tasty Topping (also makes a great donut filling)
- Ingredients:
- 8 oz. cream cheese
- 1 large box vanilla instant pudding
- 1 large tubs cool whip or 2-3 small tubs 1/4 c milk or liquid of your choice to start (I've tried pineapple juice and espresso which is yummy)
- Set cream cheese out to soften or place in microwave and soften to where it's mixable Whisk in cool whip. Mix until smooth.
- Add 1/2 the vanilla instant pudding and whisk. Add 2+ TBS liquid if needed to loosen the mixture. Once mixed add the remainder of the vanilla pudding and whisk until smooth. You will need to add liquid until you reach the consistency you want of the mixture.
- If you want something stiff use less liquid, more of a dip, add more liquid. This tastes great on just about anything you want to put it on.

102. Chocolate Lava Cake With Warm Liquid Center Recipe

Serving: 2 | Prep: | Cook: 10mins | Ready in:

Ingredients

- 2 regular size dark chocolate bars with 75% cocoa
- 2 eggs
- 2 tsp suar
- 2 tbs butter
- 2 cupcake sized baking tins
- raspberries (optional for serving)
- orange Slice (optional for serving)

Direction

- Take a large pot and boil the water,

- In this pot lay another small pot and melt your butter and chocolate, leaving 4 cube pieces aside (Italian word = Bango Maria)
- When melted add your sugar and stir.
- When a little warm beat your eggs in thoroughly.
- Butter your cupcake sized baking tins and pour in the mixture equally.
- (Make sure to lick the pan dry, it's too good to waste).
- Insert 2 cube pieces of chocolate into the center and let it cool for about 15 mins. Preheat your oven to about 400 degrees and put your mix in.
- Let it bake no more than 10 mins (you will see it rise a little).
- Remove from oven and let it cook for about 3 mins.
- Hold a plate on the open end of the tin and invert it.
- You should get a perfect shaped individual cake.
- Serve immediately with Raspberries and an orange slices.

103. Chocolate Layer Cake Recipe

Serving: 12 | Prep: | Cook: 30mins | Ready in:

Ingredients

- 2 cups all purpose flour
- 2 cups granulated sugar
- 3/4 cup cocoa powder
- 2 Tbsp. Clabber Girl cornstarch
- 2 Tsp. Clabber Girl baking powder
- 1 tsp. salt
- 1/2 tsp. baking soda
- 4 large eggs
- 3/4 cup vegetable oil
- 2 tsp. vanilla extract
- 1 1/4 cup water

Direction

- Preheat oven to 350 degrees F.; grease and flour two 8-inch round cake pans.
- In a large bowl stir together the flour, sugar, cocoa, cornstarch, baking powder, baking soda and salt. In a separate bowl combine eggs, oil, vanilla and water. Add to dry ingredients and mix for 2 minutes at medium speed, stopping once or twice to scrape the bowl.
- Pour batter evenly into prepared baking pans and bake for 30 to 35 minutes, or until a skewer inserted into the center comes out clean. Cool cakes in pans for 15 minutes, then turn out and cool completely on a rack.

104. Chocolate Lovers Dream Cake Recipe

Serving: 12 | Prep: | Cook: 40mins | Ready in:

Ingredients

- CAKE:
- 1 box Betty Crocker Triple chocolate fudge cake mix or your favorite Deep chocolate cake
- 3 eggs
- 1/3 cup vegetable oil
- 1 1/4 cup water
- 1 jar Hershey's hot fudge
- chocolate GANACHE:
- 1 cup milk chocolate chips or chopped baking squares
- 1/2 cup heavy cream
- 1 TBSP unsalted butter, cubed

Direction

- FOR CAKE:
- Preheat oven to 350 degrees. Butter or spray the bottom of a large baking pan (9x13). Prepare cake mix as directed. Pour into the pan making sure no air bubbles are formed. Place spoonfuls of the hot fudge sauce evenly across the top of the batter.

- Bake cake as directed. It may take a bit longer to bake than usual due to the fudge. The cake is done when a toothpick inserted into the center (be sure to miss the fudge pocket) comes out clean. Remove the cake from the oven and prepare the ganache as follows.
- FOR GANACHE:
- Place the chocolate in a heat proof bowl. Heat the cream on the stove in a small pan until it just begins to boil. Remove from the heat and pour the hot cream into the bowl with the chocolate. Stir until all the cream is incorporated and the chocolate is melted. Add the cubed butter and continue stirring until it is well incorporated. Pour the ganache over the hot cake and serve warm. This rich fudgy cake goes well with a side of ice cream and will be a favorite of any chocolate fan!
- NOTE: Leftovers are just as delicious at room temp or right out of the fridge. (IF you have any leftovers!)

105. Chocolate Macaroon Filled Cake Recipe

Serving: 12 | Prep: | Cook: 55mins | Ready in:

Ingredients

- 1 egg white
- 3 tablespoons sugar
- 2 cups flaked coconut, finely chopped
- 1 tablespoon all-purpose flour
- cake BATTER:
- 4 eggs, separated
- 1-3/4 cups sugar, divided
- 1/2 cup shortening
- 1/2 cup sour cream
- 2 teaspoons vanilla extract
- 1/2 cup cold brewed coffee
- 1/4 cup buttermilk
- 2 cups all-purpose flour
- 1/2 cup baking cocoa
- 1 teaspoon baking soda
- 1 teaspoon salt
- FROSTING:
- 1 cup semisweet chocolate chips, melted and cooled
- 3 tablespoons butter, softened
- 2 cups confectioners' sugar
- 5 tablespoons milk

Direction

- In a small bowl, beat egg white on medium speed until soft peaks form. Gradually beat in sugar, 1 tablespoon at a time, on high until stiff glossy peaks form and sugar is dissolved. Fold in coconut and flour; set aside.
- In a large bowl, beat the egg whites on medium until soft peaks form. Gradually beat in 1/2 cup sugar, 1 tablespoon at a time, on high until stiff glossy peaks form and sugar is dissolved; set aside.
- In another large bowl, cream shortening and remaining sugar until light and fluffy. Add the egg yolks, sour cream and vanilla; beat until creamy. Combine coffee and buttermilk. Combine the flour, cocoa, baking soda and salt; add to creamed mixture alternately with coffee mixture. Beat until combined. Fold in beaten egg whites.
- Pour half of the batter into an ungreased 10-in. tube pan with removable bottom. Drop coconut filling by spoonfuls over batter. Top with remaining batter.
- Bake at 350° for 55-60 minutes or until a toothpick inserted near the center comes out clean. Immediately invert cake onto a wire rack; cool completely, about 1 hour. Run a knife around side of pan and remove.
- In a small bowl, beat frosting ingredients until smooth and creamy. Spread over the top and sides of cake. Yield: 12-16 servings.

106. Chocolate Meringue Cake Recipe

Serving: 0 | Prep: | Cook: 35mins | Ready in:

Ingredients

- 1/2 c. butter
- 1 c. sugar
- 4 eggs separated
- 4 squares (1 oz.) unsweetened chocolate. melted
- 1 tsp. vanilla
- 1/2 c. cake flour
- 1/2 tsp. baking soda
- 1/4 tsp. salt
- 1/4 c. hot water
- 1 pkg. (6 oz.) chocolate bits
- whipped cream
- Shaved chocolate

Direction

- Cream butter with 3/4 cup sugar until fluffy.
- Beat in egg yolks; add melted chocolate and vanilla.
- Sift together flour, soda and salt.
- Add to mixture.
- Stir in water.
- Spread quickly into 2 greased pans. (8 inches).
- Beat egg whites, gradually beating in 1/4 cup sugar until stiff and glossy.
- Sprinkle chocolate pieces over all.
- Spread meringue over tops.
- Bake at 350 degrees about 35 minutes.
- Cool on racks 10 minutes before removing from pans.
- Assemble so that meringue layers are together with whip cream between for filling.
- Frost top with whip cream.
- Sprinkle with shaved chocolate.

107. Chocolate Meringue Surprise Cake Recipe

Serving: 10 | Prep: | Cook: 50mins | Ready in:

Ingredients

- chocolate Cake:
- 4 ounces (120 grams) unsweetened chocolate, chopped
- 1/3 cup (28 grams) unsweetened cocoa powder (not Dutch-processed)
- 1 cup (240 ml) boiling water
- 2 1/4 cups (315 grams) all purpose flour
- 2 teaspoons baking powder
- 1 teaspoon baking soda
- 1/4 teaspoon salt
- 1 cup (226 grams) unsalted butter, room temperature
- 2 cups (400 grams) granulated white sugar
- 3 large eggs
- 2 teaspoons pure vanilla extract
- 1 cup (240 ml) milk
- For the chocolate filling:
- 1 cup heavy cream
- 12 ounces (340 gram) semi-sweet chocolate, diced
- 2 ounces (60 gram) butter, at room temperature
- For the finishing and the glaze:
- ¾ cup heavy cream
- 6 ounces (180 gram) semi-sweet chocolate, diced
- For the meringue:
- 3 egg whites
- 120 grams sugar
- ¼ tsp cream of tartar
- 1 tsp vanilla

Direction

- Preheat oven to 350 degrees. Butter and line with parchment paper, a 23 x 5 cm loose bottomed baking pan. Set aside.
- In a stainless steel or heatproof bowl place the chopped chocolate and cocoa powder. Pour the boiling water over the chocolate and cocoa

powder and stir until they have melted. Set aside to cool while you make the batter.
- In a separate bowl, whisk to combine, the flour, baking powder, baking soda, and salt. Set aside.
- In the bowl of your electric mixer, cream the butter. Gradually add the sugar and continue beating until the mixture is fluffy (this will take about 3-5 minutes). Add the eggs, one at a time, mixing well after each addition. Add the vanilla extract and melted chocolate mixture and beat to combine.
- Add the milk and flour mixtures in three additions, beginning and ending with the flour mixture. Beat only until the ingredients are incorporated.
- Pour the batter in the prepared pan and smooth the top. Bake for about 35 - 40 minutes or until a toothpick inserted in the center comes out clean. Remove from oven and place on a wire rack to cool for about 10 minutes.
- When completely cooled, split the cake in half horizontally; place one half on a wire rack.
- Chocolate filling:
- Put the cream in a saucepan and turn the heat to medium. Remove the pan from the heat immediately before the cream starts boiling. Add the diced chocolate, and stir until dissolved.
- In a small bowl, using a spatula or a fork beat the butter until soft. Stir the butter into the cream and let it cool at room temperature for about 2 hours. Spread half of the filling over the cake half and sprinkle the chopped meringue over. Place the other layer on top and spread the rest of the filling on the top and sides of the cake. Place the cake in the refrigerator while you make the glaze.
- Meringue:
- On a clean stainless bowl, place the egg whites and using clean beaters, beat till frothy.
- Add the cream of tartar or lemon juice if using till soft peaks formed.
- Start adding the sugar till you reach a stiff peaks and the meringue is shiny and glossy. Spread meringue in a round shape in a cookie sheet lined with foil and bake in a 300 F

preheated oven for 1 hour till crisp to the touch. Leave in the oven with door ajar to cool for 1 hour. Once cooled, chop the meringue into small bites.
- Final glaze:
- Put the cream in a saucepan and turn the heat to medium. Remove from the heat immediately before the cream starts boiling. Add the diced chocolate, and stir until dissolved. Whisk and beat the glaze until it is very light and soft. Remove the cake from the refrigerator, cover it with the glaze, and spread it uniformly with a spatula. Garnish with meringue kisses. Put the cake back in the refrigerator for 15 – 20 minutes to allow the glaze to cool. Keep in the refrigerator until serving time tightly covered.

108. Chocolate Mint Layer Cake 1 Recipe

Serving: 8 | Prep: | Cook: 30mins | Ready in:

Ingredients

- * 1 cup Mint-chocolate chips -- Nestles
- * 1 1/4 cups water -- divided
- * 2 1/4 cups flour -- Unbleached
- * 1 teaspoon salt
- * 1 teaspoon baking soda
- * 1/2 teaspoon baking powder
- * 1 1/2 cups brown sugar -- Firmly Packed
- * 1/2 cup butter -- Softened
- * 3 eggs -- Large
- -----chocolate mint FROSTING-----
- * 1/2 cup Mint-chocolate chips -- Nestles
- * 1/4 cup butter
- * 1 teaspoon vanilla extract
- * 1/4 teaspoon salt
- * 3 cups confectioners' sugar
- * 6 tablespoons milk
- -----GARNISHES-----
- * chocolate Leaves
- * chocolate curls

- * chocolate Gratings

Direction

- CAKE:
- Preheat oven to 375 degrees F. In a small saucepan, combine mint-chocolate chips and 1/4 cup of water. Cook over medium heat, stirring constantly, until chips are melted and mixture is smooth. Cool 10 minutes.
- In medium bowl, combine flour, salt, baking soda, and baking powder; set aside. In a large bowl, combine brown sugar and butter; beat until creamy.
- Add eggs, 1 at a time, beating well after each addition. Blend in chocolate mixture. Gradually beat in flour mixture alternately with remaining 1 cup of water.
- Pour into 2 greased and floured 9-inch round baking pans.
- Bake at 375 degrees F. for 25 to 30 minutes, or until cakes test done. Cool completely on wire racks. Fill and frost with Chocolate Mint Frosting. Garnish as desired.
- CHOCOLATE-MINT FROSTING:
- Combine over hot (not boiling) water, the mint-chocolate chips and butter. Stir until chips are melted and mixture is smooth. Stir in vanilla extract and salt. Transfer to a large bowl. Gradually beat in the confectioners' sugar alternately with milk; beat until smooth. (If necessary add more milk until desired consistency is reached.)
- GARNISHES:
- Use chocolate curls and grated chocolate on top of the cake. Form a ring of grated chocolate pieces around the outside edge and use the curls in the center.
- To make chocolate leaves, select several small leaves, wash and dry them and paint one side of them with melted chocolate. Chill until firm and peel the leaf off the chilled chocolate.

109. Chocolate Mocha Mud Cake Recipe

Serving: 12 | Prep: | Cook: 100mins | Ready in:

Ingredients

- 475gm of good quality dark chocolate
- 3 cups of sugar (yes that's right!)
- 250gm of butter
- 2 cups of espresso coffee (from a machine)
- 4 eggs
- 3 cups of flour
- 3 teaspoons of baking powder
- 1 teaspoon of salt
- Icing: (for one cake)
- 2 cups of icing sugar
- 3 tablespoons of softened butter
- hot water
- Berry sauce:
- 1 packet of frozen mixed berries
- 3 tablespoons of white sugar
- 2 teaspoons of cornflour

Direction

- Cake:
- Place the chocolate, sugar and butter into a bowl then pour the hot coffee over the top and whisk ingredients until the chocolate is melted and the sugar dissolved.
- Beat the eggs into the chocolate mixture one by one until thoroughly mixed.
- Gradually add the remaining sifted ingredients until thoroughly mixed.
- Pour mixture evenly into 2 greased and lined 22cm springform tins and bake at 140 degrees Celsius
- Icing:
- Mix the icing ingredients together and microwave on high for 1 minute until runny
- Pour icing over cake and leave to set
- Berry Sauce:
- Place the berries and sugar into a saucepan and cook on low until the sugar has dissolved.
- Stir in the cornflour until sauce has thickened.

- Serve cake warm or cold with cream and drizzle berry sauce over the top....YUM

110. Chocolate Moist Cake Recipe

Serving: 16 | Prep: | Cook: 30mins | Ready in:

Ingredients

- This is a dump and pour recipe:
- 2 cups flour
- 3/4 c cocoa
- 1 1/2 tsp. baking powder
- 1 cup milk
- 1 tsp. vanilla
- 2 cup sugar
- 2 tsp baking soda
- 1/2 cup oil
- 1 cup hot coffee
- 2 eggs
- pinch salt

Direction

- Beat all together. This will be very thin. Pour in greased baking pan. Cake pans or 9 x13 is what I usually use. OR IN ROUND CAKE PANS.
- Bake 30 minutes @ 350. Do not overbake. Test before removing.
- DO NOT OVER BAKE!!! OR IT WILL NOT HAVE THAT WONDERFUL MOISTNESS.
- Top with your favorite buttercream or icing. A lot of times just Whip cream does it for us. My children who are now grown even love this with just powdered sugar. I Love it with buttercream or German Chocolate icing. Sometimes I make a Raspberry Buttercream.
- I hope you enjoy this easy recipe.

111. Chocolate Mousse Cake Recipe

Serving: 4 | Prep: | Cook: 60mins | Ready in:

Ingredients

- 500g dark chocolate
- 2 tablespoons golden syrup
- 125g unsalted butter
- 4 eggs
- 1 tablespoon caster sugar
- 1 tablespoon plain flour, sifted
- Melted chocolate, to decorate
- chocolate ice cream, to serve

Direction

- 1. Preheat oven to 220°C. Grease and line the base of a 20cm round spring-form cake pan with non-stick baking paper.
- 2. Melt the chocolate, golden syrup and butter in a bowl over a saucepan of gently simmering water. Set aside to cool slightly.
- 3. Place eggs and sugar in a bowl. Using an electric mixer, beat on high for 10 minutes until very thick and pale. Gently fold in the flour then fold in the chocolate mixture until combined. Pour into the cake pan and bake on the middle shelf of the oven for 12 minutes. Remove from oven and run a knife around the edge of the cake. Remove collar from cake pan and transfer the cake to the fridge for 1 hour to cool.

112. Chocolate Oatmeal Cake Recipe

Serving: 1 | Prep: | Cook: 55mins | Ready in:

Ingredients

- 2 cups flour
- 2 tsp baking powder
- 2 tsp baking soda

- 1 tsp salt
- 1 tsp almond extract
- 10 tbsp cocoa
- 1 cup margarine
- 3 cups brown sugar
- 4 eggs
- 1 cup oatmeal (quaker rolled oats)
- 2 cups hot water
- 1 lg greased pan

Direction

- In a dish mix oatmeal and water, set aside.
- In another dish sift dry ingredients.
- In a large bowl cream together margarine, sugar and eggs.
- To this add the oat mixture.
- Gradually blend in dry ingredients beating well.
- Add almond extract.
- Pour into greased pan.
- Bake at 350 till done.

113. Chocolate Oatmeal Cake Mix Cookies Recipe

Serving: 48 | Prep: | Cook: 12mins | Ready in:

Ingredients

- * 1 package (approx. 18.25 ounces) chocolate fudge cake mix. or use spice, or yellow cake mix for an oatmeal taste.
- (If you use the yellow cake mix add 1 tes. cinnamon spice.)
- * 1/2 cup quick oats
- * 1/2 cup vegetable oil, such as Canola or corn oil
- * 2 large eggs
- * 3/4 cup toffee chips or chocolat/white chips
- * 3/4 cup chopped walnuts or pecan
- * 1/2 cup raisins or craisins (optional)

Direction

- PREPARATION:
- Lightly grease a baking sheet. Heat oven to 350°.
- Combine the cake mix in a mixing bowl with the oats, oil, and eggs; beat with an electric mixer on low speed just until moistened. Beat on high speed for a few seconds to blend thoroughly.
- Stir in the chips of choice and chopped nuts. Drop on the prepared baking sheet. Bake for 10 to 12 minutes. Let cookies cool for 1 minute in the pan; using a spatula, carefully remove to cool completely.
- Makes about 4 dozen 2-inch cookies.

114. Chocolate Orange Cake Recipe

Serving: 12 | Prep: | Cook: 20mins | Ready in:

Ingredients

- 2tsp plus 1/3c baking cocoa, divided
- 1/3c quick-cooking oats
- 2/3c reduced-fat sour cream
- 1/3c sugar blend
- 2 eggs
- 3Tbs triple sec or orange juice
- 2Tbs butter, melted
- 5tsp canola oil
- 1tsp vanila extract
- 2/3c flour
- 1tsp baking powder
- 1/2tsp baking soda
- 1/4tsp salt
- 1/4c mini sem-sweet chocolate chips
- 2tsp grated orange peel
- Frosting:
- 4oz. reduced-fat cream cheese
- 1/4c confectioners sugar
- 2tsp grated orange peel
- 2tsp orange juice

Direction

- Coat an 8" square baking dish with cooking spray and sprinkle with 2 tsp. cocoa; set aside. Place oats in a small food processor; cover and process till ground. Set aside
- In a large bowl, beat the sour cream, sugar blend, eggs, Triple Sec, butter, oil and vanilla until well blended. Combine the flour, baking powder, baking soda, salt and remaining cocoa; gradually beat into sour cream mixture until blended. Stir in chocolate chips and orange peel.
- Transfer to reserved dish. Bake at 350 for 20-25 mins. or till toothpick comes out clean. Cool completely on wire rack.
- Frosting: In a small bowl, beat cream cheese until fluffy. Add confectioners' sugar, orange peel and juice; beat until smooth. Frost top of cake.

115. Chocolate Orange Carrot Cake Recipe

Serving: 8 | Prep: | Cook: 50mins | Ready in:

Ingredients

- 1-1/2 cups vegetable oil
- 4 large eggs
- 2-1/2 cups all purpose flour
- 2-1/4 cups granulated sugar
- 2/3 cup unsweetened cocoa powder
- 2 teaspoons baking soda
- 1 teaspoon salt
- 2 cups finely shredded peeled carrots
- 1 cup packed sweetened flaked coconut
- 1-1/2 teaspoons grated orange peel
- 11 ounce can mandarin oranges drained and cut into 1/2" pieces
- Frosting:
- 2-1/2 cups semisweet chocolate chips
- 1 cup unsalted nondairy margarine at room temperature
- 1/3 cup powdered sugar
- 1/4 cup frozen orange juice concentrate thawed
- Additional canned mandarin orange segments drained and patted very dry

Direction

- Preheat oven to 350 then spray two round cake pans with non-stick spray.
- Beat oil and eggs in large bowl until well blended and thick about 2 minutes.
- Add flour, sugar, cocoa powder, baking soda and salt then beat at low speed to blend.
- Increase speed and beat 1 minute longer.
- Stir in carrots, coconut and orange peel then orange pieces.
- Divide batter between prepared pans then bake 40 minutes and cool cakes in pan 10 minutes.
- Turn out onto racks and cool completely.
- Stir chocolate chips in heavy medium saucepan over very low heat until melted and smooth.
- Remove from heat and cool to lukewarm.
- Spoon 1/3 cup chocolate into small bowl and reserve for decoration.
- Beat margarine and sugar in medium bowl until fluffy.
- Beat in remaining melted chocolate and orange juice concentrate.
- Place 1 cake layer on platter and spread with 2/3 cup frosting.
- Top with second cake layer then spread remaining frosting over top and sides of cake.
- Arrange additional orange segments around top edge of cake.
- Reheat 1/3 cup reserved chocolate to pourable consistency if necessary.
- Drizzle orange segments with chocolate then cover cake with dome and refrigerate.

116. Chocolate Passion Cake Recipe

Serving: 8 | Prep: | Cook: 45mins | Ready in:

Ingredients

- Cake:
- 5 eggs
- 150 grams sugar
- 1 1/4 cup flour
- 1/3 cup cocoa powder
- 175 grams grated carrots
- 50 grams chopped walnuts
- 2 tbsp vegetable oil
- Filling:
- 350 grams cream cheese softned
- 1 cup icing(powder) sugar
- 175 grams milk or dark chocolate, melted

Direction

- Preheat oven to 375 F. Lightly grease and line the base of a 20cm deep cake pan.
- Place the eggs and sugar in a large mixing bowl set over a pan of gently simmering water and whisk till very thick.
- Remove from heat and sieve the flour and cocoa powder into the bowl and carefully fold in.
- Fold in the walnuts and carrots and oil till all combined.
- Pour in the cake pan and bake for 45 minutes till springy to the touch. Cool completely.
- Filling:
- Beat together the cheese and the sugar till combined.
- Beat in the melted chocolate. Split the cake in half, spread half of the filling on it, top with the other cake half and cover with the remainder of the filling swirling with a knife or a teaspoon to make a decorative look. Chill

117. Chocolate Peach Cake Recipe

Serving: 8 | Prep: | Cook: 35mins | Ready in:

Ingredients

- 1 box Duncan Hines dark chocolate fudge cake (Any other chocolate cake mix will do but I prefer this one)
- 1 1/3 cup water
- 1/2 cup veg. oil
- 3 lg. eggs
- 1 tbls. expresso powder
- 1 lg. can sliced peaches
- 1 container Cool Whip
- chocolate shavings

Direction

- Prepare cake according to directions for a 2 layer 8 In. cake using first 5 ingredients
- Cool on rack
- Cut 1/2 can of peaches into bite size pieces.
- On plate, frost first layer of cake with cool whip
- Scatter peach pieces over top of 1st layer.
- Put 2nd layer on and frost whole cake with remaining cool whip
- Arrange remaining peaches on top of cake. (I do so in a fan fashion)
- Finish with chocolate shavings over the top

118. Chocolate Peanut Butter Swirl Cake Recipe

Serving: 16 | Prep: | Cook: 30mins | Ready in:

Ingredients

- 2-1/4 cups all purpose flour sifted
- 1-1/2 cups sugar
- 1/3 cup cocoa
- 1-1/2 teaspoons baking soda
- 1/2 teaspoon salt

- 1-1/2 cups water
- 1/2 cup vegetable oil
- 4-1/2 teaspoons white vinegar
- 1-1/2 teaspoons vanilla extract
- 4 ounces softened cream cheese
- 1/4 cup creamy peanut butter
- 1/4 teaspoon peanut butter flavoring
- 1/3 cup sugar
- 1 egg
- 1/8 teaspoon salt
- 1/2 cup semisweet chocolate chips
- 1/2 cup pecans chopped
- 1 tablespoon sugar

Direction

- Combine dry ingredients.
- Stir in oil, water, vinegar and vanilla.
- Mix well.
- When well mixed pour into greased rectangular baking pan.
- Beat cream cheese, peanut butter, flavoring, sugar, egg and salt until smooth.
- Stir in chocolate chips and drop by tablespoons over cake batter.
- Cut through batter with a knife to swirl.
- Sprinkle with pecans and remaining sugar.
- Bake at 350 for 30 minutes.
- Cool before cutting.
- Refrigerate any leftovers.

119. Chocolate Peanut Ripple Cake Recipe

Serving: 12 | Prep: | Cook: 35mins | Ready in:

Ingredients

- cake
- 1 pkg. Fudge Marble cake mix
- 1 cup dairy sour cream
- 1/2 cup creamy peanut butter
- 1/4 cup water
- 3 eggs
- 1/2 cup chopped peanuts
- frosting
- 1 can chocolate Fudge frosting Supreme
- 2 T creamy peanut butter
- 1 T chopped peanuts

Direction

- Heat oven to 350F. Grease and flour two 8 or 9-inch round cake pans.
- In large bowl, blend cake mix (reserve marble pouch), sour cream, ½ cup peanut butter, water and eggs until moistened. Beat 2 minutes at highest speed. Fold in 1/2 cup chopped peanuts.
- Pour 3/4 of batter into prepared pans.
- To the remaining batter add marble pouch and 2 T water; blend well. Spoon randomly over yellow batter. Marble by pulling knife through batter in wide curves, then turn pan and repeat.
- Bake at 350F. for 35 to 45 minutes, or until toothpick inserted in center comes out clean.
- Cool upright in pan 15 min; then remove. Cool completely.
- Blend frosting with 2 T peanut butter. Spread small amount (about 1/3 cup) between cake layers. Frost sides and top with remaining frosting. Garnish with 1 T chopped peanuts.

120. Chocolate Pistachio Nut Marble Cake Recipe

Serving: 12 | Prep: | Cook: 50mins | Ready in:

Ingredients

- 1 box Duncan Hines butter cake mix
- 1 small package pistachio instant pudding
- 4 eggs
- 1 cup sour cream
- 1/2 cup oil
- 1/2 teaspoon almond extract
- 1/4 cup Hershey's chocolate syrup (to go in half the batter)

Direction

- In large mixing bowl, combine all ingredients EXCEPT chocolate syrup.
- Blend with mixer for 30 seconds.
- Beat at medium for 2 minutes.
- Pour 1/2 batter into a separate bowl.
- Stir into this batter 1/4 cup chocolate syrup.
- Spoon batters alternately into a greased and floured 10 tube or Bundt pan.
- Zigzag spatula through batter to marble.
- Place in oven and bake at 350 degrees for 50 minutes or until center springs back when lightly touched.
- Cool 15 minutes before removing from pan.
- MAY ICE WITH A FAVORITE CHOCOLATE ICING AND TOP WITH CRUSHED PISTACHIOS.
- Cake is delicious served without icing and chocolate ice cream.

121. Chocolate Polenta Cake Recipe

Serving: 8 | Prep: | Cook: 35mins | Ready in:

Ingredients

- 12 ounces semisweet chocolate
- 3/4 pound sweet butter
- 8 egg yolks
- 1 cup brown sugar
- 1/3 cup white sugar
- 1/3 cup ground almonds
- 1 tablespoon all purpose flour
- 1/4 cup cornmeal
- 8 egg whites
- 1 tablespoon cream of tartar

Direction

- In large saucepan over very low heat melt chocolate.
- Add butter then stir until melted and remove from heat.
- In large bowl combine egg yolks, brown sugar and white sugar then stir until well mixed.
- Add chocolate and stir well until combined.
- In small bowl combine almonds, flour and cornmeal then stir until well mixed.
- Pour into chocolate and stir until combined.
- In large bowl with electric mixer beat egg whites with cream of tartar until they form stiff peaks.
- Fold egg whites into chocolate in three batches.
- Bake in a buttered floured springform pan for 5 minutes at 400.
- Reduce heat to 350 and bake another 25 minutes.
- Let cool completely before removing from pan.

122. Chocolate Potato Cake Recipe

Serving: 16 | Prep: | Cook: 40mins | Ready in:

Ingredients

- 3/4 cup butter or margarine, softened
- 1-1/2 cup sugar, divided
- 4 eggs, separated
- 1 cup hot mashed or riced potatoes (no milk, butter or seasoning added)
- 1-1/2 cups all-poupose flour
- 1/2 cup baking cocoa
- 2 teaspoons baking powder
- 1 teaspoon ground cinnamon
- 1/2 teaspoon ground nutmeg
- 1/4 teaspoon ground cloves
- 1 cup milk
- 1 teaspoon vanilla extract
- 1 cup chopped nuts
- FLUFFY WHITE FROSTING:
- 2 egg whites
- 1-1/2 cups sugar
- 1/3 cup water
- 2 teaspoons light corn syrup

- 1/8 teaspoon salt
- 1 teaspoon vanilla extract

Direction

- In a mixing bowl, cream butter and 1 cup sugar.
- Add egg yolks; beat well.
- Add potatoes and mix thoroughly.
- Combine flour, cocoa, baking powder, cinnamon, salt, nutmeg and cloves; add to creamed mixture alternately with milk, beating until smooth.
- Stir in vanilla and nuts.
- In a mixing bowl, beat egg whites until foamy.
- Gradually add remaining sugar; beat until stiff peaks form. Fold into batter.
- Pour into a greased and floured 13-in. x 9-in. x 2-in. baking pan.
- Bake at 350 degrees for 40-45 minutes or until cake tests done.
- Cool.
- Combine first five frosting ingredients in top of a double boiler.
- Beat with electric mixer for 1 minutes.
- Place over boiling water; beat constantly for 7 minutes, scraping sides of pan occasionally.
- Remove from heat.
- Add vanilla; beat 1 minute.
- Frost cake.
- Yield: 16-20 servings.
- Editor's Note: Cake is moist and has a firm texture.

123. Chocolate Pound Cake Recipe

Serving: 8 | Prep: | Cook: 70mins | Ready in:

Ingredients

- 1/4 cup shortening
- 2 sticks butter softened
- 3 cups granulated sugar
- 5 eggs
- 3 cups all purpose flour
- 1/2 cup cocoa
- 1 teaspoon baking powder
- 1 cup buttermilk
- 2 teaspoons vanilla extract

Direction

- Preheat oven to 350.
- Cream shortening, butter and sugar together until light and fluffy.
- Add eggs one at a time beating for 1 minute after each addition.
- Measure flour and sift it together with cocoa and baking powder.
- Sift again.
- Mix buttermilk and vanilla together in a cup then add to creamed mixture alternating with dry ingredients in thirds.
- Mix gently just until well blended.
- Pour into a greased and floured 10-inch tube pan.
- Bake for 1 hour and 10 minutes.

124. Chocolate Praline Cake Recipe

Serving: 8 | Prep: | Cook: 35mins | Ready in:

Ingredients

- 1 cup firmly packed brown sugar
- 1/2 cup butter
- 1/4 cup whipping cream
- 1/2 cup finely chopped pecans
- 1 package devil's food cake mix with pudding
- 1-1/4 cups water
- 1/3 cup vegetable oil
- 3 large eggs
- Filling and Topping:
- 3/4 cup whipping cream
- 1/4 cup sifted powdered sugar
- 1/4 teaspoon vanilla extract

- pecan halves
- chocolate curls

Direction

- Combine first 3 ingredients in a medium saucepan.
- Cook over medium heat until sugar and butter melt stirring occasionally.
- Pour mixture evenly into 2 round cake pans then sprinkle evenly with chopped pecans.
- Combine cake mix, water, oil and eggs in a large mixing bowl.
- Beat at high speed of an electric mixer 2 minutes or until blended then pour into prepared pans.
- Bake at 325 for 35 minutes then cool in pans on wire racks 5 minutes.
- Turn out carefully onto racks and allow to cool completely.
- Beat whipping cream until foamy then gradually add sugar and vanilla.
- Beat well until soft peaks form.
- Spread filling and topping mixture between layers and on top of cake.
- Top with pecan halves and chocolate curls then store in refrigerator.

125. Chocolate Praline Mousse Cake Recipe

Serving: 6 | Prep: | Cook: 210mins | Ready in:

Ingredients

- *Cook time inlcudes 30 minutes should you decide to make your own cake base: genoise, sponge, or a biscuit.
- Ingredients:
- Cake:
- 4 yolks
- 30g sugar
- 1 tbsp Frangelico hazelnut Liquer/rum
- Pinch of salt
- 80ml warm water
- 4 tbsp warm corn oil
- 75g cake flour
- 25g hazelnut meal
- less than 1/2 tsp baking powder
- 4 egg whites
- 35g sugar
- 1/2 tsp cream of tartar
- chocolate Praline:
- 110g chocolate
- 90g praline
- 70g milk + 50g whipping cream
- 30g sugar
- 1 tbsp Frangelico hazelnut Liquer/rum/Grand Marnier
- 250g whipping cream (whipped)
- 10g gelatine sheet
- chocolate Ganache:
- 95g chocolate
- 25g butter
- 55g skim milk
- Decoration:
- 8 - 12 hazelnuts roasted and skin rubbed off
- 1 cup sugar
- 1/2 cup water
- pinch of cream tartar
- 100ml sweet whipping cream + 1 tbsp cocoa powder (whipped)

Direction

- Cake:
- Cut the cake into 2 equal layers of about 2 cm thick and trim the cake to be slightly smaller than the cake pan.
- Chocolate Praline:
- Method:
- 1. Whip 250g whipping cream till mousse state and chill till ready to use.
- 2. Soak gelatine sheet in water till soft, remove from water and leave aside.
- 3. Heat 70g milk and 50g whipping cream till hot but not boiling, stir in sugar and then praline till a smooth paste is formed.
- 4. While still warm, add in the chopped chocolate pieces and stir till you get a smooth paste. You might need to warm this in a hot water bath, if the chocolate pieces are not

dissolved completely. Stir in the gelatine and liqueur. Cool the chocolate praline mousse a little.
- 5. Stir some whipped cream into the slightly warm chocolate praline mousse a few times. Pour chocolate praline into the whipped cream and mix gently till well combined. If the mixture is runny, chill in the refrigerator for 2 - 3 minutes.
- 6. Line the cake pan with a cake board and line the inner ring of the cake pan with pectin sheet or plastic cake wrapper. Put in a layer of the cake.
- 7. Pour more than 1/3 of the chocolate praline mousse on top of the cake layer and tilt the cake pan left and right so that the mousse will fill up all around the cake layer. Chill for 2 - 3 minutes.
- 8. Top it with another layer of the cake and then all the mousse and do the tilting to even out the mousse.
- 9. Chill the cake for about 2 - 3 hours till set.
- Chocolate Ganache:
- Method:
- 1. Warm butter and chopped chocolate over a basin of hot water and stir till a smooth chocolate paste is formed.
- 2. Stir in milk a third at a time.
- 3. Stirring the ganache constantly till it is slightly warm, smooth and runny, pour this ganache over the chilled and set cake from above. Tilt pan left and right gently to even out the ganache. Chill till set.
- Decoration:
- Method:
- 1. Roast whole hazelnuts at 160C for 5 - 6 minutes. Rub off skin and leave aside to cool.
- 2. Cook sugar, water and a pinch of cream of tartar in a saucepan, stirring till all sugar dissolved.
- Leave it to boil without stirring till syrup is bubbling and golden in color.
- 3. Leave syrup to cool till bubbles have settled, dip hazelnuts into the toffee and lie them on a baking sheet to set and cool. You may spoon more toffee onto the pattern formed and create any designs you like on the hazelnuts.
- 4. Dip a fork into the toffee and do zigzag design on baking sheet. When cooled and set, break them up and these will be the decorations for the side of the cake.
- 5. If the toffee has thicken, you can warm it up to regain the runny texture.
- 6. Whip sweet whipping cream with cocoa powder till stiff.
- 7. Make some rosettes on the chilled cake and top it up with hazelnut toffee.
- 8. Decorate the side of the cake with the zigzag toffee pieces.
- Notes:
- I used Valrhona 70% Guanaja in Beans (Dark Couvertures) dark chocolate all the way through.
- I would suggest Valrhona 40% (Milk Couvertures) for the mousse and Valrhona 66% or 70% for the ganache.
- Best to use hazelnut liqueur for that nutty aroma.

126. Chocolate Prune Cake 1 Recipe

Serving: 12 | Prep: | Cook: 40mins | Ready in:

Ingredients

- * 9 (1 ounce) squares bittersweet chocolate
- * 2/3 cup unsalted butter
- * 3 eggs
- * 3/4 cup white sugar
- * 1/3 cup all-purpose flour
- * 3/4 cup finely ground almonds
- * 1/2 cup prunes, pitted and chopped
- * 1/2 cup brandy
- * 3 tablespoons water

Direction

- 1. Soak prunes overnight in brandy. Melt chocolate and butter or margarine with water.

- 2. In a large bowl, beat egg yolks and sugar until pale. Stir in chocolate mixture. Gently mix in flour and ground nuts. Stir in prunes.
- 3. In another bowl, beat egg whites to stiff peaks. Carefully fold into cake mixture. Pour into a greased 9 inch round cake tin.
- 4. Bake at 375 degrees F (175 degrees C) for 30 - 40 minutes. Remove from oven, and cool on a wire rack. Frost with Chocolate Ganache Frosting.

127. Chocolate Pudding Cake And Hazelnut Sauce Recipe

Serving: 9 | Prep: | Cook: 35mins | Ready in:

Ingredients

- 1 cup All Purpose flour
- ½ cup granulated sugar
- 1 cup dark chocolate morsels (used Giaradelli)
- ¼ teaspoon salt
- 1 tablespoon baking powder
- 1 cup toasted walnut halves
- 1 cup sundried cranberries
- 3 eggs
- 2 tablespoons butter, softened
- 3/4 cup half and half
- ************FOR hazelnut SAUCE:1 cup store bought hazelnut chocolate, ¼ cup half and half

Direction

- Pre heat the oven to 350 F.
- Combine the dry ingredients in a mixing bowl and set aside.
- Whisk eggs, butter and half and half until well combined.
- Combine both wet and dry ingredients.
- Pour into a baking dish, put in a baking pan, situate the pan on a rack in the bottom part of the oven.
- Bake for 35 minutes until set.
- Let cool just until warm.
- Divide into 8 to 10 pieces. Drizzle the sauce on top and around.
- Dust with confectioner's sugar and cocoa powder and serve.
- Pair with pistachio and vanilla ice cream for a complete indulgement.
- ************DIRECTIONS FOR HAZELNUT SAUCE: While the cake is baking, heat the half and half in a small sauce pot; 30 seconds to 1 minute.
- Add hazelnut and continue to whisk until the cream and hazelnut are well incorporated.
- Cool it down to room temperature and serve with the cake

128. Chocolate Pudding Cake Recipe

Serving: 12 | Prep: | Cook: 40mins | Ready in:

Ingredients

- 1 box chocolate fudge cake mix
- water, vegetable and eggs called for on cake mix box
- 4 ounce size milk chocolate instant pudding mix
- 2 cups cold milk

Direction

- Preheat oven to 350. Make and cool cake as directed on box for rectangular pan. Poke cake with handle of wooden spoon in several places. In medium bowl beat pudding mix and milk with wire whisk for about 2 minutes. Pour pudding evenly over cake. Run knife around sides of pan to loosen cake. Refrigerate 2 hours. Store loosely covered in refrigerator.

129. Chocolate Raspberry Ice Cream Cake Recipe

Serving: 12 | Prep: | Cook: 45mins | Ready in:

Ingredients

- 1 recipe Clara's chocolate cake (see my recipes)
- 1 jar Fudge Topping Or Ganache (1 c SS chocolate 1 c 35 % Cream)
- 1 jar Seedless raspberry jam
- 1 pint chocolate ice cream or enough to make a 1 " layer
- 16 chocolate Fudge cream-filled cookies, crushed to pea size

Direction

- Bake cake using a 10 inch spring-form pan instead of 9x13.
- Be sure to dust pan with cocoa, not flour.
- Cool completely and remove outer ring only
- Using heavy thread or fishing line, cut cake in 1/2 horizontally
- Replace ring
- Place crushed cookies on cake bottom and press down lightly
- Cover crumbs with 1 inch of the best chocolate ice cream you can afford
- Place in freezer
- With cake top up-side-down on a piece of waxed paper, spread the bottom (side facing up) with enough jam to cover without running off.
- Remove bottom from freezer, place jam-covered top over ice cream, and press down lightly. Remove waxed paper.
- Cover top with Chocolate Fudge topping or Ganache
- Return to freezer for 4 hours or overnight.
- To serve, remove cake from freezer 1/2 an hour before and remove outer ring
- Using a sharp, heavy knife dipped in hot water (dry off), cut in 12 and serve.
- Keep leftovers frozen.
- Return cake to freezer.

130. Chocolate Ribbon Cake Recipe

Serving: 15 | Prep: | Cook: 25mins | Ready in:

Ingredients

- FOR THE cheese LAYER
- 8 ounces low-fat cream cheese, softened
- 1/4 cup granulated sugar
- FOR THE cake
- 2 cups all-purpose flour
- 1/4 cup unsweetened cocoa powder
- 1 teaspoon baking powder
- 1 teaspoon baking soda
- 1 cup granulated sugar
- 1/2 cup margarine, softened
- 2 large eggs
- 1 cup skim milk
- FOR THE frosting
- 3 cups confectioners' sugar
- 1/2 cup skim milk
- 2 squares (2 ounces) semisweet chocolate, melted

Direction

- Preheat oven to 350° F.
- Spray a 13- x 9-inch baking pan with vegetable cooking spray.
- To prepare cheese layer, beat cream cheese and sugar until smooth.
- To prepare cake, in a large bowl, combine flour, cocoa, baking powder, and baking soda. Using an electric mixer set on medium speed, beat sugar and butter until light. Beat in eggs. Alternately, beat in flour mixture and milk until smooth.
- Pour half of batter into prepared pan. Spread cheese mixture over batter; top with remaining batter. Bake until set, about 25 minutes. Place pan on a wire rack to cool completely.
- To prepare frosting, beat confectioners' sugar, milk, and chocolate until smooth. Spread over cake.

131. Chocolate Sandwich Cake Triggers Passion Recipe

Serving: 10 | Prep: | Cook: 25mins | Ready in:

Ingredients

- 4-5 oz milk chocolate
- 8-oz soft margarine
- 8-oz superfine caster sugar
- 7-oz self raising flour
- 1-oz cocoa powder
- 1 -teaspoons baking powder
- 1 -tablespoon milk
- 6 -eggs
- 1-1/4 tsp salt
- 2 tsp vanilla

Direction

- Preheat a 350 degrees F/ 180 degrees C/Gas 4 oven. Line 3.8 x 1 ½m (20 x 3 cm) round tins with greaseproof paper and grease.
- Dust evenly with flour and spread with a brush. Set aside.
- Melt the butter over a low heat. With a spoon, skin off any foam that rises to the surface. Set aside.
- Sift the float, cocoa, baking powder and salt together 3 times and set aside.
- Place the eggs and sugar in a large heatproof bowl set over a pan of hot water. With an electric mixer, heat until the mixture doubles in volume and is thick enough to leave a ribbon trail when the beaters are lifted, about 10 minutes. Add the vanilla.
- Sift over the dry ingredients in 3 batches, folding in carefully, after each addition. Fold in the butter.
- Divide the mixture between the tins and bake until the cakes pull away from the sides of the tin, about 25 minutes. Transfer in a rack.
- ***.
- For the icing, melt the chocolate in the top of a double boiler, or in a heat proof bowl set over hot water.
- Off the heat, stir in the butter and egg yolks. Return to a low heat and stir until thick.
- Remove from the heat and set aside.
- Whip the cream until firm, set aside. In another bowl, beat the egg whites until stiff. Add thaw sugar and heat until glossy.
- Fold the cream into the chocolate mixture, then carefully fold in the egg.
- Refrigerate for 20 minutes to thicken the icing.
- Tip: Line baking pans with foil so that they're easy to clean.
- *******for the icing
- 3 eggs
- 3 tablespoons caster sugar
- 1 cup whipping cream
- 1/4 cup of butter
- 4-5 ounces milk chocolate as above

132. Chocolate Sandwich Cake Recipe

Serving: 8 | Prep: | Cook: 30mins | Ready in:

Ingredients

- 175 gmgolden caster sugar
- 150 gm butter , diced
- 3 Large eggs
- 1 tsp vanilla essence
- 1 tbsp thick milk
- 1/2 tbsp golden syrup
- 150 gm self raising flour
- 25 gm cocoa pwd
- ....
- 2 tbsp black cherry jam
- 2 tbsp cream
- ....
- 2 tbsp finely grated dark chocolate or
- 1 tbsp icing sugar for dusting
- ....

Direction

- Pre heat oven at 170 deg C.
- Beat the butter and sugar until creamy.
- Add the eggs and essence.
- Beat until thick.
- Add the flour, cocoa and the milk.
- Mix well.
- Pour into a 9 inch greased pan.
- Bake for 35 mins.
- Cool.
- Cut into 2 layers.
- Spread the jam and then the cream on a layer and sandwich with the other layer.
- Dust with icing sugar or sprinkle the chocolate shaving on top.

133. Chocolate Sheath Cake With Chocolate Frosting Recipe

Serving: 12 | Prep: | Cook: 30mins | Ready in:

Ingredients

- 1/2 teaspoon cinnamon
- 2 cups granulated sugar
- 2 cups flour
- 1 teaspoon baking soda
- 1 stick oleo
- 1/2 cup shortening
- 2 tablespoons cocoa
- 1 cup water
- 1/2 cup buttermilk
- 2 eggs
- 1 teaspoon vanilla
- Frosting:
- 1 can vanilla creamy supreme frosting
- 3 ounces white baking chocolate melted
- 1 teaspoon vanilla
- 8 ounces frozen whipped topping thawed

Direction

- Preheat oven to 375.
- Sift together cinnamon, sugar, flour and baking soda.
- Bring to boil then oleo, shortening, cocoa and water then pour over the flour mixture.
- Mix well then add buttermilk, eggs and vanilla.
- Mix well and pour into a well-greased shallow pan and bake for 30 minutes.
- When cool frost with icing.
- To prepare frosting beat frosting at medium speed.
- Gradually add the white chocolate and beat at high speed for 30 seconds.
- Fold in vanilla and whipped frosting then refrigerate until ready to ice cake.
- Store iced cake in refrigerator.

134. Chocolate Snickerdoodle Cake With Cinnamon Chocolate Cream Cheese Frosting Recipe

Serving: 12 | Prep: | Cook: 32mins | Ready in:

Ingredients

- 1 pkg dark chocolate fudge cake mix
- 3/4 cup milk
- 3/4 cup oil
- 3 large eggs
- 2 tsp cinnamoon
- 1 tsp vanilla
- Frosting:
- 1 pkg (8 ounces) light cream cheese, at room temp
- 1 stick butter, at room temp
- 1/2 cup unsweetened cocoa powder
- 1 tsp cinnamon
- 1 tsp vanilla
- 4 cups powdered sugar

Direction

- Preheat oven to 350 degrees. Generously grease and flour 2 - 9 inch cake pans.

- Place cake mix, milk, oil eggs, cinnamon, and vanilla in mixing bowl. Blend with mixer for 1 minute. Scrape down sides and beat 2 minutes more.
- Divide batter evenly between prepared pans.
- Bake 28 - 32 minutes.
- Remove from oven and cool 10 minutes. Run a dinner knife around the edge of each layer and invert onto a rack, then invert again onto another rack----so both are right side up. Allow to cool 30 minutes.
- Meanwhile, place cream cheese and butter in mixing bowl. Blend on low speed 30 seconds. Add cocoa powder, cinnamon, vanilla and 3 3/4 cups sugar. Blend with mixer on low speed until all ingredients are moistened, 30 seconds. Add more sugar if frosting seems too thin. Increase the speed to medium and beat until the frosting is fluffy, 2 minutes more.
- Place one cake layer, right side up, on a serving platter. Spread the top with frosting. Place the second layer, right side up, on top of the first layer and frost the top and sides of the cake.
- Place this cake, uncovered, in the refrigerator until the frosting sets, 20 minutes. The store at room temp for 3 days or in the refrigerator for 1 week.

135. Chocolate Soda Pop Cake Recipe

Serving: 12 | Prep: | Cook: 25mins | Ready in:

Ingredients

- Boxed cake mix
- Can of soda pop
- oil for pan
- Dusting of cocoa powder, Confectioners sugar-whatever

Direction

- Preheat oven as instructed on the box.
- Let's say I am making a chocolate cake:
- Oil and dust the pan (oil: any cocoa mix).
- Put mix into bowl.
- Dump 3/4 of the can of soda and fold until all is moist.
- Add rest of soda and hand mix.
- Pour in prepared pan.
- For baking directions follow directions on the box (I usually turn oven down a few degrees and keep an eye on it for doneness. Do not over bake; keep moist.
- I use these cakes especially for trifles, it is unbelievably moist.
- SUGGESTIONS:
- Carrot Cake-Orange Soda
- Red Velvet Cake-Cherry Soda
- White Cake-Ginger Ale
- Spice cake-Ginger Ale
- And on and on
- If you are a vegan (or have to cook for one every day) there are great mixes on the market
- Make whatever frosting you like
- For Vegan: Tofutti-Better than Cream Cheese, soy milk, powdered sugar. Add any crushed fruit to the icing.

136. Chocolate Sour Cream Cake Recipe

Serving: 12 | Prep: | Cook: 35mins | Ready in:

Ingredients

- 2c sugar
- 1 3/4c cake flour
- 2Tbs cornstarch
- 1tsp baking soda
- 1/4tsp salt
- 2/3c unsweetened cocoa
- 1tsp instant coffee
- 1tsp boiling water
- 1/2c sour cream
- 1tsp vanilla
- 4lg. egg whites, at room temp.

- 14Tbs butter, melted
- ice cream, to serve

Direction

- Adjust oven rack to lower-middle position and heat oven to 350. Spray 2 8" cake pans with vegetable cooking spray, then dust pans with flour, knocking out excess.
- Whisk sugar, flour, cornstarch, baking soda and salt and set aside.
- In another medium bowl, measure cocoa and coffee, then whisk in water to form smooth paste. Stir in sour cream and vanilla; set aside.
- In a third bowl, using hand mixer, beat egg whites to soft peaks. Add melted butter to dry ingredients; without cleaning the beaters, mix until butter is completely incorporated.
- Immediately add cocoa mixture; beat until batter is smooth, 2-3 mins. Carefully fold egg whites into batter with rubber spatula until just incorporated.
- Divide batter evenly between the 2 pans and bake until skewers inserted in center of each cake comes out with still moist crumbs, 30-35 mins. Remove from oven, let cakes cool slightly in pans, about 5 mins. Invert each cake onto a plate and back to rack so it sits top side up. Cool completely.
- Double wrap one cake and freeze for another use. Serve remaining cake in wedges with ice cream.
- Note: This cake is firm on bottom and soft on top, so it's important to invert it back on wire rack to cool. Otherwise, the top may stick to the rack and tear as removed

137. Chocolate Sourkrout Cake Recipe

Serving: 8 | Prep: | Cook: 37mins | Ready in:

Ingredients

- 2 1/4 c. flour
- 1 tsp. baking soda
- 1 tsp. baking powder
- 1 1/2 c. sugar
- 2/3 c. shortening
- 3 eggs
- 1 1/4 tsp. vanilla
- 1/4 tsp. salt
- 1/2 c. unsweetened cocoa
- 1 c. water
- 1 c. sauerkraut, rinsed, drained and chopped

Direction

- Sift together flour, baking soda and baking powder, set aside. Cream sugar and shortening, add eggs, mix well, and then add vanilla, salt and cocoa. Mix well.
- Alternately add flour mixture and water. Add sauerkraut. Bake in greased and floured pan. For two or 3, 8 inch square pans, bake at 325 degrees for 25-30 minutes.
- For 1 Bundt pan or angel food pan, bake 45-50 minutes at 375 degrees.
- TOPPINGS:
- May spread with favorite icing. I use White Buttercream or 7 min, or Thickened whipped cream.

138. Chocolate Sponge Cake Recipe

Serving: 12 | Prep: | Cook: 25mins | Ready in:

Ingredients

- 4 L egg whites
- 1/2 tsp salt
- ....
- 100g caster sugar
- 125 g olive margarine
- 4 L egg yolks
- 1 tsp vanilla essence
- ....
- 200 g self raising flour

- 1/2 tsp baking pwd and baking soda - sifted
- ....
- 1 C water with mango (essence) fruit drink base
- 3 tbsp chocolate syrup
- ....
- Filling :
- 2 tbsp cream cheese
- 1 tbsp mango (essence) fruit drink base
- ....
- Ganache :
- 150 g baking chocolate
- 3/4 C heavy cream
- ....
- chocolate shavings
- Dragees Gold

Direction

- Pre heat the oven at 200 deg C.
- Grease and line 2 round pans.
- Beat egg whites with salt until stiff peak form and set aside.
- Beat the sugar and margarine until creamy.
- Now add the yolks and essence until it mix well.
- Add half of the dry ingredients along with half of the juice.
- Beat 30 secs.
- Add the rest of the dry ingredients and juice.
- Mix the syrup in.
- Fold in the egg whites.
- Pour in the tin and bake for 20 mins.
- Mix the filling and spread on top of a layer.
- Keep the other layer on top.
- Microwave the cream and add the chocolate.
- Beat it after 5 mins and pour over the cake evenly.
- Now decorate and chill until ready to serve.

139. Chocolate Sponge Cake With Fresh Fruit Recipe

Serving: 12 | Prep: | Cook: 20mins | Ready in:

Ingredients

- cake Ingredients:
- 1 cup powdered sugar
- 4 eggs, room temperature
- 1 egg yolk, room temperature
- 1 tablespoon creme de cacao*
- 1/2 cup all-purpose flour
- 1/4 cup Dutch process unsweetened cocoa
- 1/8 teaspoon salt
- 2 tablespoons LAND O LAKES® butter, melted
- Topping Ingredients:
- 1 pint strawberries, hulled, cut in half
- 1 kiwifruit, peeled, sliced 1/8-inch, cut in half
- 1/2 cup fresh blueberries
- 1/2 cup fresh raspberries
- 1 (10-ounce) jar apple jelly, melted

Direction

- Heat oven to 375°F. Grease and flour 10-inch tart pan with removable bottom. Place pan on baking sheet. Set aside.
- Combine powdered sugar, eggs, egg yolk and crème de cacao in large bowl. Beat at high speed until mixture is very thick and double in volume (5 to 8 minutes). (Mixture should be light yellow and consistency of soft whipped cream.)
- Stir together flour, cocoa and salt in medium bowl. Gently stir flour mixture into egg mixture by hand, 1/4 cup at a time, just until flour mixture disappears. Gently stir melted butter into batter.
- Gently spoon batter into prepared pan. Bake for 20 to 23 minutes or until toothpick inserted in center comes out clean. Cool completely.
- To serve, decoratively arrange fresh fruit on top of cake. Drizzle melted jelly over top of cake and fruit.
- *Substitute 1 teaspoon vanilla.

140. Chocolate Strawberry Cake The Ultimate Combination Recipe

Serving: 1518 | Prep: | Cook: 45mins | Ready in:

Ingredients

- chocolate Sponge:
- eggs -3
- sugar - 75gms /powdered
- cornflour - 1 tbsp
- cocoa - 2 tbsp
- flour - 75 gms minus 3 tbsps
- baking powder - 1 tsp
- Pinch of salt
- vanilla essence - 1 tsp
- Strawberry Sponge:
- eggs - 3
- sugar - 75 gms
- cornflour - 1 tbsp
- flour - 75gms minus 1 tbsp
- baking powder - 1 tsp
- Pinch of salt
- Strawberry essence - 1 tsp
- Method : Similar to above.
- Filling :
- Cream - 400ml (35% fat)
- Strawberry essence -1 tsp (optional)
- powdered sugar - 2-3 tbsp (increase if strawberries are tart)
- strawberries - 200gms/ chopped; reserve 3-4 for decoration
- Ganache:
- dark chocolate - 200gms
- Cream - 200ml

Direction

- Line & grease an 8" spring form tin.
- Sift the cornflour + flour + cocoa + baking powder + salt 3 times. Keep aside.
- Preheat the oven to 180 degrees C.
- Beat the eggs & sugar well till it holds thick ribbons; about 10 minutes.
- Beat in the vanilla essence.
- Gently fold in the flour mix, a tbsp. at a time, in figure 8 hand movements so that the beaten air doesn't escape.
- Turn into the prepared tin & bake for 25-30 minutes/ until done.
- Remove from tin after 5 minutes, take off the lining & cool completely on rack.
- Filling:
- Whip cream, essence & sugar till it holds peaks.
- Reserve 1-2 tbsp. cream in a baggie for the spiral/ web on top.
- Fold in the strawberries.
- Don't make this too much in advance, since strawberries macerate with sugar, & might make the cream runny.
- Ganache:
- Put the chocolate & cream in a pan. Keep on low heat, stirring constantly, till the chocolate melts. Remove & stir vigorously with a spoon.
- If you want to pipe decorations on top, pass about 1/4 cup through a sieve & reserve separately. I've found that unless you sieve the ganache, it's not easy to pipe it through an icing set. It's fine for spreading though.
- Set aside to cool. It will thicken as it cools & get a spreadable consistency.
- Finishing off:
- Cut each sponge into 2, so there are a total of 4 layers.
- Sandwich them with the strawberry cream, using 1/3 each time.
- Spread the ganache over the top & sides of cake. Use sprinkles on the sides if desired.
- For the marbling, see pictures. Draw a spiral, with the cream in the baggie reserved from the filling, beginning from the centre outwards
- Then drag a wooden pick from the centre outwards, at a 60 degree angle, to equal points on the edge.
- Do the same in the opposite direction (i.e. outwards to the centre) between the earlier lines. This will create a webbed pattern.
- Pipe a ganache edging if you like. Then finish off with sliced strawberries & flaked chocolate etc. Chill till required.

141. Chocolate Supreme Layer Cake Recipe

Serving: 12 | Prep: | Cook: 30mins | Ready in:

Ingredients

- 1 3/4 cups all-purpose flour
- 1 cup less 1 tablespoon unsweetened cocoa powder
- 1 1/4 teaspoons baking soda
- 1/8 teaspoon salt
- 3/4 cup (1 1/2 sticks) butter, softened
- 2/3 cup granulated sugar
- 2/3 cup firmly packed brown sugar
- 2 large eggs
- 2 teaspoons vanilla extract
- 1 1/2 cups buttermilk
- For the frosting and Garnish
- 1/2 cup (1 stick) butter, softened
- 1 cup confectioners' sugar, sifted
- 3 ounces (3 squares) unsweetened chocolate, melted
- 2 teaspoons vanilla extract
- chocolate shavings (optional)
- Tips
- chocolate shavings
- To make chocolate shavings, scrape a vegetable peeler along the edge of a piece of semisweet chocolate that is at room temperature.

Direction

- 1. Preheat oven to 350F. Line bottoms of two 9-inch round cake pans with waxed paper. Grease paper and sides of pans. Dust with flour.
- 2. Mix flour, cocoa, baking soda, and salt. In another bowl, beat butter, granulated sugar, and brown sugar at medium speed until light and fluffy. Add eggs, 1 at a time, beating well after each addition. Add vanilla.
- 3. At low speed, alternately beat flour mixture and buttermilk into butter mixture just until blended. Divide batter equally between prepared pans.
- 4. Bake cakes until a toothpick inserted in center comes out clean, 25 to 30 minutes. Transfer pans to wire racks to cool for 10 minutes. Turn out onto racks. Remove paper. Turn layers top-side up and cool completely.
- 5. To prepare frosting, beat butter and confectioners' sugar at medium speed until light and fluffy. Add melted chocolate and vanilla; continue beating until shiny and smooth.
- 6. Place 1 cake layer on a serving plate; spread with frosting. Top with remaining cake layer. Spread frosting on top and sides of cake. Let cake stand for at least 30 minutes before sprinkling with chocolate shavings and slicing.

142. Chocolate Syrup Bundt Cake Recipe

Serving: 12 | Prep: | Cook: 80mins | Ready in:

Ingredients

- 3 cups flour
- 1/2 tsp baking soda
- 1/2 tsp baking powder
- 2 3/4 cups sugar
- 1/2 cup oil
- 5 eggs
- 1 cup buttermilk
- 2/3 cup chocolate syrup
- 1 tsp vanilla
- chocolate buttercream drizzle recipe (see below)
- 2 Tbs chocolate syrup
- buttercream drizzle:
- 3 Tbs softened butter
- 1 1/2 cups powdered sufgar
- 1/2 tsp vanilla
- 2 Tbs chocolate syrup

- milk if needed

Direction

- Sift together dry ingredients and set aside.
- In another bowl, beat sugar and oil till well blended and add eggs, one at a time
- Alternating, beat in flour with buttermilk.
- Blend in chocolate syrup and vanilla.
- Pour batter into a greased and floured 10 inch Bundt pan.
- Bake in a preheated 325F oven about 90 minutes or cake tested done in centre with toothpick.
- Cool on rack 15 minutes.
- Remove from pan and completely cool.
- Drizzle with chocolate buttercream and just before serving drizzle with the chocolate syrup.
- Buttercream:
- Beat butter with 1/2 cup powdered sugar.
- Beat in the syrup, and vanilla and then beat in 3/4 cup powdered sugar.
- If too thick, thin with some milk until mixture drapes off spoon.

143. Chocolate Syrup Cake Recipe

Serving: 10 | Prep: | Cook: 75mins | Ready in:

Ingredients

- 3 cups all-purpose flour
- 1/4 tsp. baking powder
- 1/4 tsp. baking soda
- 2-3/4 cups sugar
- 1/2 cup cooking oil
- 5 eggs
- 1 cup buttermilk
- 2/3 cup chocolate syrup
- 1 tsp. vanilla
- 1 recipe Chocolate-Buttercream Drizzle
- 2 Tbsp. chocolate syrup

Direction

- Preheat oven to 325 degrees F.
- Grease and flour a 10-inch fluted tube pan; set aside.
- In bowl stir together flour, baking powder, baking soda, and 1/4 teaspoon salt; set aside.
- In a large mixing bowl beat sugar and oil with an electric mixer on medium to high speed for 1 minute or until evenly moistened.
- Add eggs one at a time, beating well after each addition; beat until smooth.
- Alternately beat in flour mixture and buttermilk.
- Add the 2/3 cup chocolate syrup and vanilla; beat well. Pour into pan. Bake 1-1/4 to 1-1/2 hours or until a wooden toothpick inserted in center comes out clean. Cool on wire rack 15 minutes. Remove from pan; cool completely on rack. Transfer cake to platter; drizzle with Chocolate-Buttercream.
- Just before serving, drizzle 2 tablespoons syrup around top edge.

144. Chocolate Toffee Cake Recipe

Serving: 10 | Prep: | Cook: 35mins | Ready in:

Ingredients

- 1 box chocolate cake mix (I use Duncan Hines Devils Food)
- 1 1/3 cup water
- 1/2 cup vegetable oil
- 3 eggs
- 6 toffee candy bars, frozen (Heath or Skor)
- 1 container Cool Whip
- almonds, chopped to garnish

Direction

- Cook cake according to box directions.
- Crush candy bars.
- Fold into cool whip.

- Frost cooled cake with cool whip mixture.
- Garnish top with almonds.

145. Chocolate Triple Layer Cake With Fluffy Chocolate Frosting Recipe

Serving: 8 | Prep: | Cook: 45mins | Ready in:

Ingredients

- 1 ounce unsweetened chocolate
- 2 cups cake flour
- 6 tablespoons unsweetened cocoa powder
- 1-3/4 teaspoons baking powder
- 1/2 teaspoon baking soda
- 1/4 teaspoon salt
- 1/4 cup vegetable oil
- 2-1/2 tablespoons unsalted butter
- 1-1/2 cups granulated sugar
- 1 large egg
- 4 egg whites
- 1/4 cup room temperature coffee
- 2-1/4 teaspoons vanilla extract
- 3/4 cup plain yogurt
- 2 tablespoons plain yogurt
- Frosting:
- 3 large egg whites
- 1/2 ounce unsweetened chocolate
- 2-1/2 tablespoons light corn syrup
- 3/4 cup granulated sugar
- 1/8 teaspoon salt
- 3/4 teaspoon vanilla extract
- 1/4 teaspoon instant coffee powder
- 1 teaspoon hot water
- 1/4 cup powdered sugar
- 3 tablespoons unsweetened cocoa powder

Direction

- Preheat oven to 350.
- Grease three round cake pans.
- In a small heavy saucepan over lowest heat melt chocolate stirring constantly until smooth.
- Set aside.
- Sift together flour, cocoa powder, baking powder, baking soda and salt onto a sheet of wax paper.
- In a large mixer bowl with mixer set on medium speed beat oil, butter and sugar until fluffy.
- Beat in chocolate then beat in egg and then egg whites, coffee and vanilla until smooth.
- Gently stir half of the dry ingredients then yogurt into the mixture just until mixed.
- Stir in remaining dry ingredients just until well blended and smooth.
- Divide batter among pans spreading to edges.
- Bake in middle of the oven for 25 minutes.
- Transfer pans to racks and let stand until completely cooled.
- To make frosting place egg whites in a large mixer bowl.
- Set bowl in a large bowl of very hot tap water and let stand for 10 minutes stirring occasionally.
- In a small heavy saucepan set over low heat melt chocolate stirring constantly until smooth.
- Set aside to cool slightly.
- Combine corn syrup, 1/4 cup water and sugar in a saucepan stirring until well blended.
- Bring to a simmer over medium high heat.
- Cover and boil 2 minutes to allow steam to wash any sugar from pan sides.
- Uncover and continue simmering without stirring for 2 minutes.
- Immediately remove pan from heat and set aside.
- With mixer set on medium speed beat egg whites until very frothy and opaque.
- Raise speed to high and beat until whites just begin to stand in soft peaks.
- Return syrup to burner and reheat just to boiling.

- Beating whites on high speed and immediately begin pouring boiling syrup stream down side.
- Pour rapidly enough that all syrup is incorporated in about 15 seconds.
- Add salt and continue beating on high speed until mixture is stiffened glossy and cooled to warm.
- Beat in vanilla and coffee mixture until evenly incorporated.
- Sift powdered sugar and cocoa onto a sheet of wax paper.
- A bit at a time whisk into egg white mixture.
- Whisk in melted chocolate just until smoothly incorporated.
- Frost cake immediately or store frosting in airtight container up to 48 hours.

146. Chocolate Turtle Cake Recipe

Serving: 12 | Prep: | Cook: 32mins | Ready in:

Ingredients

- unsweetened cocoa
- 1 (18.25-oz.) package devil's food cake mix
- 1 (3.9-oz.) package chocolate instant pudding mix
- 3 large eggs
- 1 1/4 cups milk
- 1 cup canola oil
- 2 teaspoons vanilla extract
- 1 teaspoon chocolate extract
- 1 teaspoon instant coffee granules
- 1 (6-oz.) package semisweet chocolate morsels
- 1 cup chopped pecans
- 1 (16-oz.) container ready-to-spread cream cheese frosting
- 1/2 cup canned dulce de leche
- 2 (7-oz.) packages turtle candies
- 1 (16-oz.) can ready-to-spread chocolate fudge frosting
- 1 (12 oz.) jar dulce de leche ice cream topping
- 1/4 cup pecan halves, toasted

Direction

- Preparation
- 1. Preheat oven to 350°. Grease 2 (9-inch) round cake pans, and dust with cocoa. Set aside.
- 2. Beat cake mix and next 7 ingredients at low speed with an electric mixer 1 minute; beat at medium speed 2 minutes. Fold in chocolate morsels and chopped pecans. Pour batter into prepared pans.
- 3. Bake at 350° for 30 to 32 minutes or until a wooden pick inserted in center comes out clean. Cool in pans on wire racks 10 minutes. Remove from pans to wire racks, and cool completely. Wrap and chill cake layers at least 1 hour.
- 4. Whisk together cream cheese frosting and canned Dulce de Leche in a small bowl until well blended. Set aside. Cut 6 turtle candies in half, and set aside for garnish. Dice remaining turtle candies.
- 5. Using a serrated knife, slice cake layers in half horizontally to make 4 layers. Place 1 layer, cut side up, on cake plate. Spread with 1/2 cup cream cheese frosting mixture; sprinkle with one-third diced turtle candies. Repeat procedure twice. Place final cake layer on top of cake, cut side down. Spread chocolate fudge frosting on top and sides of cake. Cover and chill in refrigerator until ready to serve. Just before serving, drizzle Dulce de Leche ice cream topping over top of cake. Garnish with remaining halved turtle candies and pecan halves. Store in refrigerator.

147. Chocolate Upside Down Cake Recipe

Serving: 8 | Prep: | Cook: 35mins | Ready in:

Ingredients

- 2 ounces chocolate squares
- 1-1/3 cup sweetened condensed milk
- 1-1/2 cups cake flour sifted
- 1/4 teaspoon salt
- 2 teaspoons baking powder
- 6 tablespoons shortening
- 1 cup sugar
- 2 eggs well beaten
- 1 teaspoon vanilla
- 1/2 cup milk

Direction

- Melt chocolate then add condensed milk and mix well.
- Line greased pans with paper and grease paper.
- Pour chocolate mixture into pans and cool.
- Sift flour, salt and baking powder together.
- Cream shortening with sugar until fluffy then add eggs and vanilla and beat thoroughly.
- Add sifted dry ingredients and milk alternately in small amounts.
- Beat thoroughly after each addition.
- Pour carefully over chocolate mixture and bake at 350 for 35 minutes.

148. Chocolate Valentines Day Cake Recipe

Serving: 12 | Prep: | Cook: 40mins | Ready in:

Ingredients

- Cake:
- 1 (16-ounce) package pound cake mix
- 3/4 cup milk
- 2 large eggs
- 1/2 cup pistachios, chopped
- 1 teaspoon vanilla extract
- Filling:
- 1/3 cup butter or margarine, at room temperature
- 2/3 cup unsifted powdered sugar
- 1 large egg yolk
- 3 ounces white chocolate squares, chopped
- 2 tablespoons heavy cream
- glaze & Topping:
- 3 ounces dark chocolate (bittersweet or semi-sweet), chopped
- 1/4 cup heavy cream
- 1/2 cup raspberries
- 1/4 cup pistachios, chopped

Direction

- Cake:
- Beat cake mix with milk and 2 eggs as package directs.
- Mix in pistachios and vanilla extract. Grease bottoms of two small 6-inch diameter (approximately 3 cup) baking dishes.
- Pour batter into dishes.
- Bake at 350*F for 40 minutes or until done.
- Cool 15 minutes in dishes then invert onto wire racks and cool.
- Wrap and freeze one cake for use another time.
- Filling:
- Beat butter with powdered sugar and 1 egg yolk until smooth.
- Melt white chocolate with cream in saucepan, stirring over low heat, then beat smooth with wire whip.
- Beat into butter mixture and cool until spreadable consistency.
- Glaze:
- In saucepan, combine chocolate and cream; stir over low heat until melted.
- Cool until it begins to thicken, then spread on top and sides of cake.
- (To soften glaze, warm over hot water.)
- Assembly:
- Split one cake into three thin layers and divide filling between two center layers.
- Cover cake with plastic wrap and chill until set.
- Spread with Dark Chocolate Glaze, then decorate top with raspberries and chopped pistachios.

- Cake is best served when it has been at room temperature at least 30 minutes.
- Cover and chill any leftovers.

149. Chocolate Voodoo Drunken Zombie Cake Recipe

Serving: 1012 | Prep: | Cook: 145mins | Ready in:

Ingredients

- chocolate Voodoo cake
- 1 cup raisins
- 1/2 cup Myers dark rum
- 1/2 pound plus 2 tablespoons unsalted butter
- (2 tablespoons melted)
- 1 cup all purpose flour
- 1/4 cup unsweetened cocoa
- 2 teaspoons baking powder
- 1/2 teaspoon ground cinnamon
- 1/2 teaspoon ground allspice
- 1/8 teaspoon salt
- 10 ounces semisweet chocolate, broken into 1/2-ounce pieces
- 1 cup tightly packed light brown sugar
- 4 large eggs
- 1 teaspoon pure vanilla extract
- *Mocha rum Mousse*
- 8 ounces semisweet chocolate, broken into 1/2-ounce pieces
- 1/4 cup brewed full-strength coffee
- 2 tablespoons Myers dark rum
- 1 cup heavy cream
- 3 large egg whites
- 2 tablespoons granulated sugar
- *Blackened molasses Glaze*
- 3/4 cup heavy cream
- 3 tablespoons unsalted butter
- 2 tablespoons black strap molasses
- 6 ounces semisweet chocolate, broken into 1/2-ounce pieces
- *chocolate caramel Voodoo Needles*
- 1 cup granulated sugar
- 1/4 teaspoon lemon juice
- 1/2 ounce semisweet chocolate

Direction

- Measuring cup, measuring spoons, small non-stick pan, 1-quart plastic container with tight-fitting lid, pastry brush, two 9 x 1-1/2 inch round cake pans, parchment paper, sifter, wax paper, double boiler, plastic wrap, whisk, electric mixer with paddle and balloon whip, rubber spatula, toothpick, 2 cardboard cake circles, 5-quart stainless steel bowl, 1-1/2 quart saucepan, cake spatula, 3-quart stainless steel bowl, 4 non-stick baking sheets, plastic container with lid, serrated slicer.
- *Why We Call It Drunken*
- Combine 1 cup raisins and 1/2 cup dark rum in a plastic container with a tight-fitting lid. Allow to stand at room temperature for 6 hours or overnight.
- *Make the Drunken Zombie Cake*
- Preheat the oven to 325 degrees Fahrenheit.
- Lightly coat the insides of two 9 x 1-1/2 inch cake pans with melted butter. Line each pan with parchment paper, then lightly coat the parchment paper with more melted butter. Set aside.
- Combine together in a sifter 1 cup flour, 1/4 cup cocoa, 2 teaspoons baking powder, 1/2 teaspoon ground cinnamon, 1/2 teaspoon allspice and 1/8 teaspoon salt. Sift onto wax paper and set aside.
- Heat 1 inch of water in the bottom half of a double boiler over medium heat. Place 10 ounces semisweet chocolate in the top half of the double boiler. Tightly cover the top with plastic wrap. Allow to heat for 8 minutes. Remove from the heat and stir until smooth. Keep at room temperature until ready to use.
- Place the remaining 1/2 pound butter and 1 cup brown sugar in the bowl of an electric mixer fitted with a paddle. Beat on medium for 2 minutes. Use a rubber spatula to scrape down the sides of the bowl. Beat on high for 2 minutes. Scrape down the sides of the bowl. Add the 4 eggs, one at a time, beating on medium for 30 seconds and scraping down the

sides of the bowl after each addition. Add 1 teaspoon vanilla extract and beat on high for 30 seconds. Add the melted chocolate and beat on medium for 30 seconds. Operate the mixer on low while gradually adding the sifted dry ingredients. Once all the dry ingredients have been incorporated, turn off the mixer, add the rum-infused raisins, and mix on medium for 30 seconds (at this point, the aromas wafting up from the mixing bowl are quite extraordinary). Remove the bowl from the mixer and use a rubber spatula to finish mixing the batter until smooth and thoroughly combined.

- Immediately divide the cake batter between the prepared pans, spreading evenly. Bake on the center rack in the preheated oven until a toothpick inserted in the center of the cakes comes out clean, about 32 to 35 minutes. Remove the cakes from the oven and cool in the pans for 15 minutes at room temperature. Invert the cakes onto cake circles. Carefully remove the parchment paper. Place the cakes in the freezer for 1 hour or in the refrigerator for at least 2 hours (the cakes must be thoroughly cooled before adding the mousse, as described later).
- *Make the Mocha Rum Mousse*
- Heat 1 inch of water in the bottom half of a double boiler over medium heat. Place 8 ounces semisweet chocolate, 1/4 cup coffee, and 2 tablespoons dark rum in the top half of the double boiler. Tightly cover the top with plastic wrap. Allow to heat for 5 to 6 minutes. Remove from the heat and stir until smooth. Transfer the chocolate mixture to a 5-quart stainless steel bowl and keep at room temperature until ready to use.
- Place 1 cup heavy cream in the well-chilled bowl of an electric mixer fitted with a well-chilled balloon whip. Whisk on high for 1 minute until peaks form. Set aside for a few moments.
- Whisk 3 egg whites in a 3-quart stainless steel bowl until soft peaks form, about 2-1/2 to 3 minutes. Add 2 tablespoons sugar and continue to whisk until stiff peaks form, 1 to 1-1/2 minutes. Use a rubber spatula to quickly fold one third of the whisked egg whites into the melted chocolate. Then place the whipped cream and the remaining egg whites on top of the chocolate and use a rubber spatula to fold together until smooth and completely combined. Refrigerate the mocha rum mousse for 30 to 45 minutes (the mousse must be refrigerated until slightly firm before beginning to assemble the cake).
- *Begin Assembling the Cake*
- Remove the cake layers from the freezer or refrigerator and the mousse from the refrigerator. Reserve 1 cup of mousse and set aside in the refrigerator for a few moments. Spoon the remaining mousse onto one of the inverted cake layers, using a cake spatula to spread evenly to the edges. Place the other inverted cake layer on top of the mousse and press gently into place. Use a cake spatula to coat the top and sides of the cake with the reserved cup of mousse. Place the cake in the freezer while preparing the blackened molasses glaze and the voodoo needles.
- *Prepare the Blackened Molasses Glaze*
- Heat 3/4 cup heavy cream, 3 tablespoons butter, and 2 tablespoons molasses in a 1-1/2-quart saucepan. Stir to dissolve the molasses, then bring to a boil. Place 6 ounces semisweet chocolate in a 3-quart stainless steel bowl. Pour the boiling cream mixture over the chocolate and allow to stand for 5 minutes. Stir until smooth. Keep the glaze at room temperature for an hour before using (the glaze will thicken to the desired texture during that time period).
- *Prepare the Chocolate Caramel Voodoo Needles*
- Combine 1 cup sugar and 1/4 teaspoon lemon juice in a 1-1/2-quart saucepan. Stir with a whisk to combine (the sugar will resemble moist sand). Caramelize the sugar for 5-1/2 to 6 minutes over medium high heat, stirring constantly with a whisk to break up any lumps (the sugar will first turn clear as it liquefies, then light brown as it caramelizes). Remove the saucepan from the heat, add the chocolate,

and stir to dissolve. Dip a wire whisk into the chocolate caramel and drizzle the hot caramel, in long thin lines, onto 4 non-stick baking sheets, one sheet at a time (move the whisk back and forth over the length of the baking sheets). Continue drizzling—making an effort to create as many individual long, thin, and separate chocolate caramel strips as possible—until all the caramel is used. Allow the strips to harden at room temperature, about 15 minutes. Break the strips into the desired size voodoo needles (3- to 4-inch needles make for delightful sticking). The voodoo needles may be stored in a tightly sealed plastic container in the freezer until needed (which may be sooner than you think, especially if an intruder sticks a finger into the glaze).

- *Finish Assembling the Cake*
- Remove the cake from the freezer. Pour the glaze over the top of the cake. Use a cake spatula to spread a smooth coating of glaze over the top and sides of the voodoo cake. Refrigerate the cake for 1 hour to set the glaze.
- *To Serve*
- Heat the blade of a serrated slicer under hot running water and wipe the blade dry before cutting each slice. Place a piece of Chocolate Voodoo Cake in the center of each serving plate. Randomly stick the chocolate caramel voodoo needles into the cake slices (avoid thinking about your enemies at this time, if at all possible). Dispatch immediately.
- Aunt Lena says:
- There is no witchcraft going on here, just a little fun. We tried to catch the spirit of the islands with this confection by using lots of rum, molasses, spices, and chocolate.
- Although other brands of dark rum may be used, I prefer Myer's dark, with its no-nonsense, straightforward flavor that lives on beyond the baking of the cake—especially if you accompany each slice with a glass of this smooth island beverage.
- The black strap molasses of choice for the glaze is Plantation "The Original" Brand. The rap on black strap is that it comes from the dregs of the barrel, its bitter flavor better suited for non-confectionary use. Not so with Plantation brand. This turbid syrup has a refined and specific taste that gives a subtle finish to the completed dessert. Failing to locate this particular brand, I would suggest choosing another flavorful but not overpowering molasses.
- Chocolate Voodoo Cake may be produced over a period of two to three days, rather than all in one day. The chocolate caramel voodoo needles may be prepared several days in advance, cool the needles thoroughly and store in a tightly sealed plastic container in the freezer (you never know when you may need them). The Chocolate Voodoo Cake may be baked one to two days in advance. Wrap the baked and cooled layers in plastic wrap and refrigerate until assembly.
- After assembly, you may refrigerate this cake for two to three days before serving.

150. Chocolate Walnut Apple Cake Recipe

Serving: 8 | Prep: | Cook: 45mins | Ready in:

Ingredients

- 2 cups sifted flour
- 1-1/2 cups granulated sugar
- 1/4 cup cocoa
- 1 teaspoon baking soda
- 1 teaspoon salt
- 1 teaspoon ground cinnamon
- 1/2 teaspoon ground nutmeg
- 1/4 teaspoon ground allspice
- 2 eggs
- 3/4 cup cooking oil
- 3 cups peeled diced apples
- 1 cup chopped walnuts

Direction

- Resift flour with sugar, cocoa, baking soda, salt, cinnamon, nutmeg and allspice.

- Add eggs, oil and 1 cup of apples then beat three minutes at medium speed scraping bowl.
- Stir in remaining apples and walnuts then turn into greased rectangular baking pan.
- Bake at 350 for 40 minutes then cool and sprinkle with powdered sugar.

151. Chocolate Walnut Cake Recipe

Serving: 12 | Prep: | Cook: 45mins | Ready in:

Ingredients

- 8 large eggs, at room temperature
- 1 cup granulated sugar, divided
- 1/2 cup packed dark brown sugar
- 1 1/2 cups toasted ground walnuts (about 2 cups walnut halves; see Tip)
- 2 teaspoons vanilla extract
- 6 tablespoons all-purpose flour
- 1/3 cup cocoa powder, sifted
- 1/2 teaspoon salt
- 1/4 teaspoon ground cinnamon
- 3/4 cup orange marmalade or other jam, such as apricot or raspberry
- 1 teaspoon confectioners' sugar

Direction

- 1. Preheat oven to 375 degrees F. Lightly oil and flour a 9-inch springform pan, tapping out any excess flour.
- 2. Crack 2 eggs into a large bowl. Separate 2 more eggs, placing the whites in a second large bowl and adding the yolks to the bowl with the whole eggs. Separate the remaining 4 eggs, adding the whites to the other whites (reserve the 4 yolks for another use.) You should have 6 whites in one bowl, 2 whole eggs plus 2 yolks in the other bowl.
- 3. Beat the egg whites with an electric mixer at high speed until foamy. Add 1/3 cup granulated sugar and continue beating until soft peaks form. Set aside.
- 4. Clean and dry the beaters. Add brown sugar and the remaining 2/3 cup granulated sugar to the eggs and yolks and beat with the mixer at medium speed until thick and light in color, about 3 minutes. Scrape down the sides of the bowl with a rubber spatula; beat in the toasted ground nuts and vanilla until combined. Beat in flour, cocoa powder, salt and cinnamon just until combined, scraping down the sides as needed. Fold in 1 cup of the beaten whites with a rubber spatula until smooth, then fold in the remaining whites with very gentle arcs, just until incorporated (some white streaks may still be visible). Gently pour the batter into the prepared pan.
- 5. Place the pan in the oven and reduce heat to 325 degrees F. Bake the cake until set, puffed and spongy but nonetheless firm, 40 to 45 minutes. Transfer to a wire rack and let cool completely, about 2 hours. As it cools, the cake will shrink away from the sides of the pan.
- 6. Remove the pan's side. Release the cake from the pan's bottom using a long, thin, metal spatula and carefully transfer it to a serving plate. Slice the cake horizontally into two layers with a long, thin knife. Gently lift off the top. Spread the marmalade (or jam) over the bottom layer and replace the top. Do not press down. Sprinkle with confectioners' sugar just before serving.
- TIP: Tip: To toast and grind walnuts, spread them on a baking sheet and bake at 350 degrees F, stirring once, until fragrant, 7 to 9 minutes. Let the nuts cool on a plate then grind into a coarse meal in a food processor or blender.

152. Chocolate Wave Cake Recipe

Serving: 6 | Prep: | Cook: 15mins | Ready in:

Ingredients

- 3/4 cup butter

- 1 cup semisweet chocolate chips
- 1 cup sugar
- 2 1/2 teaspoons cornstarch
- 4 eggs
- 4 egg yolks
- 1 1/2 teaspoons Grand Marnier
- **
- For the white-chocolate truffle:****************
- 6 ounces white chocolate
- 3 tablespoons heavy cream
- 3 tablespoons softened butter
- 2 tablespoons Grand Marnier

Direction

- 1. Melt butter in a double boiler over medium-low heat.
- 2. Add chocolate chips, heating until mixture is melted.
- 3. Combine sugar and cornstarch in a large mixing bowl.
- 4. Add chocolate mixture to sugar mixture and beat well.
- 5. In a separate bowl, combine four eggs, four yolks, and Grand Marnier. Add this to the chocolate mixture and beat until well mixed. Cover and chill overnight.
- 6. Melt the white chocolate and heavy cream in a double boiler over low heat. Add butter and Grand Marnier and stir until smooth. Chill overnight.
- 7. Butter and flour six 5-ounce ramekins. Fill 1/3 of each with the chilled chocolate mixture.
- 8. Add a rounded tablespoon of the truffle mixture. Fill to the top with the chocolate mixture.
- 9. Bake at 450 degrees for 15 minutes.
- Let the cakes sit for 15 to -20 minutes before inverting. Run a knife around the edges to loosen. Serve with chocolate sauce, raspberries, and /or ice cream if desired.
- Serves 6.

153. Chocolate Zucchini Cake Recipe

Serving: 912 | Prep: | Cook: 30mins | Ready in:

Ingredients

- 1 and 3/4 c whole wheat pastry flour
- 1 and 1/2 tsp baking powder
- 1/2 tsp baking soda
- 1/4 tsp salt
- 2 eggs
- 1/2 c sugar
- 1/2 c low-fat vanilla yogurt
- 1/3 c canola oil
- 1 tsp vanilla extract
- 1 and 1/2 c shredded zucchini
- 2 c semisweet miniature chocolate chips, divided (MUFA) (divide 3 cups of chocolate chips, if you are a serious advocate of chocolate)

Direction

- Preheat the oven to 350°F. Coat an 11" x 8" baking pan with cooking spray
- Combine the flour, baking powder, baking soda, and salt in a large bowl.
- Whisk the eggs, sugar, yogurt, oil, and vanilla extract in a medium bowl. Whisk in the zucchini and 1 to 1 ½ cups of the chips. Stir into the flour mixture just until blended. Spread into the prepared pan and bake for 30 minutes or until lightly browned and a wooden toothpick inserted in the center comes out clean
- Remove from the oven and sprinkle the remaining 1 to 1 ½ cups chips over the cake. Spread with a small spatula as they melt to form an icing, placing back into the warm oven, if needed, for about 1 minute.
- Nutrition Info Per Serving (1/12 of cake): 361 Cal, 5 g pro, 47 g carbs, 17 g fat, 4 g fiber, 175 mg sodium

154. Chocolate And Raspberry Cake Recipe

Serving: 8 | Prep: | Cook: 35mins | Ready in:

Ingredients

- 2 cups flour
- 1/2 cup baking cocoa
- 1/4 tsp salt
- 1 cup sugar
- 1 tsp baking soda
- 6 Tbs, white vegetable shortening
- 2 large eggs
- 1 tsp pure vanilla
- 6 oz milk
- 1 cup fresh or fresh frozen raspberries
- Garnish:
- Raspberry syrup
- whipped cream
- chocolate shavings

Direction

- In a large bowl sift in all the dry ingredients.
- Beat in shortening with an electric mixer.
- Then add remaining ingredients (except berries) and beat all well.
- Fold in berries.
- Batter will be thick.
- Spread into a greased 9 inch square pan (or 2 cake layer pans) and bake in a preheated 325F oven until cake springs back in the center and test done in center, about 35 to 45 minutes.
- Do not overbake.
- Cool cake completely.
- For a layer cake, spread layers with raspberry preserves and frost as desired.
- For cut from the pan pieces: drizzle with raspberry syrup and add whipped cream.
- Garnish if desired with fresh berries and chocolate shavings.

155. Chocolate Banana Mousse Cake Recipe

Serving: 10 | Prep: | Cook: | Ready in:

Ingredients

- 1 23cm chocolate sponge cake
- 1 ½ tsp gelatine
- 3 tbsp cold water
- 2 cups heavy cream
- 4 tbsp powder sugar
- 2 ripe banana, mashed
- 2 bananas, sliced
- Decoration:
- Melted chocolate
- icing sugar

Direction

- In a small heatproof bowl, sprinkle the gelatine over the cold water and leave for 5 minutes until spongy. Set the bowl over a small saucepan with simmering water and stir until the gelatine dissolves. Set aside to cool.
- In the same time, beat the heavy cream and the powder sugar until peaks form. Add the cooled gelatine and beat until only combined. Fold in the mashed bananas until combined.
- Split the chocolate sponge cake horizontally. Set the base of the cake in a 23cm spring form cake ring. Arrange sliced bananas over the top, pour over the cream filling and smooth the top with a spatula. Cover with the domed half of the sponge cake making sure to put it right in the center leaving ¼ inch in the edges. Arrange the rest of the sliced bananas all around the edge, inserting them in the empty spaces between the ring and the filling. Chill for 3-4 hours
- Sift icing sugar over the top and use the melted chocolate to decorate the sliced bananas in the edges. Best served at the same day.

156. Chocolate Cake Vegen Recipe

Serving: 810 | Prep: | Cook: 35mins | Ready in:

Ingredients

- 1 cup all-purpose flour
- 2 teaspoons baking powder
- 1/2 teaspoon baking soda
- 1/4 teaspoon salt
- 1 cup sugar, divided
- 1/2 cup Dutch processed cocoa powder, divided
- 1/2 cup plain soy milk
- 1/4 cup canola oil
- 1 teaspoon vanilla extract
- 1 teaspoon rum extract (or just use 1 more teaspoon vanilla if you don't have rum)
- 1/2 cup boiling water
- 1/2 cup pure maple syrup
- 1/4 cup light rum

Direction

- Boil some water in a teakettle, preheat oven to 350°F, and grease a 9-inch springform round cake pan.
- Sift together flour, baking powder, baking soda, salt, 3/4 cup of the sugar, and 1/4 cup of the cocoa. Add the soy milk, oil, and extracts, and mix into a thick batter.
- Spread batter into cake pan. Sprinkle the top with the remaining cocoa and sugar.
- Pour the boiling water into a glass measuring cup, add the maple syrup and rum to the water, and pour this mixture on top of the cake batter.
- Place cake on a cookie sheet in case of pudding overflow and bake for 30 to 35 minutes. Let cool just a bit; while the cake is still warm, place it on a large plate (your plate should have a slight edge to prevent spillage).
- Throw on a scoop of vanilla soy ice cream if you like, and you've got yourself one impressive dessert.

157. Chocolate Cake Wit Blueberry Topping Recipe

Serving: 8 | Prep: | Cook: 45mins | Ready in:

Ingredients

- 175 gmgolden caster sugar
- 150 gm butter , diced
- 3 Large eggs
- 1 tsp vanilla essence
- 1 tbsp thick milk
- 1/2 tbsp golden syrup
- 150 gm self raising flour
- 25 gm cocoa pwd
- ....
- whipped cream
- ....
- A bowl of fresh blueberries
- 1/3 cup sugar
- 1 tablespoon fresh lemon juice
- 1/2 teaspoon vanilla extract
- 1 tsp cornflour

Direction

- Pre heat oven at 170 deg C.
- Beat the butter and sugar until creamy.
- Add the eggs and essence.
- Beat until thick.
- Add the flour, cocoa and the milk.
- Mix well.
- Pour into a 9 inch greased pan.
- Bake for 35 mins.
- Cool.
- Cut into 2 layers.
- Spread the whipped cream on top of one layer.
- Arrange another layer on top.
- Spread the rest on the cream on top and the sides.
- ....
- Wash the blueberries
- Add sugar, lemon juice and mix well.
- In a small saucepan, bring blueberry mixture to a boil.

- Add the cornflour.
- Boil 1 minute until slightly thicken.
- Add vanilla.
- Chill and pour over the cake.
- Serve over puddings, cake, or ice cream.

158. Chocolate Cherry Bavarian Cake Recipe

Serving: 10 | Prep: | Cook: 50mins | Ready in:

Ingredients

- chocolate genoise:
- 1/3 cup cake flour
- 1/3 cup cornstarch
- 1/4 cup unsweetened alkalized cocoa powder
- 3 large eggs plus 3 large egg yolks, at room temperature
- 3/4 cup sugar
- Pinch of salt
- chocolate filling:
- 1/2 cup heavy cream
- 3 bars (1.5 ounces each) Godiva dark chocolate, coarsely chopped
- 2 tablespoons butter
- Cherry Bavarian:
- 2 cans (12 ounces each) cherry in syrup, drain and reserve syrup
- 3/4 cup sugar
- 1 1/2 tbsp unflavored gelatin powder
- 2 cups heavy cream + tbsp powder sugar
- Assembly:
- Godiva dark chocolate, coarsely grated
- 1/2 pint fresh cherries

Direction

- Make the genoise:
- Preheat oven to 350°F. Butter bottom and side of 9-inch round baking pan. Line with parchment or waxed paper.
- Sift together cake flour, cornstarch and cocoa.
- Beat together whole eggs, egg yolks, sugar and salt in heatproof bowl, using hand-held electric mixer at medium speed. Place bowl over pan of simmering water and continue beating until the mixture is lukewarm, about 100°F. Remove from water. Increase speed to high and beat until mixture is cooled and increased in volume, about 3 to 4 minutes.
- Sift dry ingredients over egg mixture in three additions, gently folding with a rubber spatula. Spread batter in prepared pan.
- Bake for 30 minutes or until cake springs back when touched with finger. Cool in pan on wire rack for 10 minutes. Loosen edge with knife and invert cake onto a rack. Carefully remove paper. Place another rack on cake and invert again. Cool completely.
- Make the chocolate filling:
- Heat heavy cream in saucepan to a boil over medium heat. Remove from heat. Add chocolate and let stand 30 seconds. Whisk in butter until smooth.
- Make the Raspberry Bavarian:
- Combine cherries and sugar in a saucepan. Heat to a boil and simmer 10 minutes. Strain mixture through a fine-meshed sieve into bowl. Cool to room temperature and process in the food processor. Combine 1/3 cup of the reserved syrup and gelatine in heatproof cup and let stand 5 minutes. Place over a saucepan with simmering water and stir until gelatine is dissolved. Whisk into cherry purée.
- Beat heavy cream in bowl until soft peaks form, using electric mixer at high speed. Fold whipped cream into cherry mixture.
- Assembly:
- Cut genoise horizontally into two equal layers. Place one layer in bottom of 9-inch springform pan, cut side up. Brush with 2 tbsp. of the reserved cherry syrup. Whisk cooled chocolate filling to lighten it and spread half of filling over cake. Top with half of the cherry Bavarian. Top with other cake layer, cut side down. Repeat layers. Cover and refrigerate until mixture sets, about 2 hours.
- To serve: Run a small knife between dessert and pan. Remove side of springform pan.

Press chocolate shavings around sides and sprinkle 8 portions over the top Arrange cherries over each portion and one in the center

159. Chocolate Coconut Cake Recipe

Serving: 1224 | Prep: | Cook: 35mins | Ready in:

Ingredients

- One box delux chocolate pudding cake
- One can cream of coconut
- Cool Whip
- 1 bag shredded coconut

Direction

- Make cake per package directions
- Open can of cream of coconut stir very well because it is very thick
- When cake comes out of oven poke holes with end of wooden spoon then pour cream of coconut over the cake and refrigerate for 1 hour at least. Longer is better I found.
- Top cake with cool whip and toasted coconut.
- Keep in fridge.
- Chocolate curls look really nice with the toasted coconut.
- I have also done this cake with caramel sauce too and that is really good too.

160. Chocolate Moist Bundt Cake Recipe

Serving: 10 | Prep: | Cook: 40mins | Ready in:

Ingredients

- * 1 1/2 sticks butter
- * 1 cup flour
- * 3/4 cups sugar
- * 3 eggs
- * 1 cup confectioners sugar
- * 1/2 cup cocoa powder
- * 1 cup chopped walnuts

Direction

- Preheat the oven to 350.
- Grease and flour the cake pan.
- Butter should be soft, at room temperature, mix it together with the sugar in a large bowl.
- When the butter and sugar are mixed together, add the eggs one at a time, beating them in before adding the next.
- Add the confectioners' sugar gradually, while continuously mixing the batter. Next, add the flour, the cocoa, and the walnuts, and stir these in by hand.
- Pour the batter into the cake pan. Put the cake in the oven, and bake it for about 40 minutes.
- Remove the cake from the oven, and let it cool in its pan for an hour or so. You can serve the cake as is, or glaze it with a mixture of one cup confectioners' sugar and two tablespoons milk. Add 3 tab. coco if you want chocolate glaze.

161. Chocolate N Cheese Tunnel Cake Recipe

Serving: 12 | Prep: | Cook: 60mins | Ready in:

Ingredients

- 1 (18.25 ounce) box chocolate cake mix with pudding
- 1/3 cup butter or margarine
- 16 ounces cream cheese, softened
- 1/2 cup granulated sugar
- 2 eggs
- 2 teaspoons butter or margarine, melted
- 2 ounces semisweet chocolate
- 2 teaspoons corn syrup

Direction

- Heat oven to 350 degrees F.
- Prepare cake mix according to package directions, substituting butter for oil. Reserve 1 cup of batter. Pour remaining batter into a 12-cup greased and floured fluted tube pan.
- Combine cream cheese and sugar, mixing well at medium speed on an electric mixer until well blended. Blend in eggs, one at a time. Pour over batter in the pan. Spoon reserved batter over cream cheese mixture.
- Bake 1 hour or until a wooden pick inserted in center comes out clean. Cool 30 minutes; remove to a wire rack.
- Combine butter, chocolate and corn syrup in a small saucepan. Cook over low heat until chocolate is melted. Pour over cooled cake.

162. Chocolate Peppermint Truffle Cake Recipe

Serving: 12 | Prep: | Cook: 50mins | Ready in:

Ingredients

- 150g dark chocolate, chopped
- 150g butter, chopped
- 3/4 cup firmly packed brown sugar
- 2 eggs, lightly beaten
- 1 cup plain flour
- 2/3 cup self-raising flour
- 2 tablespoons cocoa powder
- 2 x 35g peppermint crisp chocolate bars, finely crushed
- chocolate ganache:
- 250g dark chocolate, chopped
- 2/3 cup thickened cream

Direction

- Preheat oven to 160°C/140°C fan-forced. Grease a 6cm-deep, 20cm round cake pan. Line base and side with baking paper.
- Place chocolate, butter, sugar and 1/2 cup cold water in a saucepan over medium-low heat. Cook, stirring, for 3 to 4 minutes or until smooth. Transfer to a bowl. Cool for 10 minutes.
- Add eggs. Stir to combine. Add flours and cocoa. Stir to combine. Pour mixture into prepared pan. Bake for 50 minutes or until a skewer inserted in the centre comes out with moist crumbs clinging. Stand for 10 minutes in pan. Turn out onto a wire rack to cool.
- Meanwhile, make ganache Place chocolate and cream in a saucepan over low heat. Cook, stirring, for 2 to 3 minutes or until smooth. Divide mixture between 2 bowls. Refrigerate 1 bowl for 2 hours or until firm. Stand remaining bowl at room temperature for 2 hours or until thick enough to spread. Spread over top and side of cake.
- Place peppermint crisp in a shallow bowl. Roll heaped teaspoons of chilled chocolate mixture into 12 balls. Roll each ball in peppermint crisp. Arrange balls on top of cake. Serve.

163. Chocolate Profiteroles Cake Recipe

Serving: 8 | Prep: | Cook: 75mins | Ready in:

Ingredients

- 1 9inch butter chocolate cake or Devil's food chocolate cake, split in half.
- Profitteroles:
- 1 c. water
- Pinch of salt
- 1/2 c. butter
- 2 tbsp. sugar
- 1 c. all-purpose flour
- 3-4 eggs
- 1 tsp. baking powder
- Filling:
- 300ml heavy cream
- 2 tbsp powder sugar

- 1 banana
- 2 tbsp powder sugar
- sugar glaze:
- ½ cup sugar
- 1 tbsp water
- 4 tbsp crushed hazelnuts
- 2 tbsp cocoa powder
- Cream layer:
- ½ cup heavy cream whipped with 2 tbsp powder sugar to soft peaks
- Top chocolate layer:
- 16 oz plain chocolate, chopped
- 1 ½ heavy cream
- 2 tbsp butter

Direction

- Place half of the split cake in a loose cake ring on your serving platter and set aside.
- Make the profiteroles first:
- Grease and flour a baking sheet. Combine water, salt, butter and sugar in a saucepan. Bring to a boil. Remove from heat. Add flour and baking powder all at once. Cook, stirring vigorously until mixture leaves sides of pan, about 1 minute. Remove from heat. Turn into a large bowl. Add eggs, one at a time, beating well after each addition until smooth and shiny. Let cool.
- Drop batter by spoonfuls in 2 inch rounds onto prepared baking sheet or squeeze through a decorating bag with large round tube. Bake on middle oven rack at 400 degrees for about 40 minutes. Make a small hall on each immediately after baking. Let cool.
- Make filling:
- Whip cream with the powder sugar until soft peaks. Mash the banana with the rest of the powder sugar and fold into the cream. Place the filling into a piping bag fitted with a long thin nozzle and pipe each profiteroles cookie with the filling. Put in the fridge while you make the sugar glaze.
- Sugar glaze:
- Mix sugar and water on a medium saucepan and stir over a medium heat until sugar melts. Let cool slightly and use to coat each cookie on the top. Sprinkle with the crushed hazelnuts. Put in the fridge while you make the chocolate topping.
- Chocolate topping:
- Heat the heavy cream over low heat until simmering point then pour over the chopped chocolate. Stir until melted. Add the butter and stir again. Let cool completely stirring occasionally until thickened.
- Assemble the cake:
- Spread whipped cream over chocolate cake half. Arrange enough profiteroles cookies to cover all the surface pressing lightly over them. Pour the thickened chocolate topping over them. Give the cake ring a shake to evenly distribute the chocolate mixture. Arrange 7-8 profiteroles cookies over the top pressing lightly over each. Chill for 4-5 hours. Sift cocoa powder over the top and score into wedges.

164. Chocolate Truffle Cake With White Chocolate Truffles Recipe

Serving: 10 | Prep: | Cook: 25mins | Ready in:

Ingredients

- white chocolate truffles:
- 2 tbsp butter
- 5 tbsp heavy cream
- 225 grams good quality white chocolate, broken into pieces.
- 1 tbsp orange – flavored liqueur
- To finish:
- 100 grams white chocolate melted
- Method:
- Line a loaf tin with parchment paper. Place the butter and the cream in a saucepan and bring slowly to the boil, stirring constantly. Boil for 1 minute, then remove the pan from the heat. Add the chocolate pieces to the mixture, stir till melted, then beat in the liqueur If using (1

didn't use it).Pour the mixture in the prepared tin and chill for 2 hours till firm. Using a teaspoon, roll small amounts of the mixture into balls. Chill for another 30 minutes.
- To finish:
- Dip the balls in the chocolate, allowing the excess to drip back into the bowl. Place on nonstick baking parchment , swirl the chocolate with the tines of a fork and leave to harden.
- chocolate Truffle cake
- 75grams butter
- 75grams caster sugar
- 2 eggs, lightly beaten
- 75 grams self raising flour
- ½ tsp baking powder
- 25 grams cocoa powder
- 50 grams ground almonds
- Truffle Topping
- 350 grams plain chocolate
- 100 gram butter
- 1 ¼ cups of heavy cream
- 75 grams chocolate cake crumbs

Direction

- Preheat oven to 350 F.
- Lightly grease 20 cm cake pan and line the base. Beat together the butter and sugar until light and fluffy. Gradually add the eggs, beating well after each addition.
- Sieve the flour, baking powder and cocoa powder together and fold into the mixture along with the ground almonds. Pour into the prepared pan and bake for 25 minutes or until springy to the touch. Leave to cool completely. Wash and dry the pan and return the cooled cake to the pan.
- Topping:
- Heat the chocolate, butter and cream in a heavy based pan and stir until smooth. Cool, and then chill for 30 minutes. Beat well with a wooden spoon and chill for a further 30 minutes. Beat the mixture again, and then add the cake crumbs, beating until well combined. Spoon over the sponge base .Arrange the truffles over the mixture and press slightly

.Sift some cocoa powder over the truffles in a decorative way. Chill.

165. Chocolate Covered OREO Cookie Cake Recipe

Serving: 16 | Prep: | Cook: 60mins | Ready in:

Ingredients

- 1 (18.25 ounce) package devil's food chocolate cake mix
- 4 (1 ounce) squares BAKER'S Semi-Sweet baking chocolate
- 1/4 cup butter, cut up
- 1 (8 ounce) package PHILADELPHIA cream cheese, softened
- 1/2 cup sugar
- 2 cups thawed Cool Whip whipped topping
- 12 OREO chocolate Sandwich cookies, coarsely crushed

Direction

- Preheat oven to 350 degrees F.
- Prepare and bake cake mix in two (9-inch) round cake pans as directed on package.
- Cool in pans 5 min. Invert onto wire racks; remove pans. Cool layers completely.
- Place chocolate and butter in small microwaveable bowl. Microwave on HIGH 2 min. or until butter is melted. Stir until chocolate is completely melted.
- Cool 5 min.
- Beat cream cheese and sugar in large bowl with electric mixer on medium speed until well blended.
- Add the whipped topping and cookie crumbs; mix lightly.
- Place 1 of the cake layers, top-side down, on serving plate; spread with the cream cheese mixture.
- Cover with the remaining cake layer, top-side up.
- Spoon glaze over top of cake.

- Let stand until set.

166. Chocolate Espresso Layer Cake With Mocha Marscapone Frosting Recipe

Serving: 10 | Prep: | Cook: 60mins | Ready in:

Ingredients

- Cake:
- 2 cups cake flour
- 3/4 cup natural unsweetened cocoa powder
- 1 1/2 teaspoons baking soda
- 3/4 teaspoon salt
- 3/4 cup (1 1/2 sticks) unsalted butter, room temperature
- 2 cups (packed) golden brown sugar
- 3 large eggs
- 1 1/2 teaspoons vanilla extract
- 1 cup buttermilk
- 4 teaspoons instant espresso powder dissolved in 3/4 cup hot water
- Frosting:
- 1/3 cup natural unsweetened cocoa powder
- 1 tablespoon instant espresso powder
- 1 1/2 cups chilled heavy whipping cream, divided
- 1 1/3 cups sugar
- 2 8-ounce containers chilled mascarpone cheese*
- bittersweet chocolate curls (optional)

Direction

- For cake:
- Position rack in center of oven; preheat to 325°F. Generously butter two 9-inch cake pans with 2-inch-high sides; dust with flour, tapping out any excess. Line bottom of pans with parchment paper.
- Sift 2 cups cake flour, cocoa, baking soda, and salt into medium bowl. Using electric mixer, beat butter in large bowl until smooth. Add brown sugar and beat until well blended, about 2 minutes. Add eggs 1 at a time, beating well after each addition. Mix in vanilla. Add flour mixture in 3 additions alternately with buttermilk in 2 additions, beating just until blended after each addition. Gradually add hot espresso-water mixture, beating just until smooth.
- Divide batter between pans; smooth tops. Bake cakes until tester inserted into center comes out clean, about 40 minutes. Cool cakes in pans on rack 15 minutes. Run small knife around sides of pans to loosen cakes. Invert cakes onto racks; lift pans off cakes and remove parchment. Place wire rack atop each cake; invert again so top side is up. Cool completely.
- For frosting:
- Sift cocoa powder into large bowl; add espresso powder. Bring 1 cup cream to boil in small saucepan. Slowly pour cream over cocoa mixture, whisking until cocoa is completely dissolved, about 1 minute. Add 1/2 cup cream and sugar; stir until sugar dissolves. Chill until cold, at least 2 hours. DO AHEAD: Can be made 1 day ahead. Cover; keep chilled.
- Add mascarpone to chilled cocoa mixture. Using electric mixer, beat on low speed until blended and smooth. Increase speed to medium-high; beat until mixture is thick and medium-firm peaks form when beaters are lifted, about 2 minutes (do not overbeat or mixture will curdle).
- Using pastry brush, brush off crumbs from cakes. Place 1 cake layer, top side up, on platter. Spoon 1 3/4 cups frosting in dollops over top of cake. Using offset spatula, spread frosting to edges. Top with second cake layer, top side up, pressing to adhere. Spread thin layer of frosting over top and sides of cake. Chill 10 minutes. Using offset spatula, spread remaining frosting over top and sides of cake, swirling decoratively. Top with chocolate curls, if desired.

167. Chocolate Malt Ice Cream Cake Recipe

Serving: 16 | Prep: | Cook: | Ready in:

Ingredients

- 1 quart light vanilla ice cream, slightly softened
- 1/4 cup malted milk powder
- 1 quart light chocolate ice cream
- 1/3 cup fat-free fudge topping
- 1 cup chopped malted milk balls

Direction

- You'll need an 8-inch springform pan. In large bowl, stir vanilla ice cream and malted milk powder until blended.
- Spoon chocolate ice cream into bottom of pan; pack into a fairly even layer. Place spoonfuls of the fudge sauce over top. Sprinkle with 1/2 cup of the chopped malt balls.
- Spread vanilla ice cream mixture over top. Freeze at least 4 hours or until firm.
- To serve: Remove sides of pan. Place on serving plate. Arrange remaining malt balls around edge.
- Per serving: 204 calories; 4 g fat; 35 g carb

168. Chocolate Peanut Butter Cake With Cream Cheese And Butterfinger Frosting Recipe

Serving: 12 | Prep: | Cook: 25mins | Ready in:

Ingredients

- Filling
- 2 1/4 cups heavy whipping cream
- 1/2 cup (packed) golden brown sugar
- 12 ounces bittersweet or semisweet chocolate, finely chopped
- 1/2 cup old-fashioned (natural) chunky peanut butter
- cake
- 2 1/2 cups all purpose flour
- 1 teaspoon baking powder
- 1 teaspoon baking soda
- 1/2 teaspoon salt
- 10 tablespoons (1 1/4 sticks) unsalted butter, room temperature
- 1/2 cup old-fashioned (natural) chunky peanut butter
- 1 pound golden brown sugar
- 4 large eggs
- 1 teaspoon vanilla extract
- 1 cup buttermilk
- frosting
- 1 1/2 8-ounce packages cream cheese, room temperature
- 2 cups powdered sugar, divided
- 6 tablespoons (3/4 stick) unsalted butter, room temperature
- 1 teaspoon vanilla extract
- 3/4 cup chilled heavy whipping cream
- butterfinger candy bars, coarsely chopped
- glazed peanuts

Direction

- For filling:
- Bring cream and sugar to simmer in saucepan, whisking to dissolve sugar. Remove from heat. Add chocolate; let stand 1 minute. Whisk until smooth. Whisk in peanut butter. Chill uncovered overnight.
- For cake:
- Preheat oven to 350°F. Butter three 9-inch-diameter cake pans with 1 1/2-inch-high sides. Line bottoms with parchment paper. Sift first 4 ingredients into medium bowl. Using electric mixer, beat butter and peanut butter in large bowl until blended. Beat in sugar. Beat in eggs, 1 at a time, then vanilla. At low speed, beat in flour mixture in 4 additions alternately with buttermilk in 3 additions.
- Divide batter among pans and spread evenly. Bake cakes until tester inserted into center comes out clean, about 25 minutes. Cool cakes 5 minutes. Turn out onto racks; peel off parchment. Cool cakes completely.

- For frosting:
- Using electric mixer, beat cream cheese, 1 1/4 cups powdered sugar, butter, and vanilla in large bowl to blend. Whisk whipping cream and 3/4 cup powdered sugar in bowl until mixture holds medium-firm peaks. Fold into cream cheese mixture in 3 additions; chill until firm but spreadable, about 1 hour.
- Place 1 cake layer, bottom side up, on 9-inch tart pan bottom. Spread with half of filling. Place another layer, bottom side up, on work surface. Spread with remaining filling; place atop first layer. Top with remaining cake layer, bottom side up.
- Spread frosting over top and sides of cake. (Can be made 1 day ahead. Cover with cake dome; chill. Let stand at room temperature 2 hours before continuing.) Press candy and peanuts onto top of cake.

169. Chocolate Peanut Butter Refrigerator Cake Recipe

Serving: 810 | Prep: | Cook: | Ready in:

Ingredients

- 2 1/2 cups heavy (whipping) cream
- 1 bag (10 oz) peanut butter chips
- 18 whole chocolate graham crackers

Direction

- 1. Heat 2/3 cup cream in a large microwave-safe bowl until steaming. Add chips; whisk until smooth. Slowly whisk in remaining cream. Chill 15 minutes.
- 2. Beat with mixer just until soft peaks form. Arrange 3 crackers, side by side, long edges touching, on serving plate. Spread evenly with 1/2 cup cream mixture. Repeat for 4 more layers; add 1 more layer crackers. Chill 1 hour. Chill remaining cream.
- 3. Spread top and sides of cake with cream. Chill 4 hours or up to 2 days.
- 4. Decorate with peanut butter chips, if desired. Slice with a serrated knife using a sawing motion.

170. Chocolate Raspberry Cake Recipe

Serving: 12 | Prep: | Cook: 35mins | Ready in:

Ingredients

- 1 cup whole grain pastry flour
- 1/2 cup sugar
- 3 tablespoons unsweetened cocoa powder
- 1 teaspoon baking powder
- 1/4 teaspoon salt
- 1 container (8 ounces) low-fat vanilla yogurt
- 2 tablespoons canola oil
- 2 large egg yolks, at room temperature
- 1 teaspoon vanilla extract
- 2 large egg whites, at room temperature
- 1 1/4 cups reduced-fat whipped topping
- 1 1/2 cups raspberries
- 1/2 cup raspberry all-fruit preserves, melted
- mint sprigs for garnish (optional)

Direction

- Preheat the oven to 350°F. Coat an 8" round baking pan with cooking spray. 2. In a medium bowl, mix the flour, sugar, cocoa, baking powder, and salt. 3. In a large bowl, mix the yogurt, oil, egg yolks, and vanilla. 4. Place the egg whites in a medium bowl. Using an electric mixer on high speed, beat until stiff peaks form. 5. Stir the flour mixture into the yogurt mixture just until blended. Fold in the egg whites until no streaks of white remain. Pour into the prepared pan. 6. Bake for 35 minutes, or until a wooden pick inserted in the center comes out clean. Cool on a rack for 5 minutes. Remove from the pan and place on the rack to cool completely. 7. To serve, split the cake horizontally into 2 layers. Spread 1 cup of the whipped topping over 1 layer. Top with 1 cup of the raspberries and drizzle with the preserves. Top with the remaining cake layer and spoon 12 dollops of the remaining whipped topping around the cake. Top each with a few of the remaining raspberries and garnish with the mint (if using).

171. Chocolate Glazed Hazelnut Mousse Cake Recipe

Serving: 8 | Prep: | Cook: 25mins | Ready in:

Ingredients

- For Shortbread Base:
- 2 tablespoons hazelnuts, toasted and skins rubbed off
- 3 tablespoons sugar
- 1/2 cup all-purpose flour
- 1/2 stick (1/4 cup) unsalted butter, softened
- 2 tablespoons unsweetened Dutch-process cocoa powder
- 1/8 teaspoon salt
- ~~~~
- For Mousse:
- 1 teaspoon unflavored gelatin (from a 1/4-oz envelope)
- 3 tablespoons cold water
- 1/2 cup chocolate hazelnut spread such as nutella (5 oz)
- 1/2 cup mascarpone (1/4 lb)
- 1 1/2 cups chilled heavy cream
- 2 tablespoons unsweetened Dutch-process cocoa powder
- 3 tablespoons sugar
- ~~~~
- For Ganache:
- 1/4 cup plus 1 tablespoon heavy cream
- 3 1/2 oz fine-quality bittersweet chocolate (not unsweetened), chopped
- ~~~~
- Needed: an 8-inch (20-cm) springform pan; parchment paper

Direction

- Make Shortbread Base:
- Put oven rack in middle position and preheat oven to 350°F.
- Invert bottom of springform pan (to make it easier to slide shortbread base off bottom), then lock on side of pan and line bottom with a round of parchment paper.
- Pulse hazelnuts with sugar in a food processor until nuts are finely chopped. Add flour, butter, cocoa, and salt and pulse just until a dough forms.
- Press dough evenly onto bottom of springform pan with your fingers. Prick all over with a fork, then bake until just dry to the touch, about 18 to 20 minutes.
- Transfer base in pan to a rack to cool completely, about 30 minutes.
- Remove side of pan and carefully slide out parchment from under shortbread, then reattach side of pan around shortbread base.
- ~~~~
- Make Hazelnut Mousse while shortbread cools:
- Sprinkle gelatine over water in a 1- to 1 1/2-quart heavy saucepan and let stand until softened, about 5 minutes.
- Heat gelatine mixture over low heat, stirring, just until gelatine is melted, about 2 minutes.
- Whisk in chocolate hazelnut spread until combined and remove from heat.
- Whisk together mascarpone and chocolate hazelnut mixture in a large bowl.
- Beat together cream, cocoa powder, and sugar in another large bowl with an electric mixer at low speed until just combined, then increase speed to high and beat until cream just holds soft peaks.
- Whisk one third of whipped cream into mascarpone mixture to lighten, then fold in remaining whipped cream until well combined.
- Spoon filling onto shortbread base in pan, gently smoothing top, then chill, covered, at least 3 hours.
- ~~~~

- Make Ganache and Glaze Cake:
- Bring cream to a simmer in a small heavy saucepan and remove from heat. Add chocolate and let stand 1 minute, then gently whisk until completely melted and smooth.
- Transfer ganache to a small bowl and cool, stirring occasionally, until slightly thickened but still pourable, about 20 minutes.
- Run a warm thin knife around inside of springform pan, then remove side. Slide cake off bottom of pan and transfer to a serving plate.
- Pour ganache onto top of cake and spread, allowing excess ganache to drip down sides.
- ~~~~
- Notes:
- ~ Cake, without glaze, can be chilled up to 2 days.
- ~ Cake can be glazed 6 hours ahead and chilled, uncovered.

172. Chocolate Peanut Butter Cake With Cream Cheese And Butterfinger Frosting Recipe

Serving: 12 | Prep: | Cook: 35mins | Ready in:

Ingredients

- Filling:
- 2 1/4 cups heavy whipping cream
- 1/2 cup (packed) golden brown sugar
- 12 ounces bittersweet or semisweet chocolate, finely chopped
- 1/2 cup old-fashioned (natural) chunky peanut butter
- ~~~~
- Cake:
- 2 1/2 cups all purpose flour
- 1 teaspoon baking powder
- 1 teaspoon baking soda
- 1/2 teaspoon salt
- 10 tablespoons (1 1/4 sticks) unsalted butter, room temperature
- 1/2 cup old-fashioned (natural) chunky peanut butter
- 1 pound golden brown sugar
- 4 large eggs
- 1 teaspoon vanilla extract
- 1 cup buttermilk
- ~~~~
- Frosting:
- 1 1/2 8-ounce packages cream cheese, room temperature
- 2 cups powdered sugar, divided
- 6 tablespoons (3/4 stick) unsalted butter, room temperature
- 1 teaspoon vanilla extract
- 3/4 cup chilled heavy whipping cream
- ~~~~
- Garnish:
- butterfinger candy bars, coarsely chopped
- glazed peanuts

Direction

- For Filling:
- Bring cream and sugar to simmer in saucepan, whisking to dissolve sugar.
- Remove from heat. Add chocolate; let stand 1 minute.
- Whisk until smooth. Whisk in peanut butter.
- Chill uncovered overnight.
- ~~~~
- For Cake:
- Preheat oven to 350°F.
- Butter three 9-inch-diameter cake pans with 1 1/2-inch-high sides. Line bottoms with parchment paper.
- Sift first 4 ingredients into medium bowl.
- Using electric mixer, beat butter and peanut butter in large bowl until blended.
- Beat in sugar. Beat in eggs, 1 at a time, then vanilla.
- At low speed, beat in flour mixture in 4 additions alternately with buttermilk in 3 additions.
- Divide batter among pans and spread evenly.
- Bake cakes until tester inserted into center comes out clean, about 25 minutes.

- Cool cakes 5 minutes. Turn out onto racks; peel off parchment. Cool cakes completely.
- ~~~~
- For Frosting:
- Using electric mixer, beat cream cheese, 1 1/4 cups powdered sugar, butter, and vanilla in large bowl to blend.
- Whisk whipping cream and 3/4 cup powdered sugar in bowl until mixture holds medium-firm peaks.
- Fold into cream cheese mixture in 3 additions; chill until firm but spreadable, about 1 hour.
- Place 1 cake layer, bottom side up, on 9-inch tart pan bottom.
- Spread with half of filling.
- Place another layer, bottom side up, on work surface. Spread with remaining filling; place atop first layer. Top with remaining cake layer, bottom side up.
- Spread frosting over top and sides of cake.
- **Note: Can be made 1 day ahead. Cover with cake dome; chill. Let stand at room temperature 2 hours before continuing.
- ~~~~
- To Garnish:
- Press candy and peanuts onto top of cake.

173. Chocolate Peanut Ice Cream Cake Recipe

Serving: 8 | Prep: | Cook: 8mins | Ready in:

Ingredients

- 2 -cups purchased chocolate cookie crumbs ....
- 1/2- cup butter, melted ....
- 1/4 -cup sugar ....
- 1 -quart vanilla ice cream................
- 1-1/2 -cups chocolate-covered peanuts, chopped ....
- 1- quart chocolate ice cream ....
- chocolate and peanut butter Sauce below.............
- chocolate-covered or plain peanuts, chopped for topping..............

Direction

- Preheat oven to 350 degrees F.
- For crust, in a medium bowl, combine cookie crumbs, melted butter, and sugar.
- Press crust mixture onto the bottom and 1 to 2 inches up the side of a 9x3-inch springform pan.
- Bake for 8 to 10 minutes or until crust is set.
- Cool on a wire rack for 15 minutes.
- Freeze for 30 minutes.
- Let vanilla ice cream stand at room temperature for 15 minutes. In a large bowl, use a wooden spoon to stir vanilla ice cream just enough to soften.
- Spoon softened ice cream into frozen crust, spreading ice cream evenly.
- Sprinkle with the 1-1/2 cups chocolate-covered peanuts.
- Freeze about 1 hour or until firm.
- Let chocolate ice cream stand at room temperature for 15 minutes. In a large bowl, use a wooden spoon to stir chocolate ice cream just enough to soften.
- Spoon softened chocolate ice cream on top of chocolate-covered peanut layer, spreading ice cream evenly.
- Cover and freeze for 4 hours.
- Using a thin metal spatula, loosen crust from side of pan; remove side of pan.
- Let ice cream cake stand at room temperature for 20 to 25 minutes to soften slightly.
- To serve, cut the ice cream cake into wedges and top with Chocolate and Peanut Butter Sauce.
- If desired, sprinkle with additional chocolate-covered peanuts. Makes 12 servings.
- ***
- Chocolate and Peanut Butter Sauce:
- _____
- In a small saucepan, combine one 12-ounce jar fudge ice cream topping and 3 tablespoons creamy peanut butter.

- Cook and stir over medium-low heat until heated through.
- Serve over cake.
- ***
- Make-Ahead Tip: Prepare ice cream cake as directed.
- Wrap in moisture proof and vapor proof wrap and freeze for up to 1 week.
- Loosen cake from pan and remove side of pan.
- Let stand at room temperature for 20 to 25 minutes to soften slightly. Cut into wedges and serve as directed.

174. Coconut Cake With Chocolate Chunks And Coconut Drizzle Recipe

Serving: 12 | Prep: | Cook: 70mins | Ready in:

Ingredients

- Cake:
- 1 3/4 cups all purpose flour
- 2 tsp baking powder
- 1 tbs fine sea salt
- 1 cup unsweetened shredded coconut
- 3/4 cup sugar
- 1/2 cup (1 stick) unsalted butter, room temperature
- 2 tsp (packed) finely grated orange peel
- 2 large eggs
- 1 tsp vanilla extract
- 1 cup canned unsweetened coconut milk
- 6 oz bittersweet chocolate bars (do not exceed 61% cacoa), broken to 1/2-inch irregular pieces, divided.
- 1/2 cup sweetened flaked coconut
- coconut Drizzle:
- 3/4 cup powdered sugar
- 2 tbs (or more) canned unsweetened coconut milk
- 1/2 tsp vanilla extract
- vanilla ice cream

Direction

- Cake:
- Preheat oven to 350 degrees. Generously butter 9-inch cake pan with 2-inch sides, dust pan with flour, shaking out excess.
- Sift 1 3/4 cups flour baking powder, and sea salt into a medium bowl. Stir in unsweetened shredded coconut and set aside.
- Using an electric mixer, beat sugar, butter, and orange peel in large bowl until light and fluffy. Add eggs 1 at a time, beating well after each addition. Beat in vanilla. Add flour mixture in 3 additions alternately with coconut milk in 2 additions, beating just until blended after each addition. Fold in half of bittersweet chocolate pieces. Spread batter evenly in cake pan. Sprinkle remaining chocolate pieces over batter, then sprinkle with sweetened flaked coconut.
- Bake until golden for about 60-70 minutes. Tent with sheet of foil if top browns too quickly.
- Transfer cake to rack and cool in pan 45 minutes.
- Coconut Drizzle:
- Whisk powdered sugar, 2 tbsp. unsweetened coconut milk, and vanilla in small bowl to blend well, adding more coconut milk by 1/2 teaspoonfuls until mixture is thin enough to drizzle over cake.
- Carefully place cake on a platter, coconut side up. Using a small spoon, drizzle powdered sugar mixture decoratively over cake. Cool cake completely on platter. Serve with vanilla ice cream.

175. Coffee Cake With Chocolate Recipe

Serving: 8 | Prep: | Cook: 60mins | Ready in:

Ingredients

- 280 grs butter

- 300 grs sugar
- grated zest of 1/2 lemon
- 4 eggs + 1 yolk
- 6 tbsp VERY strong made coffee
- 300 grs plain flour
- 1 tsp baking powder
- *
- 100 grs plain chocolate
- 1.5 dl cream
- *
- raspberries
- chocolate shavings

Direction

- Whisk together the butter, sugar and lemon zest.
- Add the eggs and the yolk plus the coffee.
- Sieve the flour and baking powder together and add to the mixture.
- Pour into a prepared tin (24cm) and bake at 180°C for 45-60 minutes.
- In the meantime, break the chocolate in small pieces and add the cream.
- Cook mixing continuously until the chocolate has melted and you have a glossy mixture - DO NOT LET IT BOIL.
- When the cake is cold, unmould onto a cake dish and pour the chocolate sauce over it.
- Decorate with raspberries and the chocolate shavings.
- A swirl of chantilly would go well

176. Coffee Chocolate Layer Cake With Mocha Mascarpone Frosting Recipe

Serving: 12 | Prep: | Cook: 40mins | Ready in:

Ingredients

- 2 cups cake flour
- 3/4 cup natural unsweetened cocoa powder
- 1 1/2 teaspoons baking soda
- 3/4 teaspoon salt
- 3/4 cup (1 1/2 sticks) unsalted butter, room temperature
- 2 cups (packed) golden brown sugar
- 3 large eggs
- 1 1/2 teaspoons vanilla extract
- 1 cup buttermilk
- 4 teaspoons instant espresso powder dissolved in 3/4 cup hot water
- Frosting:
- 1/3 cup natural unsweetened cocoa powder
- 1 tablespoon instant espresso powder
- 1 1/2 cups chilled heavy whipping cream, divided
- 1 1/3 cups sugar
- 2 8-ounce containers chilled mascarpone cheese*
- bittersweet chocolate curls (optional)

Direction

- For cake:
- Position rack in center of oven; preheat to 325°F. Generously butter two 9-inch cake pans with 2-inch-high sides; dust with flour, tapping out any excess. Line bottom of pans with parchment paper.
- Sift 2 cups cake flour, cocoa, baking soda, and salt into medium bowl. Using electric mixer, beat butter in large bowl until smooth. Add brown sugar and beat until well blended, about 2 minutes. Add eggs 1 at a time, beating well after each addition. Mix in vanilla. Add flour mixture in 3 additions alternately with buttermilk in 2 additions, beating just until blended after each addition. Gradually add hot espresso-water mixture, beating just until smooth.
- Divide batter between pans; smooth tops. Bake cakes until tester inserted into center comes out clean, about 40 minutes. Cool cakes in pans on rack 15 minutes. Run small knife around sides of pans to loosen cakes. Invert cakes onto racks; lift pans off cakes and remove parchment. Place wire rack atop each cake; invert again so top side is up. Cool completely. DO AHEAD: Can be made 1 day

ahead. Wrap each cake in plastic and store at room temperature.
- For frosting:
- Sift cocoa powder into large bowl; add espresso powder. Bring 1 cup cream to boil in small saucepan. Slowly pour cream over cocoa mixture, whisking until cocoa is completely dissolved, about 1 minute. Add 1/2 cup cream and sugar; stir until sugar dissolves. Chill until cold, at least 2 hours.
- DO AHEAD: Can be made 1 day ahead. Cover; keep chilled.
- Add mascarpone to chilled cocoa mixture. Using electric mixer, beat on low speed until blended and smooth. Increase speed to medium-high; beat until mixture is thick and medium-firm peaks form when beaters are lifted, about 2 minutes (do not overbeat or mixture will curdle).
- Using pastry brush, brush off crumbs from cakes. Place 1 cake layer, top side up, on platter. Spoon 13/4 cups frosting in dollops over top of cake. Using offset spatula, spread frosting to edges. Top with second cake layer, top side up, pressing to adhere. Spread thin layer of frosting over top and sides of cake. Chill 10 minutes. Using offset spatula, spread remaining frosting over top and sides of cake, swirling decoratively.
- Top with chocolate curls, if desired.
- DO AHEAD: Can be made 1 day ahead. Cover with cake dome; chill. Let stand at room temperature 20 minutes before serving.
- *An Italian cream cheese; sold at many supermarkets and at Italian markets.

177. Crazy Chocolate Lava Cake Recipe

Serving: 0 | Prep: | Cook: 35mins | Ready in:

Ingredients

- 2 large eggs and 1 egg yolk
- 6 tbsp melted butter
- 3 tablespoons sugar
- 1 cup chocolate chips(its better if you use dark chocolate)
- 3 tablespoons flour
- 1 tbsp cocoa powder
- pinch of salt

Direction

- Preheat your oven to 450 degrees F.
- Grease your molds or a muffin tin that you will use for this recipe (grease very well, because these cakes like to stick).
- Now, melt your 1 cup chocolate chips along with the 6 tbsp. butter in a microwave for 30 seconds, making sure to mix the chocolate after 15 seconds, until it's completely melted.
- Now, to the melted chocolate, add 1 tbsp. cocoa powder and salt and leave it aside for 5 minutes to cool it down a bit.
- Now, while the chocolate mixture in cooling, beat your eggs with the sugar for 3 minutes.
- Now add your chocolate to the egg mixture and mix fast!
- Now add the 3 tbsp. flour to the mixture.
- Now, pure the batter in to the 4 greased molds or 5 sections of a muffin tin.
- Place it in the freezer for 5 minutes.
- Now take the cakes out of the freezer and put it in the hot oven right away for 10 minutes. (Don't over bake. the max time is 15 minutes, no MORE)
- Take them out of the oven and set on the counter for 10 minutes.
- Serve them in the molds or on the plate when their warm.
- ENJOY.

178. Crazy Green Watercress Sponge Cake And Chocolate Sauce Recipe

Serving: 8 | Prep: | Cook: 40mins | Ready In:

Ingredients

- Cake:
- 4 cups watercress, roughly chopped
- 4 egg yolks, 4 egg whites, 1 whole egg
- 6 tbsp oil
- 4 tbsp milk
- 1 cup sugar
- 1 cup flour
- 1 tsp baking powder
- 2 tbsp port wine or Madeira
- 1 pinch each: cinnamon, cloves, cardamom
- chocolate sauce:
- 4 oz 70% cocoa chocolate, broken into small pieces
- 6 tbsp Grand Marnier
- 1 tsp butter
- 3 tbsp confectioner's sugar
- 7 tbsp sour cream

Direction

- Preheat oven. Prepare a baking pan of your favorite format.
- Mix the egg yolks, egg, watercress, sugar, milk and port in a food processor until the ingredients become a fine paste.
- Transfer the paste to a bowl and add the flour, spices and baking powder.
- Finally whisk the egg whites until stiff (similar to meringue) and add gently to the watercress mix.
- Bake for 30 to 40 minutes. Keep an eye on the baking process so your cake don't get burned.
- Chocolate sauce: Melt chocolate with sugar and the Grand Marnier over low heat (8 minutes). Take it off the heat and add butter and cream. It is ready to serve.

179. DUNCAN HINES DEEP CHOCOLATE CAKE Recipe

Serving: 1 | Prep: | Cook: 35mins | Ready in:

Ingredients

- 1 Duncan Hines deep chocolate cake mix
- 1 Duncan Hines family size brownie mix
- 4 eggs
- 1/2 c. oil
- 1 c. mayonnaise
- FROSTING:
- 1 sm. tub of Cool Whip
- 1 pkg. Jello instant vanilla pudding
- 1 c. milk
- 1/4 c. confectioners' sugar

Direction

- CAKE:
- Put all ingredients into a large mixing bowl and mix on high for 4 minutes. Grease and flour 9 x 13 inch pan. Bake approx. 35-40 or till toothpick comes out clean.
- FROSTING:
- Combine pudding, milk and confectioners' sugar. Beat approximately 3 minutes until pudding thickens. Fold in Cool Whip.

180. Dark Chocolate Amaretto Cake Recipe

Serving: 16 | Prep: | Cook: 65mins | Ready in:

Ingredients

- 1 package devil's food cake mix with pudding (18.25 oz)
- 1 package chocolate fudge instant pudding mix (5.9 oz)
- 1 1/4 cups water
- 1/2 cup canola oil
- 1 Tablespoon almond extract
- 4 large eggs
- 3 cups semisweet chocolate morsels, divided
- 1/2 cup Amaretto flavored liquid non dairy creamer
- 3 Tablespoons sliced natural almonds, toasted

Direction

- Combine first 6 ingredients in a large mixing bowl; beat at medium speed with an electric mixer for 2 minutes.
- Stir in 2 cups chocolate morsels.
- Pour batter into greased and floured 12 cup Bundt pan.
- Bake at 350 degrees for 55 to 65 minutes or until a wooden pick inserted in center of cake comes out clean.
- Cool in pan on a wire rack 10 minutes; remove from pan, and cool completely on wire rack.
- Combine remaining 1 cup chocolate morsels and amaretto flavored creamer in a small saucepan.
- Cook over medium heat, stirring constantly, until chocolate morsels melt.
- Remove from heat; let stand 15 minutes.
- Drizzle chocolate glaze over cake; sprinkle with almonds.
- Yield: one 10 inch cake

181. Dark Chocolate Cake With Rich Chocolate Frosting Recipe

Serving: 12 | Prep: | Cook: 35mins | Ready in:

Ingredients

- 2 cups cake flour
- 2 cups white sugar
- 1 cup baking cocoa
- 1 teaspoon baking powder
- 1/2 teaspoon salt
- 2 teaspoons baking soda
- 3 eggs
- 1 teaspoon vanilla extract
- 1 cup cold brewed coffee
- 1 cup buttermilk
- 1/2 cup vegetable oil
- Rich Chocolate Frosting:
- 1 cup butter softened, no substitutes
- 1 cup baking cocoa
- 1 teaspoon vanilla extract
- 1/2- 1 cup milk
- 4 cups confectioners' sugar

Direction

- Cake:
- Preheat oven to 350 degrees.
- Grease and flour two 9" cake pans or one 9x13 pan.
- In a large mixing bowl, combine flour, baking powder, salt, soda, cocoa, and sugar.
- Make a well in the center and add the eggs, coffee, buttermilk, vanilla, and oil.
- Mix until well combined. Batter will be thin.
- Pour batter into prepared pan(s).
- Bake 35-40 minutes or until toothpick inserted in center comes out clean.
- Let layers set for 10 minutes then turn out onto wire cooling racks.
- Cool completely.
- Frosting:
- In a large mixing bowl, cream butter.
- Gradually beat in confectioners' sugar, cocoa, and vanilla.
- Add milk until frosting reaches spreading consistency.
- Frost cake.

182. Dark Chocolate Chip Pound Cake Recipe

Serving: 12 | Prep: | Cook: 90mins | Ready in:

Ingredients

- 2 cups white sugar
- 1 cup shortening
- 4 eggs
- 2 teaspoons vanilla extract
- 2 teaspoons butter flavored extract
- 1 cup buttermilk
- 3 cups sifted all-purpose flour

- 1/2 teaspoon baking soda
- 1 teaspoon salt
- 1 cup dark chocolate chips
- 1 cup milk chocolate chips
- powdered sugar

Direction

- Preheat oven to 300 degrees. Grease and flour 2 - 9 inch loaf pans. Sift flour, baking soda and salt together and set aside.
- In a large bowl, cream shortening and sugar until light and fluffy. Beat in the eggs one at a time, then stir in the vanilla and butter flavoring. Add the flour mixture, alternating with the buttermilk, and mix well. Finally, stir in the chocolate chips.
- Divide batter into 2 - 9 inch loaf pans. Bake at 300 degrees F for 1 hour and 30 minutes, or until a toothpick inserted into the center of cake comes out clean. Remove from oven and let cool completely. Sift powdered sugar over the top and serve.

183. Dark Chocolate Chip Whole Wheat Loaf Cake With Chocolate Frosting Recipe

Serving: 6 | Prep: | Cook: 45mins | Ready in:

Ingredients

- Cake:
- 1 c. white whole wheat flour
- 1/8 tsp. salt
- 1/2 tsp. baking soda
- 1/3 c. dark brown sugar
- 1/4 c. olive oil
- 1/4 c. 100% pure maple syrup
- 1/3 c. applesauce
- 1/2 tsp. vanilla
- 1 egg
- 1/4 c. milk
- 1/2 c. dark chocolate chips
- Frosting:
- 1/2 c. honey or blue agave (for a milder taste)
- 3 T. cornstarch
- 3 T. unsweetened cocoa powder
- 1/2 tsp. salt
- 1/2 c. water
- 1 T. olive oil
- 1/4 tsp. vanilla

Direction

- Cake:
- Put all ingredients (except chocolate chips) into large bowl.
- Beat with electric mixer until well blended, then another 60 seconds.
- Add chocolate chips and stir until blended.
- Pour into ungreased loaf pan.
- Bake at 350 F for 45 minutes.
- Frosting:
- **Type of honey matters. I used wildflower the first time and it was way to strong so I switched it to good ol' plain and it was a much tamer flavor. Also if you find the chocolate flavor not strong enough add more cocoa powder.
- Put first 4 ingredients into small saucepan.
- Whisk water into mixture.
- Heat over medium constantly stirring.
- Once it thickens & is smooth remove from heat.
- Stir in oil and vanilla.
- Spread hot frosting over cooled cake.

184. Death By Chocolate Cake Recipe

Serving: 1 | Prep: | Cook: 60mins | Ready in:

Ingredients

- 4 eggs
- 1 cup sour cream
- 1/2 cup water

- 1/2 cup oil
- 1 package chocolate cake mix
- 1 package chocolate instant pudding
- 12 ounces semisweet chocolate chips
- Confectioners's sugar

Direction

- Beat eggs, sour cream, water and oil together in a large bowl until thoroughly mixed. Add cake mix and pudding mix. Beat until smooth. Stir in chocolate chips. Pour into Bundt or tube pan and bake at 350F for 1 hour. When cool, sift powdered sugar on top of cake.

185. Decadent Lil Chocolate Cheese Cakes Recipe

Serving: 24 | Prep: | Cook: 30mins | Ready in:

Ingredients

- Lil Cakes:
- 6 cups white flour
- 4 cups sugar
- 1 cup cocoa
- 1 tbsp salt
- 4 tsp baking soda
- 4 tsp vinegar
- 1 1/3 cup grapeseed oil
- 4 tsp vanilla
- 2 1/2 cups buttermilk
- 1 1/2 cups water
- Topping:
- 3 cups cream cheese
- 2/3 cup sugar
- 1 cup chocolate chips
- 2 eggs
- Warm water as needed
- 1/2 cup sliced almonds
- Cream topping:
- 3 1/2 cups whipped cream (or Cool Whip Topping)
- 1/4-1/2 cup chocolate syrup
- Grated chocolate

Direction

- Preheat oven 350*.
- Using large muffin cups or custard cups butter or line with muffin liners.
- Add first 4 ingredients of Lil Cakes batter in mixer gently mix till all is combined.
- Make a small trough into the flour mixture add Baking Soda to it.
- Pour vinegar directly on the soda and allow to stand 2 minutes to get a really good reaction. If it does not foam up the soda is old and you have to begin again.
- Now with mixer running slowly add the oil, vanilla, buttermilk, and the water last.
- Scrape down the sides of the bowl halfway through the addition of the liquid. Pour batter into a container with spout and prepare the topping.
- Topping:
- Whip together the cream cheese, eggs and sugar on medium add chocolate chips and just a little warn water to loosen it up but be very cautious because it can become too runny if you add too much.
- Set aside.
- Pour batter into dishes or muffin cups filling halfway.
- Place a dollop of cream cheese mixture on top of batter.
- Pour more batter over top of cheese mixture filled to the 3/4 mark now in cups.
- Top with more cream cheese spreading over top to edges completely covering the batter.
- Push a few sliced almonds down into cheese topping.
- Bake 15 minutes in preheated oven rotate containers and bake another 15 minutes until done toothpick will come out clean when done. Cool Completely.
- Whip Cream or if using cool whip add enough chocolate syrup to give a nice chocolate flavor.
- Add a generous dollop of chocolate cream on top of cakes when serving and sprinkle cream

with a few more sliced almonds and grated chocolate.

186. Decadent Chocolate Cake Recipe

Serving: 10 | Prep: | Cook: 22mins | Ready in:

Ingredients

- 1 box milk chocolate cake mix
- 1 (3-ounce) box instant vanilla pudding
- 3 eggs
- 1 cup whole milk
- 1/2 cup vegetable oil
- frosting
- 1 (12-ounce) container Cool Whip, thawed
- 1 (8-ounce) package cream cheese, softened
- 1 cup powdered sugar
- 1/2 cup granulated sugar
- 4 chocolate bars with almonds, crushed
- 1 cup chopped pecans
- 2 chocolate bars

Direction

- Preheat oven according to directions on the cake box. Combine cake mix, pudding, eggs, milk and oil. Pour batter into 3 greased and floured cake pans. Bake for about 22 minutes or according to directions on the box. Let cakes cool.
- For the frosting, mix together whipped topping and cream cheese. Set aside. Stir together powdered sugar and granulated sugar and combine with first mixture. Stir in the crushed chocolate bars and nuts. Spread between layers and on top and sides of cake. Break 2 chocolate bars into large chunks and garnish top of cake. Refrigerate.

187. Deep Chocolate Cake By Better Homes Amp Gardens Recipe

Serving: 14 | Prep: | Cook: 20mins | Ready in:

Ingredients

- * 1/2 cup unsweetened cocoa powder
- * 2 cups all-purpose flour
- * 1 teaspoon baking powder
- * 1/2 teaspoon baking soda
- * 2/3 cup butter, softened
- * 1-3/4 cups sugar
- * 3 eggs
- * 4 ounces unsweetened chocolate, melted and cooled
- * 2 teaspoons vanilla
- * 1-1/2 cups milk
- * 12 ounces semisweet chocolate pieces (2 cups)
- * 1/2 cup butter
- * 8 ounces dairy sour cream
- * 4-1/2 cups sifted powdered sugar (about 1 pound)
- * chocolate curls (optional)
- * Chocolate-sour cream frosting *
- * fresh raspberries (optional)**
- * Fresh mint sprigs (optional)

Direction

- 1. Grease three 9-inch round baking pans, three 8X8X2-inch square baking pans; lightly dust each pan with 1 teaspoon of the cocoa powder. In a medium bowl, stir together the remaining cocoa powder, flour, baking powder, and baking soda. Set aside.
- 2. Preheat oven to 350 degrees F. In a large bowl, beat the butter with an electric mixer on medium to high speed for 30 seconds. Add sugar; beat until combined. Add eggs, one at a time, beating for 30 seconds after each addition.
- 3. Beat in chocolate and vanilla. Alternately add flour mixture and milk to chocolate

mixture, beating on low speed until well mixed. (Batter will be thick.)

- 4. Divide batter among prepared pans; spread evenly. Bake in the preheated oven for 20 to 25 minutes or until a toothpick inserted near the centers comes out clean. Cool in pans on wire racks for 10 minutes. Remove from pans. Cool completely on wire racks.
- 5. Make chocolate curls, if using. Arrange curls in an even layer on a waxed paper-lined tray and set aside in a cool, dry place. To assemble cake, spread Chocolate-Sour Cream Frosting on tops of two of the layers; stack. Add top layer; frost the top and sides of the cake. If desired, while frosting is still moist, use a 4- to 6-inch wooden skewer or tweezers to lightly press chocolate curls into frosting around the bottom two-thirds of the cake. If desired, garnish top with raspberries and mint. Store, covered, in the refrigerator. Makes 12 to 16 servings.
- 6. *In a large saucepan melt chocolate and butter over low heat, stirring frequently. Cool for 5 minutes. Stir in sour cream. Gradually add powdered sugar, beating until smooth. This frosts tops and sides of two 8- or 9-inch cake layers.
- 7. **Chocolate-Mint Sour Cream Frosting: Prepare as above except stir in 1/2 teaspoon mint extract with the sour cream. Makes about 4-1/2 cups.

188. Deep Chocolate Triple Layer Cake Recipe

Serving: 14 | Prep: | Cook: 20mins | Ready in:

Ingredients

- 1/2 cup unsweetened cocoa powder
- 2 cups all-purpose flour
- 1 teaspoon baking powder
- 1/2 teaspoon baking soda
- 2/3 cup butter, softened
- 1-3/4 cups sugar
- 3 eggs
- 4 ounces unsweetened chocolate, melted and cooled
- 2 teaspoons vanilla
- 1-1/2 cups milk
- 12 ounces semisweet chocolate pieces (2 cups)
- 1/2 cup butter
- 8 ounces dairy sour cream
- 4-1/2 cups sifted powdered sugar (about 1 pound)
- chocolate curls (optional)
- Chocolate-sour cream frosting *
- fresh raspberries (optional)**
- Fresh mint sprigs (optional)

Direction

- Grease three 9-inch round baking pans, three 8X8X2-inch square baking pans; lightly dust each pan with 1 teaspoon of the cocoa powder. In a medium bowl, stir together the remaining cocoa powder, flour, baking powder, and baking soda. Set aside.
- Preheat oven to 350 degrees F. In a large bowl, beat the butter with an electric mixer on medium to high speed for 30 seconds. Add sugar; beat until combined. Add eggs, one at a time, beating for 30 seconds after each addition.
- Beat in chocolate and vanilla. Alternately add flour mixture and milk to chocolate mixture, beating on low speed until well mixed. (Batter will be thick.)
- Divide batter among prepared pans; spread evenly. Bake in the preheated oven for 20 to 25 minutes or until a toothpick inserted near the centers comes out clean. Cool in pans on wire racks for 10 minutes. Remove from pans. Cool completely on wire racks.
- Make chocolate curls, if using. Arrange curls in an even layer on a waxed paper-lined tray and set aside in a cool, dry place. To assemble cake, spread Chocolate-Sour Cream Frosting on tops of two of the layers; stack. Add top layer; frost the top and sides of the cake. If desired, while frosting is still moist, use a 4- to

6-inch wooden skewer or tweezers to lightly press chocolate curls into frosting around the bottom two-thirds of the cake. If desired, garnish top with raspberries and mint. Store, covered, in the refrigerator. Makes 12 to 16 servings.

- *In a large saucepan melt chocolate and butter over low heat, stirring frequently. Cool for 5 minutes. Stir in sour cream. Gradually add powdered sugar, beating until smooth. This frosts tops and sides of two 8- or 9-inch cake layers.
- **Chocolate-Mint Sour Cream Frosting: Prepare as above except stir in 1/2 teaspoon mint extract with the sour cream. Makes about 4-1/2 cups.

- Pour into a greased and floured 10" Bundt pan (fluted tube pan)
- Bake at 350 for 45-50 minutes, or until a toothpick comes out clean.
- {Check last 15 minutes, the last time I made this it took less than 45.}
- Let cool in pan 10 minutes before removing from pan to a wire rack to cool completely.
- When cool dust with powdered sugar or glaze with a chocolate glaze.
- *Recommended glaze on this site is Elle's "Shiny Chocolate Glaze"
- For cupcakes; bake 18-20 minutes

189. Deep Dark Chocolate Bundt Cake Recipe

Serving: 12 | Prep: | Cook: 60mins | Ready in:

Ingredients

- 1 cup white sugar
- 1 cup dark brown sugar
- 1 3/4 cups flour
- 3/4 cup baking cocoa
- 1/4 Tsp. cinnamon
- 2 Tsps. baking powder
- 1 Tsp. baking soda
- 1 Tsp. salt
- 2 eggs
- 1 cup strong brewed coffee, cooled
- 1 cup buttermilk
- 1/2 cup vegetable oil
- 2 Tsps. vanilla

Direction

- In a large mixing bowl combine first 8 ingredients
- Add eggs, coffee, buttermilk, oil and vanilla, beat at medium speed for 2 minutes. Batter will be somewhat thin.

190. Deep Dark Chocolate Cake Recipe

Serving: 28 | Prep: | Cook: 30mins | Ready in:

Ingredients

- 2 cups sugar
- 1¾ cups cake flour
- ¾ cup cocoa powder
- 1½ teasp baking powder
- 1½ teasp baking soda
- 1 teasp salt
- 2 eggs
- 1 cup milk
- ½ cup vegetable oil
- 2 teasp vanilla extract
- 2 oz unsweetened chocolate, melted
- 1 cup boiling water

Direction

- Preheat oven to 350oF.
- Grease and flour two 9" round pans.
- In a large bowl, stir together sugar, flour, cocoa, baking powder, baking soda and salt.
- Add eggs, milk, oil, melted chocolate, and vanilla. Beat on medium speed of electric mixer 2 minutes.
- Stir in water. Batter will be thin.

- Pour batter evenly into prepared pans.
- Bake 30 to 35 minutes or until a wooden pick inserted in center comes out clean.
- Cool 10 minutes and remove from pans to wire racks to finish cooling.
- Frost.

191. Deep Fried Chocolate Pound Cake Recipe

Serving: 16 | Prep: | Cook: 20mins | Ready in:

Ingredients

- 2 cups corn flakes, finely crushed
- 1 1/2 tablespoons sugar
- 3 1/2 teaspoons ground cinnamon
- 2 eggs
- 1 teaspoon water
- Bag Lady's Favorite chocolate Pound cake, recipe follows
- oil, for deep-frying
- powdered sugar, for sprinkling
- chocolate syrup, for drizzling

Direction

- Mix cereal, sugar and cinnamon. Divide equally between 2 pie plates or other shallow containers. Beat eggs with water in another pie plate or shallow bowl. Cut pound cake into bite-sized square pieces.
- Press each square in cereal mixture and press coating into cake.
- Dip coated square in egg wash, then roll in second container of cereal mixture. Again press coating onto cake.
- Freeze coated cake squares on a waxed paper lined baking sheet until solid, 4 to 6 hours. Deep-fry frozen coated cake squares for 45 seconds.
- Sprinkle with powdered sugar and drizzle with chocolate syrup.
- Serve with whipped cream and a cherry.

192. Differently Delicious Chocolate Cake Recipe

Serving: 12 | Prep: | Cook: 45mins | Ready in:

Ingredients

- 2/3 cup cocoa powder
- 3/4 cup boiling water
- 1 1/2 sticks plain butter cut up, softened
- 3 eggs
- 1 tsp vanilla
- 2 cups flour
- 1/4 cup cornstarch
- 1 1/2 cups sugar
- 1 1/2 tsp baking soda
- dash salt
- 1/2 tsp baking powder
- Filling: seedless black raspberry jam or apricot preserves from a jar
- topping: your favorite bottle chocolate ice cream topping or chocolate sauce
- Your favorite chocolate frosting or ganache for sides of cake
- Jimmes for decorating

Direction

- Combine boiling water with the cocoa and whisk smooth.
- Add butter and stir to melt and softened butter and blend smooth.
- Mixture will be thick.
- In another bowl combine, eggs, vanilla and beat to blend.
- Using an electric mixer, combine remaining ingredients, add to the cocoa mixture and beat smooth.
- Place mixture in a cocoa dusted springform pan and bake in middle oven rack, 350F degrees until tested done in center with tooth pick 40 to 60 minutes or tested done.
- Cool in pan, but while warm drizzle with chocolate ice cream topping or chocolate syrup

- and sprinkle on some chocolate chips and use tooth pick to swirl chips into a pattern.
- Add jimmies to decorate if desired.
- When cool remove sides of springform, cool completely and chill cake.
- When cold slice cake in half horizontally, being carefully not to disturb top.
- Either spread bottom layer with seedless raspberry jam or apricot jam.
- Place on top half of cake carefully.
- Make a favorite chocolate ganache or chocolate frosting and smooth around sides of cake and seal any separations.
- Chill well but bring to room temperature before serving.
- Note: may be baked in two separate layer pans but I often use a springform to make one layer and then split it. Which I find just as easy.
- Do what is easier for yourself!

193. Disneys Chocolate Chip Crumb Cakes Recipe

Serving: 3 | Prep: | Cook: 40mins | Ready in:

Ingredients

- 1 1/2 tablespoons + 2 teaspoons sifted cake flour
- 1 cup cornstarch
- 1/2 teaspoon baking powder
- 1 1/2 cups granulated sugar
- 1 1/4 cups (2 1/2 sticks) butter at room temp
- 1 1/4 teaspoons pure vanilla extract
- 1/2 teaspoon lemon extract
- 4 large eggs
- 1 cup semi-sweet chocolate chips

Direction

- Preheat oven to 350°F. Lightly grease and flour three 3" x 5" mini loaf pans.
- . In a medium bowl combine 1 cup plus 2 teaspoons of the cake flour with the cornstarch and baking powder.
- In a medium bowl, using an electric mixer beat 1 cup sugar and 1 cup plus 2 table spoons of the butter, 1/2 teaspoon vanilla, and the lemon extract for about 5 minutes or until light and creamy.
- Add the eggs one at a time, beating well after each addition and adding 2 to 3 tablespoons of the flour mixture with the last egg; the mixture may seem curdled. Beat for 3 or 4 minutes or until creamy again.
- With a rubber spatula, fold in the remaining flour mixture until thoroughly incorporated. Stir in the chocolate chips.
- In a small bowl, with a fork mix together the remaining 1/4 sugar, 2 tablespoons butter and 3/4 teaspoons vanilla. Add the remaining 1/2 cup flour and mix until crumbly.
- . Fill the prepared loaf pans with the crumb cake batter and sprinkle the crumb mixture over the top
- Bake the crumb cake for 35 to 40 minutes or until the middle of the cake springs back when touched lightly or a wooden toothpick inserted in the center comes out clean.

194. Double Chocolate Gooey Butter Cake Recipe

Serving: 12 | Prep: | Cook: 40mins | Ready in:

Ingredients

- 16 tablespoons butter melted
- 1 package chocolate cake mix
- 3eggs
- 8 ounce package cream cheese softened
- 4 tablespoons cocoa powder
- 16 ounce box powdered sugar
- 1 teaspoon vanilla extract
- 1 cup chopped nuts

Direction

- Preheat oven to 350. Lightly grease a rectangular baking pan. In a large bowl combine cake mix, 1 egg and 1 stick melted butter and stir until well blended. Pat mixture into prepared pan and set aside. In a stand mixer or with a hand mixer beat cream cheese until smooth. Add remaining 2 eggs and the cocoa powder. Lower the speed of the mixer and add the powdered sugar. Continue beating until ingredients are well mixed. Slowly add the remaining 1 stick of melted butter and the vanilla continuing to beat the mixture until smooth. Stir in nuts with a rubber spatula. Spread filling over cake mixture in pan. Bake for 45 minutes. Be careful not to overcook the cake the center should still be a little gooey when finished baking. Let cake partially cool on a wire rack before cutting into pieces.

195. Double Chocolate Lava Cakes Recipe

Serving: 6 | Prep: | Cook: 20mins | Ready in:

Ingredients

- 3/4 cup butter
- 6 ounces semisweet chocolate pieces (1 cup)
- 1 recipe Praline Sauce (see below)
- 3 eggs
- 3 egg yolks
- 1/3 cup sugar
- 1 1/2 teaspoons vanilla
- 1/3 cup all-purpose flour
- 3 tablespoons unsweetened cocoa powder
- 1/3 cup pecan halves, toasted

Direction

- Preheat oven to 400 degrees F. Lightly grease and flour six 1- to 1 1/4-cup soufflé dishes or six 10-ounce custard cups. Place soufflé dishes or custard cups in a shallow baking pan and set pan aside. In a heavy small saucepan melt butter and semisweet chocolate over low heat, stirring constantly. Remove from heat and cool.
- Meanwhile, prepare Praline Sauce, cover and keep warm until needed.
- In a large mixing bowl beat eggs, egg yolks, sugar, and vanilla with an electric mixer on high speed about 5 minutes or until thick and lemon colored. Beat in cooled chocolate mixture on medium speed. Sift flour and cocoa over chocolate mixture; beat on low speed just until combined. Divide batter evenly into prepared dishes or cups.
- Bake 10 minutes. Pull cakes out of oven. Using a small spatula or table knife, puncture top of each partially-baked cake and gently enlarge to make a dime-sized hole. Slowly spoon about 1 tablespoon Praline Sauce into center of each cake. Return cakes to oven. Bake 5 minutes more or until cakes feel firm at the edges.
- Cool in dishes on a wire rack for 5 minutes. Using a small spatula or knife, loosen cake edges from sides of dish or cup and slip cake out upright onto individual dessert plates. Stir 1/3 cup toasted pecan halves into the remaining Praline Sauce. If necessary, stir 1 to 2 tablespoons hot water into remaining sauce to thin. Spoon warm Praline Sauce on top of cakes. Top with pecan halves and sweetened whipped cream. Serve immediately. Makes 6 servings.
- Praline Sauce: In a heavy medium saucepan combine 1/2 cup sugar, 1/3 cup packed brown sugar and 2 tablespoons dark colored corn syrup. Stir in 1/2 cup whipping cream. Cook over medium-high heat until boiling, stirring constantly to dissolve sugar. Reduce heat. Cook, uncovered, 10 minutes or until thickened, stirring occasionally. Makes 1 cup sauce

196. Double Chocolate Rum Cake With Rasberry Rum Glaze Recipe

Serving: 10 | Prep: | Cook: 51mins | Ready in:

Ingredients

- cake
- 1 18-1/2 oz package chocolate cake mix
- 1 3-1/2 oz. package chocolate instant pudding mix
- 1/2 cup rum
- 3/4 cup of water
- 1/2 cup of vegetable oil
- 12 oz. package semi-sweet chocolate chips, divided
- RASPBERRY GLAZE:
- 1 cup of raspberry preserves
- 1/2 cup rum
- chocolate icing
- Remainder of semi-sweet chocolate chips from cake recipe
- 2 Tbsp. shortening
- 1 oz. white chocolate

Direction

- CAKE:
- Preheat oven to 350°.
- Grease 10-inch tube pan or spring form pan.
- Combine cake mix, pudding mix, 1/2 cup of BACARDI Select Rum, water and oil in bowl.
- Using an electric mixer, beat at a low speed until moistened. Beat for 2 minutes at a medium speed then stir in 1 cup of chocolate chips.
- Pour batter into pan and cook 50 minutes.
- Cool in pan 15 minutes then remove from pan and cool on rack.
- RASPBERRY GLAZE
- In small saucepan, heat preserves and BACARDI Select Rum. Strain through sieve to remove seeds.
- Place cake on serving plate and prick surface of cake with fork. Brush glaze evenly over cake, until all glaze has been absorbed.
- CHOCOLATE ICING
- In a glass bowl combine remaining chocolate chips and shortening. Microwave on medium high until melted, about 1 minute. Stir until smooth. (Or heat over hot, not boiling, water until melted.)
- Spoon chocolate icing over cake. Let stand 10 minutes.
- Melt white chocolate and drizzle on top of chocolate icing.

197. Double Chocolate Zucchini Cake Recipe

Serving: 12 | Prep: | Cook: 45mins | Ready in:

Ingredients

- 1/2 cup butter or margarine, softened
- 1 3/4 cup Sugar
- 1/2 cup vegetable oil
- 2 eggs
- 1/4 cup milk
- 1/4 cup sour cream
- 1 tsp vanilla
- 2 1/2 cups flour
- 1/2 tsp baking powder
- 1/2 tsp baking soda
- 4 Tbs. baking cocoa
- 1/2 tsp cinnamon
- 1/2 tsp ground cloves
- 2 cups finely shredded zucchini
- 1 cup chocolate chips

Direction

- Mix butter, sugar and oil until blended. Add eggs, vanilla, milk and sour cream; beat well with mixer.
- Combine dry ingredients and add to egg mixture, beating well. Stir in shredded zucchini. Turn into greased, floured,
- 9 x 13 inch pan and sprinkle with chocolate chips.

- Bake at 350 degrees for 40 - 45 minutes or until cake tests done.

198. Double Dark Fudge Brownie Cake With Chocolate Glaze Recipe

Serving: 8 | Prep: | Cook: 30mins | Ready in:

Ingredients

- 1/2 cup light corn syrup
- 1 stick butter
- 5 squares semisweet baking chocolate
- 3/4 cup granulated sugar
- 3 eggs
- 1 teaspoon vanilla
- 1 cup flour
- 1 cup chopped walnuts
- Glaze:
- 3 squares semisweet baking chocolate
- 1 tablespoon butter
- 2 tablespoons corn syrup
- 1 teaspoon milk

Direction

- Preheat oven to 350 then grease and flour a 9" layer cake pan.
- In large saucepan over medium heat bring corn syrup and butter to boil stirring occasionally.
- Remove from heat then add chocolate and stir until melted.
- Add sugar then stir in eggs one at a time then vanilla, flour and nuts.
- Pour into prepared pan then bake at 350 for 30 minutes and cool in pan 10 minutes.
- Remove from pan and drizzle with chocolate glaze and cool completely before serving.
- To make glaze melt chocolate in saucepan over low heat then add butter and stir often.
- Remove from heat and stir in corn syrup and milk until smooth.
- Pour over top of cake and spread over sides then allow to stand 1 hour before serving.

199. Dr Pepper Chocolate Cake Recipe

Serving: 8 | Prep: | Cook: 45mins | Ready in:

Ingredients

- 1 box chocolate cake mix
- 1 can dr. pepper soda
- Frosting:
- 1 small container frozen whipped topping thawed
- 1 small box instant chocolate pudding

Direction

- Combine cake mix according to package directions substituting soda for water.
- Bake in a rectangular baking pan according to package directions.
- Combine whipped topping and pudding then mix well.
- Cool cake completely then spread topping over cake and serve.

200. Dr Pepper Chocolate Cake Recipe

Serving: 8 | Prep: | Cook: 45mins | Ready in:

Ingredients

- 1 box chocolate cake
- 1 box of chocolate pudding
- 1 can of dr. pepper
- 4 eggs
- 3/4 cup of oil

Direction

- Grease a bunt pan heat oven to 350.
- Mix all ingredients well for 30 sec then mix on medium for 2 minutes.
- Pour into prepared pan and bake for 45 to 55 minutes or until toothpick comes out clean!
- Sprinkle with powdered sugar if you like or top with cherry pie filling and whipped cream. Personally I like it plain!

201. EASY Decadent Chocolate Pudding Cake Recipe

Serving: 8 | Prep: | Cook: 40mins | Ready in:

Ingredients

- 1 cup flour
- 3/4 cup granulated sugar
- 3 tablespoons cocoa
- 2 teaspoons baking powder
- 1/4 teaspoon salt
- 1/2 cup milk
- 2 tablespoons vegetable oil
- 1 teaspoon vanilla
- 3/4 cup brown sugar
- 1/4 cup cocoa
- 1 3/4 cups boiling water

Direction

- Directions for chocolate pudding cake
- Heat oven to 350°.
- In a mixing bowl, stir together flour, sugar, 3 tablespoons cocoa, baking powder and salt.
- With a fork, mix in milk, oil and vanilla.
- Spread the batter evenly in a lightly buttered 9-inch square baking pan.
- Combine brown sugar and 1/4 cup cocoa; sprinkle over the batter. Slowly pour boiling hot water over the batter and brown sugar-cocoa mixture.
- Bake chocolate pudding cake for 40 minutes. Let chocolate pudding cake stand for 5 minutes.
- Spoon into dessert dishes or cut into squares.
- Top chocolate pudding cake with ice cream or whipped cream.

202. Earthquake Cake Aka A Quick Version Of German Chocolate Cake Recipe

Serving: 12 | Prep: | Cook: 50mins | Ready in:

Ingredients

- 1c. coconut
- 1c. chopped pecans
- 1 box chocolate cake mix
- 1 stick of butter
- 1 8oz. pkg. sofened cream cheese
- 2c. powdered sugar

Direction

- Grease and flour 13x9in. pan.
- Put coconut and pecans in bottom of pan evenly.
- Prepare cake mix as instructed on box.
- Spread over coconut and pecans.
- Mix butter, powdered sugar and cream cheese.
- Spoon cheese mixture in dollops over cake.
- Bake in preheated oven at 350 for 50 min.
- Serve with whipped cream.

203. Easy Chocolate Mousse Cake Eagle Brand Recipe

Serving: 12 | Prep: | Cook: 30mins | Ready in:

Ingredients

- 1 box of chocolate cake mix
- 1 14-ounce can EAGLE BRAND® sweetened condensed milk
- 2 1-ounce squares unsweetened chocolate, melted

- 1/2 cup cold water
- 1 4-serving size package instant chocolate pudding mix
- 1 cup of heavy cream, stiffly whipped

Direction

- Preheat oven to 350°F. Prepare and bake cake mix as package directs for two 9-inch layers. Remove cakes from pans; cool.
- In large bowl, beat EAGLE BRAND® and chocolate until well blended.
- Gradually beat in water and pudding mix until smooth.
- Chill 30 minutes.
- Beat until smooth. Fold in whipped cream.
- Chill at least one hour.
- Place one cake layer on serving plate; top with 1 1/2 cups mousse mixture.
- Top with remaining cake layer.
- Frost side and top of cake with remaining mousse mixture.

204. Easy Chocolate Peanut Butter Cake Recipe

Serving: 12 | Prep: | Cook: 30mins | Ready in:

Ingredients

- 1 box devil's food cake mix
- 1 3oz box instant chocolate pudding mix
- 3 eggs
- 1/2 cup plus 1 tablespoon vegetable oil- divided
- 1 cup milk
- 1 cup peanut butter
- 1 16oz tub chocolate frosting

Direction

- Preheat oven to 350 degrees.
- Grease and flour a 9" x 13" baking pan.
- In a large mixing bowl, sift together cake mix and pudding mix.
- Add 1/2 cup vegetable oil, eggs, and milk.
- Beat for 3 minutes.
- Pour batter into prepared pan.
- Bake 30-35 minutes or until inserted toothpick comes out clean.
- In a small bowl, stir together peanut butter and remaining tablespoon of oil until smooth. Spread over warm cake. Cool completely.
- Microwave frosting until runny and carefully pour over cake. Spread evenly.
- Let frosting set.
- Serve with ice cream if desired.

205. Eggless Chocolate Cake Recipe

Serving: 14 | Prep: | Cook: 50mins | Ready in:

Ingredients

- 1 tablespoon plus 1/2 cup baking cocoa, divided
- 3 c all-purpose flour
- 2 c sugar
- 2 t baking soda
- 1 t salt
- 1/4 t cinnamon
- 2 c cold brewed coffee
- 1/3 c canola oil
- 2 T white vinegar
- 2 t vanilla extract
- 1/2 c semisweet chocolate chips
- 1/2 t shortening

Direction

- Coat a 10-in. fluted tube pan with cooking spray and dust with 1 tablespoon cocoa; set aside.
- In a large bowl, combine the flour, sugar, baking soda, salt, cinnamon and remaining cocoa.
- Stir to blend well.

- In another bowl, combine the coffee, oil, vinegar and vanilla.
- Stir into dry ingredients just until combined.
- Pour into prepared pan.
- Bake at 350° for 40-50 minutes or until a toothpick inserted near the center comes out clean.
- Cool for 10 minutes before removing from pan to a wire rack to cool completely.
- In a microwave or heavy saucepan, melt chocolate chips and shortening; stir until smooth.
- Drizzle over cake.

206. Ever So Moist Chocolate Cake With Chocolate Sour Cream Frosting Recipe

Serving: 12 | Prep: | Cook: 30mins | Ready in:

Ingredients

- The cake
- Solid vegetable shortening for greasing the pans
- flour for dusting the pans
- 1 package (18.25 ounces) devil's food cake mix with pudding
- 1 cup sour cream
- ¾ cup water
- ½ cup vegetable oil
- 3 large eggs
- 1 teaspoon pure vanilla extract
- chocolate sour cream frosting
- Makes 3 cups, enough to frost a 2- or 3-layer cake or 30 cupcakes
- Preparation Time: 10 minutes
- easy
- RECIPE INGREDIENTS
- 8 tablespoons (1 stick) butter, cut into 8 pieces
- 2/3 cup unsweetened cocoa powder
- 3 cups confectioners' sugar, sifted
- 1/3 cup sour cream
- 1 teaspoon pure vanilla extract

Direction

- Place a rack in the center of the oven and preheat the oven to 350° F.
- Generously grease two 9-inch round cake pans with solid vegetable shortening, then dust with flour.
- Shake out the excess flour.
- Set the pans aside.
- Place the cake mix, sour cream, water, oil, eggs, and vanilla in a large mixing bowl.
- Blend with an electric mixer on low speed for 1 minute.
- Stop the machine and scrape down the sides of the bowl with a rubber spatula.
- Increase the mixer speed to medium and beat 2 minutes more, scraping down the sides again if needed.
- The batter should look well combined.
- Divide the batter between the prepared pans, smoothing it out with the rubber spatula.
- Place the pans in the oven side by side.
- Bake the cakes until they spring back when lightly pressed with your finger, 28 to 32 minutes.
- Remove the pans from the oven and place them on wire racks to cool for 10 minutes.
- Run a dinner knife around the edge of each layer and invert each onto a rack, then invert again onto another rack so that the cakes are right side up.
- Allow to cool completely, 30 minutes more.
- Meanwhile, prepare the Chocolate Sour Cream Frosting.
- When frosting is ready
- Place one cake layer, right side up, on a serving platter.
- Spread the top with frosting.
- Place the second layer, right side up, on top of the first layer and frost the top and sides of the cake with clean, smooth strokes
- DIRECTIONS FOR CAKE TOPPING AND FILLING
- . Melt the butter in a small saucepan over low heat or melt it in a large glass bowl in the microwave oven on high power for 45 seconds.

- Place the melted butter in a large mixing bowl and add the cocoa powder.
- Whisk until smooth.
- Add the confectioners' sugar alternately with the sour cream, blending with an electric mixer on low speed for 1 to 1½ minutes, or until incorporated.
- Stop the machine and add the vanilla. Increase the mixer speed to medium and beat until light and fluffy, 1 minute more.
- Use the frosting to frost the top and sides of the cake
- Store this cake in a cake saver or under a glass dome, in the refrigerator for up to 1 week
- .Or freeze it, in a cake saver, for up to 6 months.
- Thaw the cake overnight in the refrigerator before serving.

207. Extreme Coffee Chocolate Mousse Cake Recipe

Serving: 8 | Prep: | Cook: 45mins | Ready in:

Ingredients

- Ingredients for the Cake:
- 7 eggs, separated
- pinch of salt
- 3/4 cup granulated sugar
- 1/2 cup good quality Dutch cocoa
- 1/2 cup finely ground hazelnuts or almonds
- Mousse Ingredients:
- 8 ounces bittersweet chocolate
- 1/2 cup brewed coffee
- 4 eggs, separated

Direction

- Finely grind the nuts and set aside.
- Separate the eggs.
- In a cold copper or very clean cold glass bowl, beat the egg whites with the salt until stiff peaks form.
- In a separate bowl, beat the egg yolks until thick and pale yellow in color.
- Add sugar to the egg yolks, beating constantly.
- Add the coca and mix thoroughly.
- Gently fold in the egg whites into the chocolate mixture.
- Pour in to a 9" springform pan and bake at 325°F. oven for 45 minutes.
- Remove the pan from the oven and allow to cool in the pan.
- Cake may fall in center which is okay.
- Directions for mouse:
- In a double boiler, melt the chocolate and set aside to cool.
- Brew the coffee and set aside to cool.
- Separate the eggs.
- In a medium size bowl beat the egg whites until peaks form.
- In a separate bowl, mix together the chocolate, coffee, and egg yolks until well incorporated.
- Gently fold in the egg whites, chill in the refrigerator until firm.
- To assemble, using a spatula, scoop out the mousse from the bowl and put into the center of the cake.
- Refrigerate the cake until ready to serve. Remove from the pan and slice with a very sharp knife.

208. Fabulous Chocolate Flourless Cake Recipe

Serving: 8 | Prep: | Cook: 25mins | Ready in:

Ingredients

- 1/8 c. cocoa powder
- 4 oz. (stick) sweet butter
- 10 oz. semi sweet chocolate
- 8 eggs, separated
- 1/3 c. sugar
- Pinch of cream of tartar
- 1 (9 inch) springform pan

Direction

- Heat oven to 275 degrees. Lightly butter the springform pan and dust with 1/8 cup cocoa powder, remove excess by shaking pan. Set aside.
- In top of double boiler melt chocolate and butter together until smooth. Remove from heat. Quickly whisk egg yolks into melted chocolate.
- Beat egg whites and cream of tartar until foamy with an electric mixer on high speed. Then slowly add sugar and beat until medium peaks form when beaters are lifted. Do not overbeat.
- In thirds, gently fold egg whites into melted chocolate mixture. Pour into prepared pan and bake for 20 to 30 minutes. Test for doneness with a toothpick.

209. Flan Chocolate Cake Recipe

Serving: 20 | Prep: | Cook: 60mins | Ready in:

Ingredients

- For the caramel sauce:
- 1 cup sugar.
- 60 grams butter.
- 1 cup whipping cream.
- For the flan:
- 1 can sweetend condensed milk(410grams).
- 200 grams evaporated milk.
- 200 grams heavy cream.
- 5 eggs.
- 48 grams cream cheese cold
- 1 tsp vanilla extract.
- For the cake:
- 1 box devil's food cake mix or fudge chocolate cake mix.

Direction

- Method:
- 1-Heat the sugar over medium heat till it all dissolve and turn golden color, add the butter in small pieces stirring with a wooden spoon, add the cream in a steady stream so slowly while stirring. Pour the caramel in the pan and keep aside till cooled.
- 2-In a mixer, combine all the flan ingredients and keep aside.
- 3-Make the cake batter by following the instructions on the box.
- 4-Pour the cake batter over the caramel sauce in the pan. Using a large spoon, add the flan mixture so slowly on top. Don't be surprised, here is the trick steps, the flan and the cake batter will flip while baking leaving the caramel on the base.
- 5-Put the pan in a bigger tin and add boiling water to the tin till it comes 2cm of the pan base. Bake for 50-60minutes till a skewer inserted in the center comes out clean.
- 6-Take out of oven and flip in a glass dish. Serve warm or cold. Can be stored covered in the refrigerator for 3 days.

210. Flourless Chocolate Cake With Toasted Marshmallows Recipe

Serving: 8 | Prep: | Cook: 40mins | Ready in:

Ingredients

- 8 ounces bittersweet chocolate (not unsweetened), chopped into small pieces
- 1 cup (2 sticks) unsalted butter
- 1 1/2 cups sugar
- 6 large eggs, room temperature
- 1 cup unsweetened cocoa powder
- 30 marshmallows
- ~~~~~~~~~~~~~~~~~~~~~~~
- Variations
- For a mocha twist, stir 2 Tablespoons of instant espresso into the melted chocolate and butter mixture.

Direction

- Place rack in the middle of the oven and preheat oven to 375 degrees F. Butter a 10 inch round spring-form pan. Line the bottom of the pan with a round piece of wax paper, and butter the paper.
- In a double boiler (or metal bowl set over a saucepan of barely simmering water), melt the chocolate with the butter, stirring until smooth.
- Remove the top of the double boiler from the heat and whisk the sugar into the chocolate mixture. Add the eggs one at a time and whisk well after adding each egg.
- Sift 1/2 cup of the cocoa powder over the chocolate mixture from step 3, and whisk until just combined. Repeat with the remaining 1/2 cup cocoa powder. Pour the batter into the spring form pan and bake on the middle rack of the oven for 35-40 min, or until the top has formed a thin crust and a wooden pick inserted into the cake comes out with moist crumbs.
- Cool the cake in the pan on a cooling rack for 10 minutes (cake will deflate slightly). Then remove the spring-form sides, leaving the cake on the bottom of the pan.
- Place the cake (still on its springform base0 on a sheet pan or cookie sheet. Top the cake with marshmallows while it is still warm, leaving one inch free around the edge. Return cake on cookie sheet back in oven and bake at 375 for 5-10 minutes, or until the marshmallows are golden brown. Remove from oven and place on a cooling rack until completely cooled, about 1 hour
- ***When serving
- The marshmallows will be sticky. Lightly coat your knife with cooking spray or oil and carefully wipe off the blade before slicing, continuing to wipe the blade between each slice.

211. Flourless Chocolate Cake With Chocolate Mousse And Raspberry Sauce Recipe

Serving: 14 | Prep: | Cook: 45mins | Ready in:

Ingredients

- Flourless chocolate Cake:
- 8 bars (1.5 ounces each) Godiva® dark chocolate, chopped
- 1 1/2 cups (3 sticks) unsalted butter, softened
- 3 cups confectioners' sugar
- 12 eggs, separated
- Pinch of salt
- chocolate Mousse:
- 1 1/2 cups milk
- 1/2 cup granulated sugar
- 7 bars (1.5 ounces each) Godiva® dark chocolate, chopped
- 3 tablespoons vegetable oil
- 1 teaspoon vanilla extract
- 1 1/2 cups heavy cream
- Raspberry Sauce:
- 1/2 cup water
- 1/2 cup granulated sugar
- 1 1/2 cups fresh or frozen raspberries
- 1/2 teaspoon vanilla extract
- 1/2 teaspoon finely grated orange peel

Direction

- Make Flourless Chocolate Cake:
- Position rack in center of oven and preheat to 350°F. Lightly grease a 10 x 3-inch springform pan.
- Place chocolate in a microwavable bowl. Microwave on HIGH for 1 to 1 1/2 minutes or until almost melted. Let stand 1 minute and stir until smooth.
- Beat butter and 2 cups confectioners' sugar with mixer at high speed for about 3 minutes or until light and fluffy. Add egg yolks, one at a time, beating well after each addition.
- Beat egg whites and salt with mixer at medium speed in a dry, clean bowl until frothy. Gradually add remaining

confectioners' sugar. Increase speed to high and beat until stiff peaks form.
- Fold melted chocolate into butter mixture. Gently fold egg whites into chocolate-butter mixture. Do not overmix (the mixture should have a few streaks of whites in it). Pour batter into springform pan. Bake for 45 minutes, or until a toothpick inserted in center has a few moist crumbs clinging to it. Be careful not to overbake or cake will be dry. Cool completely in pan on a wire rack. Upon cooling, the center of the cake will sink
- Make Chocolate Mousse:
- 1. Heat the milk and granulated sugar in a small saucepan over medium heat to a boil. Remove from heat. Add chocolate. Let stand for 5 minutes. Stir until melted and smooth. Stir in oil and vanilla. Let cool for about 10 minutes or until tepid.
- 2. Beat cream in a chilled bowl with mixer at high speed until stiff peaks form. Gently fold one-half of the whipped cream into the tepid chocolate mixture. Gently fold in the remaining cream, being careful not to overmix. Carefully spoon mousse on top of cake, spreading evenly with a spatula. Refrigerate for at least 2 hours or until cold
- Make Raspberry Sauce:
- 1. Heat the water and granulated sugar in a small saucepan over medium heat to a boil. Add 1 cup raspberries, vanilla and orange peel. Let stand for 10 minutes. Strain raspberry mixture through a fine-meshed sieve into a bowl. Refrigerate until cold. Stir in remaining raspberries.
- 2. To serve, run a thin-bladed knife around edge of cake to loosen it from sides of springform pan. Remove side from springform pan. With a sharp thin-bladed knife, slice cake, wiping blade clean between each cut. Place the slices on serving plates and top with some of the raspberry sauce.

212. Flourless Chocolate Decadence Cake Recipe

Serving: 20 | Prep: | Cook: 45mins | Ready in:

Ingredients

- 12.5 oz chocolate covertures 66%
- 12.5 oz butter unsalted
- 5 oz Castor sugar
- 6 eggs
- mint leafs for garnish
- chocolate shavings for garnish
- Couverture chocolate is a very high quality chocolate that contains extra cocoa butter (32-39%).

Direction

- Instructions
- In one bowl, melt the butter and chocolate gently over steam. In another bowl whisk together sugar and eggs. Don't whisk the mixture foamy just combine well.
- Combine the two mixtures. Line a fireproof baking dish with greaseproof paper, then pour the mixture into the lined dish and bake by 300 Fahrenheit for 40 to 45 minutes. Best results are achieved if the mixture is just under done when removed from the oven and the cake is allowed to "set" during the cooling process. Cool in the refrigerator.
- The high amount of butter in the cake will make it fairly solid when chilled and easy to handle when cutting and portioning.
- Cut to size and let come to room temperature before garnishing and serving. In order to keep the cutting surface nice and clean, you need to heat your knife in hot water for a few seconds, wipe it clean and then cut the chocolate cake to size with the heated knife.
- This recipe will make approximately 20 to 25 cakes at about 1 1/2 ounces each.

213. Flourless Chocolate Almond Cake Recipe

Serving: 10 | Prep: | Cook: 35mins | Ready in:

Ingredients

- ⅔ cup brown sugar, packed
- 3 ounces bittersweet chocolate, coarsely chopped
- ½ cup unsweetened cocoa (not Dutch)
- ⅓ cup boiling water
- 2 large egg yolks, room temperature
- ¾ cup whole almonds
- 1 teaspoon xanthan gum
- 4 large egg whites, room temperature
- ¼ teaspoon cream of tartar
- 1 tablespoon brown sugar
- 1 teaspoon vanilla extract
- ½ teaspoon almond extract
- powdered sugar, for dusting

Direction

- Preheat oven to 375 degrees. Line bottom of 8-inch springform pan with parchment paper. Spray parchment paper and sides of pan with cooking spray.
- Combine 2/3 cup brown sugar, chocolate, cocoa and boiling water in a small bowl. Stir until chocolate is melted. Let cool to room temperature. Whisk in egg yolks. Set aside.
- Finely grind almonds in food processor or clean coffee grinder. Add xanthan gum. Set aside.
- Using electric mixer, beat egg whites and cream of tartar until soft peaks form. Add 1 tablespoon brown sugar, vanilla extract and almond extract. Beat until stiff but not dry.
- Carefully whisk almond mixture into chocolate mixture. Fold in egg whites in two additions.
- Transfer batter to prepared springform pan. Wrap bottom in aluminum foil to prevent leaking. Place in larger pan of boiling water so that water comes up one inch on outer sides of springform pan.
- Bake 35 minutes or until toothpick inserted into center comes out clean. Cool cake in pan on rack. Dust with powdered sugar. Cut around edge of cake to loosen from pan edges. Release pan sides. Cut into 10 slices.

214. Fondant Chocolate Cake Recipe

Serving: 10 | Prep: | Cook: 40mins | Ready in:

Ingredients

- cake ingredients:
- 60 grams plain chocolate, chopped
- 15 grams unsweetened cocoa powder (not Dutch-processed)
- ½ cup boiling water
- 160 grams all purpose flour
- 1 teaspoon baking powder
- 1/2 teaspoon baking soda
- Pinch of salt
- 115 grams unsalted butter, room temperature
- 1 cup granulated white sugar
- 2 eggs
- 1 teaspoon pure vanilla extract
- ½ cup milk
- Fondant ingredients:
- 600 grams good quality plain or dark chocolate such as Lindt, chopped
- ¾ LITRE (not cup) whipping cream divided in ¼ +1/2
- Decoration:
- almonds blanched
- cocoa powder
- icing sugar

Direction

- Cake:
- Preheat oven to 350 degrees. Butter, and line with parchment paper, a 23 x 5 cm loose bottomed baking pan. Set aside.

- In a stainless steel or heatproof bowl place the chopped chocolate and cocoa powder. Pour the boiling water over the chocolate and cocoa powder and stir until they have melted. Set aside to cool while you make the batter.
- In a separate bowl, whisk to combine, the flour, baking powder, baking soda, and salt. Set aside.
- In the bowl of your electric mixer, cream the butter. Gradually add the sugar and continue beating until the mixture is fluffy (this will take about 3-5 minutes). Add the eggs, one at a time, mixing well after each addition. Add the vanilla extract and melted chocolate mixture and beat to combine.
- Add the milk and flour mixtures in three additions, beginning and ending with the flour mixture. Beat only until the ingredients are incorporated.
- Pour the batter in the prepared pan and smooth the top. Bake for about 35 - 40 minutes or until a toothpick inserted in the center comes out clean. Remove from oven and place on a wire rack to cool for about 10 minutes.
- When completely cooled, split the cake in half horizontally; place one half in the same baking pan after you have washed it and save the other half for another use. Decorate the inside edges of the cake ring with some almonds.
- Chocolate fondant:
- Bring ¼ litre to simmering point in a saucepan over medium heat, pour over the chopped chocolate and let stand for 2-3 minutes. Stir till chocolate melts and mixture is smooth. Set aside for 20 minutes till cooled slightly. Whisk the chocolate mixture till slightly thickened.
- Whip the remaining ½ litre cream till stiff, fold in the chocolate mixture carefully till all is combined and no white streaks exist. Pour the mixture over the cake in the pan and level the top. Chill for 4 hours. Use your imagination for decoration with cocoa powder, almonds, chocolate chips or chocolate curls.

215. French Chocolate Coffee Cake Recipe

Serving: 1216 | Prep: | Cook: 55mins | Ready in:

Ingredients

- 1/2 cup butter, softened
- 1/2 cup butter- flavored shortening or margarine
- 11/2 cups sugar
- 5 eggs
- 1 teaspoon vanilla extract
- 3 cups flour
- 2 teaspoons baking powder
- 1 teaspoon baking soda
- 1 cup sour cream
- TOPPING:
- 1/2 cup sugar
- 1 teaspoon cinnamon
- 2 ounces unsweetened baking chocolate, grated
- powdered sugar

Direction

- Preheat oven to 350 degrees. Grease a 10- or 12 inch tube pan or Bundt pan.
- In large bowl of an electric mixer, cream butter, shortening and sugar. Beat in eggs, one at a time. Then beat in vanilla.
- In a separate bowl, sift together flour, baking powder, and baking soda. Add flour mixture to butter mixture alternately with sour cream. Mix well.
- For the topping:
- In a small bowl, mix sugar, cinnamon and grated chocolate.
- Put one- third to one- half of the thick batter in the bottom of the prepared pan. Sprinkle batter with half the topping. Repeat with the rest of the batter and topping. Run a knife through the topping and batter once to marbleize the cake.
- Bake about 55 minutes or until toothpick or knife inserted into the center comes out clean. Cool pan for 10 minutes or more before

inverting on a serving plate. Dust with powdered sugar before serving.

216. Frozen Chocolate Bar Cookie Cake Recipe

Serving: 9 | Prep: | Cook: | Ready in:

Ingredients

- 1 package of your favorite chocolate chip cookies
- 1 Litre tub of frozen whipped topping
- Some milk (for dunking the cookies…about a cup and a half)
- 3 chocolate bars like Butterfinger, Skor or Crispy Crunch (I use Crispy Crunch) — put in the blender to make chunky crumbs

Direction

- First, make sure you leave the frozen topping in the fridge for the day so that it's soft and spreadable…or leave on the counter for a few hours. You also need a 9×9 inch square dish that is okay to put in the freezer.
- Take a cookie and dunk completely in some milk, but don't make it soggy. Place on the bottom of the dish…repeat until you have a layer of cookies.
- Cover the cookies with half of the softened whipped topping and sprinkle half of the chocolate bar crumbs. Next, repeat with another layer of cookies and whipped topping and finally top with the remaining chocolate crumbs…AND YOU'RE DONE!! Just place in the freezer and wait a few hours until frozen. Enjoy!

217. Fudge Fudge Chocolate Syrup Cake Recipe

Serving: 12 | Prep: | Cook: 30mins | Ready in:

Ingredients

- 1 cup sugar
- 1 cup oil
- 4 eggs, *beaten*
- 1 teaspoon baking powder
- 1-16 ounce can chocolate syrup
- 1 teaspoon vanilla
- 1 cup flour

Direction

- In large bowl, combine all ingredients.
- Blend well.
- Pour into greased and floured 9 x 13 inch pan.
- Bake 30-35 minutes.
- Please do not overcook.
- Frost with favorite frosting.
- Toasted nuts, optional.
- Great with vanilla ice cream.

218. Fudgy Chocolate Layer Cake Recipe

Serving: 12 | Prep: | Cook: 27mins | Ready in:

Ingredients

- 1 3/4 cups all-purpose flour
- 1 cup less 1 Tbsp unsweetened cocoa powder
- 1 1/4 tsp baking soda
- 1/8 tsp salt
- 3/4 cup (1 1/2 sticks) butter, softened
- 2/3 cup granulated sugar
- 2/3 cup firmly packed brown sugar
- 2 large eggs
- 2 tsp vanilla extract
- 1 1/2 cups buttermilk
- frosting and Garnish:
- 1/2 cup (1 stick) butter, softened

- 1 1/2 cup confectioners' sugar, sifted
- 3 oz (3 squares) unsweetened chocolate, melted
- 2 tsp vanilla extract
- chocolate shavings

Direction

- Preheat oven to 350 degrees.
- Line bottom of two 9-inch round cake pans with waxed paper. Grease paper and sides of pans. Dust with flour.
- Mix flour, cocoa, baking soda, and salt.
- In another bowl, beat butter, granulated sugar, and brown sugar at medium speed until light and fluffy.
- Add eggs, one at a time, beating well after each addition. Add vanilla.
- At low speed, alternately beat flour mixture and buttermilk into butter mixture just until blended.
- Divide batter equally between prepared pans.
- Bake cakes until a toothpick inserted in center comes out clean, about 25 to 30 minutes.
- Transfer pans to wire racks to cool for 10 minutes. Turn out onto racks and remove paper. Turn layers right side up and cool completely.
- To prepare frosting, beat butter and confectioners' sugar at medium speed until light and fluffy.
- Add melted chocolate and vanilla; continue beating until shiny and smooth.
- Place one cake layer on a serving plate; spread with frosting.
- Top with remaining cake layer.
- Spread frosting on top and sides of cake.
- Let cake stand for at least 30 minutes before sprinkling with chocolate shavings and slicing.

219. German Chocolate Cake Recipe

Serving: 16 | Prep: | Cook: 180mins | Ready in:

Ingredients

- 4 oz Baker's German's sweet chocolate, broken into squares
- 1/2 cup water
- 2 cups all purpose flour
- 1 1/2 teaspoons baking soda
- 1/4 teaspoon salt
- 4 large eggs, separated, at room temperature
- 1 cup butter, softened
- 2 cups sugar
- 1 teaspoon vanilla extract
- 1 cup buttermilk
- 1 1/2 cans evaporated milk
- 6 egg yolks
- 2 cups sugar
- 1 cup butter, cut into small pieces
- 2 teaspoons vanilla extract
- 4 cups sweetened, shredded coconut
- 2 cups coarsely chopped pecans

Direction

- Preheat oven to 350.
- Grease and flour 3 9x2 inch round cake pans, then line bottoms with wax paper.
- In a small saucepan over low heat, combine the chocolate with the water, stirring to melt the chocolate, and blend well. Set aside and cool for 10 minutes.
- Meanwhile, in a medium sized bowl, sift together the flour, the baking soda, and the salt. Set aside.
- In a small bowl, lightly beat the egg yolks, about 1 minute.
- In a large bowl, on the medium speed of an electric mixer, cream the butter and the sugar until light and fluffy, about 3 minutes.
- Add the egg yolks, beating until well combined.
- Add the chocolate mixture and the vanilla extract.
- Add the dry ingredients in thirds, alternating with the buttermilk, beating after each addition, until smooth.

- In a separate bowl, beat the egg whites on the high speed of an electric mixer until soft peaks form. Gently fold into batter.
- Divide batter among the prepared pans.
- Bake for 25-30 minutes or until a cake tester comes out clean. Be careful not to over bake, as this cake has a different, lighter texture than most.
- Let cake cool in pans for 10 minutes.
- Remove from pans and cool completely on wire rack.
- In a large saucepan, beat together the evaporated milk and the egg yolks.
- Stir in the sugar, the butter, and the vanilla extract.
- Stir over medium heat about 15-18 minutes or until thickened and bubbly and golden in color. Remove from heat.
- Stir in the coconut and pecans.
- Transfer to a large bowl and cool until room temperature and of good spreading consistency (about 2 hours.)
- When cake has cooled, spread frosting between layers and over top of cake.

220. German Chocolate Pound Cake Recipe

Serving: 12 | Prep: | Cook: 47mins | Ready in:

Ingredients

- 1 German cake mix (without pudding)
- 1 tub 15oz coconut pecan frosting
- 1 cup water
- 1/3 cup oil
- 3 eggs

Direction

- Mix all ingredients together, including frosting. Grease Bundt pan and bake at 350 for 45 to 50 minutes. This cake is very moist, and so delicious.

221. German Chocolate Pound Cake Recipe Recipe

Serving: 10 | Prep: | Cook: 65mins | Ready in:

Ingredients

- For Cake:
- 4 ounces Baker's German sweet chocolate
- 2-3/4 cups sifted cake flour
- 1-3/4 cups sugar
- 1 teaspoon salt
- 3/4 teaspoon cream of tartar
- 1/2 teaspoon baking soda
- 1/4 teaspoon cinnamon
- 1 cup softened butter
- 3/4 cup milk
- 1 teaspoon vanilla extract
- 3 eggs
- 1 egg yolk
- For chocolate Glaze:
- 4 ounces Baker's German sweet chocolate
- 1 tablespoon butter
- 1/4 cup water
- 1 cup confectioners' sugar, sifted
- 1/8 teaspoon salt
- 1/2 teaspoon vanilla extract

Direction

- Preheat oven to 350 degrees.
- Melt chocolate in double boiler. Cool. Sift dry ingredients. Cream softened butter. Add dry ingredients, milk, and vanilla extract, mixing only to combine. Beat two minutes at medium speed with an electric mixer. Add eggs, egg yolk, and chocolate. Beat one minute longer. Pour batter into a greased and floured 10-inch tube pan which has been lined with waxed paper. Bake about 65 minutes. Cool in pan for 15 minutes. Turn out of pan, remove waxed paper, and cool completely. Frost with chocolate glaze.
- To make glaze, melt chocolate, butter, and water in a double boiler over low heat

Combine confectioner's sugar and salt. Gradually stir in chocolate mixture and vanilla extract, blending well. Pour over cooled cake.

222. German Chocolate Upside Down Cake Recipe

Serving: 0 | Prep: | Cook: |Ready in:

Ingredients

- 1 cup coconut
- 1 cup pecans, chopped
- 1 box German chocolate cake mix
- 1 stick butter
- 8 oz. package cream cheese
- 1 box powdered sugar

Direction

- Grease a 9 x 13 baking dish. Mix coconut and pecans together and spread evenly in the bottom of dish. Mix cake according to directions on box.
- Pour cake mixture over the coconut/pecan mixture. Soften butter and cream cheese and blend together until smooth.
- Add box of powdered sugar to butter/cream mixture and blend together until smooth.
- Dribble this mixture over the top of the cake mixture. Bake according to the directions on the cake mix box.

223. German Chocolate Upside Down Cake Recipe

Serving: 12 | Prep: | Cook: 45mins |Ready in:

Ingredients

- 1 cup shredded coconut
- 1 cup chopped pecans
- 1 (8-ounce) package cream cheese, room temperature
- 1/2 cup (1 stick) butter, melted
- 1 (1-pound) box confectioners' sugar
- 1 (18.25-ounce) package German chocolate cake mix, plus ingredients listed on the package (eggs, oil, water)

Direction

- Preheat oven to 350 degrees. Spray a 9-by-13-inch pan with cooking spray. Sprinkle the coconut and pecans evenly over the bottom of the pan.
- In a mixing bowl, combine the cream cheese, butter and confectioners' sugar; beat with a wooden spoon or electric mixer until well-combined. Spread the cream cheese mixture over the coconut and nuts.
- Prepare the cake batter according to the package directions. Pour the batter over the cream cheese mixture. Bake for 45 to 55 minutes, until cake tests done. Cool at least 20 minutes or to room temperature.
- To serve, cut the cake into squares. Lift each square with a spatula and flip onto a dessert plate so that the gooey coconut good stuff is on top.
- Store the cake in the baking pan.
- Notes:
- Tip: If the gooey stuff at the bottom sticks to the pan, gently warm the pan on the stove over low heat for 30 seconds.

224. German Chocolate Yum Yum Cake Recipe

Serving: 1 | Prep: | Cook: 25mins |Ready in:

Ingredients

- 1 box German chocolate cake mix
- 1 can sweetened condensed milk (Eagle Brand)
- 1 jar caramel ice cream topping
- 1 (8 oz) container Cool Whip

- 6 oz crushed Heath Bar
- 6 oz. crushed plain hershey bar

Direction

- Bake cake as directed in a 9x13 pan.
- Take the handle of a wooden spoon and poke holes all over the cake while it's still warm. Pour can of condensed milk over warm cake, then repeat with caramel topping. Refrigerate for 6 hours.
- Frost cake with Cool Whip topping and sprinkle with crushed Hershey bar. Serve immediately.

225. German Chocolate Upside Down Cake Recipe

Serving: 12 | Prep: | Cook: 45mins | Ready in:

Ingredients

- 1 cup flaked coconut
- 1 cup chopped pecans
- 1 package German chocolate cake mix
- 8 0z cream cheese (room temp)
- 1/2 cup butter (room temp)
- 1 pound box powdered sugar

Direction

- Grease and flour 9 x13 pan.
- Sprinkle coconut and pecans evenly over bottom of pan.
- Prepare cake mix according to package directions.
- Pour cake batter over coconut and pecans.
- Beat together cream cheese, butter, and powdered sugar.
- Drop by spoonfuls over the top of the cake batter.
- Bake about 45 minutes or until a toothpick comes out clean when inserted in the center.
- To serve: cool cake, cut into serving size pieces and turn upside down on dessert plates

- ENJOY!!!

226. Giannas Chocolate Whipped Cream Cake Recipe

Serving: 8 | Prep: | Cook: 35mins | Ready in:

Ingredients

- 1 3/4 cup(s) all-purpose flour
- 2 1/4 cup(s) granulated sugar
- 2 tablespoon granulated sugar
- 3/4 cup(s) unsweetened cocoa
- 1 1/2 tablespoon(s) unsweetened cocoa
- 1 teaspoon(s) salt
- 1 1/2 teaspoon(s) baking powder
- 1 1/2 teaspoon(s) baking soda
- 1/2 cup(s) canola oil
- 1 cup(s) milk
- 2 large eggs
- 2 teaspoon(s) vanilla extract
- 2 tablespoon(s) anisette liqueur
- 1 1/2 cup(s) heavy cream, cold
- 1 1/2 teaspoon(s) confectioners' sugar
- 1/3 cup(s) mini chocolate chips

Direction

- Make the cake: Heat oven to 350 degrees F. Butter the bottoms of two 9-inch round cake pans and fit with two circles of parchment paper. Butter the paper and pan sides and dust with flour. Set aside. Bring a small saucepan of water to a boil and maintain. Combine the flour, 2 cups granulated sugar, 3/4 cup cocoa, salt, baking powder, and baking soda in a large bowl. Beat in the oil, milk, eggs, vanilla, and anisette liqueur using a mixer set on medium speed for 2 minutes. Reduce mixer speed to low and add 1 cup of the boiling water. Divide the batter between the prepared pans and bake until a wooden skewer inserted into the middle of each cake comes out clean -- about 35 minutes. Cool the cakes in pans on a wire rack for 10 minutes. Unmold the cakes

- and return to the wire rack until completely cool.
- Make the frosting:
- Beat the heavy cream and confectioners' sugar until soft peaks form. Gently fold in the remaining 1/4 cup plus 2 tablespoons granulated sugar and 1 1/2 tablespoons cocoa until combined.
- Assemble the cake:
- Place one layer on a cake plate. Spread a third of the frosting over the layer. Sprinkle with half of the chocolate chips. Top with the remaining layer and spread the remaining frosting over the top and sides of the cake. Sprinkle with the remaining chocolate chips. Serve immediately or store in the refrigerator until ready to serve

227. Golden Chocolate Cake Recipe

Serving: 12 | Prep: | Cook: 35mins | Ready in:

Ingredients

- 1 golden cake mix, withouth pudding
- 1 (3.4-ounce) box instant vanilla pudding
- 1/2 cup vegetable oil
- 1/2 cup water
- 4 eggs
- 1 (8-ounce) carton sour cream
- 3 Hershey Bars (or other milk chocolate bars), chopped
- 1 cup semisweet chocolate chips
- 1 cup chopped walnuts
- 1 cup shredded coconut
- Confectioners' sugar, optional

Direction

- Heat oven to 350 degrees.
- Grease a 12-cup Bundt pan.
- Combine cake and pudding mixes, oil, water and eggs in the large bowl of a mixer.
- Beat on low 30 seconds. Increase speed to high and beat 2 minutes.
- Mix in sour cream.
- Stir in chocolate, chocolate chips, walnuts and coconut.
- Pour into prepared pan and bake 60 to 65 minutes.
- Cool in pan 15 minutes before turning out onto a wire rack to cool completely.
- Dust with confectioners' sugar, if desired.

228. Heavenly Chocolate Hazelnut Cake Gluten Free Recipe

Serving: 16 | Prep: | Cook: 30mins | Ready in:

Ingredients

- Cake:
- 2 1/2 cups real semi-sweet chocolate chips Nestle's is GF
- 1/2 cup LAND O LAKES® butter
- 1/2 cup toasted finely chopped hazelnuts or filberts, skins removed
- 2 tablespoons sugar
- 4 eggs, slightly beaten
- glaze Ingredients:
- 4 (1-ounce) squares semi-sweet baking chocolate
- 1/4 cup whipping cream
- Garnish Ingredients:
- Melted chocolate, if desired
- toasted chopped hazelnuts, if desired

Direction

- Heat oven to 350°F. Grease bottom and sides of 8-inch springform pan; dust with powdered sugar.
- Combine chocolate chips and butter in 2-quart saucepan. Cook over low heat, stirring constantly, until smooth (4 to 6 minutes). Stir

in nuts, sugar and eggs. Pour into prepared pan.
- Bake for 28 to 32 minutes or until edges begin to pull away from sides of pan. Cool completely. Remove sides of springform pan; place cake onto serving plate.
- Meanwhile, combine baking chocolate and whipping cream in small saucepan. Cook over low heat, stirring constantly, until smooth (3 to 4 minutes). Cool 5 minutes. Pour over top and sides of cooled cake. Refrigerate until set (at least 1 hour).
- To serve, drizzle plate with melted chocolate, if desired. Sprinkle with hazelnuts, if desired.
- Recipe Tip
- To toast hazelnuts, bake at 350°F. for 9 to 11 minutes. Rub in a wet dish towel to remove skins. If skins don't come off, continue baking for an additional 5 minute

229. Heavenly Deep Dark Chocolate Cake Recipe

Serving: 5 | Prep: | Cook: 35mins | Ready in:

Ingredients

- Ingredients:
- 2 cups sugar
- 1-3/4 cups all-purpose flour
- 3/4 cup cocoa or dark cocoa
- 1-1/2 teaspoons baking powder
- 1-1/2 teaspoons baking soda
- 1 teaspoon salt
- 2 eggs
- 1 cup milk
- 1/2 cup vegetable oil
- 2 teaspoons vanilla extract
- 1 cup boiling water
- ONE-BOWL BUTTERCREAM frosting(recipe follows)

Direction

- Directions:
- 1. Heat oven to 350°F. Grease and flour two 9-inch round pans or one 13x9x2-inch baking pan.
- 2. Stir together sugar, flour, cocoa, baking powder, baking soda and salt in large bowl. Add eggs, milk, oil and vanilla; beat on medium speed of electric mixer 2 minutes. Stir in boiling water (batter will be thin). Pour batter into prepared pans.
- 3. Bake 30 to 35 minutes for round pans, 35 to 40 minutes for rectangular pan or until wooden pick inserted in center comes out clean. Cool 10 minutes; remove from pans to wire racks. Cool completely. (Cake may be left in rectangular pan, if desired.) Frost with ONE-BOWL BUTTERCREAM FROSTING. 8 to 10 servings.
- ONE-BOWL BUTTERCREAM FROSTING
- 6 tablespoons butter or margarine, softened
- 2-2/3 cups powdered sugar
- 1/2 cup Cocoa or Dutch Processed Cocoa
- 1/3 cup milk
- 1 teaspoon vanilla extract
- Beat butter in medium bowl. Add powdered sugar and cocoa alternately with milk, beating to spreading consistency (additional milk may be needed). Stir in vanilla. About 2 cups frosting.
- HIGH ALTITUDE DIRECTIONS (Cake):
- -- Decrease sugar to 1-3/4 cups
- -- Increase flour to 1-3/4 cups plus 2 tablespoons
- -- Decrease baking powder to 1-1/4 teaspoons
- -- Decrease baking soda to 1-1/4 teaspoons
- -- Increase milk to 1 cup plus 2 tablespoons
- -- Bake at 375°F, 30 to 35 minutes for both pan sizes

230. Hersheys Perfectlatey Chocolate Cake Recipe

Serving: 810 | Prep: | Cook: 30mins | Ready in:

Ingredients

- 2 cups sugar
- 1 3/4 cups flour
- 3/4 cups of cocoa (I used Hershey's brand)
- 1 1/2 tsp baking powder
- 1 1/2 tsp baking soda
- 1 tsp salt
- 2 eggs
- 1 cup milk
- 1/2 vegetable oil
- 2 tsp vanilla extract
- 1 cup boiling water
- Perfectly chocolate frosting(recipe below)

Direction

- Heat oven to 350*. Grease and flour two 9-inch round baking pans
- Stir together sugar, flour, cocoa, baking powder, baking soda and salt in large bowl.
- Add eggs, milk, oil and vanilla; beat on medium speed of mixer for 2 minutes.
- Stir in water (batter will be thin).
- Pour batter evenly into prepared pans.
- Bake for 30 to 35 minutes or until wooden pick inserted into center comes out clean.
- Cool 10 minutes; remove from pans to wire racks and cool completely.
- Prepare frosting
- 1/2 cup butter
- 2/3 cup cocoa
- 3 cups powdered sugar
- 1/3 cup milk
- 1 tsp. vanilla extract
- Melt butter.
- Stir in cocoa.
- Alternately add powdered sugar and milk, beating to spreading consistency.
- Add small amount additional milk, if needed.
- Stir in vanilla.
- Spread frosting between layers and over top and sides of cake.

231. Hersheys Perfectly Chocolate Cake Recipe

Serving: 1 | Prep: | Cook: 30mins | Ready in:

Ingredients

- 2 cups sugar
- 1 3/4 cups flour
- 3/4 cup Hershey's cocoa
- 1 1/2 teaspoons baking powder
- 1 1/2 teaspoons baking soda
- 1 teaspoon salt
- 2 eggs
- 1 cup milk
- 1/2 cup vegetable or canola oil
- 2 teaspoons vanilla
- 1 cup boiling water

Direction

- Heat oven to 350 degrees.
- Combine dry ingredients in large bowl. Add eggs, milk, oil, and vanilla. Beat for 2 minutes on medium speed. Stir in boiling water. (Batter will be thin).
- Pour into two 9" round greased and floured pans. Bake 30-35 minutes. Cool 10 minutes.
- Remove from pans to wire rack. Cool completely.
- Frost with your favorite frosting.

232. Holy Cow Cake Recipe

Serving: 0 | Prep: | Cook: 1hours35mins | Ready in:

Ingredients

- 1 box German chocolate cake mix
- 1 can sweetened condensed milk
- 2-3 miniature butterfinger candy bars, crushed
- caramel sauce
- Cool Whip

Direction

- Prepare and bake cake according to directions. Punch holes in the hot cake with a wooden pick. Pour sweetened milk over cake. Drizzle caramel topping on top of the milk layer then refrigerate for at least a few hours.
- When you are ready to serve, spread cool whip over the cake and sprinkle with crushed candy bars.

233. Homemade Candy Bar Cake Recipe

Serving: 12 | Prep: | Cook: 2hours | Ready in:

Ingredients

- For the cake
- 1 3/4 cups all-purpose flour
- 3/4 cup plus 2 tablespoons unsweetened cocoa powder
- 2 cups plus 2 tablespoons sugar
- 1 1/2 teaspoons baking powder
- 1 1/2 teaspoons baking soda
- 1 1/2 teaspoons salt
- 2 large eggs
- 1 cup milk
- 1/2 cup vegetable oil
- 1 tablespoon pure vanilla extract
- 3/4 cup plus 2 tablespoons boiling water
- For the filling
- 1/3 cup sliced almonds
- 1/2 cup confectioners' sugar
- 2 large egg whites
- 1 tablespoon granulated sugar
- 1/2 cup salted roasted peanuts, coarsely chopped
- 1 cup creamy peanut butter
- 2 tablespoons unsalted butter, softened
- 3 ounces milk chocolate, chopped
- 1 cup Rice Krispies
- For the ganache
- 1 1/4 pounds milk chocolate, chopped
- 1 3/4 cups plus 2 tablespoons heavy cream, warmed

Direction

- Preheat the oven to 350
- In a large bowl, whisk together, flour, cocoa, sugar baking powder, baking soda and salt.
- In a medium bowl, whisk the eggs, milk, oil and vanilla. Pour the wet ingredients into the dry and mix just until combined. Add the boiling water and stir until combined - the batter will be fairly thin. Pour the mixture into a 9" x 13" baking pan coated with non-stick spray.
- Bake until a toothpick placed near the center of the cake comes out mostly clean with a couple moist crumbs attached, about 40 to 50 minutes. Remove from the oven and let cool completely. Turn the cake out of pan and place the cake, top side up, on a wire rack.
- To make the filling
- Reduce the oven temperature to 325
- On a large piece of parchment, trace a rough 9" x 13" rectangle onto the paper and place it on a large baking sheet.
- Add the almonds and confectioners' sugar into the bowl of a food processor - pulse until they're finely ground.
- In a medium mixing bowl, beat the egg whites at medium speed until soft peaks form. Add the granulated sugar and beat until the whites are stiff and glossy, about 2 minutes. Gently fold in the ground almond mixture. Scoop the meringue onto the parchment paper and use an offset spatula to fill out the outline you traced on the paper. Scatter the chopped peanuts on top. Bake until lightly browned and firm, about 15 to 20 minutes. Remove from the oven and let cool.
- In a medium bowl set over a saucepan of simmering water, heat the peanut butter with the butter and milk chocolate, stirring constantly, until smooth and melted. Remove from the heat and fold in the Rice Krispies. Spread the mixture all over the meringue rectangle. Place in the freezer and let harden.
- To make the ganache
- In a medium bowl set in a saucepan of simmering water, melt the chocolate. Whisk in

the cream until smooth. Remove from the heat and place the bowl into the refrigerator for 1 to 1 1/2 hours, whisking occasionally, until thick enough to spread.
- To assemble the cake
- Using a serrated knife, carefully slice the cake horizontally in half.
- Place the bottom cake layer, cut side up, on a large board. Spread about one-third of the ganache over the cake. Invert the filling onto the cake and peel off the parchment paper. Spread half of the remaining ganache over the filling, then top with the second cake layer. Refrigerate until firm, at least 1 hour. Using a serrated knife, trim the edges. Spread the remaining ganache over the top and sides of the cake and refrigerate to set.

234. Homemade Chocolate Cake With Homemade Chocolate Frosting Recipe

Serving: 12 | Prep: | Cook: 35mins | Ready in:

Ingredients

- Cake:
- 2 cups all-purpose flour
- 1¾ cups sugar
- ½ cup Special dark cocoa
- ½ teaspoon salt
- 1 tablespoon baking soda
- 1 teaspoon cinnamon
- 1 egg
- ⅔ cup vegetable oil
- 1 cup buttermilk
- 1 cup strong, hot coffee
- 1 teaspoon vanilla extract
- Frosting:
- 6 tablespoons butter, melted
- 4 cups powdered sugar
- ¼ to ½ cup Special dark cocoa, depending on how chocolatey you like your frosting
- 1 teaspoon vanilla extract

- enough ½ and ½ to make the frosting spreadable (about ¼ cup or so)

Direction

- Stir together the first 6 cake ingredients in a large mixing bowl.
- Add egg, oil, buttermilk; mix on medium speed until blended.
- Add coffee and vanilla; mix until smooth.
- Pour batter into a lightly greased 9x11 pan.
- Bake at 350° for about 35 minutes, or until toothpick can be poked into center of cake and it comes out "clean".
- While cake is baking, prepare the frosting.
- Melt butter in the microwave in a glass mixing bowl.
- Add powdered sugar, cocoa and vanilla.
- Slowly begin mixing on low speed, adding ½ and ½ until frosting is right consistency.
- Frost cooled cake.

235. Homemade Yellow Cake With Chocolate Buttercream Frosting Recipe

Serving: 8 | Prep: | Cook: 45mins | Ready in:

Ingredients

- 4 cups cake flour
- 2-1/2 cups granulated sugar
- 1-3/4 cup shortening
- 1-3/4 cup milk
- 3 teaspoons baking powder
- 1-1/2 teaspoon salt
- 1-1/2 teaspoon vanilla
- 5 eggs
- 14 ounce can sweetened condensed milk
- Frosting:
- 5-1/3 cups powdered sugar
- 1 cup baking cocoa
- 3/4 cup butter softened
- 2/3 cup milk

- 2 teaspoons vanilla

Direction

- Preheat oven to 350 then grease and flour 3 round cake pans.
- Mix flour, sugar, shortening, milk, baking powder, salt, vanilla and eggs in a large bowl.
- Beat on low speed 30 seconds scraping bowl occasionally.
- Beat on medium speed 2 minutes scraping bowl occasionally then pour batter into pans.
- Bake 35 minutes then cool 10 minutes and remove from pans.
- Poke a number of holes halfway through each layer using the handle of a wooden spoon.
- Pour milk into holes then cool completely.
- Combine all frosting ingredients and beat until frosting is smooth and spreadable.
- Frost between layers and on top and sides of cake.

236. Hot Chocolate Pudding Cake A La Mode Recipe

Serving: 8 | Prep: | Cook: 45mins | Ready in:

Ingredients

- 3/4 stick (6 T) unsalted butter
- 1 oz. semisweet baking chocolate, chopped
- Yolk from 1 large egg
- 1 cup all-purpose flour
- 1 1/4 cups granulated sugar
- 2/3 cup unsweetened Dutch-process cocoa powder
- 2 tsps baking powder
- 1/4 tsp salt
- 2 1/2 cups milk
- 2 tsps vanilla extract
- 1/3 cup packed light brown sugar
- 1 1/2 pt. vanilla ice cream

Direction

- Heat oven to 350. You'll need a shallow 2-qt. baking dish.
- Microwave butter and chocolate in a small bowl just until melted; stir with a whisk to combine, then stir in yolk until well blended.
- Whisk flour, 3/4 cup granulated sugar, 1/3 cup cocoa, the baking powder and salt in a medium bowl until blended. Stir in 1/2 cup milk, the butter mixture and vanilla until smooth. Spread batter in ungreased baking dish.
- Mix remaining 1/2 cup granulated sugar, remaining 1/3 cup cocoa and the brown sugar in small bowl with fingers or a fork until blended. Sprinkle over batter.
- Heat remaining 2 cups milk in microwave just until simmering. Slowly pour over mixture in baking dish-DON'T STIR.
- Bake 45 minutes. Spoon into dessert bowls. Top each serving with a small scoop of ice cream. Serve immediately or pudding layer will be absorbed by cake layer.
- Per serving (serious dieters, do not continue reading, look away look away!!): 481 calories; 20 g fat; 73 g carb

237. Hush Chocolate Cake Recipe

Serving: 6 | Prep: | Cook: 35mins | Ready in:

Ingredients

- 4 eggs
- 2 cups sifted all purpose flour
- 1&1/2 cup sugar
- 1&1/2 cups oil
- 1&1/4 warm milk
- 5 tablespoons cocoa powder
- 3 teaspoons vanilla
- 3 teaspoons baking powder
- sprinkle of salt
- Bitter or semisweet chocolate shavings for garnish

- and Hershey chocolate sauce

Direction

- 1- Heat your oven to 180 C
- 2- Whisk the eggs with sugar vanilla baking powder and oil very well for ten minutes.
- 3- Dissolve the cocoa powder in the liquid milk and slowly spoon in the sifted flour till you get a homogeneous mixture then fold in the eggs vanilla sugar batter.
- 4- Paint a cake tin with oil and dust lightly with flour then shake off the excess and pour the batter into the cake tin & tap thrice on the counter to get all the batter to settle into the tin.
- 5- Bake for 35-minutes lower thermostat then turn on the upper thermostat for 5 minutes.
- 6- Let the cake cool before taking it out of the tin.
- 7- Flip the cake over to get it out of the tin and decorate. Let the cake chill in the fridge for 20 minutes then serve.

238. I Love A Nutty German Chocolate Cake Recipe

Serving: 16 | Prep: | Cook: 30mins | Ready in:

Ingredients

- 4 eggs
- 3/4 cup butter
- 1-3/4 cups all purpose flour
- 3/4 cup pecans, toasted & ground
- 1 teaspoon baking soda
- 1/4 teaspoon baking powder
- 1/4 teaspoon salt
- 2 cups sugar
- 1 4-oz pkg. sweet baking chocolate, chopped, melted & cooled
- 1 cup buttermilk
- 1/2 cup strong coffee or water
- ****coconut pecan Frosting****
- 2 eggs
- 1-1/3 cups half & half
- 1-1/3 cups sugar
- 1/2 cup butter
- 7-oz package (2 2/3 cups) coconut
- 1 cup chopped toasted pecans

Direction

- Separate eggs. Let eggs & butter stand at room temperature 30 minutes.
- Preheat oven to 350 degrees F.
- Grease bottoms of three 9-inch round cake pans.
- Line with waxed or parchment paper; grease & flour bottoms & sides.
- Set aside.
- In large mixing bowl, beat egg whites until stiff peaks form; set aside.
- In medium bowl, stir together flour, pecans, baking soda, baking powder and 1/4 teaspoon salt.
- In 4 quart bowl, beat butter on medium high for 30 seconds.
- Gradually add sugar; beat until light & fluffy.
- Add egg yolks one at a time, beating well after each addition.
- Beat in chocolate on low.
- In bowl, combine buttermilk and coffee.
- Alternately add with flour mixture to butter mixture; beat well after each. With spatula fold in egg whites.
- Spread batter in pans.
- Bake 25 minutes or until toothpick inserted in center tests done.
- Cool in pans 10 minutes. Remove and peel off paper.
- Cool on wire racks.
- *******Coconut Pecan Frosting Directions******
- In saucepan slightly beat 2 eggs.
- Stir in 1-1/3 cups half & half, 1-1/3 cups sugar and 1/2 cup butter.
- Cook and stir over medium heat 10 minutes, until slightly thickened and bubbly. Remove from heat, stir in 7-oz package (2 2/3 cups) coconut and 1 cup chopped toasted pecans.
- Cover and cool.
- Makes 3-1/2 cups frosting.

239. Individual Chocolate Melting Cakes Recipe

Serving: 8 | Prep: | Cook: 15mins | Ready in:

Ingredients

- 10 ounces semisweet or bittersweet chocolate, chopped
- 4 tablespoons unsalted butter
- 5 eggs
- 1/2 cup sugar
- 3/4 cup all-purpose flour
- 1 1/2 teaspoons baking powder
- 1/8 teaspoon salt
- caramel sauce
- coffee ice cream

Direction

- Heat oven to 325° F.
- Lightly coat a 12-cup muffin tin with vegetable cooking spray.
- Melt the chocolate and butter in a large bowl over a saucepan of simmering water.
- Remove from heat. In another large bowl, beat the eggs and sugar at medium-high speed until light and fluffy. Add the flour, baking powder, salt, and melted chocolate.
- Mix with a spoon until well blended.
- Divide the batter evenly into 8 muffin tins and bake until the cakes have just cooked through, about 15 minutes. The cakes will still look a bit moist on top.
- Remove from the oven and let cool 5 minutes. Serve warm with the caramel sauce and ice cream.

240. Irish Cream Chocolate Cake Recipe

Serving: 12 | Prep: | Cook: 30mins | Ready in:

Ingredients

- Sponge:
- 6oz self-rising flour
- 1/2 tsp salt
- 2oz dark chocolate
- 4oz butter
- 6oz caster sugar (very fine sugar)
- 3oz cooked mashed potato
- 2 eggs, beaten
- 4tbs milk
- Filling and topping:
- 4oz dark chocolate
- 4fl oz double cream (whipping creams can be used in recipes which call for double cream)
- 2oz icing sugar
- 3tbsp irish cream liqueur

Direction

- Preheat oven to 375°F, and grease and line two 8 inch cake tins. Sift flour and salt into a mixing bowl. Melt chocolate in a bowl placed over a saucepan of hot water. In a separate bowl, cream butter and sugar together until fluffy, then beat in the chocolate and mashed potato. Gradually beat in the eggs, adding a little flour with each addition. Fold in the rest of the flour and stir in the milk.
- Divide mixture between cake tins and bake for 25-30 minutes or until top is firm but springy to the touch. Remove from oven and after a few minutes, turn out on a cooling rack. While the cake is cooling, make the filling. Melt the chocolate as before, stir in the other ingredients and mix well. Use the filling to sandwich the sponge layers together and coat the top and sides of the cake.
- You can also torte the cakes and make it several layers.

241. Italian Chocolate Cake Recipe

Serving: 10 | Prep: | Cook: 45mins | Ready in:

Ingredients

- 100 g butter
- 350 g Italian chocolate
- 3 tbsp cocoa pwd
- 1 tbsp instant coffee pwd
- ....
- 5 L eggs
- 250 g caster sugar
- 5 tbsp ground walnut or walnut meal
- 1 tbsp cocoa icing sugar

Direction

- Pre heat the oven at 180 deg C and grease a 20 cm pan.
- Melt the butter and the chocolate.
- Whisk in the cocoa and coffee powder.
- ....
- In a mixer beat the eggs and sugar until thick and pale.
- Fold in the walnut meal.
- Now fold in the chocolate mixture.
- Bake for 40 mins.
- ....
- Dust with the sugar.
- Serve warm.

242. Its A Chocolate Wonder Cake With Chocolate Cream Cheese Frosting Recipe

Serving: 10 | Prep: | Cook: 35mins | Ready in:

Ingredients

- ***************chocolate Wonder Cake******************
- 1 - 3 oz. square baking chocolate
- 1 cup sugar
- 1/2 cup buttermilk
- 2 1/2 cups flour(all purpose)
- 1 1/2 teaspoons baking powder
- 3/4 teaspoon baking soda
- ***************
- 1/2 teaspoon salt
- 1/2 cup butter
- 3/4 cup sugar(yes....another sugar addition. Stay with me!)
- 3 eggs, beaten
- 1 cup buttermilk
- 1 teaspoon vanilla
- ******************chocolate Wonder Frosting*****************
- 1 - 3oz. package cream cheese
- 2 or 3 Tablespoons milk
- 2 cup confectioners powdered sugar
- 2-3oz squares chocolate
- dash of salt

Direction

- Melt chocolate.
- Add 1 cup sugar & buttermilk. Cool.
- Sift flour, baking powder, baking soda and salt.
- Cream butter, 1/2 cup sugar.
- Add eggs and 1/4 cup flour.
- Add chocolate mixture.
- Add rest of flour mixture alternately with buttermilk.
- Add vanilla
- Bake at 350 for 30 minutes.
- Ice with the Chocolate Wonder Frosting.
- Cream the cream cheese; add sugar, salt and melted chocolate.
- Add enough milk to make the right consistency to spread
- **
- -The race is not for the swift. - Ecclesiastes 9:11
- **

243. Jack Daniels Chocolate Cake Recipe

Serving: 8 | Prep: | Cook: 45mins | Ready in:

Ingredients

- 1 box dark chocolate cake mix
- OR
- Your favorite chocolate cake recipe
- 4 eggs, lightly beaten
- 1/2 cup Jack Daniel's whiskey
- 1/2 cup black coffee
- 1/4 cup broken pecan pieces
- 1 very ripe banana
- 1 stick butter, softened

Direction

- Preheat oven to 350F degrees.
- Grease and flour Bundt cake pan.
- In a large mixing bowl combine all ingredients except the pecan pieces.
- Mix on medium-high 1-2 minutes until you get a ribbon like consistency (do not overmix).
- Put pieces of nuts in the bottom of the Bundt pan.
- Pour batter into the pan.
- Bake 45-50 min or until toothpick inserted in center is nearly clean.
- Let cool for 15-20 minutes and then invert on to cooling rack to cool completely.

244. Jetts Chocolate Peanut Butter Cake Recipe

Serving: 16 | Prep: | Cook: 40mins | Ready in:

Ingredients

- Cake:
- cooking spray
- 2 cups all-purpose flour
- 2/3 cup unsweetened cocoa powder
- 2 teaspoons baking soda
- 1 teaspoon baking powder
- 1/2 teaspoon salt
- 2/3 cup vegetable oil
- 2 cups granulated sugar
- 2 eggs
- 1 cup 2% reduced-fat milk
- 1 cup brewed coffee, cooled to room temperature
- 1 teaspoon vanilla extract
- Frosting:
- 1 (8-ounce) package cream cheese, softened
- 1/4 cup creamy peanut butter
- 2 cups powdered sugar
- 2 tablespoons 2% reduced fat milk
- 1/2 teaspoon vanilla extract
- miniature chocolate chips (optional)

Direction

- Instructions
- 1. Preheat oven to 350F. Coat a 13 x 9-inch glass baking pan with cooking spray.
- 2. To prepare cake, sift together flour, cocoa, baking soda, baking powder and salt into a large bowl.
- 3. Combine oil and sugar in a large mixing bowl. Using a mixer, beat at medium speed until well combined. Add eggs; beat well. Add flour mixture alternately with milk, beginning and ending with flour mixture, beating well after each addition and scraping down the sides of the bowl. Stir in the coffee and vanilla (batter will be thin).
- 3. Pour batter into prepared pan. Bake 35 to 40 minutes, until a wooden toothpick inserted near the center comes out clean. Cool completely on a wire rack.
- 4. To prepare frosting, combine cream cheese and peanut butter in a large mixing bowl. Using a mixer, beat at medium speed until smooth. Add powdered sugar, milk and vanilla; beat until smooth. (If frosting is too thin, add more powdered sugar; if it is too thick, add more milk.) Spread frosting over top of cooled cake and sprinkle with chocolate

chips, if using. Store in the refrigerator. Serves 16.
- Nutritional Information
- Nutritional facts per serving: 350 calories, 18g fat, 5g protein, 49g carbohydrates, 1g fiber, 350mg sodium.

245. Jubilee Chocolate Cake Recipe

Serving: 12 | Prep: | Cook: 30mins | Ready in:

Ingredients

- 3/4 teaspoon baking soda
- 1 cup buttermilk or sour milk*
- 1-1/2 cups cake flour or 1-1/4 cups all-purpose flour
- 1-1/2 cups sugar, divided
- 1/2 cup HERSHEY'S cocoa
- 1/2 teaspoon salt
- 1/2 cup vegetable oil
- 2 eggs, separated
- 1/2 teaspoon vanilla extract
- vanilla ice cream
- QUICK AND EASY FLAMING CHERRY SAUCE
- FLAMING CHERRY SAUCE
- QUICK AND EASY FLAMING CHERRY SAUCE: Combine 1 can (21 oz.) cherry pie filling with 1/4 cup orange juice in chafing dish or medium saucepan; heat thoroughly. Gently heat 1/4 cup kirsch (cherry-flavored liqueur) in small saucepan; pour over cherry mixture. Carefully ignite with match. Stir gently; serve as directed. (Repeat procedure for sufficient amount of sauce for entire cake.) 6 to 8 servings.
- FLAMING CHERRY SAUCE
- 1 can (16 or 17 ounces) pitted dark or light sweet cherries, drained
- (reserve 3/4 cup liquid)
- 1-1/2 tablespoons sugar
- 1 tablespoon cornstarch
- Dash salt
- 1/2 teaspoon freshly grated orange peel
- 1/4 cup cherry-flavored liqueur or brandy
- Stir together reserved cherry liquid, sugar, cornstarch and salt in chafing dish or medium saucepan. Cook over medium heat, stirring constantly, until mixture boils, about 1 minute. Add cherries and orange peel; heat thoroughly.
- Gently heat liqueur in small saucepan over low heat; pour over cherry mixture. Carefully ignite with match. Stir gently; serve as directed. (Repeat procedure for sufficient amount of sauce for entire cake.) 4 to 6 servings.

Direction

- Heat oven to 350°F. Grease and flour 13x9x2-inch baking pan.
- Stir together flour, 1 cup sugar, cocoa and salt. Add oil, buttermilk mixture, egg yolks and vanilla; beat until smooth. Beat egg whites in small bowl until soft peaks form; gradually add remaining 1/2 cup sugar, beating until stiff peaks form. Gently fold egg whites into chocolate batter. Pour batter into prepared pan.
- Bake 30 to 35 minutes or until cake springs back when touched lightly in center. Cool in pan. Cut into squares; top each square with scoop of ice cream and serving of FLAMING CHERRY SAUCE, or QUICK AND EASY FLAMING CHERRY SAUCE
- 12 to 15 servings.
- * To sour milk: Use 1 tablespoon white vinegar plus milk to equal 1 cup.

246. Killer Chocolate Marshmallow Cake Recipe

Serving: 16 | Prep: | Cook: 40mins | Ready in:

Ingredients

- 1 chocolate fudge cake mix & required ingredients
- 8 oz. can sweetended condensed milk
- 1 bag mini marshmallows
- 8 oz. semi-sweet chocolate chips

Direction

- Prepare & bake cake in 9x13" pan according to package directions. Let cool.
- Meanwhile, prepare frosting.
- Spray a saucepan with non-stick spray.
- Melt sweetened condensed milk & chocolate chips over med-low heat.
- Add marshmallows & stir until completely melted.
- Remove from heat.
- Let frosting cool slightly and pour onto cooled cake.
- Frosting will set up as in continues to cool.

247. Layered Chocolate Tortilla Cake Recipe

Serving: 6 | Prep: | Cook: 180mins | Ready in:

Ingredients

- 1 package of large tortillas (flour)
- 11.5 ounce bag of milk chocolate or semi-sweet chips
- 16 ounce container of sour cream
- 1/4 cup confectioners sugar (sifted)

Direction

- Melt chocolate chips.
- Add sour cream and confectioners' sugar to the melted chocolate chips.
- Mix well to blend.
- Put one tortilla on plate and spread with some of the chocolate mixture.
- Continue to layer the tortillas and chocolate with the chocolate ending up on top.

- Refrigerate for 3 hours (at least) before serving.

248. Liezels Chocolate Cake Recipe

Serving: 10 | Prep: | Cook: 30mins | Ready in:

Ingredients

- 1/2 cup + 3 tablespoons cocoa (170 ml) or
- 1/4 cup + 3 tablespoons cocoa if you want it lighter (100 ml)
- 1 cup boiling water (250 ml)
- 2 cups cake flour (500 ml)
- 1 teaspoon salt (5 ml)
- 1 tablespoon baking powder, heaped (15 ml)
- 2 cups brown sugar (500 ml)
- 1/2 cup + 3 tablespoons oil (160 ml)
- 1/4 cup honey (60 ml) - to keep cake moist
- 3 tablespoons brandy (50 ml)
- 7 eggs, seperated
- 1 teaspoon vanilla (5 ml)
- Filling:
- caramel condesed milk or cooked condensed milk
- Icing:
- 1/4 cup + 3 tablespoons soft butter (100 ml)
- 4 cups icing sugar (1000 ml)
- 1/2 cup cocoa powder (125 ml)
- 2 tablespoons milk (25 ml)
- 2 teaspoons vanilla (10 ml)

Direction

- Mix boiling water and cocoa.
- Set aside to cool down.
- Sift flour, salt and baking powder.
- Stir in the sugar.
- Separate the eggs.
- Pour the egg yolks into the same bowl of the cocoa mixture.
- Pour the oil, vanilla, honey and brandy into the cocoa mixture.

- Mix well.
- Whisk the egg whites.
- Mix cocoa mixture with flour mixture very well.
- Fold in the egg whites.
- Pour into cake pans.
- Bake at 360 deg F (180 deg C) for 30 minutes.
- Let it cool down.
- Filling:
- Put caramel or cooked condensed milk in the middle.
- Icing:
- Sift icing sugar.
- Add the icing sugar bit by bit to the butter while mixing.
- Add cocoa powder.
- Mix well.
- Add milk and vanilla.
- Mix well.
- Add a bit more milk if mixture seems to stiff.
- Put over cake.

249. Mango Chocolate Mousse Cake Recipe

Serving: 10 | Prep: | Cook: 30mins | Ready in:

Ingredients

- 20 cm jocond cake
- For jocond cake base:
- Follow my white chocolate opera cake post:
- cake.html">white chocolate Opera cake
- Mousse:
- 11 ounces semi-sweet chocolate
- 3 ounces melted butter, unsalted
- 1 cup heavy cream
- 4 egg whites
- 1 cup whipping cream
- 2 tbsp powder sugar
- Can mango halves in syrup, cut into thin slices.
- chocolate glaze:
- 6 oz plain chocolate, chopped
- ½ cup heavy cream
- chocolate curls and cocoa powder for decoration

Direction

- In a medium-size saucepan, mix chocolate, cream and butter together until smooth. Remove from heat and let cool.
- In a large bowl, beat egg whites until stiff peaks form. In another bowl, beat whipping cream and powder sugar until stiff peak form; fold into egg whites. Fold egg white/whipping cream mixture into cooled chocolate mixture.
- Place the jocund base on a loosed bottom cake ring. Arrange the mango slices over the cake. Pour the chocolate mixture over and smooth top. Chill.
- Make topping glaze:
- Heat cream in a heavy saucepan until simmering point. Pour over chopped chocolate and stir until smooth. Set aside to cool completely, stirring occasionally. Pour over the top of the chilled cake, let it set and decorate with chocolate curls cocoa powder.

250. Maroon Chocolate Cake Recipe

Serving: 12 | Prep: | Cook: 30mins | Ready in:

Ingredients

- 1/3 cup packed brown sugar
- 2/3 cup sugar
- 1/4 cup butter
- 1/3 cup unsweetened applesauce
- 2 eggs
- 1 tbsp vanilla
- 2 tbsp red food colouring
- 1 tbsp pure beet juice
- 2 tbsp water
- 1/4 cup cocoa, sifted
- 1 1/4 cups flour

- 1 cup Kamut flour
- 1/4 tsp salt
- 1 cup low-fat buttermilk
- 1 1/2 tbsp apple cider vinegar
- 2 tsp baking soda

Direction

- Preheat oven to 350 F. Grease two round 9" cake pans.
- Cream sugars, butter and applesauce until fluffy.
- Add eggs and vanilla, beat well.
- Make a paste of the food colouring, beet juice, water and cocoa powder, scrape into above mixture and beat well.
- Whisk together flours and salt in a separate bowl.
- Add dry ingredients alternately with the buttermilk to the creamed mixture.
- In a small dish, mix vinegar and baking soda well (it will foam).
- Add to the batter and fold in gently but thoroughly.
- Bake 30 minutes, cool completely in pans before turning out.

251. Mary Starrs Chocolate Wet Cake Recipe

Serving: 20 | Prep: | Cook: 25mins | Ready in:

Ingredients

- cake
- 2 c. flour (plain)
- 2 c. sugar
- 1 c. water
- 1/4 c. or 1 stick butter
- 1/2 c. Crisco
- 1/4 c. cocoa
- 2 whole eggs
- 1 1/8 tsp. soda
- 1 1/8 tsp. cinnamon
- 1/2 c. buttermilk
- 1 1/8 tsp. vanilla
- icing
- about half a box powdered sugar (approx 2 cups)
- 1/8 c. milk (or 2 T)
- 1/8 c. cocoa (or 3 T)
- 1 stick butter
- 1 1/8 tsp. vanilla

Direction

- CAKE:
- Combine sugar and flour in mixer bowl.
- Melt butter and Crisco in sauce pan.
- Stir cocoa and water in with melted butter and Crisco.
- Bring to boil and pour over sugar and flour.
- Add buttermilk, soda, cinnamon, vanilla and eggs to ingredients in bowl.
- Mix together (batter will be thin and may spatter).
- Pour into 9"x13" pan that has been greased and floured.
- Bake at 400 degrees for about 25 minutes, until toothpick comes out clean.
- ICING:
- Pour powdered sugar in mixer bowl.
- Melt butter in saucepan.
- Stir in milk and cocoa and bring to boil.
- Add to powdered sugar in mixer bowl.
- Add vanilla.
- Beat well and spread on cooled cake.

252. Mayo Chocolate Syrup Cake Recipe

Serving: 8 | Prep: | Cook: 25mins | Ready in:

Ingredients

- Beat together the following ingredients:
- ½ Cup mayonnaise
- 1 Cup sugar

- 4 eggs beaten in one at a time
- 1 16-ounce can Hershey's chocolate syrup
- 1 cup plus one tablespoon flour
- Pour into a greased and floured 9x 13 pan; bake 25 minutes at 350 degrees.

Direction

- Frosting:
- 1 Stick melted butter
- 2/3 Cup Cocoa Powder
- 3 Cups Powdered Sugar
- 1/3 Cup Milk
- 1 tsp. vanilla extract
- Stir Cocoa powder into butter; alternately add powdered sugar and milk while beating on medium speed; add vanilla. Beat until desired consistency. Adding very small amounts of milk if necessary to make it a spreading consistency

253. Merry Cherry Dense Chocolate Black Forest Easy Cake Recipe

Serving: 12 | Prep: | Cook: 25mins | Ready in:

Ingredients

- EASY BLACK FOREST cake
- 1 package Duncan Hines fudge cake mix
- 1 can Comstock (or other) cherry pie filling
- 3 eggs
- chocolate icing
- 1 cup granulated sugar
- 5 tablespoons butter
- 1/3 cup milk
- 6 oz. semi-sweet chocolate chips
- NOTE: For a STAR IN THE SHOW presentation, bake in bundt pan, place on pedestal, spoon on and DRIZZLE icing, letting it cascade down sides, spoon on more cherry pie filling, making a ring on top, Spoon big dollops of whipped cream in ring on top of cherry filling, and place a stemmed maraschino cherry in the center of each dollop right before serving. If using whipped cream, refrigerate.

Direction

- Pour cake mix into large bowl, and whisk to get out the lumps.
- In medium bowl whisk the 3 eggs with wire whisk until blended well.
- Add cherry pie filling to the eggs and blend.
- Add eggs and pie filling to the dry cake mix, and only STIR until well blended.
- Pour into a greased and floured 9 x 13 in pan (can bake in Bundt).
- Bake until sides shrink from pan (about 25 minutes).
- Cool.
- ICING
- On stovetop, bring to boil, sugar, butter, milk and boil 1 MINUTE ONLY.
- Remove and add chocolate chips.
- Spread on cooled cake.
- THIS IS A VERY GOOD, DENSE CHOCOLATE, EASY CAKE THAT CAN BECOME THE STAR OF THE SHOW IN PRESENTATION.

254. Mexican Chocolate Icebox Cake Recipe

Serving: 12 | Prep: | Cook: 15mins | Ready in:

Ingredients

- 60 sponge-cake-type ladyfingers (from three 3-ounce packages)
- 2 3/4 cups chilled whipping cream
- 4 ounces unsweetened chocolate, chopped
- 1/4 cup sugar
- 1 cup plus 2 tablespoons powdered sugar
- 1/2 cup (1 stick) unsalted butter, room temperature
- 2 teaspoons vanilla extract

- 1 teaspoon ground cinnamon
- 1 ounce semisweet chocolate, grated

Direction

- Line bottom of 9-inch-diameter springform pan with ladyfingers.
- Line sides of pan with ladyfingers, standing ladyfingers side by side and rounded side out.
- Stir 3/4 cup whipping cream, unsweetened chocolate and 1/4 cup sugar in heavy small saucepan over low heat until chocolate melts and mixture is smooth. Remove saucepan from heat and cool to room temperature.
- Using electric mixer, beat 1 cup powdered sugar, butter and 1 teaspoon vanilla in large bowl until blended.
- Beat in cooled chocolate mixture.
- Combine remaining 2 cups cream, 2 tablespoons powdered sugar, 1 teaspoon vanilla and cinnamon in another large bowl.
- Using clean dry beaters, beat until firm peaks form. Fold half of whipped cream mixture into chocolate mixture.
- Spread half of chocolate filling in ladyfinger-lined pan. Top with layer of ladyfingers, then remaining chocolate filling.
- Pipe or spread remaining whipped cream mixture over filling.
- Sprinkle with grated semisweet chocolate.
- Refrigerate until firm, at least 3 hours. (Can be made 1 day ahead. Cover and keep refrigerated.)
- Remove pan sides from cake and serve.

255. Microwave Chocolate Cake Recipe

Serving: 6 | Prep: | Cook: 10mins | Ready in:

Ingredients

- 1 1/2 cups all purpose flour
- 1 cup sugar
- 3 Tbs baking cocoa
- 1 tsp baking soda
- 1/4 tsp salt
- 1 cup cold water/ or cold brewed coffee
- 1/3 cup oil
- 1 tsp vanilla or almond flavor

Direction

- Combine the dry ingredients.
- Combine the liquids.
- Stir both together till well blended.
- Pour into a slightly oiled 9 inch square glass or Pyrex pan or small microwave fluted mold or a small microwave tube pan for a festive look.
- Cook high heat (use turntable) 6 to 8 minutes or until cake tests done in center.
- Cool completely in pan.
- Store airtight as microwave baked goods tend to dry out faster.
- To serve, cut in pieces and serve with a chocolate pudding or sauce over the pieces.
- Note: I have had this recipes for years and of course used a much lower microwave wattage? 650 watts I believe.
- My suggestion is cook in less time and check for doneness.

256. Milk Chocolate Bar Cake Recipe

Serving: 12 | Prep: | Cook: 25mins | Ready in:

Ingredients

- 1 package Swiss chocolate cake mix
- 1 package cream cheese, softened (I used low-fat and it was fine)
- 1 cup icing sugar
- 1/2 cup sugar
- 10 milk chocolate bars with almonds (50g each)
- 1 container frozen whipped topping, thawed

Direction

- Prepare cake mix according to package directions. Pour into 3 greased and floured 8" round cake pans.
- Bake at 325F for 20-30 mins or until wooden toothpick inserted in centre comes out clean. Cool in pans on wire racks for 10 mins. Remove from pans, and cool completely on racks.
- Beat cream cheese and both sugars at medium speed of electric mixer until creamy.
- Finely chop 8 of the chocolate bars. Fold, along with cream cheese mixture, into whipped topping.
- Spread icing between layers and on top and sides of cake.
- Chop remaining 2 chocolate bars and sprinkle half over top of cake. Press remaining along bottom edge of cake.

257. Mini Chocolate Bundt Cakes With Peanut Butter Filling And Chocolate Glaze Recipe

Serving: 12 | Prep: | Cook: 25mins | Ready in:

Ingredients

- 1 stick butter
- 1 3/4 cups sugar
- 2 cups all-purpose flour
- 1 teaspoon baking powder
- 1 teaspoon baking soda
- Pinch salt
- 2 eggs
- 4 ounces melted unsweetened chocolate
- 1 teaspoon pure vanilla extract
- 1 1/4 cups milk
- 1/2 cup peanut butter chips
- 1/4 cup cocoa powder
- 1 cup powdered sugar
- 2 to 3 tablespoons milk

Direction

- Preheat the oven to 350 degrees. Grease and lightly flour 12 individual (about 1 cup size) Bundt tins.
- In the bowl of an electric mixer, fitted with a paddle, cream the butter and sugar together.
- In a small mixing bowl, sift together the flour, baking powder, baking soda and salt and set aside. Add the eggs, one at a time, to the butter mixture. Mix well after each egg.
- Add the chocolate and vanilla. Mix well.
- Add the sifted flour mixture, 1/2 cup at a time, alternating with the milk. Mix well.
- Fill each tin 1/2 full with the batter.
- Place some of the peanut butter chips in the centre of the batter.
- Pour the remaining batter over the chips.
- Place in the oven and cook for about 18 to 20 minutes.
- Remove from the oven and cool for a couple of minutes in the pan. Invert the cakes onto a wire rack.
- In a small mixing bowl, combine the cocoa powder, powdered sugar and milk. Mix until smooth. Spoon some of the glaze over each Bundt cake. Allow the glaze to set, then serve.

258. Mini Chocolate Christmas Cakes Recipe

Serving: 24 | Prep: | Cook: 30mins | Ready in:

Ingredients

- 1/3 cup apple juice
- 375g mixed dried fruit
- 1/4 finely chopped dried apricots
- 100g butter
- 1/3 cup brown sugar
- 1/2 tspn vanilla essence
- 1 egg
- 100 slivered almonds
- 1/2 cup self raising flour
- 1/2 tspn mixed spice
- 1/2 cup dark cooking chocolate bits/pieces

- 150g dark cooking chocolate extra

Direction

- Preheat oven to 160C.
- Lightly grease 24 hole mini-muffin pan.
- Heat apple juice in large microwave safe bowl on high for 1 minute, add mixed fruit and apricots, stand for 30 minutes.
- Beat butter, brown sugar and vanilla until creamy. Beat in egg,
- Stir in fruit mix and almonds then add sifted flour, spice and choc bit then mix well.
- Spoon mixture into muffin pans to completely fill. Try to keep surfaces smooth for easy coating later. Bake for 25 - 30 minutes, turn out onto wire rack to cool.
- Spread tops of cakes with melted chocolate and allow to set.

259. Miracle Orange Chocolate Mini Cakes Recipe

Serving: 24 | Prep: | Cook: 25mins | Ready in:

Ingredients

- For the caramel sauce:
- 1 cup sugar.
- 6 tbsp butter.
- 1/3 cup whipping cream.
- For the flan:
- 1 can sweetened condensed milk (390grams/14oz)
- 1 can evaporated milk (195 grams/7oz)
- 1 ¼ cups heavy cream.
- 5 eggs.
- 3 ½ oz cream cheese
- Zest of 1 orange
- 1 tsp vanilla extract.
- For the cake:
- 1 box devil's food cake mix or fudge chocolate cake mix.

Direction

- Preheat oven to 375F. Fill 2 (12 muffins tray) with paper cups or silicon cups.
- Heat the sugar over medium heat till it all dissolve and turn golden color, add the butter in small pieces stirring with a wooden spoon, add the cream in a steady stream so slowly while stirring. Pour the caramel in the muffins tray and keep aside till cooled.
- In a food processor, mix all the flan ingredients for 2 minutes and set aside.
- Make the cake batter by following the instructions on the box.
- Pour the cake batter over the caramel sauce in the pan. Using a large spoon, add the flan mixture so slowly on top. Don't be surprised, here is the trick steps, the flan and the cake batter will flip while baking leaving the caramel on the base. Isn't a Miracle!!
- Bake for 25 minutes or until a skewer inserted in the center comes out clean.
- Take out of oven and flip in a glass dish. Serve warm or cold. Can be stored covered in the refrigerator for 3 days.

260. Mississippi Chocolate And Coffee Cake Recipe

Serving: 10 | Prep: | Cook: 75mins | Ready in:

Ingredients

- For the Cake:
- 2 c. all-purpose flour
- 1 t. baking soda
- Pinch of salt
- 1 3/4 c. strong brewed coffee
- 1/4 c. bourbon
- 5 oz. unsweetened chocolate
- 1 c. butter
- 2 c. sugar
- 2 large eggs, lightly beaten
- 1 t. vanilla extract
- For chocolate Icing:
- 6 1/2 oz. semisweet chocolate

- 4 1/2 T. butter

Direction

- For the Cake: Preheat the oven to 350 degrees F. Grease a 9-inch round cake pan. Line pan with parchment paper. Grease sides of cake pan.
- In a mixing bowl, sift together the flour, baking soda, and salt.
- In the top of a double boiler, I use a metal bowl set on top of a pan of simmering water, heat the coffee, bourbon, chocolate, and butter, stirring until the chocolate and butter are melted and the mixture is smooth. Remove the pan from the heat and stir in the sugar. Let the mixture cool for 3 minutes and transfer to an electric mixer. Add the flour mixture to the chocolate mixture, half a cup at a time, and beat medium speed for 1 minute. Add the eggs and vanilla and beat until smooth.
- Pour into the prepared pan and bake for 1 hour and 10 to 15 minutes, or until a skewer inserted in the center comes out clean. Let the cake cool completely in the pan. When cooled, turn out onto a serving plate.
- For Chocolate Icing: Combine the chocolate and butter in the top of a double boiler or bowl resting over a pan of simmering water and stir over low heat until they are melted and combined. Cool slightly and the ice cake.

261. Mocha Layer Cake With Chocolate Rum Filling Recipe

Serving: 16 | Prep: | Cook: 20mins | Ready in:

Ingredients

- Filling and Topping:
- 4 cups whipping cream
- 1/2 stick unsalted butter
- 1/4 cup sugar
- 20 ounces semisweet chocolate, finely chopped-plus 2 ounces chopped separately
- 1/3 cup rum
- 2 teaspoons vanilla extract
- Syrup:
- 1/4 cup water
- 2 tablespoons sugar
- 2 tablespoons rum
- Cake:
- 1 1/2 teaspoons vanilla extract
- 1 teaspoon instant coffee
- 2/3 cup cake flour
- 3 tablespoons cocoa powder
- 1/2 teaspoon baking soda
- 3 large eggs-separated
- 3/4 cup sugar
- 1/4 teaspoon cream of tartar
- 1/4 teaspoon salt

Direction

- Filling:
- Stir first 3 ingredients in large saucepan over medium-high heat until sugar dissolves and cream comes to a simmer.
- Remove from heat. Add 20 ounces chocolate. Whisk until melted and smooth.
- Whisk in vanilla and rum.
- Transfer 1 cup warm chocolate mixture to small bowl. Whisk in remaining 2 ounces of chocolate. Cover, set aside, and let stand at room temperature. This will be the topping.
- Transfer remaining chocolate mixture to a large bowl for the filling.
- Chill until cold and thick. At least 6 hours.
- Syrup:
- Stir water and sugar in small saucepan over low heat just until sugar dissolves.
- Remove from heat and mix in rum. Let stand.
- Cake:
- Preheat oven to 350 degrees.
- Grease and flour 9"x 9" x 2" cake pan.
- Combine vanilla and coffee powder in a small bowl or cup. Swirl to dissolve coffee.
- Sift flour, cocoa, and baking soda into small bowl.
- Using an electric mixer, beat egg yolks and 1/2 cup sugar in medium mixing bowl until thick

and light in color, about 3 minutes. Beat in coffee/vanilla mixture.
- Using clean dry beaters, beat egg whites, cream of tartar, and salt in large bowl until soft peaks form.
- Gradually add 1/4 cup sugar and continue beating until stiff but not dry. Fold egg whites into yolk mixture alternating with flour mixture.
- Pour batter into prepared pan.
- Bake for 18 minutes.
- Cool cake in pan. Cake will shrink slightly.
- Turn cake out onto flat surface and cut in half horizontally using serrated knife. Place bottom half on plate cut side up.
- Drizzle half of syrup over layer.
- Using electric mixer, beat cold chocolate filling until thick, creamy, and spreadable. Spread all of filling evenly over cake layer. Filling layer will be about an inch thick.
- Drizzle remaining syrup over cut side of second cake layer.
- Place layer syrup side down on top of filling. Press gently.
- Rewarm topping until just pourable and pour over center of cake.
- Using a knife or spatula, carefully spread to edges. It's okay if a little runs over.
- Cover with cake dome and chill until ready to serve.

262. Moist Red Beet Chocolate Cake With Chocolate Cream Cheese Frosting Recipe

Serving: 1 | Prep: | Cook: 20mins | Ready in:

Ingredients

- Cream 1 1/2 cups sugar with 3 eggs and add 1 cup Wesson Oil blended with 1 1/2 cups canned beets cut into small pieces, also add 2 squares melted chocolate.
- Sift together 1 3/4 cup flour, 1 1/2 tsp baking soda, and 1/2 tsp. salt. Add this to above along with 1 tsp vanilla
- Bake in 2 greased and floured layer plans in a 350 oven for 20 - 25 min. Very good and moist.
- chocolate cream cheese frosting
- 2 tablespoons softened butter
- 2 small packages (3 ounces each) cream cheese, softened
- 1 pound confectioners' sugar
- 2 ounces unsweetened chocolate, melted
- 1 to 2 tablespoons milk
- 1 teaspoon vanilla

Direction

- Chocolate Cream Cheese Frosting Directions:
- Cream butter and cream cheese; gradually add part of the sugar, alternating with chocolate then milk, until well blended and spreading consistency is reached. Beat in 1 teaspoon vanilla.
- Frosts 2 9-inch round layers.

263. Molten Chocolate Cake Recipe

Serving: 8 | Prep: | Cook: 15mins | Ready in:

Ingredients

- 4 squares Semi-Sweet baking chocolate
- 1/2 cup (1 stick) butter
- 1 cup powdered sugar
- 2 eggs
- 2 egg yolks
- 6 Tbsp. flour
- 1/2 cup thawed whipped topping

Direction

- PREHEAT oven to 425°F. Butter four 3/4-cup custard cups or soufflé dishes. Place on baking sheet.

- MICROWAVE chocolate and butter in large microwaveable bowl on HIGH 1 min. or until butter is melted. Stir with wire whisk until chocolate is completely melted. Stir in sugar until well blended. Blend in eggs and egg yolks with wire whisk. Stir in flour. Divide batter among prepared custard cups.
- BAKE 13 to 14 min. or until sides are firm but centers are soft. Let stand 1 min. Carefully run small knife around cakes to loosen. Invert cakes onto dessert dishes. Serve immediately, topped with whipped topping.

264. Molten Chocolate Cake With Peanut Butter Filling Recipe

Serving: 4 | Prep: | Cook: 16mins | Ready in:

Ingredients

- 1 stick plus 1 tablespoon unsalted butter, plus melted butter for brushing
- 1 tablespoon unsweetened cocoa powder
- 1/4 cup plus 1 tablespoon all-purpose flour
- 6 ounces dark chocolate (70 percent cacao), chopped
- 3 tablespoons creamy peanut butter
- 1 tablespoon confectioners' sugar, plus more for sprinkling
- 1/2 cup granulated sugar
- 3 large eggs, at room temperature
- Pinch of salt

Direction

- Preheat the oven to 425°.
- Brush four 6-ounce ramekins with melted butter.
- In a small bowl, whisk the cocoa powder with 1 tablespoon of the flour; dust the ramekins with the cocoa mixture, tapping out the excess.
- Transfer the ramekins to a sturdy baking sheet.
- In a medium saucepan, melt 1 stick of butter with the chocolate over very low heat, stirring occasionally.
- Let cool slightly.
- In a bowl, blend the peanut butter with the 1 tablespoon of confectioners' sugar and the remaining 1 tablespoon of butter.
- In a bowl, using an electric mixer, beat the granulated sugar with the eggs and salt at medium-high speed until thick and pale yellow, 3 minutes.
- Using a rubber spatula, fold in the melted chocolate until no streaks remain.
- Fold in the 1/4 cup of flour.
- Spoon two-thirds of the batter into the prepared ramekins, then spoon the peanut butter mixture on top.
- Cover with the remaining chocolate batter.
- Bake in the center of the oven for 16 minutes, until the tops are cracked but the centers are still slightly jiggly.
- Transfer the ramekins to a rack and let cool for 5 to 8 minutes.
- Run the tip of a small knife around each cake to loosen. Invert a small plate over each cake and, using pot holders, invert again. Carefully lift off the ramekins.
- Dust the warm cakes with confectioners' sugar and serve immediately.

265. Molten Chocolate Cakes Recipe

Serving: 4 | Prep: | Cook: 30mins | Ready in:

Ingredients

- 4 squares BAKER'S Semi-Sweet baking chocolate
- 1/2 cup (1 stick) butter
- 1 cup powdered sugar
- 2 eggs
- 2 egg yolks
- 6 Tbsp. flour

- 1/2 cup thawed Cool Whip whipped topping
- How to to Bake cakes in Muffin Cups:
- Prepare batter as directed; pour evenly among nine well-greased medium muffin cups. Bake at 425°F for 7 min. or until sides are firm but centers are soft. Let stand 1 min. Loosen cakes and remove from pan as directed.

Direction

- Preheat oven to 425°F. Butter four 3/4-cup custard cups or soufflé dishes. Place on baking sheet.
- Microwave chocolate and butter in large microwaveable bowl on HIGH 1 min. or until butter is melted. Stir with wire whisk until chocolate is completely melted. Stir in sugar until well blended. Blend in eggs and egg yolks with wire whisk. Stir in flour. Divide batter among prepared custard cups.
- Bake 13 to 14 min. or until sides are firm but centers are soft. Let stand 1 min. Carefully run small knife around cakes to loosen. Invert cakes onto dessert dishes. Serve immediately, topped with whipped topping.

266. Moms Chocolate Souffle Cake Recipe

Serving: 12 | Prep: | Cook: 30mins | Ready in:

Ingredients

- CAKE:
- unsalted butter, 3/4 CUP PLUS 1 TABLESPOON
- bittersweet chocolate, CHOPPED, 14 OUNCES. I USE THE DARKEST CHOCOLATE I CAN, I USUALLY USE 70%
- eggs, LARGE, 7
- sugar, 3/4 CUP PLUS 2 TABLESPOONS
- salt, 1/4 TEASPOON
- GANACHE TOPPING (OPTIONAL)
- bittersweet chocolate, CHOPPED, 4 OUNCES
- heavy cream, 1/2 CUP
- OPTIONAL:(BEFORE GANACHE GOES ON cake
- preserves, CHERRY, apricot, STRAWBERRY. I BUY THIS PRESERVE FROM LONDON IT IS STRAWBERRY champagne.
- OPTIONAL: TO SERVE
- HOMEMADE whipped cream
- fresh strawberries

Direction

- NOTE:
- SUCCESS OF THIS CAKE DEPENDS ON TWO THINGS:
- FIRST, YOU MUST INCORPORATE AIR INTO THE EGG YOLK AND SUGAR MIXTURE, WHIPPING THEM TO A THICK RIBBON, OR THE CAKE WILL NOT HAVE THE CORRECT LIGHT TEXTURE WHEN IT IS BAKED.
- SECOND, YOU MUST BE CAREFUL NOT TO OVERBAKE THE CAKE, OR IT WILL TURN OUT DRY. MANY COOKS ARE INCLINED TO TURN THE MIXER TO HIGH SPEED FOR BEATING EGG WHITES TO STIFF PEAKS. BUT, YOU WILL FIND THAT IF YOU WHIP WHITES ON MEDIUM SPEED AND TAKE A LITTLE LONGER, THE WHITES WILL HAVE A TIGHTER, MORE STABLE STRUCTURE AND HAVE FEWER LARGE IRREGULAR AIR POCKETS.
- CAKE:
- PREHEAT OVEN TO 325
- LINE THE BOTTOM OF A 10-INCH SPRINGFORM PAN WITH 3 INCH SIDES WITH PARCHMENT PAPER CUT TO FIT EXACTLY.
- (AT THIS POINT YOU COULD PLACE IN A LAYER OF CHOCOLATE CAKE, THIN OR SPRINKLE IN 3/4 CUPS TOASTED FINELY CHOPPED PECANS OR WALNUTS, I HAVE NOT USED EITHER OF THESE)
- IN SMALL SAUCEPAN, MELT THE BUTTER OVER MEDIUM HEAT AND THEN ADD THE CHOCOLATE. STIR AS THE CHOCOLATE MELTS, BLENDING IT WITH

- THE BUTTER. REMOVE FROM THE HEAT AND SET ASIDE.
- SEPARATE THE EGGS, PLACING THE YOLKS AND WHITES IN SEPARATE MIXING BOWLS. ADD HALF OF THE SUGAR TO THE EGG YOLKS. USING A MIXER FITTED WITH THE WHISK ATTACHMENT. BEAT THE YOLK MIXTURE ON HIGH SPEED UNTIL LIGHT AND FLUFFY, AND THE MIXTURE TRIPLES IN VOLUME AND FALLS FROM THE BEATER INA WIDE RIBBON THAT FOLDS BACK ON ITSELF AND SLOWLY DISSOLVES ON THE SURFACE,4 TO 5 MINUTES. USING A RUBBER SPATULA, FOLD THE CHOCOLATE MIXTURE INTO THE EGG YOLKS. DONT WORRY ABOUT THE MIXTURE BEING PERFECTLY BLENDED IN AT THIS POINT BECAUSE YOU WILL BE FOLDING IN THE WHITES NEXT.
- USING THE MIXER, BEAT THE EGG WHITES ON MEDIUM SPEED UNTIL SOFT PEAKS FORM. ADD THE REST OF THE SUGAR AND THE SALT AND BEAT UNTIL THE WHITES HOLD MEDIUM-STIFF, GLOSSY PEAKS. STIR ONE-THIRD OF THE WHITES INTO THE CHOCOLATE-YOLK MIXTURE TO LIGHTEN IT, ANDTHEN GENTLY FOLD IN THE REMAINING WHITES UST UNTIL NO WHITE STREAKS ARE VISIBLE. IMMEDIATELY TURN THE BATTER INTO THE PREPARED PAN.
- BAKE UNTIL THE TOP OF THE CAKE IS NO LONGER SHINY, BEING CAREFUL NOT TO LET IT "SOUFFLE"(PUFF UP AND EXPAND BEYOND IT ORIGINAL VOLUME), 30 TO 40 MINUTES. LET COOL COMPLETELY IN THE PAN ON A WIRE RACK. AS THE CAKE COOLS, IT WILL BECOME FIRMER. COVER AND REFRIGERATE UNTIL WELL CHILLED, AT LEAST 3 HOURS OR FOR UP TO OVERNIGHT.
- GANACHE: (OPTIONAL, I ALWAYS MAKE THIS FOR THE CAKE)
- REMOVE THE CAKE FROM THE REFRIGERATOR, UNCOVER IT, AND LET IT SIT ON THE COUNTERTOP FOR ABOUT 15 MINUTES TO WARM UP JUST A BIT BEFORE YOU TOP IT. I SPREAD ON THE PRESERVES AT THIS POINT (OPTIONAL, I ALWAYS DO)
- PLACE CHOCOLATE IN A HEATPROOF BOWL. HEAT THE CREAM IN A SMALL SAUCEPAN AND BRING TO JUST UNDER A BOIL. POUR THE CREAM OVER THE CHOCOLATE. LET THE MIXTURE SIT FOR ABOUT 2 MINUTES WITHOUT STIRRING UNTIL THE CHOCOLATE MELTS, AND THEN STIR GENTLY WITH A RUBBER SPATULA (SO AS TO INCORPORATE AS LITTLE AIR AS POSSIBLE) UNTIL SMOOTH. POUR THE GANACHE OVER THE CAKE, AND TILT AND TURN THE CAKE PAN TO COVER THE TOP EVENTLY. THE COLD TEMPERATURE OF THE CAKE WILL HELP THE GANACHE SET UP. WHEN THE CHOCOLATE IS SET, AFTER 20 MINUTES, RUN A THIN KNIFE BLADE AROUND THE INSIDE EDGE OF THE PAN TO LOOSEN THE CAE SIDES. (OR, YOU CAN INSTEAD WRAP A DAMP, WARM TOWEL AROUND THE PAN SIDES, OR USE A KITCHEN TORCH TO WARM THE METAL; BOTH WILL LOOSEN THE CAKE SIDES). RELEASE AND LIFT OFF THE PAN SIDES. USING A WIDE METAL SPATULA, TRANSFER THE CAKE TO A SERVING PLATE, IF USING OR LEAVE IT IN THE PAN BASE (I LEAVE IT IN THE PAN).
- TO SERVE:
- SERVE THE CAKE AT ROOM TEMPERATURE OR COLD. IF SERVED COLD, SLICE THE CAKE WITH A WARM KNIFE (HAE A TALL CONTAINER FILLED WITH VERY HOT WATER FOR DIPPING THE KNIFE BEFORE EACH CUT AND A TOWEL TO WIPE THE KNIFE CLEAN AFTER EACH CUT). IF YOU PREFER TO SERVE THE CAKE A LITTLE WARMER, IT WILL HAVE A LIGHTER, MORE MOUSSELIKE CONSISTENCY, WHICH IS MORE DIFFICULT TO CUT (I HAD NO PROBLEM, I LOVE THIS CAKE AT ROOM TEMP, EVEN AFTER THE 3 HOURS IT

RESTS BEFORE IT HITS THE REFRIGERATOR. I USUALLY ONLY REFRIGERATE THE LEFT OVERS)
- IT KEEPS FOR UP TO 1 WEEK. WRAP WELL FOR STORAGE; CHOCOLATE ABSORBS REFRIGERATOR ODORS.
- I SERVE THIS WITH WHIPPED CREAM, LIGHTLY SWEET OR NO SUGAR IN IT. CAKE IS SWEET AND RICH. I CUT UP STRAWBERRIES WITH THIS AND SERVE ON SIDE WITH WHIPPED CREAM.
- THIS IS MY MOST REQUESTED RECIPE ALONG WITH MY CHEESECAKE AND APPLE PIE.

267. Moosewoods Six Minute Vegan Chocolate Cake Recipe

Serving: 12 | Prep: | Cook: 30mins | Ready in:

Ingredients

- cake
- 1 1/2 cups unbleached white flour
- 1/3 cup cocoa powder
- 1 teaspoon baking soda
- 1/2 teaspoon salt
- 1 cup sugar
- 1/2 cup vegetable oil
- 1 cup cold water or brewed coffee
- 2 teaspoons vanilla extract
- 2 tablespoons vinegar
- glaze
- 1/2 lb bittersweet chocolate
- 3/4 cup hot water or milk
- 1/2 teaspoon vanilla extract

Direction

- Preheat the oven to 375°F.
- Sift the flour, cocoa, baking soda, salt and sugar into an ungreased 8 inch square or 9 inch round baking tin.
- In a 2 cup measuring cup, measure and mix the oil, water or coffee and vanilla.
- Pour the liquid ingredients into the baking tin and mix the batter with a fork or small whisk.
- When the batter is smooth, add the vinegar and stir quickly. Pale swirls will occur where the vinegar and baking soda react. Stir just until the vinegar is even distributed throughout the batter.
- Bake for 25-30 minutes. Set aside the cake to cool.
- If you are making the glaze, reset the oven to 300°F.
- Melt the chocolate in small ovenproof bowl or heavy skillet in the oven for about 15 minutes. Stir the hot liquid and vanilla into the chocolate until smooth.
- Spoon the glaze over the cooled cake. Refrigerate the glazed cake for a minimum of 30 minutes before serving.

268. Most Dangerous Chocolate Cake In The World Minute Chocolate Mug Cake Recipe

Serving: 1 | Prep: | Cook: 3mins | Ready in:

Ingredients

- 1 - coffee Mug
- 4 - tablespoons flour......(that's plain flour, not self-rising)
- 4 - tablespoons sugar
- 2 - tablespoons baking cocoa
- 1 - egg
- 3 - tablespoons milk
- 3 - tablespoons oil
- 3 -4 - tablespoons chocolate chips
- Small splash of vanilla extract

Direction

- Add dry ingredients to mug, and mix well. Add the egg and mix thoroughly.
- Pour in the milk and oil and mix well.

- Add the chocolate chips (if using) and vanilla, and mix again.
- Put your mug in the microwave and cook for 2 minutes at 1000 watts. Try 1/1/2 - 2 minutes first so it's not so dry ok.
- The cake will rise over the top of the mug, but don't be alarmed!
- Allow to cool a little, and tip out onto a plate if desired.
- EAT! (This can serve 2 if you want to share!) But who wants too!
- And why is this the most dangerous cake recipe in the world? Because now we are all only 5 minutes away from chocolate cake at any time of the day or night! Yikes!!!!!!!!

269. Mothers Day Chocolate Peanut Ice Cream Cake Recipe

Serving: 12 | Prep: | Cook: 38mins | Ready in:

Ingredients

- 2 cups purchased chocolate cookie crumbs
- 1/2 cup butter, melted
- 1/4 cup sugar
- 1 quart vanilla ice cream
- 1-1/2 cups chocolate-covered peanuts, chopped
- 1 quart chocolate ice cream
- chocolate and peanut butter Sauce
- chocolate-covered or plain peanuts, chopped (optional)

Direction

- Preheat oven to 350 degrees F. For crust, in a medium bowl, combine cookie crumbs, melted butter, and sugar. Press crust mixture onto the bottom and 1 to 2 inches up the side of a 9x3-inch springform pan. Bake for 8 to 10 minutes or until crust is set. Cool on a wire rack for 15 minutes. Freeze for 30 minutes.
- Let vanilla ice cream stand at room temperature for 15 minutes. In a large bowl, use a wooden spoon to stir vanilla ice cream just enough to soften. Spoon softened ice cream into frozen crust, spreading ice cream evenly. Sprinkle with the 1-1/2 cups chocolate-covered peanuts. Freeze about 1 hour or until firm.
- Let chocolate ice cream stand at room temperature for 15 minutes. In a large bowl, use a wooden spoon to stir chocolate ice cream just enough to soften. Spoon softened chocolate ice cream on top of chocolate-covered peanut layer, spreading ice cream evenly. Cover and freeze for 4 hours.
- Using a thin metal spatula, loosen crust from side of pan; remove side of pan. Let ice cream cake stand at room temperature for 20 to 25 minutes to soften slightly.
- To serve, cut the ice cream cake into wedges and top with Chocolate and Peanut Butter Sauce. If desired, sprinkle with additional chocolate-covered peanuts. Makes 12 servings.
- Chocolate and Peanut Butter Sauce: In a small saucepan, combine one 12-ounce jar fudge ice cream topping and 3 tablespoons creamy peanut butter. Cook and stir over medium-low heat until heated through.
- Make-Ahead Tip: Prepare ice cream cake as directed. Wrap in moisture proof and vapour proof wrap and freeze for up to 1 week. Loosen cake from pan and remove side of pan. Let stand at room temperature for 20 to 25 minutes to soften slightly. Cut into wedges and serve as directed.

270. My Chocolate Fudge Layer Cake Recipe

Serving: 18 | Prep: | Cook: 95mins | Ready in:

Ingredients

- 1 pkg. (8 squares) semisweet baking chocolate, divided
- 1 pkg. (2 layer size) chocolate cake mix

- 1 pkg. chocolate instant pudding and pie filling
- 4 eggs
- 1 cup sour cream
- 1/2 cup oil
- 1/2 cup water
- 1 tub (8-oz.) whipped topping, thawed
- 2 Tbsp. sliced almonds

Direction

- Preheat the oven to 350*F.
- Grease two 9" round cake pans.
- Chop 2 of the chocolate squares, set aside.
- Beat cake mix, dry pudding mix, eggs, sour cream, oil and water in large bowl with electric mixer on low speed just until moistened. Beat on medium speed 2 minutes. Stir in chopped chocolate squares, spoon into prepared pans.
- Bake for 35 minutes or until wooden toothpick inserted in center comes out clean.
- Cool on wire racks 10 minutes.
- Loosen cakes from sides of pans. Invert onto racks, gently remove pans. Cool cakes completely.
- Place frozen whipped topping and remaining 6 chocolate squares in microwaveable bowl. Microwave on high 1-1/2 minutes or until chocolate is completely melted and mixture is smooth, stirring after 1 minute.
- Let stand 15 minutes to thicken.
- Place 1 cake layer on serving plate, top with 1/4 of the chocolate mixture and the second cake layer.
- Spread top and sides with remaining chocolate mixture.
- Garnish with almond slices.
- Store in refrigerator.

271. My Favorite Chocolate Cake Recipe

Serving: 12 | Prep: | Cook: 25mins | Ready in:

Ingredients

- 1 1/2 cup all-purpose flour
- 1 cup sugar
- 1/2 teaspoon salt
- 1 teaspoon baking soda
- 1/4 cup cocoa powder
- 1/2 cup chocolate chips
- 1 cup cold water
- 1 tablespoon vinegar, white or apple cider
- 5 tablespoons of neutral oil
- 1 teaspoon vanilla extract

Direction

- Preheat your oven to 350 degrees F.
- Line your pan(s) with parchment paper or cupcake papers and spray lightly with spray oil. This recipe makes (1) 8 to 9 inch round or square or 12 cupcakes or (2) 6 inch round cakes.
- Sift together the flour, sugar, salt, baking soda and cocoa. You can also just stir them well with a wire whisk.
- Add in the chips and stir until distributed.
- Add in the water, vinegar, oil and vanilla. Mix with a whisk or wooden spoon until just combined.
- Pour or spoon into pans and bake. 25-30 minutes for large round, 20-25 for cupcakes or 6 inch rounds. Check for doneness with a wood skewer and remove when only a few crumbs cling to the skewer.
- Cool for 5-10 minutes and then invert onto a plate or remove and cool on a wire rack.

272. My Moms Chocolate Mayo Cake Recipe

Serving: 10 | Prep: | Cook: 35mins | Ready in:

Ingredients

- 2 C. flour
- 1 ½ tsp. baking soda

- 1 C. sugar
- ½ C. baking cocoa
- ¾ C. mayonnaise
- 1 C. cold water
- 1 tsp. vanilla

Direction

- Sift together flour, sugar, soda and cocoa into a mixing bowl.
- Add the remaining ingredients and beat until smooth.
- Put batter in a 9x13 cake pan.
- Bake at 350 for 35 min.

273. Non Butter Chocolate Cake Recipe

Serving: 6 | Prep: | Cook: 50mins | Ready in:

Ingredients

- fresh cream (double cream)   200ml
- sugar   200g
- egg   4
- chocolate (shaved or crushed) 40g
- plain flour   140g
- coco powder   40g
- BP 2tsp

Direction

- Pre-heat oven 180 degree C.
- Whip fresh cream and sugar, very hard.
- Add eggs by each one.
- Add shaved chocolate and shifted flour and coco powder.
- Pour it into tin (buttered and floured or lined) and put into oven for 40~50min.

274. Nougat Chocolate Cake Recipe

Serving: 10 | Prep: | Cook: 10mins | Ready in:

Ingredients

- 1 20cm chocolate cake.
- Nougat filling:
- 1-1/2 cups heavy cream or crème fresh
- 5 egg whites
- 1/8 tsp cream of tartar
- 1/2 cup sugar, plus 3 tbsp for the white
- 4 Tbsp water
- 4 Tbsp honey or maple syrup
- 3/4 cup chopped toasted hazelnuts
- 3/4 cup candied cherries or fresh red cherries, chopped.
- 1/3 cup caramel sauce
- chocolate glaze:
- 7 oz plain chocolate, chopped
- ¾ cup heavy cream

Direction

- Split chocolate cake in half and place the bottom half in a cake ring into your serving platter. Spread half of the caramel sauce over the top and set aside.
- Nougat filling:
- Beat the cream to stiff peaks and refrigerate. Beat the whites until frothy. Add the cream of tartar and beat until stiff peaks forms, then sprinkle over the 3 tablespoons of sugar and continue beating to a stiff, glossy meringue. Set aside with electric beaters at the ready.
- Bring the remaining 1/2 cup/110 g of sugar to a boil with the water. Let it boil until the syrup forms a ball when thrown in cold water, 4 minutes (250°F/120°C/firm-ball stage on a candy thermometer). Now add the honey and bring back to the boil. Run towards the egg whites...
- With the electric beaters running in the whites, slowly pour the syrup in a stream straight into the beaters or down the side of the bowl for the beaters to pick up. Continue beating until

the meringue has cooled, which you can tell by feeling the bottom of the bowl. It will take 10 minutes.
- Scatter the fruits and nuts over the meringues. Dump the whipped cream on top, and fold everything together gently until evenly mixed. Spoon mixture over the split cake and smooth the top. Chill for 3 hours.
- Release the cake ring and drizzle the rest of the caramel sauce over the top. Chill again while you make the chocolate glaze.
- Make the chocolate glaze:
- Heat the cream to a simmering point and pour over the chopped chocolate. Stir until chocolate melts and mixture is smooth. Once cooled completely, pour over the cake keeping 3-4 tbsp. aside. Chill cake for 30 minutes and then drizzle the rest of the chocolate glaze with a tbsp. over the top creating a decorative pattern.

275. Old Fashioned Chocolate Cake And Frosting Recipe

Serving: 24 | Prep: | Cook: 1hours | Ready in:

Ingredients

- Cake:
- 2 cups sugar
- 1 tsp baking soda
- 1 tsp cinnamon
- 1 stick butter
- 1/2 cup buttermilk
- 1 tsp vanilla
- 2 cups all-purpose flour
- 1/4 tsp salt
- 1 cup water
- 4 TBS cocoa powder
- 2 beaten eggs
- Frosting:
- 1/4 cup cocoa powder
- 1/4 cup milk
- 1 cup toasted pecans, chopped
- 1 cup sugar
- 1 stick butter
- pinch salt

Direction

- Preheat oven 400.
- In a medium to large bowl, combine the sugar, flour, soda, salt and cocoa.
- In a small pot, boil the water and butter together and pour directly into the bowl containing the flour mixture.
- Beat eggs and add to the chocolate batter along with the buttermilk, vanilla and cinnamon. Mix well.
- Pour into a greased and floured 13x9 pan. Bake 20 minutes.
- Frosting: Start the frosting shortly before the cake is done, because you will pour it directly over the cake.
- In a medium saucepan bring to boil, sugar, butter, milk, cocoa, and a pinch of salt. Once the boil has started, boil for exactly 1 minute. Remove from heat and beat until thick. Stir in pecans.
- When cake come out of the oven, punch holes on the top with a fork. Spread the frosting over the cake. Cut and serve.

276. Omas Chocolate Pudding Cake Recipe

Serving: 12 | Prep: | Cook: 35mins | Ready in:

Ingredients

- cake
- 3/4 cup granulated sugar
- 5 1/4 oz package Cook and Serve chocolate pudding mix
- 4 eggs lightly beaten
- 2 tsp. baking powder
- 1 cup vegetable oil (or 1/2 c. oil and 1/2 c applesauce)
- 3/4 c milk

- icing
- 3/4 cup powdered sugar
- 1/2 tsp vanilla
- 2-4 tsp water

Direction

- Preheat oven to 350 degrees.
- Stir all ingredients together, mix with spoon until fairly smooth.
- A few lumps are OK.
- Pour batter into non-stick Bundt cake pan.
- Bake for 35 - 40 minutes - until toothpick comes out clean.
- Mix icing ingredients together, add just enough water to allow icing to drizzle over cake.

277. Ooey Gooey Double Chocolate Butter Cake 1 Recipe

Serving: 8 | Prep: | Cook: 45mins | Ready in:

Ingredients

- 8 tablespoons (1 stick) butter, melted, plus 8 more
- tablespoons (1 stick) butter, melted, plus additional
- butter, for greasing pan
- 1 (18.25 ounce) package chocolate cake mix
- 1 egg, plus 2 eggs
- 1 (8 ounce) package cream cheese, softened
- 3 to 4 tablespoons cocoa
- 1 (16 ounce) box powdered sugar
- 1 teaspoon vanilla
- 1 cup chopped nuts

Direction

- Preheat oven to 350 degrees. Lightly grease a 13 x 9-inch baking pan.
- In a large bowl, combine the cake mix, 1 egg and 1 stick melted butter, and stir until well blended. Pat mixture into prepared pan and set aside. In a stand mixer, or with a hand mixer, beat the cream cheese until smooth. Add the remaining 2 eggs, and the cocoa powder. Lower the speed of the mixer, and add the powdered sugar. Continue beating until ingredients are well mixed.
- Slowly add the remaining 1 stick of melted butter, and the vanilla extract, continuing to beat the mixture until smooth. Stir in nuts with a rubber spatula.
- Spread filling over cake mixture in pan. Bake for 40 to 50 minutes. Be careful not to overcook the cake; the center should still be a little gooey when finished baking. Let cake partially cool on a wire rack before cutting into pieces.

278. Ooh La La Adult Chocolate Cake Recipe

Serving: 1 | Prep: | Cook: 60mins | Ready in:

Ingredients

- 8 oz. of good bittersweet chocolate
- 1 cup (2 sticks) of unsalted butter, softened
- 1 1/2 cup sugar
- 5 eggs

Direction

- Grease a cake pan (8 1/4" X 1 1/2" deep and in diameter).
- Break the chocolate into a large bowl.
- Set over a sauce pan of barely simmering water until melted.
- Remove from the heat and cool slightly.
- Cut the butter into little pieces and beat into the chocolate.
- Add the sugar and blend well, beating thoroughly.
- In another bowl, beat the eggs until frothy and foamy, then gently fold into the chocolate mixture; make sure everything is thoroughly combined.

- Pour the mixture into the cake pan and place in a bain marie (roasting pan containing enough water to come up to 1 inch of the cake pan's side).
- Bake at 350 degrees for 1 hour, then let it cool completely in the pan. When cool remove from the bain marie and refrigerate overnight.
- When ready to eat, run a thin metal spatula around the edge of the pan and with a thump unmold the cake. As written from "Cooking with 2 Fat Ladies"

279. Orange And Chunksa Dark Chocolate Pound Cake Recipe

Serving: 12 | Prep: | Cook: 30mins | Ready in:

Ingredients

- 1 3/4 Cups flour
- 3/4 Cups sugar
- 1/2 Cup butter (Room Temp.)
- 2 eggs (Prebeaten)
- 1 1/2 teaspoons baking powder
- 1 teaspoon vanilla
- 1/2 Cup orange juice
- 2 Tablespoons orange zest
- 3 Tablespoons Grand Manier (Optional. If you omit then add 1 more Tablespoon Zest)
- 1 Large dark chocolate Bar (Cut into big chunks. Save the dust for the top)

Direction

- Preheat Oven to 375.
- Grease & flour a 9X5 Bread Pan even if it's non-stick.
- In a large Bowl mix the Flour into the softened Butter.
- Add in Sugar, Eggs, Baking Powder & mix.
- Then add in the Vanilla, Orange Juice, Zest & Grand Marnier & mix.
- If using an electric beater then mix on low for 1 minute & then for 1 1/2-2 minutes on medium.
- If mixing by hand then beat mixture for 4 minutes & 1 minute as hard as you can.
- Pour 1/2 batter into prepared Bread Pan.
- Cover the Batter in Bread Pan with Dark Chocolate chunks.
- Pour in remaining batter & sprinkle the Chocolate Dust over the top of the Bread batter.
- Put in oven
- At 25 Minutes stick a knife into the center of the Pound Cake. If the knife comes out clean then it's done. If the knife isn't clean continue to bake, checking at 5 minute intervals.
- When done, remove from oven & allow it to stand for 10 minutes.
- Remove from pan, slice yourself a couple of slices & get out of the way of anyone else in the house.
- Do not expect any leftovers.

280. Orange Cola Chocolate Cake Recipe

Serving: 12 | Prep: | Cook: 30mins | Ready in:

Ingredients

- 1 package (18-1/4 ounces) devil's food cake mix
- 3 eggs
- 1-1/3 cups cola
- 1/2- cup canola oil
- 1 -tablespoon orange extract
- chocolate-COVERED STRAWBERRIES:
- 1/2 -cup semisweet chocolate chips
- 1 -teaspoon shortening
- 12- fresh strawberries
- **************************
- FROSTING:
- 1/2 -cup butter, softened
- 3 3/4- cups confectioners' sugar

- 3- tablespoons instant chocolate drink mix
- 1/4- cup cola
- 1/2- teaspoon orange extract

Direction

- In a large bowl, combine the cake mix, eggs, cola, oil and extract.
- Beat on low speed for 30 seconds; beat on medium for 2 minutes. Pour into a greased 13-in. x 9-in. baking pan.
- Bake at 350° for 30-35 minutes or until a toothpick inserted near the center comes out clean.
- Cool on a wire rack.
- In a small microwave-safe bowl, melt chocolate chips and shortening; stir until smooth.
- Wash strawberries and pat dry.
- Dip each strawberry into chocolate; allow excess to drip off.
- Place on a waxed paper-lined baking sheet; refrigerate until set, about 30 minutes.
- In a small bowl, combine the frosting ingredients; beat until smooth. Frost cake.
- Garnish each serving with a chocolate-covered strawberry.
- Yield: 12 servings.
- Note: diet cola is not recommended for this recipe!!

281. Oreo Buttermilk Bundt Cake With Chocolate Glaze Recipe

Serving: 12 | Prep: | Cook: 30mins | Ready in:

Ingredients

- 1 1/4 cup butter (200 gm)
- 1 cup superfine sugar (160 gm)
- 4 eggs
- 2 cups plain flour (200 gm)
- 1 level tsp baking soda
- 2 level tsp cream of tartar
- 2/3 cup buttermilk
- 2 tsp vanilla extract
- 1 pack Oreo Double Stuff cookies (11 cookies/170 gm)
- **
- glaze
- 200 gms (about 8 oz) dark chocolate
- 2 Tbsp butter

Direction

- Preheat oven at 180 degrees C. Thoroughly grease a 10 cup capacity Bundt tin.
- Cream butter and sugar with a hand whisk, in large bowl till pale and fluffy. Whisk in eggs one by one till well mixed.
- Combine flour with baking soda and cream of tartar then sieve over butter and egg mixture in two lots and stir in gently with whisk till well mixed.
- Combine buttermilk and vanilla and add to batter. Stir gently into batter till combined. Break Oreos into quarters and fold through batter.
- Scrape batter into Bundt tin and bake at 180 C for 20 minutes. Lower heat to 165 C and bake for another 10 - 15 minutes.
- Remove from oven and cool 20 minutes before turning out. Allow to cool completely.
- Break chocolate up into a microwave safe bowl and microwave with the butter for 1 minute on high. Stir chocolate. If not completely melted, repeat 1 minute on medium and stir till completely melted. Let cool till warm but still liquid then pour over cake. Allow to set before cutting cake.
- Note: I used a dark cake pan which bakes faster. An ordinary cake pan may need a further 10 minutes baking.

282. Organic Chocolate Fudge Brownie Cake Recipe

Serving: 10 | Prep: | Cook: 40mins | Ready in:

Ingredients

- 1 Box Organic chocolate cake
- chocolate graham crackers
- butter
- little marshmallows
- dark chocolate bits
- peanut butter
- unsalted butter
- ----
- Alton Brown makes a pastry bag out of a large glad bag by putting mixture in and cutting the tip out after.

Direction

- Prepare packaged cake according to directions.
- Put aside.
- Crush one sleeve of chocolate grahams between 2 sheets of wax paper.
- Melt enough unsalted butter in pan to make a crust while adding crushed crackers.
- In a 9x13 Pyrex baking dish that has been greased very well.
- Spread cracker mixture.
- Add a layer of the chocolate bits and a layer of marshmallows.
- Pour cake mix over.
- Bake according to directions about 40 minutes.
- Allow to cool.
- When almost cool prepare the following.
- Melt butter with peanut butter in a saucepan and keep thick enough to put in pastry bag and make a checkerboard pattern or whatever pattern you wish.

283. Original German Chocolate Cake With Coconut Pecan Frosting Recipe

Serving: 8 | Prep: | Cook: 40mins | Ready in:

Ingredients

- 4 ounces German sweet chocolate squares
- 1/2 cup boiling water
- 1 cup butter
- 2 cups granulated sugar
- 4 eggs separated
- 1 teaspoon vanilla extract
- 2 cups all purpose flour
- 1 teaspoon baking soda
- 1/2 teaspoon salt
- 1 cup buttermilk
- Filling and Topping:
- 14 ounce can sweetened condensed milk
- 1/2 cup water
- 3 egg yolks
- 1 tablespoon vanilla extract
- 1/2 cup unsalted butter
- 1-1/3 cups pecans chopped
- 10 whole pecans halves for garnish
- 1-3/4 cup flaked coconut

Direction

- Melt chocolate in water then cool.
- Cream butter and sugar then beat in egg yolks.
- Stir in vanilla and chocolate.
- Mix flour, soda and salt then beat in flour mixture alternately with buttermilk.
- Beat egg whites until stiff peaks form then fold into batter.
- Pour batter into three cake pans lined on bottoms with waxed paper.
- Bake at 350 for 30 minutes then cool 15 minutes and remove and totally cool on wire rack.
- For filling cook milk, eggs and water over a double boiler until thickened.
- Add vanilla and butter then whisk until it is melted and smooth.
- Add the chopped pecans and coconut.

- Spread between layers and over tops and sides of cake.
- Garnish with pecan halves.

284. PISTACHIO CHOCOLATE CAKE Recipe

Serving: 8 | Prep: | Cook: 45mins | Ready in:

Ingredients

- 1/2-cup orange juice
- 1/2 cup water
- 4 eggs
- 1 white cake mix
- 1 pkg pistachio pudding
- 1/2 cup chocolate syrup

Direction

- Mix all ingredients except the pistachio pudding & chocolate syrup.
- Divide.
- Add pudding mixture to one half.
- Grease and flour loaf pan.
- Pour pistachio part into a loaf pan.
- Mix the remaining cake mix with the chocolate syrup and pour evenly over the pistachio mixture.
- Bake at 375 degrees for 45-50 minutes.
- Test to make sure it is done.
- Top with a dollop of whip cream if desired.

285. Party Size One Bowl Chocolate Cake Recipe

Serving: 12 | Prep: | Cook: 30mins | Ready in:

Ingredients

- Cake:
- 2 eggs
- 1 c oil
- 1 c Hot tap water (or brewed coffee for a mocha flavor)
- 2 c sugar
- 2 c flour
- 1 c baking cocoa
- 2 ts baking soda
- 1 c sour milk (or buttermilk)
- (to make sour milk: add 2 tsp vinegar to Sweet milk (whole milk) and let thicken 5 minutes)
- whipped cream
- Mocha whipped cream Topping
- (which may be used for any cake or dessert - not a buttercream but can easily be made into one by adding butter!)
- 3 cups chilled heavy cream
- 1 1/2 cups powdered sugar
- 3/4 cup sifted baking cocoa
- 2 tsp. rum
- 2 tsp. instant coffee powder

Direction

- This is so easy and tastes wonderful!
- In a large bowl simply mix all together (either by hand mixing or electric mixer medium speed) just until well combined.
- Pour batter (it will be a bit thin) into a large 9 x13 or 10 x 14 pan.
- Bake 350F, 45 minutes OR until tested done.
- Remove pan to rack to cool completely.
- Top cold cake with a whipped cream frosting or mocha type frosting which is great with this moist chocolate cake.
- There are many versions of this sour milk cake but our family enjoys this one the best!
- This cake tastes best the day after being baked and freezes very well.
- Note: may be baked in round layer cake pans (baking time will decrease) and filled and frosted as desired.
- Serves 12 to 24!

286. Paul Neumans Chocolate Cake Recipe

Serving: 12 | Prep: | Cook: 20mins | Ready in:

Ingredients

- 1 pk Dark choc cake mix Or
- 1 Recipe favorite 9 x 13 chocolate cake (I used this as I don't care for mixes) Or yellow or butter cake
- 1 14 oz can sweetened condensed milk (not evaporated)
- (I use about 1/2 can)
- 1 ,16 0z jar butterscoth ice cream topping
- 1 ,8 0z Cool Whip (I use 12 oz whipped topping)
- 3 Heath candy bars (crushed in the wrappers)
- 1.4 oz each (English toffee and milk chocolate)
- chocolate jimmies (sprinkles)

Direction

- Prepare cake for 9 x 13 pan and bake and completely cool.
- If using mix follow package directions.
- Or prepare your favorite scratch yellow, butter or chocolate cake recipe.
- I place the batter into 2, 9 or 10 inch round cake pans since I vary the recipe for a layer cake and not a 9 x 13 pan kind.
- When completely cool:
- Using large blunt end of a chop stick, poke holes all over cake and pour the condensed milk over cake (1 can was just too much for the layer cake and 1/2 can was sufficient) .
- But try the entire jar if you wish for the 9 x 13 pan.
- Then spread over the caramel topping (used whole jar) and spread evenly with the cool whip.
- For the layers, use whipped topping to frost entire cake and not in between layers.
- Sprinkle top of cake with the crushed candy (helps to chill bars first then crush).
- I sprinkled top of each layer with the crushed candy bars plus reserved some extra to sprinkle over the whipped topping.
- Chill cake for several hours (I prepared mine a day ahead) before slicing.
- This is an extremely moist cake from all that milk and caramel. I also used some chocolate jimmies to decorate the cake.
- If you love chocolate this is probably one of the most delicious cakes to try.
- It also came out extremely delicious with the yellow or butter cake recipes. But the chocolate is extra special.
- Note: with layer cake:
- Some of the caramel will ooze out of the layers as you spread it on layers and this is just fine.
- It adds to the attractiveness of the cake.
- Work quickly to frost and cover the entire cake with the whipped topping and throw on jimmies and crushed heath bars all over the cake including sides.
- Then immediately chill to set the caramel etc.
- The cake tastes best when allowed to chill overnight.

287. Peanut Butter Bundt Cake With Chocolate Peanut Butter Ganache Recipe

Serving: 12 | Prep: | Cook: 60mins | Ready in:

Ingredients

- cake
- 1 ¼ C smooth peanut butter
- ¾ C butter, softened
- 2 C brown sugar, packed
- 4 large eggs
- 1 ½ tsp vanilla
- 3 C flour
- 3 tsp baking powder
- 1 tsp baking soda
- ½ tsp salt
- 1 ½ C buttermilk

- chocolate peanut butter Ganache
- 10 ounces dark or semi-sweet chocolate, finely chopped
- ¾ C heavy cream
- ¼ C corn syrup
- 3 Tbl creamy peanut butter

Direction

- Cake
- 325 oven   greased and floured 12 C Bundt cake pan
- In a large mixing bowl, beat butter, peanut butter and brown sugar until light and fluffy
- Beat in eggs, one at a time, and beating well after each addition
- Beat in vanilla
- Combine dry ingredients and beating into creamed mixture, alternating with milk
- Beat well
- Spoon into prepared pan and bake for approximately 60 minutes or until a toothpick inserted in centre comes out clean and cake springs bake when touched lightly with finger
- Cool 15 minutes, then carefully remove from pan and invert on cooling rack
- Ganache
- In a saucepan, combine the cream and corn syrup and bring to a boil
- Remove from heat and whisk in chocolate until melted and smooth
- Whisk in peanut butter until well blended
- Place foil under cooled cake on rack and spoon the warm chocolate mixture over cake
- Let stand about 10 minutes before placing on cake plate
- Scrape up any excess chocolate and place in a small container, freeze or refrigerate to warm later for use over ice cream or pound cake

288. Peanut Buttery Chocolate Cake Recipe

Serving: 16 | Prep: | Cook: 40mins | Ready in:

Ingredients

- cake ....
- 2- cups all-purpose flour
- 2- teaspoons baking soda
- 1- teaspoon baking powder
- 1/2- teaspoon salt
- 2- cups granulated sugar
- 2/3- cup unsweetened cocoa powder
- 2- eggs
- 1- cup milk
- 2/3- cup vegetable oil
- 1- teaspoon vanilla extract
- 1- cup brewed coffee, cooled to room temperature,... (or 1 cup water plus 1 teaspoon instant coffee granules)
- Frosting...........
- 1- (3 ounce) package cream cheese .softened
- 1/4-- cup creamy peanut butter
- 2- cups powdered sugar
- 2- tablespoons milk
- miniature chocolate chips

Direction

- Preheat oven to 350 degrees F. grease a 9x 13 inch glass baking pan.
- To prepare the cake:
- Sift the flour, baking soda, baking powder, and salt into a large mixing bowl.
- Add the granulated sugar, cocoa, and mix well.
- Add the eggs, milk, oil and the vanilla.
- Using a mixer at medium speed, beat for 2 minutes, scraping down the sides of the bowl.
- Stir in the coffee, the batter will be thin.
- Pour the batter into the prepared pan.
- Bake for 35 to 40 minutes until a wooden pick inserted in the middle comes out clean.
- Cool completely on a wire rack.
- To prepare the frosting, combine the cream cheese and peanut butter in a large mixing bowl.
- Using a mixer, beat at medium speed until smooth.
- Beat in the powdered sugar, milk, and vanilla.
- Beat until smooth.

- Spread the frosting over the top of the cake and sprinkle with mini chocolate chips.
- Store in refrigerator.
- Serves 16.

289. Peppermint Chocolate Pound Cake Recipe

Serving: 8 | Prep: | Cook: 90mins | Ready in:

Ingredients

- 3 cups plus 2 tablespoons sifted all purpose flour
- 3 teaspoons baking powder
- 1 teaspoon salt
- 2/3 cup unsifted unsweetened cocoa powder
- 1 cup unsalted butter softened
- 3 cups granulated sugar
- 4 large eggs at room temperature
- 1 tablespoon vanilla extract
- 1 tablespoon chocolate extract
- 1 teaspoon butter flavoring
- 2 teaspoons peppermint extract
- 1-1/2 cups milk at room temperature
- 1/4 cup sour cream at room temperature

Direction

- Lightly grease and flour a tube pan.
- Line the bottom with a circle of waxed paper to fit pan.
- Grease waxed paper then preheat oven to 325.
- Sift together flour, baking powder, salt and cocoa.
- Cream butter at high speed 3 minutes then beat in sugar in three additions.
- Beat well after each addition then beat in eggs one at a time.
- Continue beating at least 3 minutes after the last egg has been added.
- Blend in vanilla, butter flavoring, pepper and chocolate extracts.
- Reduce speed to low.
- Alternately add sifted dry ingredients in three additions with milk in two additions.
- Add sour cream and beat 4 minutes on low speed.
- Carefully pour and scrape batter into tube pan then shake and tap gently to level batter.
- Bake on lower third level rack for 90 minutes.
- Allow cooling in pan 5 minutes then carefully invert on cooking rack.
- Remove waxed paper then allow to cool completely.

290. Peteys Birthday Cherry Chocolate Bundt Cake Recipe

Serving: 12 | Prep: | Cook: 60mins | Ready in:

Ingredients

- 2 sticks butter
- 1/2 cup cocoa
- 3/4 cup water
- 2 cups granulated sugar
- 1 cup sour cream
- 1 tablespoon vanilla extract
- 2 large eggs
- 2 cups all purpose flour
- 1 teaspoon baking soda
- 1/2 teaspoon salt
- 1 can of cherry pie filling
- **glaze**
- 3/4 cup chocolate chips
- 1/4 cup milk or cream
- 1/4 cup good dark brewed coffee
- 1/4 cup light corn syrup
- 1 teaspoon vanilla extract

Direction

- Grease and flour a 10-12 cup Bundt pan.
- Heat oven to 350 degrees F
- Melt butter in a large saucepan over medium-low heat.
- Add cocoa, stirring until smooth.

- Whisk in the water and remove from heat.
- To the warm cocoa mixture, add the sugar, sour cream, vanilla and eggs.
- Whisk until smooth.
- In another bowl combine the flour, soda and salt.
- Add all at once to the first mixture, whisking until well blended.
- Stir in one can of cherry pie filling.
- Pour the batter into the prepared pan.
- Bake for 1 hour, or until it feels firm to the touch and has slightly pulled away from the sides of the pan.
- Cool in pan on a rack for 20 minutes.
- Carefully loosen the cake with a knife and invert onto a large plate.
- While it is cooling, warm the milk/cream, coffee, and corn syrup on medium heat until it boils.
- Add vanilla.
- Pour over chocolate chips and let sit until chocolate melts.
- Whisk until smooth.
- Let cool to room temperature then spoon over the cooled cake.
- If too thick, thin with a little more milk/cream.

291. Pistachio Chocolate Cake Recipe

Serving: 8 | Prep: | Cook: 55mins | Ready in:

Ingredients

- yellow cake mix (Regular or Betty Crocker gluten Free)
- 1 box pistachio instant pudding
- 4 eggs
- 1 tsp. pure almond extract
- 1/2 cup water
- 1/2 cup oil
- 1/2 cup orange juice
- 1/2 cup chocolate syrup (u-bet works well-or Hershey)
- 1/2 cup Nestle chocolate Morsels

Direction

- Spray Bundt cake with GF or spray oil
- Mix cake mix, pudding, eggs, almond extract, water, oil, orange juice together until well blended. Pour 1/2 of the batter into greased pan. In remaining batter, pour 1/2 cup syrup and mix well. On top of yellow half in pan, add 1/2 cup chocolate bits. Pour remaining batter on top. Bake for 55 minutes or until toothpick comes out clean. For Gluten free mix be careful not to over bake. Cool for 1/2 hour before serving and enjoy!

292. Praline Chocolate Jar Cakes Recipe

Serving: 10 | Prep: | Cook: 25mins | Ready in:

Ingredients

- You'll Need
- Ten to twelve 1/2-pint canning jars
- Rimmed baking sheet or roasting pan
- For the cake
- 8 tablespoons (1 stick) unsalted butter, softened
- 1 1/2 cups packed light brown sugar
- 2 large eggs
- 1 teaspoon pure vanilla extract
- 6 tablespoons unsweetened cocoa powder
- 1 1/2 teaspoons baking soda
- 1/4 teaspoon salt
- 1 1/2 cups sifted cake flour
- 2/3 cup sour cream
- 2/3 cup brewed coffee (I just use the morning's leftover coffee)
- For the Praline Topping
- 2 tablespoons unsalted butter
- 3/4 cup firmly packed light brown sugar
- 1/2 cup water
- 1 cup powdered sugar
- 1/2 cup pecan halves or pieces

Direction

- Preheat the oven to 350°F. Place 10 to 12 1/2-pint glass canning jars on a rimmed baking sheet, evenly arranged with space between them. (If you have a Silpat liner, place it under the jars to prevent them from sliding around.)
- To make the cakes, in a mixer fitted with a whisk attachment, beat the butter until smooth. Add the brown sugar and eggs and mix until fluffy, about 2 minutes. Add the vanilla, cocoa, baking soda, and salt and mix until combined. Add half of the flour, then half of the sour cream, and mix until combined. Repeat with the remaining flour and sour cream. Drizzle in the coffee and mix until smooth. The batter will be thin, like heavy cream.
- Pour the batter into the jars, filling them halfway. Bake until the tops of the cakes are firm to the touch, about 25 minutes.*
- To make the topping, melt the butter in a medium saucepan over medium heat, then add the brown sugar and 1/2 cup water and stir with a wooden spoon until the sugar is dissolved, 2 to 3 minutes. Remove the pan from the heat and stir in the powdered sugar until combined, then return to the heat and bring to a boil. Stir in the nuts.
- Pour the praline topping over the cakes to cover, working quickly, because the praline hardens quickly as it cools. Let the cakes cool completely if they aren't already, before screwing on jar lids.**
- Do-Ahead
- * The cakes can be made ahead, cooled, covered, and kept at room temperature for 2 days or in the refrigerator for up to 4 days.
- ** The finished cakes will keep for up to 4 days at room temperature.

293. REAL And I Mean REAL German Chocolate Cake Recipe

Serving: 12 | Prep: | Cook: 24mins | Ready in.

Ingredients

- 3/4 cup butter or margarine, softened
- 1-1/2 cups sugar
- 3 eggs
- 1 teaspoon vanilla extract
- 2 cups all-purpose flour
- 3/4 cup baking cocoa
- 1 teaspoon baking soda
- 1 teaspoon baking powder
- 1/4 teaspoon salt
- 1 cup water
- 1 cup sauerkraut, rinsed, drained, squeezed dry and finely chopped
- 2/3 cup flaked coconut
- 1/2 cup finely chopped pecans
- FILLING/FROSTING:
- 2 cups (12 ounces) semisweet chocolate chips, melted
- 2/3 cup mayonnaise*
- 2/3 cup flaked coconut, divided
- 2/3 cup chopped pecans, divided

Direction

- In a mixing bowl, cream butter and sugar.
- Add the eggs, one at a time, beating well after each addition.
- Beat in vanilla.
- Combine dry ingredients; add to the creamed mixture alternately with water.
- Fold in sauerkraut, coconut and pecans.
- Pour into three greased and floured 9-in. round baking pans.
- Bake at 350° for 20-24 minutes or until a toothpick inserted near the center comes out clean.
- Cool for 10 minutes before removing from pans to wire racks; cool completely.
- In a bowl, combine melted chocolate and mayonnaise.
- Set aside 1-1/4 cups for frosting.

- To the remaining chocolate mixture, add half of the coconut and pecans; spread between cake layers.
- Spread reserved chocolate mixture over top and sides of cake. Combine remaining coconut and pecans; press onto sides of cake.
- Store in the refrigerator.
- Slice with a serrated knife.

294. Raspberry White Chocolate Mousse Cake Recipe

Serving: 8 | Prep: | Cook: 45mins | Ready in:

Ingredients

- 1/2 cup cake flour
- 3 ounces white chocolate chopped
- 1/4 teaspoon salt
- 2 tablespoons unsalted butter cut into bits
- 3 large eggs at room temperature
- 1/2 teaspoon vanilla
- 1/3 cup granulated sugar
- Pastry Cream:
- 4 large egg yolks
- 3 tablespoons unsalted butter softened
- 1/3 cup granulated sugar
- 9 ounces white chocolate chopped
- 3 tablespoons cornstarch sifted
- 1 cup heavy cream
- 1-1/2 cups milk scalded
- 1/4 cup framboise liqueur
- 2 teaspoons vanilla
- Raspberry Mousse:
- 3 tablespoons framboise
- 2 1/2 cups fresh raspberries
- 1/2 cup heavy cream

Direction

- Line bottom of a greased spring form pan with wax paper then grease paper and dust with flour.
- Melt chocolate with butter, vanilla, and 3 tablespoons water stirring until mixture is smooth.
- Remove bowl from heat and allow mixture to cool.
- Sift together flour and salt.
- In large bowl with an electric mixer beat eggs with sugar on high speed for 5 minutes.
- Fold flour mixture into egg mixture until batter is combined and gently fold in chocolate mixture.
- Pour batter into pan smoothing top and bake in middle of a preheated 350 oven for 25 minutes.
- Transfer cake to a rack and run sharp knife around edge and remove side of pan.
- Invert cake onto another rack and remove wax paper then invert cake onto rack and cool.
- After cake has cooled completely carefully slice cake horizontally into three equal layers.
- To prepare pastry cream whisk together yolks and sugar then add cornstarch and whisk.
- Add scalded milk then transfer mixture to a heavy saucepan and boil whisking for 1 minute.
- Pour into a bowl then stir in vanilla and butter then cover with plastic wrap and chill.
- Melt chocolate stirring occasionally and let it cool to lukewarm.
- Whisk together white chocolate and 1 cup pastry cream reserving the remaining pastry cream.
- In bowl with an electric mixer beat heavy cream until it holds soft peaks.
- Whisk one fourth of it into the white chocolate mixture then fold in remaining whipped cream.
- Line sides of an oiled spring form pan with pieces of plastic wrap letting excess hang over side.
- Invert top layer of genoise into bottom of pan then brush cake with some of the framboise.
- Spread evenly with half the white chocolate mousse.

- Invert middle layer of genoise onto mousse and brush with some of the remaining framboise.
- Chill cake and remaining white chocolate mousse while preparing the raspberry mousse.
- To prepare raspberry mousse puree raspberries with a little water then pour into a metal bowl.
- Whisk reserved pastry cream into raspberry mixture.
- With an electric mixer beat heavy cream until it holds soft peaks.
- Whisk 1/4 of the whipped cream into raspberry mixture and fold in remaining pastry cream.
- Spread raspberry mousse evenly over middle layer of genoise in the pan.
- Invert the third layer of genoise onto the mouse and brush it with the remaining framboise. Spread remaining white chocolate mousse over genoise and chill at least 6 hours.
- Remove side of pan and peel wrap carefully from side of cake and transfer to serving plate.
- Garnish cake with fresh raspberries and white chocolate curls.

295. Rich Beet Chocolate Cake Recipe

Serving: 0 | Prep: | Cook: 1hours | Ready in:

Ingredients

- For Cake:
- 2 c. all purpose flour
- 1 3/4 c. sugar
- 2/3 c. pure cocoa powder
- 1 tsp. baking powder
- 1 tsp. salt
- 3/4 c. unsalted butter
- 2 large eggs
- 1 tsp. vanilla
- 3/4 c. finely grated cooked beets
- 1 1/4 c. hot water
- For Frosting:
- 1/2 c. + 2 Tbsp. unsalted butter
- 1 c. sugar
- 3/4 c. cocoa powder
- 3/4 c. whipping cream
- 1 tsp. vanilla

Direction

- For Cake:
- 1. Preheat oven to 350*F. Grease two 8" round cake pans. Line the bottom of the pans with parchment paper and dust the sides with flour, tapping out any excess.
- 2. Sift the flour, sugar, cocoa powder, baking powder, and salt in a large bowl of stand mixer fitted with the paddle attachment. Add the butter and mix on low speed until the butter has been worked into the flour (it seems dry and crumbly).
- 3. Add the egg and vanilla, and mix slightly, then mix the beets. Add the hot water and while mixing on low speed, then increase the speed to medium high and continue to mix for 2 - 3 minutes, until the batter is thick and fluffy. Scrape the batter into the prepared pans. Spread to level the batter and tap the pans on the counter to knock out any large air pockets.
- 4. Bake the cake for about 35 minutes, until a tester inserted in the center of the cake comes out clean. Cool the cakes in their pans for 30 minutes, then turn them out onto a cooling rack to cool completely.
- For Frosting:
- 1. Melt the butter in a medium sauce pan, then whisk in the sugar and cocoa powder. Continue to whisk this over medium heat until mixture begins to bubble, then whisk in the cream. Continue to whisk until mixture return to simmer (gentle bubbles) and whisk for another 1 minute. Remove the pot from the heat and stir in the vanilla and salt. Cool the mixture (it will look like a thick fudge sauce) to a room temperature, then chill for about 1 hour, stirring occasionally while chilling. This

will set the frosting to a spreadable consistency.
- 2. To assemble, peel the parchment paper from a cake layer and place it on a platter. Spread an even layer of frosting over the top of the cake, and place the second cake layer on top. Frost the top and sides of the cake, spreading until smooth.
- 3. Chill the cake to set, but pull the cake out from the fridge an hour before slicing and serving.

296. Rich Chocolate Chip Honey Cake Recipe

Serving: 16 | Prep: | Cook: 60mins | Ready in:

Ingredients

- 1 ½ cups all-purpose flour
- 1 ½ cups whole-wheat pastry flour or spelt flour
- 2 ½ teaspoons baking powder
- 1 teaspoon baking soda
- ½ cup cocoa powder
- ½ teaspoon salt
- ½ tsp chili powder
- ½ teaspoon ground cloves
- 1 cup honey
- 1/3 cup vegetable oil
- 2/3 cup prune or apple butter
- 2/3 cup granulated sugar
- ½ cup firmly packed brown sugar
- 3 large eggs
- 1 cup Dr. pepper
- 1 ½ teaspoon vanilla
- ½ cup finely chopped, best-quality bittersweet chocolate

Direction

- Heat oven to 350 degrees. Grease a 10-inch tube pan.
- Sift the flour, baking powder, baking soda, cocoa powder, salt and spices into a medium bowl. Set aside.
- Combine honey, oil, fruit butter and the sugars in the bowl of an electric stand mixer with the paddle attachment. Mix on medium speed until smooth.
- Add the eggs, Dr. Pepper and vanilla; mix 2 minutes.
- Slowly add the flour mixture, beating on medium speed until incorporated.
- Fold in the chocolate by hand.
- Pour into prepared pan and bake 50 to 60 minutes.
- Cool in the pan 20 minutes. Invert onto a wire rack and allow to cool completely.

297. Rich Chocolate Pound Cake Recipe

Serving: 10 | Prep: | Cook: 55mins | Ready in:

Ingredients

- 2 cups (12-oz. pkg.) NESTLÉ® TOLL HOUSE® Semi-sweet chocolate
- Morsels, divided
- 3 cups all-purpose flour
- 1 tablespoon baking powder
- 1/2 teaspoon salt
- 2 cups packed light brown sugar
- 1 cup (2 sticks) butter, softened
- 1 tablespoon vanilla extract
- 4 large eggs, room temperature
- 1/2 cup milk

Direction

- PREHEAT oven to 350° F. Grease 10-inch Bundt pan.
- MICROWAVE 1 1/2 cups morsels in medium, uncovered, microwave-safe bowl on HIGH (100%) power for 1 minute; STIR. The morsels may retain some of their original shape. If necessary, microwave at additional 10- to 15-

second intervals, stirring just until morsels are melted.
- Cool to room temperature.
- COMBINE flour, baking powder and salt in medium bowl.
- Beat sugar, butter and vanilla extract in large mixer bowl until creamy. Add eggs, one at a time, beating well after each addition. Beat in melted chocolate. Gradually beat in flour mixture alternately with milk.
- Spoon into prepared Bundt pan.
- BAKE for 55 to 65 minutes or until wooden pick inserted in cake comes out clean. Cool in pan for 30 minutes. Invert cake onto wire rack to cool completely.
- MICROWAVE remaining morsels in heavy-duty plastic bag on HIGH (100%) power for 45 seconds; knead bag. Microwave at additional 10- to 15-second intervals, kneading until smooth. Cut a small hole in corner of bag; squeeze to drizzle over cake.

298. Run The Extra Mile PB And Chocolate Cake Recipe

Serving: 8 | Prep: | Cook: 35mins | Ready in:

Ingredients

- Cake:
- 1 cup butter
- 2 cups sugar
- 4 eggs
- 2-1/2 cups all-purpose flour
- 1 tablespoon baking soda
- 1/4 teaspoon salt
- 1 cup buttermilk
- 3/4 cup Hershey's® cocoa
- 2/3 cup boiling water
- 1 teaspoon vanilla
- peanut butter Cream Filling:
- 1/4 cup creamy peanut butter
- 1 tablespoon butter
- 1 teaspoon Dream Whip®
- 1/4 cup water, more if needed
- 2 tablespoons all-purpose flour
- 1/2 pound confectioners sugar
- dash of salt
- Frosting:
- 1/2 cup butter
- 1/4 cup Crisco® shortening
- 1/4 teaspoon vanilla
- 1-1/2 tablespoons Dream Whip®
- 3 tablespoons all-purpose flour
- 1-1/2 pounds confectioners sugar
- 1/2 cup Hershey® cocoa
- 1/2 cup water, approximately
- Crushed peanuts or mini Resse's Peanut Butter® cups for garnish if desired.

Direction

- Cake:
- In a bowl, cream butter, sugar and eggs.
- In a separate bowl, sift flour, baking soda and salt together.
- Add to the creamed mixture alternately with the buttermilk.
- In a separate bowl, stir the boiling water and Hershey's® cocoa together until the cocoa dissolves.
- Add vanilla. Stir and add to cake batter.
- Pour the batter into 2 8-inch round cake pans.
- Bake at 350° for 35 minutes or until toothpick test comes out clean.
- Remove from oven and cool on racks.
- Peanut Butter Filling:
- Mix all ingredients together until creamy. Add more water if necessary to get a smooth consistency.
- Spread between cooled cake layers.
- Frosting:
- Mix butter, shortening, vanilla, Dream Whip®, flour and confectioners' sugar together until creamy.
- Mix Hershey® cocoa with 1/4-1/2 cup hot water, stirring until dissolved.
- Add to the creamed mixture and continue to mix until well blended.
- Frost top and sides of cake.

- Garnish with chopped nuts OR mini Reese's Peanut Butter® cups that have been cut in half.
- Serve with a tall glass of ice cold milk :o)
- ***Digest thoroughly before taking that run!!!***

299. Russian Chocolate Strawberry Cake Recipe

Serving: 10 | Prep: | Cook: 60mins | Ready in:

Ingredients

- For the Cake:
- 6 eggs, yolks separated from the whites
- 1 1/2 cups flour
- 1 cup sugar
- 1 tbsp. corn starch
- 2 tbsp. cocoa powder
- 1 1/2 tsp. vanilla extract
- For the Cream:
- 500 gr. ricotta cheese
- 2 cups powdered sugar (add more if you prefer the cream sweeter)
- 2 tbsp. unflavored gelatine
- 1/2 to 2/3 cup milk (use a little more milk if needed)
- 1 cup heavy cream, whipped to stiff peaks
- 2 cups fresh strawberries, coarsely chopped
- For the chocolate Glaze:
- 2 semi-sweet chocolate squares (1oz each)
- 1/2 tbsp. shortening

Direction

- For the Cake:
- Sift the flour, corn starch and cocoa powder together. Set aside.
- In a separate large bowl, beat the egg yolks with half the sugar and vanilla extract. Beat the egg whites to stiff peaks with the rest of the sugar in another medium bowl.
- Fold in 1/3 of the egg white mixture into the egg yolks, then carefully fold in the sifted dry ingredients. Add the rest of the beaten egg whites to the batter, folding carefully (this will help the batter to stay light).
- Transfer the batter to a lightly greased 9-inch spring form pan. Bake in preheated 350F oven for about 1 hour, or until a wooden toothpick inserted near the center comes out clean. Remove from the oven and let cool.
- For the Cream:
- Whisk the gelatine into 2/4 cup milk in a small pan and cook over low heat until the gelatine has dissolved.
- Meanwhile, beat the ricotta cheese with the powdered sugar for a few minutes, or until smooth.
- Beat in the gelatine mixture into the ricotta, then beat in the whipped cream. Taste the cream to make sure it is sweet enough for you. Add more powdered sugar, if needed.
- Fold the chopped strawberries into the cream.
- To assemble the cake:
- Remove the side ring of the spring form pan. Slice the cake into 3-4 layers, however you prefer.
- Place the bottom layer of the cake back into the spring form pan. Close the ring back around it. This makes it easier to assemble the cake. Layer part of the cream on the bottom cake layer, place another cake layer on top, and repeat with the cream. Continue this way, finishing with the last cake layer on top.
- Place the cake in the fridge for about 2 hours, to let the cream set.
- When ready, melt the chocolate with 1/2 tbsp. shortening in a microwave safe bowl. Brush the top of the cake with the glaze. Place the cake back in the fridge for another hour.

300. Shirleyomas Fabulous Chocolate Flourless Cake Recipe

Serving: 8 | Prep: | Cook: 40mins | Ready in:

Ingredients

- 1/8 C. (15 grams) cocoa powder
- 4 oz. (115 grams) sweet butter
- 10 oz. (280 grams) best quality semi sweet chocolate, chopped
- 8 eggs, separated
- 1/3 C (75 grams) sugar
- 1 tsp vanilla extract
- Pinch of cream of tartar OR fine salt
- 1 (9 inch) springform pan

Direction

- Heat oven to 350°F (175°C) degrees. Lightly butter the springform pan and dust with cocoa powder, remove excess by shaking pan. Set aside.
- In top of double boiler melt chopped chocolate and butter together until smooth. Remove from heat. Quickly whisk egg yolks into melted chocolate.
- Beat egg whites and cream of tartar or salt until foamy with an electric mixer on high speed. Then slowly add sugar and vanilla and beat until medium peaks form when beaters are lifted. Do not overbeat.
- In thirds, gently fold egg whites into melted chocolate mixture. Pour into prepared pan and bake for 30 to 40 minutes. Test for doneness with a toothpick. Cake will have crackers on the top. This is normal in this kind of cake.
- Transfer the pan to a wire rack and cool for 10 minutes. Using a small sharp knife, cut around the sides of the cake to loosen it. Release the pan side. Invert the cake onto a wire rack. Cool the cake completely. Cake will deflate a little. Wrap in plastic and refrigerate overnight.
- NOTES: I have changed the oven temperatures as it seemed to be too low for me. It worked OK with the above stated temperature, but you may have to adjust temperature or time a little as I did.
- I have added the tsp. of vanilla extract so it mellows with the strong aroma of chocolate, but it can be omitted.
- The morning after, I split the cake in half and spread a thin layer of strawberry marmalade on one half, then I assembled the cake again and cut it into small squares. I dusted a little powder sugar on top and garnished with fresh strawberries.

301. Shortcut Chocolate Malted Cake Recipe

Serving: 15 | Prep: | Cook: 35mins | Ready in:

Ingredients

- 1 2-layer size package dark chocolate fudge or devil's food cake mix
- 1/3 cup vanilla malted milk powder
- 1 12-oz can whipped chocolate frosting
- 1/4 cup vanilla malted milk powder
- 1 1/2 cups coarsely chopped malted milk balls

Direction

- Preheat oven to 350 F.
- Grease a 13x9x2 inch baking pan.
- Prepare cake mix according to package directions, adding 1/3 cup malted milk powder to batter.
- Pour batter into prepared pan.
- Bake 30 to 35 minutes or until a toothpick inserted near the center comes out clean.
- Place pan on a wire rack and cool completely.
- In a medium bowl, stir together frosting and 1/4 cup malted milk powder.
- Spread evenly over cake.
- Top with chopped malted milk balls.

302. Silky Chocolate Truffle Cake Recipe

Serving: 8 | Prep: | Cook: 68mins | Ready in:

Ingredients

- Crust
- ·3 ounces toasted and coarsely chopped walnuts
- ·4 ounces toasted and coarsely chopped pecans
- ·½ cup firmly packed brown sugar
- ·1 pinch cinnamon
- ·4 ounces (1 stick) butter, melted
- Mousse cake
- ·20 ounces bittersweet chocolate cut into small pieces
- ·¾ cup soft butter (6 ounces or 1 ½ sticks)
- ·¾ cup sugar
- ·6 large eggs
- ·¼ cup heavy cream
- ·½ teaspoon vanilla

Direction

- Crust:
- In small stainless steel bowl, combine walnuts, pecans, brown sugar and cinnamon. Stir in melted butter. Press mixture into bottom of springform pan. Chill crust for ½ hour, until firm.
- Mousse Cake:
- Melt chocolate in double boiler. While chocolate is melting, combine butter and sugar in mixer bowl. On medium speed, cream mixture until light and fluffy. Add eggs, two at a time, mixing well after each addition. Scrape sides of bowl. Increase speed to medium high and whip for two minutes until egg mixture increases slightly in volume. When chocolate is melted, beat with hand whisk until it has cooled. It should be warm, not hot. Whisk the chocolate into egg mixture on medium low speed. Scrape sides and bottom of bowl and continue to mix until chocolate is fully incorporated. Stir in cream and vanilla. Spread this mousse filling evenly on pecan crust. Chill until firm, 6 hours to overnight.
- To Serve
- Unmold the cake by running a hot, dry knife around the inside edge of the pan and then releasing the latch of springform. Slice cake with hot, dry knife into 12 -15 servings. Clean blade of knife under very hot water, dry blade and immediately cut cake. Repeat for each slice. Top servings with dollop of whipped cream, or spread whipped cream over the entire cake before cutting.

303. Sinful Chocolate Cake Recipe

Serving: 10 | Prep: | Cook: 60mins | Ready in:

Ingredients

- 1 box chocolate cake mix- any kind
- 5.9 box chocolate instant pudding
- 1 cup sour cream (no low fat here)
- 4 large
- 1/2 cup water
- 1/2 cup veggie oil
- Combine all ingredients & beat on high for 2 minutes. Pour (will be thick) into a greased & floured bundt cake pan. (Or as from my big fat greek wedding Bundta pan) Optional: stir in 3/4 cup of chocolate chips into batter.
- Bake at 350 for 50-60 minutes. Cool for 15 minutes. Then remove from pan. Top with topping below...

Direction

- Chocolate Topping:
- 1/3 cup milk
- 1 cup sugar
- 5 tablespoons butter
- 1 cup chocolate chips
- Bring milk, butter and sugar to boil. Simmer for 2-3 minutes. Stirring constantly. Remove

from heat & immediately stir in chocolate chips. Beat smooth by hand and pour carefully over cooled cake.

- I am sure you can do many variations with this cake. IF you want vanilla/white cake mix and use vanilla pudding mix. Can use butterscotch chips or white chocolate chips. Same with topping just use white chocolate. Even for chocolate cake you can use peanut butter chips or peanut butter chips in topping. But TRUST ME....TRY THIS AS IT IS FIRST. PASS THE COLD MILK PLEASE! Or, good strong coffee.

304. Slow Cooker Chocolate Brownie Cake Recipe

Serving: 8 | Prep: | Cook: 120mins | Ready in:

Ingredients

- 1/2 cup brown sugar
- 3/4 cup water
- 2 tablespoon cocoa
- 2 1/2 cups fudge brownie mix
- 1 egg
- 1/4 cup peanut butter
- 1 tablespoon butter-soft
- 1/4 cup water
- 1 cup semisweet chocolate chips

Direction

- Combine 3/4 cup water, brown sugar, and cocoa in a saucepan. Bring to a boil.
- Meanwhile, combine remaining ingredients in a small bowl. Mix well.
- Spread batter on the bottom of a lightly buttered slow cooker.
- Pour boiling mixture over batter.
- Cover and cook on high for 2 hours.
- Turn off and let stand for 30 minutes.
- Serve warm with vanilla ice cream.

305. Slow Cooker Chocolate Cake Recipe

Serving: 6 | Prep: | Cook: 360mins | Ready in:

Ingredients

- 1 chocolate cake mix (the kind without the pudding in the mix)
- 1 package instant chocolate pudding mix
- 3/4 cup oil
- 1 cup water
- 4 eggs
- 1 (6 oz) bag of chocolate chips
- 1 pint sour cream

Direction

- Spray crockpot with non-stick spray.
- Mix all ingredients and place in crockpot.
- Cook on LOW for 6 hours.
- Try not to lift the lid.
- Serve with ice cream.

306. Slow Cooker Chocolate Peanut Butter Spoon Cake Recipe

Serving: 6 | Prep: | Cook: 120mins | Ready in:

Ingredients

- 1 cup all-purpose flour
- 2 T unsweetened cocoa powder
- 1/2 cup sugar
- 1 1/2 tsp baking powder
- pinch of salt
- 1/2 cup whole milk or chocolate milk
- 2 T canola, peanut, or walnut oil
- 1 T vanilla extract
- 1/2 cup smooth or chunky peanut butter (natural or hydrogenated)
- 1/2 cup semisweet chocolate chips

- Topping:
- 3 T unsweetened cocoa powder
- 3/4 cup sugar
- 1 1/2 cups boiling water
- vanilla ice cream for serving

Direction

- Coat the slow cooker with non-stick cooking spray
- In a medium bowl, whisk together the flour, cocoa, sugar, baking powder, and salt.
- Make a well in the center and add the milk, oil, and vanilla. Stir until well-blended.
- Continue stirring, in widening circles, incorporating the dry ingredients, until you have a smooth batter.
- Stir in the peanut butter (warm it in the microwave if it's too thick).
- Stir in the chocolate chips.
- Spread the mixture evenly in the slow cooker.
- In a medium bowl, combine the cocoa and sugar, pour in the boiling water and whisk until smooth.
- Gently pour over the batter in the cooker, do not stir.
- Cover and cook on HIGH until puffed and the top is set, 2 to 2 1/4 hours.
- Turn off the cooker and let it stand, covered, for at least 30 minutes before serving.

307. Slowbake Buttermilk Chocolate Cake Recipe

Serving: 12 | Prep: | Cook: 60mins | Ready in:

Ingredients

- 2 cups all purpose flour
- 2 cups granulated sugar
- 3/4 cup unsweetened cocoa powder
- 2 teaspoons baking soda
- 2 large eggs
- 1 teaspoon salt
- 1 cup buttermilk
- 1 cup canola oil
- 1 1/2 teaspoon vanilla extract
- 1 cup boiling water

Direction

- Preheat oven to 300 degrees - yes 300 (slow bake).
- Grease and flour a 9x13 pan.
- Easy part - put all ingredients in a big mixing bowl, and beat with a hand mixer on med until well blended and smooth.
- Pour into baking pan.
- Bake for 1 hour at, yes, 300 degrees.
- Test center to see if done.
- Allow to cool and frost with your favorite frosting.

308. Souffle Chocolate Cake 2 Recipe

Serving: 12 | Prep: | Cook: 30mins | Ready in:

Ingredients

- SOUFFLE chocolate cake PART:
- 8 ounces bittersweet chocolate, coarsely chopped
- 1/2 cup (1 stuck) unsalted butter, cut into 1-inch pieces
- 2 tablespoons cognac
- 6 large eggs, separated, at room temperature
- 1/2 cup plus 2 tablespoons granulated sugar, divided
- chocolate GLAZE:
- 4 ounces bittersweet chocolate, coarsely chopped
- 1/3 cup heavy cream
- 2 tablespoons honey
- ASSEMBLY:
- 1/3 cup seedless raspberry preserves
- GARNISH:
- 3 ounces milk chocolate, melted

Direction

- Make the flourless chocolate cake:
- Position a rack in the center of the oven and preheat to 350 degrees Fahrenheit. Butter the bottom and sides of a 9-inch springform pan. Line the bottom of the pan with a round of parchment or waxed paper; butter the paper.
- In a medium saucepan, combine the chocolate and butter. Cook over low heat, stirring constantly with a wooden spoon, until the chocolate and butter are melted. Gently whisk until smooth. Remove from heat and stir in the cognac. Let cool.
- In a medium bowl, whisk together the egg yolks and 1/2 cup of sugar until well blended. Stir in the melted chocolate mixture.
- In the 4 1/2-quart bowl of a heavy-duty electric mixer, using the wire whip attachment, beat the egg whites at medium speed until frothy. Increase the speed to medium-high and beat the egg whites until soft peaks start to form. One tablespoon at a time, beat in the remaining 2 tablespoons of sugar. Continue beating until the egg whites are still but not dry.
- Using a large rubber spatula, gently fold the beaten egg whites into the chocolate mixture in 3 additions. Do not over mix.
- Pour the batter into the prepared pan. Bake until the cake is puffed and a tester inserted into the center comes out with moist crumbs attached, about 30 minutes. Transfer the pan to a wire rack and cool for 10 minutes. Using a small sharp knife, cut around the sides of the cake to loosen it. Release the pan side. Invert the cake onto a wire rack. Peel off the parchment paper and cool the cake completely. Wrap in plastic and refrigerate overnight (let it sit a few hours then glaze. I don't like it cold fudge like, I like it airy and light)
- MAKE THE CHOCOLATE GLAZE:
- Place the chocolate in a medium bowl. In a small saucepan, bring the heavy cream to a gentle boil. Using a wire whisk, stir in the honey. Pour the hot cream mixture over the chocolate and let the mixture stand for 30 seconds to melt the chocolate. Whisk the mixture until smooth. Cover the surface of the glaze with plastic wrap and set aside at room temperature for 30 minutes or until slightly thickened.
- ASSEMBLE THE CAKE:
- Remove the cake from the refrigerator and remove the plastic wrap from the cake. Place the cake on a wire rack set over a baking sheet. Using a metal spatula, spread the raspberry preserves evenly over the top and sides of the cake Pour the chocolate glaze over the cake, covering it completely; spread evenly with a metal spatula. Drizzle the top of the glazed cake with the melted milk chocolate. Serve the cake immediately, or refrigerate. Bring the cake to room temperature before serving.

309. Sour Cream Chocolate Cake Recipe

Serving: 12 | Prep: | Cook: 35mins | Ready in:

Ingredients

- 4 1oz squares unsweetened chocolate-melted and cooled.
- 1 cup water
- 3/4 cup sour cream
- 1/4 cup shortening
- 1 teaspoon vanilla
- 3 eggs
- 2 cups cake flour
- 2 cup sugar
- 1 1/4 teaspoons baking powder
- 1/2 teaspoon baking soda
- 1 teaspoon salt
- sour cream Chocolate Frosting:
- 1/2 cup butter-softened
- 6 1oz squares unsweetened chocolate-melted and cooled
- 6 cups powdered sugar
- 1/2 cup sour cream
- 6-8 tablespoons milk
- 2 teaspoons vanilla extract

- 1/8 teaspoons salt

Direction

- In a large mixing bowl, combine chocolate, water, sour cream, shortening, vanilla, and eggs. Mix well.
- Combine flour, sugar, baking soda, salt, and baking powder. Gradually add to chocolate mixture.
- Beat on low speed until just combined. Beat on high for 3 minutes.
- Pour batter into two greased and floured 9" round cake pans.
- Bake at 350 degrees for 30-35 minutes or until inserted toothpick comes out clean.
- Cool in pans for 10 minutes then turn out onto wire rack.
- Cool completely.
- Frosting:
- In a large mixing bowl, combine frosting ingredients and beat until smooth and spreadable.
- If too thick, add more milk. If too thin, add more sugar.
- Frost cake as usual.
- Store leftovers in refrigerator.

310. Strawberry Chocolate Farm Cake Recipe

Serving: 8 | Prep: | Cook: 30mins | Ready in:

Ingredients

- 200 ml whipping cream, whipped
- ....
- 1 1/2 C cake flour and 1 tsp baking pwd, sifted
- 125 g butter
- 1 C Castor sugar
- 2 egg whites and yolks
- 1 tsp vanilla
- 1/2 C luke warm water and 3 tbsp full cream milk, mixed
- ....
- 250 g cream cheese
- 75 g caster sugar
- 75 g dark baking chocolate, melted in 4 tbsp milk / cream
- 1 tbsp gelatin pwd mixed in 5 tbsp water, mixed until dissolved
- ....
- 200 g strawberries blend
- 100 g caster sugar
- 1 tsp gelatin mixed in 5 tbsp water and dissolved
- ....
- almonds dipped in white chocolate
- hazelnut dipped in dark chocolate
- ....

Direction

- Pre heat the oven to 180 deg.
- Beat the butter and sugar until creamy.
- Add the egg yolks and vanilla.
- Fold in the flour and milk alt. starting and finishing with the flour.
- Fold in the beaten egg whites.
- Pour in a cake pan and bake for 35 mins.
- ....
- Beat cream cheese with sugar till smooth with a flat knife.
- Add 3/4 portion of the whipped cream.
- Add melted chocolate and stir till well.
- Mix the gelatine and mix well.
- Pour on top of the cake and chill.
- ....
- Blend strawberries to puree.
- Add the 1/4 of the whipped cream.
- Add sugar, gelatine. Mix well.
- Pour this mixture on top of the chocolate cheese cream
- Chill until set.
- Decorate

- It may take 4 to 6 hours
- ....

311. Stumps Chocolate Angels Food Cake Recipe

Serving: 8 | Prep: | Cook: 40mins | Ready in:

Ingredients

- 1c sifted cake flour
- 1 1/2c sifted powdered sugar
- 1/4c cocoa
- 1T instant coffee
- 1doz egg whites(1 1/2c)
- 1/2tsp salt
- 1 1/2tsp cream of tartar
- 1c granulated sugar

Direction

- Separate whites from yolks while cool and bring them to room temperature before whipping.
- Sift together the first 4 ingredients and set aside.
- Whip egg whites 3/4 the way to making peaks (frothy but not stiff).
- Add cream of tartar and salt and continue mixing.
- Slowly pour in sugar and beat slowly until graininess is gone.
- Fold in dry ingredients in three portions, mixing 15 times after each addition or until moistened/mixed.
- Do not over mix.
- Spoon into ungreased angel's food pan.
- Tap down pan on the countertop to bring up any bubbles before baking.
- Bake at 375 degrees for 35 to 40 minutes.
- When done, set upside down in the pan to cool at least an hour before removing from pan.

312. Super Chocolatey Zucchini Bread Recipe

Serving: 12 | Prep: | Cook: 2hours | Ready in:

Ingredients

- 1 cup whole wheat flour
- ½ cup all-purpose flour
- ½ tsp nutmeg
- Pinch salt
- ½ tsp baking soda
- ½ tsp baking powder
- ¼ cup unsweetened cocoa powder
- 1 egg
- 1 tsp vanilla
- 6 packets Truvia
- ½ cup brown sugar
- 3 tbsp Nutella
- ½ cup smooth ricotta (something like buttermilk-ricotta.html">Buttermilk Ricotta or even pureed cottage cheese)
- ½ cup butter.html">Roasted Apple butter (made without sugar or sweetener)
- ¼ cup semisweet chocolate chips
- 14 oz grated zucchini

Direction

- Preheat oven to 350°F and grease a loaf pan.
- In a mixing bowl, beat together the egg, Truvia, sugar, Nutella, ricotta and applesauce.
- Add the flours, nutmeg, baking soda, baking powder & cocoa, stirring just until moistened.
- Fold in chocolate chips and zucchini.
- Pour batter into prepared pan
- Bake 1 hour and 15 minutes.
- Cool in the pan for 10 minutes, then carefully turn out and cool completely on a wire rack
- I suggest serving this with Richer Ricotta Frosting or a cream cheese glaze like the one here: Monkey Bread with Cream Cheese Glaze

313. Susans Chocolate Cake Recipe

Serving: 20 | Prep: | Cook: 35mins | Ready in:

Ingredients

- 1 chocolate cake:
- 1/2 jar of Mrs. Richardsons caramel Butterscotch ice cream topping
- Mix 1 1/2 cups milk
- 1 small pkg. of chocolate instant pudding
- 1 carton of French vanilla Cool Whip .
- 1/2 pkg. of Heath chips

Direction

- 1 chocolate cake: Mix according to box directions and bake.
- Let set 15 min.
- Poke holes in the cake with a wooden spoon handle--approximately every couple of inches.
- Pour 1/2 jar of Mrs. Richardsons Caramel Butterscotch Ice cream topping into the holes.
- Let set in refrigerator until cold.
- Mix 1 1/2 cups milk with 1 small pkg. of chocolate instant pudding--let set for 10 min. before spreading on cake after the caramel layer. Refrigerate until set.
- Spread 1 carton of French vanilla Cool Whip on top of pudding layer.
- Sprinkle 1/2 pkg. of heath chips on top of Cool whip layer. Keep Refrigerated.
- ****I try to pour topping into the holes of the cake.

314. Sweet Chocolate Pound Cake Recipe

Serving: 16 | Prep: | Cook: 80mins | Ready in:

Ingredients

- 2 1/4 cups all purpose flour
- 1 1/2 cups sugar
- 1 teaspoon salt
- 3/4 teaspoon cream of tartar
- 1/2 teaspoon baking soda
- 1/4 teaspoon cinnamon
- 1 cup butter, room temperature
- 3/4 cup milk
- 1 teaspoon vanilla
- 4 eggs
- 1 package German sweet chocolate melted and cooled (4 oz)
- 1/2 cup flake coconut
- sifted confectioners sugar
- chocolate glaze

Direction

- Mix first 6 ingredients, set aside.
- Cream butter to soften; add flour mixture, milk and vanilla.
- Mix until all flour is moistened; then beat 2 minutes at medium speed with an electric mixer, scraping bowl occasionally.
- Add eggs and chocolate; beat 1 minute longer.
- Pour batter into a 10 inch fluted or straight sided tube pan which has been greased and floured.
- Bake at 325 degrees for about 1 hour and 20 minutes, or until cake is done.
- Cool in pan 15 minutes; remove from pan and finish cooling on rack.
- Sprinkle with confectioners' sugar and top with Chocolate glaze and coconut.
- Choc Glaze: Melt 3 squares semi-sweet chocolate and 1 tablespoons butter in saucepan over low heat, stirring constantly until smooth.
- Cool slightly, then drizzle from tip of teaspoon over top of cake, letting glaze run down flutes.

315. Sweet Potato Chocolate Nut Cake Recipe

Serving: 12 | Prep: | Cook: 75mins | Ready in:

Ingredients

- 4 ounces semisweet chocolate melted
- 1 teaspoon vanilla extract
- 3 cups all purpose flour
- 1-1/2 cups granulated sugar
- 2 teaspoons baking powder
- 2 teaspoons baking soda
- 2 teaspoons cinnamon
- 1/2 teaspoon ground ginger
- 1/4 teaspoon ground cloves
- 1/2 teaspoon ground nutmeg
- 2 cups mashed cooked sweet potatoes
- 1-1/2 cups oil
- 4 eggs
- 1 cup chopped nuts

Direction

- Butter and lightly flour a tube pan then mix melted chocolate together with the vanilla.
- Sift together the dry ingredients and set aside.
- In a large bowl beat the sweet potatoes and oil together then add eggs one at a time until blended.
- Slowly add the dry ingredients and mix well then stir in the nuts.
- Place 1/3 of the mixture in another bowl and stir in the chocolate mixture.
- Alternate batters in pan then swirl through layers with a knife to get a marble effect.
- Bake at 350 for 75 minutes then let cool for 10 minutes in pan.
- Remove from pan and cool completely on a rack.

316. TRIPLE CHOCOLATE MARSHMALLOW CAKE Recipe

Serving: 10 | Prep: | Cook: 60mins |Ready in:

Ingredients

- 1 pkg. chocolate cake mix
- 1 pkg. (small) chocolate instant pudding
- 1 3/4 C. milk
- 2 eggs
- 1 pkg. (12 oz.) Baker's chocolate chips
- 1 C. chocolate syrup
- 3 C. miniature marshmallows

Direction

- Preheat oven to 350°F
- Combine cake mix, pudding mix, milk, eggs, and chips in large bowl.
- Mix by hand until blended about 2 minutes.
- Pour into greased and floured 13 x 9 inch pan.
- Bake for 50 to 55 minutes or until cake springs back when lightly touched.
- Drizzle 1/2 cup of the chocolate syrup over the warm cake.
- Sprinkle marshmallows evenly over syrup and bake 5 minutes longer or until marshmallows are softened and lightly browned.
- Drizzle remaining syrup over marshmallows.
- Cool cake in pan and cut into squares, using knife dipped in warm water.

317. TWISTED GERMAN CHOCOLATE CAKE Recipe

Serving: 10 | Prep: | Cook: 35mins |Ready in:

Ingredients

- 1 box German Choc. cake mix
- 1 can sweetened condensed milk
- 1 (12 oz. jar) caramel ice cream topping
- 1/2 - 1 C. pecans
- Cool Whip Topping

Direction

- Mix and bake cake mix as directed.
- When cake is done, poke holes in top with a wooden spoon.
- Sprinkle nuts on top.
- Mix milk and syrup together.

- Pour over nuts.
- Top with cool whip.
- Refrigerate any leftover.

318. The Devil Made Me Do It Chocolate Cake Recipe

Serving: 8 | Prep: | Cook: 30mins | Ready in:

Ingredients

- The Devil Made Me Do It" chocolate cake
- Ingredients1 package Duncan Hines devil's food cake mix or brand of choice 1 large banana sliced
- 12 ounce Cool Whip Lite whipped topping thawed chocolate curls optional
- 1 can Lite cherry pie filling

Direction

- Instructions
- Prepare 2 layers of cake per instructions on package.
- When cake is cooled, spread a thick layer of whipped topping on top of one layer. Place dollops of cherry pie filling around the inside edge and in the center. Add sliced banana randomly.
- Place second layer on top of the first, and spread another layer of whipped topping on that.
- Top with chocolate curls if desired.

319. The Millionaire Chocolate Chip Pound Cake Recipe

Serving: 10 | Prep: | Cook: 60mins | Ready in:

Ingredients

- 1 box Duncan Hines butter Golden cake mix
- 1 cup oil
- 1/4 cup water
- 4 eggs
- 1 8 ounce carton sour cream
- 1 box Jello instant chocolate pudding mix
- 1 6 ounce package chocolate chips
- 1-1/2 teaspoons vanilla

Direction

- In large mixer bowl, place the cake mix, oil, water, eggs, pudding mix.
- Beat well.
- Add sour cream, beating on medium until blended in.
- Add chocolate chips, vanilla.
- Pour into a greased Bundt pan.
- Bake for 1 hour at 325 degrees.
- May drizzle with a thin chocolate glaze.
- *May add toasted chopped pecans to the glaze.

320. The Mother Of All Chocolate Cakes Recipe

Serving: 18 | Prep: | Cook: 35mins | Ready in:

Ingredients

- Cake:
- 1/2 cup (1 stick) butter, softened
- 1 cup sugar
- 4 eggs
- 1 cup all-purpose flour
- 1 teaspoon baking powder
- 1/8 teaspoon salt
- 1 teaspoon pure vanilla extract
- 1 (16-ounce) can chocolate syrup
- Frosting:
- 1/2 cup (1 stick) butter
- 1/2 cup semisweet chocolate chips
- 1 cup sugar
- 1/3 cup evaporated milk

- 1 teaspoon pure vanilla extract
- 1/2 cup chopped pecans or walnuts

Direction

- Preheat oven to 350 degrees F. Grease and flour a 13 by 9 by 2-inch pan.
- For the cake: Using an electric mixer, cream butter and sugar together until light and fluffy.
- Add eggs 1 at a time, beating well after each addition.
- Sift flour, baking powder, and salt together in another bowl.
- Add to creamed mixture, continuing to beat.
- Add vanilla and chocolate syrup to batter and mix well.
- Pour into prepared pan and bake for 25 to 30 minutes.
- Just before cake is done, prepare frosting.
- For the frosting: Put butter, chocolate chips, sugar and evaporated milk in a saucepan over medium heat and bring to a boil.
- Stirring ingredients together, boil for 2 to 3 minutes.
- Remove from heat and stir in vanilla and nuts.
- Pour over warm cake.

321. The Official Killer Chocolate Cake Recipe

Serving: 8 | Prep: | Cook: 50mins | Ready in:

Ingredients

- 1 pkg chocolate cake mix
- 4 eggs
- 1/2 C water
- 1/2 C vegetable oil
- 1 C sour cream
- 1 small pkg instant pudding (chocolate or butterscotch)
- 1 large pkg chocolate chips
- frosting (homemade or in the tub)

Direction

- Pre-heat oven 350 degrees.
- Grease pan. I like to use a Bundt pan.
- Mix ingredients.
- Pour into pan.
- Bake 50 - 60 minutes.
- Cool completely.
- Frost.

322. The Perfect Chocolate Cake Recipe

Serving: 4 | Prep: | Cook: 30mins | Ready in:

Ingredients

- Ingredients:
- 2 cups sugar
- 1-3/4 cups all-purpose flour
- 3/4 cup cocoa
- 1-1/2 teaspoons baking powder
- 1-1/2 teaspoons baking soda
- 1 teaspoon salt
- 2 eggs
- 1 cup milk
- 1/2 cup vegetable oil
- 2 teaspoons vanilla extract
- 1 cup boiling water
- "PERFECTLY CHOCOLATE" chocolate frosting(recipe follows)

Direction

- Directions:
- 1. Heat oven to 350°F. Grease and flour two 9-inch round baking pans.
- 2. Stir together sugar, flour, cocoa, baking powder, baking soda and salt in large bowl. Add eggs, milk, oil and vanilla; beat on medium speed of mixer 2 minutes. Stir in boiling water (batter will be thin). Pour batter into prepared pans.
- 3. Bake 30 to 35 minutes or until wooden pick inserted in center comes out clean. Cool 10

minutes; remove from pans to wire racks. Cool completely. Frost with "PERFECTLY CHOCOLATE" CHOCOLATE FROSTING. 10 to 12 servings.
- VARIATIONS:
- ONE-PAN CAKE: Grease and flour 13x9x2-inch baking pan. Heat oven to 350° F. Pour batter into prepared pan. Bake 35 to 40 minutes. Cool completely. Frost.
- THREE LAYER CAKE: Grease and flour three 8-inch round baking pans. Heat oven to 350°F. Pour batter into prepared pans. Bake 30 to 35 minutes. Cool 10 minutes; remove from pans to wire racks. Cool completely. Frost.
- BUNDT CAKE: Grease and flour 12-cup Bundt pan. Heat oven to 350°F. Pour batter into prepared pan. Bake 50 to 55 minutes. Cool 15 minutes; remove from pan to wire rack. Cool completely. Frost.
- CUPCAKES: Line muffin cups (2-1/2 inches in diameter) with paper bake cups. Heat oven to 350°F. Fill cups 2/3 full with batter. Bake 22 to 25 minutes. Cool completely. Frost. About 30 cupcakes.
- "PERFECTLY CHOCOLATE" CHOCOLATE FROSTING
- 1 stick (1/2 cup) butter or margarine
- 2/3 cup Cocoa
- 3 cups powdered sugar
- 1/3 cup milk
- 1 teaspoon vanilla extract
- Melt butter. Stir in cocoa. Alternately add powdered sugar and milk, beating to spreading consistency. Add small amount additional milk, if needed. Stir in vanilla. About 2 cups frosting.

323. The Best Chocolate Lovers Cake Recipe

Serving: 12 | Prep: | Cook: 30mins | Ready in:

Ingredients

- 3/4c (1 1/2 stcks) unsalted butter (or I CANT BELIEVE IT'S NOT BUTTER spread)
- 6oz bittersweet chocolate. (6 bakers chocolate squares)
- 4 eggs, separated
- pinch of salt
- 3/4c sugar
- 1/3c all purpose flour
- glaze
- 5 tbsp butter (or spread again)
- 10oz (10 squares) bittersweet OR semi-sweet OR dark chocolate cut coarsley into chunks.

Direction

- Pre-heat oven to 350*F. Grease 9-inch round cake pan, then line with parchment or wax paper.
- Melt butter and chocolate in a small saucepan over low heat on stove. Stirring occasionally until smooth. The set it aside. (You can melt it together in the microwave just be careful and stir often)
- In a medium bowl, use an electric mixer to beat the 4 egg whites with a pinch of salt until stiff peaks form and set aside.
- In another medium sized bowl, beat the yolks and sugar until light and ribbony (long strands when beaters are lifted).About 2 minutes.
- Continue to beat, while slowly adding the melted chocolate mixture until juts blended.
- Pour the batter into the prepared pan and bake for 30 minutes.
- Do not insert a toothpick into the center because it will not come out clean even when done.
- Remove the pan to a wire rack and run a knife around the sides of the cake to loosen.
- Cool for 15 minutes then remove the cake from the pan to cool completely. Be careful since it's very moist and delicate.
- FOR THE GLAZE: Melt the butter (or spread) and chocolate in a small saucepan over low heat. Stir occasionally.
- Spread warm glaze over cake and let sit for 5 minutes before serving.

324. Three Chocolate Mousse Cake Recipe

Serving: 12 | Prep: | Cook: 35mins | Ready in:

Ingredients

- Dark-chocolate layer:
- 8 oz. dark, or bitter-sweet chocolate chips
- 1/4 cup butter
- 2 tbsp. almond-flavored liqueur, or 1 tsp. almond extract
- 1/2 cup heavy cream, whipped to stiff peaks
- White-chocolate layer:
- 3/4 cup heavy cream
- 1 1/2 tsp. unflavored gelatin
- 6 oz. white chocolate chips
- 1/2 cup finely chopped almonds (can sub with walnuts)
- 1/2 cup heavy cream, whipped to stiff peaks
- Milk-chocolate layer:
- 8 0z. milk chocolate chips
- 1/4 cup butter
- 1 cup frozen raspberries, thawed, pureed and sieved to remove seeds
- 1/2 cup heavy cream, whipped to stiff peaks
- Raspberry sauce:
- 1 cup frozen raspberries, thawed
- 1 tbsp. cornstarch
- 1 tbsp. sugar
- unsweetened cocoa powder for decoration (optional)

Direction

- Grease an 8-inch loaf pan with non-stick cooking spray; line it with plastic wrap. Fill small roasting pan (or cookie pan) with dried beans. Wedge loaf pan into beans, tilting it lengthwise so that the first layer of dark chocolate mousse will be on one side of the pan. Note* instead of dried beans, I just use 2 small plates for support - one in the front and one in the back of the loaf pan. You just need something to keep it tilted until the mousse is hardened.
- Dark-chocolate layer: in saucepan over very low heat melt dark chocolate with butter, stirring constantly until smooth. Stir in liqueur or almond flavoring. Cool slightly. With a spatula, gently fold in the whipped cream. Pour mousse into loaf pan, smooth top. Refrigerate, tilted, until mousse is firm, about 1 hour.
- White-chocolate layer: In saucepan, combine 3/4 cup heavy cream and gelatine; let stand 5 minutes. Add white chocolate, heat over very low heat until melted, stirring constantly. Place pan in a bowl of ice water. Stir with a whisk until slightly thickened, for about 2 minutes. Remove from ice water, stir in almonds. With a spatula, gently fold in the whipped cream.
- Reposition the loaf pan to tilt in opposite direction. Add white chocolate mousse to the other side of the loaf pan. Chill until firm, for about 1 hour.
- Milk-chocolate layer: in saucepan over low heat, stir milk chocolate, butter and raspberry puree until smooth. Cool slightly, then fold in whipped cream with a spatula. Level the loaf pan. Add mousse over top, covering the dark and milk layers. At this point you don't need to support the loaf pan anymore. Cover the cake with the clear plastic wrap and smooth out the top. Refrigerate until firm, about 2 hours.
- Meanwhile, make the raspberry sauce: In food processor, puree thawed raspberries; strain into small saucepan so that there are no seeds. Stir cornstarch and sugar into puree. Bring to a low boil, stirring. Simmer 1 minute. Cool, refrigerate until serving.
- When the cake is firm, unmold it on a large plate, carefully remove the plastic wrap.
- When ready to serve, arrange a fork and a spoon on a plate. Dust with cocoa, remove utensils. This will make an imprint of the fork and spoon on the plate. This step is totally optional. Slice the mousse cake on the plate and drizzle some raspberry sauce.

325. To Die For Chocolate Cake Recipe

Serving: 10 | Prep: | Cook: 55mins | Ready in:

Ingredients

- 1 box devil's food cake mix
- 1 (3 oz.) box instant chocolate pudding
- 2 C. sour cream
- 5 eggs
- 1 C. melted butter
- 1 tsp. almond extract
- 1 C. chocolate chips

Direction

- In a large bowl, beat first 6 ingredients until well blended. Mixture will be thick. Stir in chocolate chips. Pour into greased Bundt pan. Bake at 350 degrees for 55 minutes. Dust with powdered sugar or chocolate glaze.

326. Triple Chocolate Cake Recipe

Serving: 12 | Prep: | Cook: 45mins | Ready in:

Ingredients

- 1 pkg(181/4oz) white cake mix
- 1/3 c sugar
- 4 eggs
- 1 c(8oz) sour cream
- 2/3 c canola oil
- 2 Tbs baking cocoa
- 1/2 c mniature semi-sweet chocolate chips
- 1 c chocolate frosting
- 2 Tbs. milk

Direction

- In large bowl, combine cake mix, sugar, sour cream and oil. Beat on low for 1 min; beat on med. for 2 mins. Pour half the batter into large bowl. Stir in cocoa till blended. Fold chocolate chips into white cake batter.
- Spoon batters alternately into greased and floured tube pan. Bake at 350 45 to 50 mins or till toothpick comes out clean.
- Cool 15 mins in pan before removing to rack to cool completely.
- In a small bowl, combine frosting and milk; spoon over top of cooled cake.

327. Triple Chocolate Coffee Cake Recipe

Serving: 9 | Prep: | Cook: 25mins | Ready in:

Ingredients

- 1 (18.25 oz) pkg devil's food cake mix
- 1 (3.9) oz pkg. chocolate instant pudding mix
- 2 c sour cream
- 1 c butter,softened
- 5 large eggs
- 1 tsp vanilla
- 3 c semi-sweet chocolate morsels,divided
- 1 c white chocolate morsels
- 1 c chopped pecans,toasted

Direction

- Preheat oven to 350 degrees. Beat first 6 ingredients at low speed with electric mixer 30 seconds or just till moistened; beat at medium speed 2 mins. Stir in 2 c semisweet chocolate morsels; pour batter evenly into 2 greased and floured 9" square cake pans.
- Bake for 25-30 mins or until a wooden pick comes out clean. Let cool completely in pans on wire racks.
- Microwave white chocolate morsels in glass bowl at high 30-60 seconds or till morsels melt, stirring at 30 second intervals until smooth. Drizzle evenly over cakes; repeat procedure

with remaining 1 c semisweet morsels. Spoon pecans over cakes. Cut in squares or wedges.
- Makes 2 cakes. 9 pieces per cake.

328. Triple Chocolate Pudding Cake With Raspberry Sauce Recipe

Serving: 8 | Prep: | Cook: 360mins | Ready in:

Ingredients

- Triple chocolate pudding cake with Raspberry Sauce
- vegetable cooking spray
- 1 package (about 18 ounces) chocolate cake mix
- 1 package (about 3.9 ounces) chocolate instant pudding and pie filling mix
- 2 cups sour cream
- 4 eggs
- 1 cup V8® 100% vegetable juice
- 3/4 cup vegetable oil
- 1 cup semi-sweet chocolate pieces
- Raspberry dessert topping
- whipped cream

Direction

- Spray the inside of a 4-quart slow cooker with the cooking spray.
- Beat the cake mix, pudding mix, sour cream, eggs, vegetable juice and oil in a large bowl with an electric mixer on medium speed for 2 minutes. Stir in the chocolate pieces. Pour the batter into the cooker.
- Cover and cook on LOW for 6 to 7 hours or until a knife inserted in the center comes out with moist crumbs. Serve with the raspberry topping and whipped cream.
- RECIPE TIPS
- Tip: Use your favorite chocolate cake mix and pudding mix flavor in this recipe: chocolate, devil's food, dark chocolate or chocolate fudge.
- Prep: 10 minutes
- Cook: 6 hours
- Makes: 12 servings (about 1/2 cup each)

329. Triple Nut Chocolate Upside Down Cake Recipe

Serving: 9 | Prep: | Cook: 40mins | Ready in:

Ingredients

- 1/4 cup butter
- 1/4 cup packed dark brown sugar
- 2/3 cup light-colored corn syrup
- 1/4 cup whipping cream
- 1/2 cup chopped pecans
- 1/2 cup chopped walnuts
- 1/2 cup chopped macadamia nuts
- 1-1/3 cups all-purpose flour
- 1/3 cup unsweetened cocoa powder
- 1 teaspoon baking powder
- 1/2 teaspoon baking soda
- 1/3 cup butter, softened
- 1 cup granulated sugar
- 2 eggs
- 1 teaspoon vanilla
- 2/3 cup milk

Direction

- Preheat oven to 350 degree F. Line a 9x9x2-inch baking pan with foil; grease foil. In a small saucepan melt 1/4 cup butter over medium heat. Stir in brown sugar. Cook and stir until sugar is dissolved. Stir in corn syrup and cream. Bring just to boiling. Stir in nuts. Spread in pan.
- Combine flour, cocoa powder, baking powder, baking soda, and 1/2 teaspoon salt; set aside. In a large mixing bowl beat 1/3 cup butter with electric mixer on medium to high speed for 30 seconds. Gradually add granulated sugar, beating on medium speed until well

combined, scraping sides of bowl. Add eggs, 1 at a time, beating after each (about 1 minute total). Beat in vanilla. Alternately add flour mixture and milk to butter mixture, beating on low speed after each addition just until combined. Pour into pan, being careful not to disturb nuts. Bake for 45 to 50 minutes or until a wooden toothpick inserted near center comes out clean. Cool in pan on wire rack 10 minutes. Remove from pan. Carefully peel off foil. Place nut side up on plate. Serve at room temperature.

330. Triple Layer Chocolate Mousse Cake Recipe

Serving: 1 | Prep: | Cook: 30mins | Ready in:

Ingredients

- cake Ingredients:
- 2 cups sugar
- 1 3/4 cups all purpose flour
- 3/4 cup cocoa
- 1 1/2 teaspoon baking powder
- 1 1/2 teaspoon baking soda
- 1 teaspoon salt
- 2 eggs
- 1 cup milk
- 1/2 cup vegetable oil
- 2 teaspoons vanilla extract
- 1 cup boiling water
- chocolate Mousse Ingredients:
- 1 envelope unflavored gelatin
- 2 tablespoons cold water
- 1/4 cup boiling water
- 1 cup sugar
- 1/2 cup cocoa
- 2 cups chilled whipping cream
- 2 teaspoons vanilla extract

Direction

- Heat oven to 350 degrees.
- Grease and flour three 8 inch round baking pans.
- In a large mixing bowl, stir together the sugar, flour, cocoa, baking soda, baking powder and salt.
- Add the eggs, milk, oil and vanilla. Beat on medium speed for 2 minutes. Stir in the boiling water (batter will be thin). Pour batter into the prepared pans.
- Bake 30 to 35 minutes or until wooden pick inserted in center comes out clean.
- Cool 10 minutes. Remove cakes from the pans and place on wire racks. Allow to cool completely.
- Prepare the chocolate mousse (recipe follows).
- Fill and frost the layers with the mousse. Garnish with almonds and chocolate curls, if desired.
- Refrigerate at least 1 hour. Cover and refrigerate leftover cake.
- Makes 10 to 12 servings.
- Mousse Directions:
- In a small bowl, sprinkle gelatine over cold water. Let stand 1 minute to soften.
- Add the boiling water. Stir until gelatine is completely dissolved and mixture is clear. Cool slightly.
- In a large cold mixing bowl, stir together sugar and cocoa.
- Add the whipping cream and vanilla. Beat on medium speed until stiff. Pour in the gelatine mixture and fold until well blended.
- Refrigerate about 1/2 hour. Makes about 4 cups.

331. Twisted German Chocolate Cake Recipe

Serving: 10 | Prep: | Cook: 35mins | Ready in:

Ingredients

- 1 box German Choc. cake mix
- 1 can sweetened condensed milk

- 1 (12 oz. jar) caramel ice cream topping
- 1/2 - 1 C. pecans
- Cool Whip Topping

Direction

- Mix and bake cake mix as directed.
- When cake is done, poke holes in top with the tip end of a wooden spoon or a big utility fork.
- Sprinkle nuts on top.
- Mix milk and ice cream topping together.
- Pour over nuts.
- Top with cool whip.
- Refrigerate any leftover.

332. Upside Down Chocolate Chip Cake Recipe

Serving: 8 | Prep: | Cook: 40mins | Ready in:

Ingredients

- 3 tablespoons butter
- 1/2 cup packed brown sugar
- 4 teaspoons water
- 1/2 cup coconut
- 1/2 cup coarsely chopped pecans
- 1 cup all-purpose flour
- 2/3 cup granulated sugar
- 1/2 cup unsweetened cocoa powder
- 1/4 cup packed brown sugar
- 2 teaspoons baking powder
- 1/2 cup milk
- 1/4 cup butter, softened
- 2 eggs
- 1 teaspoon vanilla
- 3/4 cup miniature semisweet chocolate pieces

Direction

- Preheat oven to 350 degree F. Melt the 3 tablespoons butter in a 9x1-1/2-inch round baking pan. Stir in the 1/2 cup brown sugar and the water. Sprinkle coconut and pecans in the pan. Set pan aside.
- In a medium mixing bowl stir together flour, granulated sugar, cocoa powder, the 1/4 cup brown sugar, and the baking powder. Add milk, the 1/4 cup butter, the eggs, and vanilla. Beat with an electric mixer on low speed until combined. Beat on medium speed for 1 minute. By hand, stir in 1/2 cup of the chocolate pieces. Spread batter into the prepared pan.
- Bake for 40 to 45 minutes or until cake feels firm in center when lightly touched. Cool on a wire rack for 5 minutes. Loose sides; invert onto a plate. Immediately sprinkle remaining miniature chocolate pieces over the topping. Let stand about 30 minutes before slicing. Serve warm.

333. Valentine Chocolate Cake Recipe

Serving: 8 | Prep: | Cook: 25mins | Ready in:

Ingredients

- 75grams butter
- 75grams caster sugar
- 2 eggs, lightly beaten
- 75 grams self raising flour
- ½ tsp baking powder
- 25 grams cocoa powder
- 50 grams ground almonds
- Truffle Topping
- 350 grams plain chocolate
- 100 gram butter
- 1 ¼ cups of heavy cream
- 75 grams chocolate cake crumbs
- 1/3 cup hazelnuts,crushed
- 100 grams white chocolate, melted
- 6-8 strawberries

Direction

- Preheat oven to 350 F.
- Lightly grease 20 cm cake pan and line the base. Beat together the butter and sugar until

light and fluffy. Gradually add the eggs, beating well after each addition.

- Sieve the flour, baking powder and cocoa powder together and fold into the mixture along with the ground almonds. Pour into the prepared pan and bake for 25 minutes or until springy to the touch. Leave to cool completely. Wash and dry the pan and return the cooled cake to the pan.
- Topping:
- Heat the chocolate, butter and cream in a heavy based pan and stir until smooth. Cool, and then chill for 30 minutes. Beat well with a wooden spoon and chill for a further 30 minutes. Beat the mixture again, and then add the cake crumbs and the hazelnuts, beating until well combined. Spoon over the sponge base.
- Dip each strawberry till half in white chocolate and arrange in a decorative way over the top.

334. Vegan Chocolate Cake Recipe

Serving: 8 | Prep: | Cook: 30mins | Ready in:

Ingredients

- 1 1/2 cups organic, unbleached flour, sifted(regular flour works)
- 3 Tablespoons organic cocoa powder, sifted(regular cocoa works)
- 1 tsp baking powder
- 1/2 tsp baking soda
- 3/4 cup evaporated cane juice (organic sugar) (regular sugar works)
- 1/4 tsp salt
- 5 T canola oil (may substitute safflower oil)
- 2 tsp raspberry vinegar *optional
- 1 tsp vanilla extract or 1/2 tsp almond extract
- 1 1/4 cup vanilla soy milk (if batter seems too thick, add more)

Direction

- Preheat oven to 350 F.
- Place flour, cocoa, baking powder and soda, sugar and salt in a medium size mixing bowl. Whisk to combine.
- Pour the soy milk, oil, vinegar, and vanilla into the flour mixture.
- Whisk the wet and dry ingredients together until smooth, then pour into a 9 x 9 inch baking pan. (Spray cake pan with non-stick cooking spray before pouring in cake batter.)
- Bake at 350 F for about 25 - 30 minutes; test with a toothpick. It is done when toothpick comes out clean. Cool on a cooling rack, then remove from pan. I find that cakes easily slip out of glass baking dishes once they have thoroughly cooled.

335. Vegan Chocolate Snack Cake Recipe

Serving: 9 | Prep: | Cook: 42mins | Ready in:

Ingredients

- 1 2/3 Cups flour
- 1 Cup brown sugar (packed)
- 1/4 Cup cocoa powder
- 1 Teaspoon baking soda
- 1/4 Teaspoon salt
- 1 Cup water
- 1/3 Cup vegetable oil
- 1 Teaspoon vinegar
- 1/2 Teaspoon vanilla
- powdered sugar (to taste)

Direction

- Preheat the oven to 350 degrees F, with the rack set to the center.
- Place all dry ingredients (flour, sugar, cocoa, baking soda, & salt) into an 8" square pan and mix thoroughly with a fork. Small balls of sugar and flour will form, make sure to crush them.

- Create a "crater" at the center of the pan, and add all liquid ingredients (water, oil, vanilla, & vinegar). Mix entire pan well, ensuring to scrape the sides and bottom.
- Bake for 35 to 40 minutes (your oven will vary some), or until a toothpick inserted into the center comes out clean.
- Lightly dust top of cake with powdered sugar.
- Variants to come in future recipe entries.

336. Very Rich Chocolate Fudge Cake Recipe

Serving: 8 | Prep: | Cook: 40mins | Ready in:

Ingredients

- 1 box devil's food cake mix
- 1 cup water
- 3 eggs
- 1/3 cup corn oil
- 1/3 cup sour cream
- 2 teaspoons vanilla
- 1/2 teaspoon kosher salt
- 1 cup semisweet chocolate chips
- Icing:
- 2 cups semisweet chocolate chips
- 2 cups granulated sugar
- 2/3 cup milk
- 2 sticks unsalted butter cut into pieces
- 1/4 teaspoon kosher salt
- 1 teaspoon vanilla

Direction

- Heat oven to 350.
- Butter 3 non-stick 8" cake pans
- Combine cake mix, water, eggs, oil, sour cream, vanilla and kosher salt in bowl of mixer.
- Fit with paddle attachment and beat on low speed until well blended.
- Increase speed to medium and beat for 2 minutes then stir in chocolate chips.
- Pour batter into pans and bake 25 minutes.
- To make icing put chocolate chips in metal bowl of a stand mixer fitted with whisk attachment.
- Combine sugar, milk, butter and salt in medium saucepan over high heat and bring to a boil.
- Stir occasionally then allow to boil vigorously for exactly 1 minute.
- Pour hot sugar mixture over chocolate then add vanilla.
- Beat on medium speed for 10 to 15 minutes.

337. White Chocolate Cake With Raspberry Filling Recipe

Serving: 12 | Prep: | Cook: 45mins | Ready in:

Ingredients

- 4 egg whites
- 1-3/4 cup all purpose flour
- 1 tablespoon finely shredded lemon peel
- 2 teaspoons baking powder
- 1/4 teaspoon salt
- 3 ounce white baking bar chopped
- 3/4 cup light cream
- 1/3 cup butter
- 1 cup granulated sugar
- 1 teaspoon vanilla
- 4 egg yolks
- 1 cup fresh raspberries
- 3 tablespoons raspberry liqueur
- 1/3 cup seedless raspberry jam
- 1/2 cup fresh raspberries
- powdered sugar
- White Chocolate Frosting:
- 4 ounce white baking bar chopped
- 1-1/2 cups whipping cream
- 1 tablespoon cold water
- 1/2 teaspoon unflavored gelatin
- 3 tablespoons granulated sugar

Direction

- In medium mixing bowl let egg whites stand at room temperature for 30 minutes.
- In a small mixing bowl stir together flour, lemon peel, baking powder and salt.
- Set flour mixture aside.
- Melt white baking bar with 1/4 cup cream in small saucepan over low heat stirring constantly.
- When chocolate starts to melt remove from heat and stir in remaining cream then allow to cool.
- In large mixing bowl beat butter with electric mixer on high speed until softened.
- Add sugar and vanilla then beat until combined.
- Add egg yolks one at a time beating until combined.
- Alternately add flour mixture and white baking bar mixture beating after each addition.
- Beat just until combined then was beaters.
- In medium mixing bowl beat egg whites with electric mixer on high speed until stiff peaks form.
- Gently fold egg whites into batter then spread into 2 greased and lightly floured round cake pans.
- Bake at 350 for 30 minutes then cool cakes in pans on racks 10 minutes then remove from pan.
- Cool cakes completely on racks.
- In small bowl combine berries and raspberry liqueur then set aside.
- To prepare frosting chill medium mixing bowl and beaters of an electric mixer.
- Place white baking bar and 1/4 cup cream in small heavy saucepan over very low heat.
- Stir constantly until baking bar starts to melt then remove from heat and stir until smooth.
- Cool completely.
- In a 1 cup glass measure combine cold water and unflavored gelatine and let stand 2 minutes.
- Place cup in saucepan of boiling water then heat and stir until gelatine is completely dissolved.
- In the chilled mixing bowl beat remaining cream and sugar with chilled beaters on medium speed while gradually drizzling gelatine over cream mixture then beat until soft peaks form.
- Continue beating gradually adding cooled baking bar mixture until stiff peaks form.
- To assemble cake place one cake layer on a cake plate.
- Drain liqueur from berries and drizzle liqueur over cake layer on plate then stir jam to soften.
- Spread jam over cake layer then top with 1/3 of the frosting and spoon 1 cup berries on top.
- Top berries with remaining cake layer then frost top and sides with remaining frosting.
- Gently place the chocolate curls on frosting on top of cake then refrigerate until serving time.
- Just before serving sprinkle cake with 1/2 cup berries and sift powdered sugar lightly over cake.

338. White Chocolate Cake With White Chocolate Frosting Recipe

Serving: 12 | Prep: | Cook: 45mins | Ready in:

Ingredients

- 1/3 Cup white chocolate (cut in small pieces)
- 1/2 Cup hot water
- 1 Cup butter(no substitutes!)
- 1 1/2 Cup white granulated sugar
- 4 egg yolks, unbeaten
- 1 teaspoon vanilla
- 2 1/2 Cups cake flour
- 1 teaspoon baking soda
- 1 Cup buttermilk
- 4 egg whites, stiffly beaten
- Frosting:
- 1/2 Cup plus 2 tablespoons sugar
- 6 Tablespoons evaporated milk
- 1/4 Cup butter
- 2 Cups white chocolate(cut in small pieces)

- 1 1/2 teaspoons vanilla
- white chocolate curls for garnish(optional)
- toasted nuts for garnish(optional)

Direction

- Preheat oven to 350 degrees F.
- Grease and flour 3 -9 inch layer pans.
- Melt white chocolate in hot water; cool.
- Cream butter and sugar until light and fluffy.
- Add egg yolks. Beat.
- Add white chocolate and vanilla.
- Sift flour and soda together, add alternately with buttermilk to creamed mixture.
- Fold in stiffly beaten egg whites.
- Frosting:
- Combine milk, sugar, and butter in saucepan. Bring to full, rolling boil and boil 1(one) minute. Remove from heat and add white chocolate and vanilla. Stir until candy is melted. Beat until spreading consistency. Frost 3-layer cake.
- Spread slowly, cool if icing is too loose, heat if too stiff.
- Garnish with the chocolate curls and/or nuts.
- Use a serrated edge knife to cut cake.

339. White Chocolate Coconut Cake Recipe

Serving: 8 | Prep: | Cook: 35mins | Ready in:

Ingredients

- 1 cup butter
- 2 cups sugar
- 4 eggs, beaten
- 4 ounces white chocolate, melted
- 2 1/2 cups flour
- 1 teasp. baking powder
- 1 teasp. vanilla extract
- 1 cup buttermilk
- 1 cup pecans or walnuts, chopped
- 1 cup flaked coconut

Direction

- Cream butter and sugar with an electric mixer.
- Add eggs and melted chocolate, blend well.
- Add flour, baking powder, vanilla, buttermilk, chopped nuts and the coconut. Blend well.
- Pour into 3 greased 9-inch round cake pans.
- Bake at 350'F for 35 minutes.
- Cool cake.
- Ice with white chocolate icing* or your favorite icing and garnish with white chocolate or milk chocolate curls.
- * Recipe to follow

340. White Chocolate Fruit Cake Recipe

Serving: 48 | Prep: | Cook: 45mins | Ready in:

Ingredients

- 2/3 cup sliced almonds
- 1 1/4 cups brazil nuts - coursely chopped
- 1 1/2 cups coconut
- 1 cup dried apricots - chopped
- 1 cup currants
- 1/4 cups all-purpose flour
- 250g white chocolate - melted
- 1/2 cup apricot jam
- 1/2 cup honey
- .
- 1 Tblspn icing sugar

Direction

- Pre-heat oven between 325 - 350 degrees.
- Lightly grease 19cm x 29cm baking pan.
- Line base with wax paper & grease paper.
- Combine melted chocolate, jam & honey in a small bowl - set aside.
- Combine nuts, coconut, fruit & flour in a large bowl.
- Stir in chocolate mixture until well combined.
- Spread evenly in prepared pan

- Bake 45 mins or until a toothpick inserted in center comes out clean.
- Cool in pan on wire rack.
- When completely cool, dust with the 1 Tbsp. icing sugar.
- Can be kept in the fridge for 1 week or in the freezer for 2 months.

341. White Chocolate Mousse Cake Recipe

Serving: 14 | Prep: | Cook: 10mins | Ready in:

Ingredients

- 3 Tablespoons butter, divided
- 3/4 cup chocolate wafer crumbs
- 1/2 cup water
- 12 ounces white chocolate, chopped
- 4 eggs(I use Davidson's pasteurized eggs), separated at room temperature
- 3 tablespoons white Creme de Cacao liqueur
- 2 squares(1 ounce each) unsweetened chocolate,chopped
- 3 cups heavy or whipping cream
- White and dark chocolate curls or grated chocolate for garnish
- 1/8 tsp cream of tartar
- pinch salt
- 2 tbsp sugar

Direction

- Preheat oven to 350degreesF. In a small saucepan melt 2 tbsp. butter over low heat. Stir crumbs. Pat evenly in the bottom of a deep 9-inch springform pan. Bake 10 minutes. Cool 10 minutes.
- In saucepan bring the water to a boil. Add white chocolate and stir until partially melted. Remove from heat and beat until smooth. Cool slightly. Beat in egg yolks; cool completely. Beat in liqueur.
- In small saucepan melt unsweetened chocolate and remaining 1 tablespoon butter over low heat. Cool. In bowl beat cream until stiff peaks form. In another bowl beat egg whites until frothy. Add cream of tartar and salt. Gradually add sugar, beating constantly, until stiff but not dry. Fold one third of the egg whites into white chocolate mixture; fold back into egg whites. Fold in whipped cream.
- To make dark chocolate layer, transfer about 3 cups mixture to a medium bowl. Fold about 1/2 cup into dark chocolate; fold back into reserved mixture.
- Pour half the white chocolate mixture evenly into prepared pan. Carefully pour on dark chocolate mixture, gently spread with spatula. Pour remaining white chocolate mixture in pan; smooth top. Place in freezer 1 hour or until top begins to set. Garnish top with chocolate curls. Wrap well and freeze 24 hours. (Can be made ahead. Cover and freeze up to 1 week)
- Let stand at room temperature 20 minutes before serving.

342. White Chocolate Mousse Sweet Potato Cake Recipe

Serving: 10 | Prep: | Cook: 80mins | Ready in:

Ingredients

- 2 pounds sweet potatoes * 2 pounds of pumpkin can be substituted for sweet potatoes
- 1/4 cups vegetable oil
- unsalted butter for pans
- 2 cups cake flour, (not self rising) plus more for pans
- 4 large eggs
- 2 cups sugar
- 2 tablespoons baking powder
- 1 teaspoon salt
- 1 tablespoon ground cinnamon
- 1 teaspoon nutmeg
- 2 teaspoons pure vanilla extract

- 3 tablespoons Nocello walnut liqueur or brandy
- 1/12/ cups unsalted macadamia nuts, toasted, coarsely chopped
- 1 pound white chocolate
- 1/2 pound dark chocolate (for leaves) optional
- 2 cups heavy cream

Direction

- 1. Heat oven to 400 degrees. Coat potatoes with 1/4 cup vegetable oil, and place on baking sheet. Bake until tender, 30 to 40 minutes. When cool enough to handle, remove skin, and mash flesh with a fork into coarse puree.
- 2. Lower oven temperature to 325 degrees. Butter two 8-by-1 1/2 -inch round cake pans, dust with flour, and set aside. In the bowl of an electric mixer fitted with the paddle attachment, beat eggs and sugar together on medium-high speed until light and fluffy, about 5 minutes. Add remaining 1 cup vegetable oil; beat on medium speed until well combined. Add the cooled sweet potatoes; mix until combined.
- 3. Sift together cake flour, baking powder, salt, cinnamon, and nutmeg; mix into sweet potato mixture. Mix in vanilla and Nocello until combined. Remove batter from mixer; fold in 1 cup macadamia nuts by hand.
- 4. Evenly distribute cake batter into prepared pans, and transfer to the oven. Bake until a toothpick inserted in center comes out clean, 40 to 45 minutes. Let pans cool on a wire rack 10 minutes. Invert cakes onto rack; cool completely, about 1 1/4 hours.
- 5. Meanwhile, chop white chocolate into small pieces; set aside. Bring 1 cup cream to a boil; pour over chocolate, whisking until chocolate is melted. Chill for 30 to 40 minutes.
- 6. When chocolate mixture has cooled, pour remaining cup cream into an electric mixer; whip on medium until soft peaks form, about 3 minutes. Fold whipped cream into chocolate mixture until fully incorporated.
- 7. Cut each cake layer in half horizontally, creating four layers. Spread 2/3 cup chocolate frosting on one layer, then stack next layer on top, and frost. Repeat frosting-and-stacking process until each layer is frosted. Spread remaining frosting on sides and top of cake.
- 8. Cut out 6 leaf shapes using parchment paper.
- 9. Melt dark chocolate in microwave and brush on cut out parchment leaf shapes, then place them onto a soup bowl that has been turned over.
- 10 place leaves in freezer for 3 minutes repeat coating leaves with chocolate 3 more times and set aside.
- 11 carefully remove leaves from soup bowl and place on top of cake.
- Drizzle some melted dark chocolate with a teaspoon over cake top.
- Arrange remaining 1/2 cup macadamia nuts on top of cake, and serve. Serves 8 to 10. (I had to guess on prep time)

343. White Chocolate Mud Cake Recipe

Serving: 12 | Prep: | Cook: 60mins | Ready in:

Ingredients

- 250 grs butter
- 150 grs white chocolate, chopped coarsely
- 2 cups caster sugar
- 1 cup milk
- 2 cups self-raising flour
- 1 tsp vanilla essence
- 2 eggs lightly beaten
- *****
- For the white chocolate ganache:
- 1/2 cup cream
- 300 grs white chocolate, chopped coarsely

Direction

- Grease a deep 20 cm-round cake pan.

- Line base and side with baking paper.
- Combine butter, chocolate, sugar and milk in medium saucepan.
- Stir over low heat, WITHOUT BOILING, until smooth.
- Transfer mixture to a large bowl.
- Cool 15 minutes.
- Pre-heat oven to moderately slow.
- Whisk flower into mixture, together with vanilla and eggs.
- Pour mixture into prepared pan.
- Cover pan with foil.
- Bake for 45 minutes.
- Remove foil and bake further 15 minutes.
- Stand cake in pan for 30 minutes.
- Turn onto wire rack to cool.
- Spread top and side of cold cake with white chocolate ganache.
- ***
- White chocolate ganache:
- Bring cream to a boil in small saucepan. Pour over chocolate in small bowl, stirring until chocolate melts.
- Cover.
- Refrigerate, stirring occasionally, about 30 minutes or until spreadable.

344. White Chocolate Sweet Potato Cake Recipe

Serving: 10 | Prep: | Cook: 40mins | Ready in:

Ingredients

- 2 pounds sweet potatoes, (about 3)
- 1 1/4 cups vegetable oil
- unsalted butter, for pans
- 2 cups cake flour, (NOT self-rising), plus more for pans
- 4 large eggs
- 2 cups sugar
- 2 teaspoons baking powder
- 1 teaspoon salt
- 1 tablespoon ground cinnamon
- 1 teaspoon ground nutmeg
- 2 teaspoons pure vanilla extract
- 3 tablespoons brandy
- 1 1/2 cups unsalted macadamia nuts, toasted, coarsely chopped
- 1 pound white chocolate
- 2 cups heavy cream

Direction

- Heat oven to 400 degrees. Coat potatoes with 1/4 cup vegetable oil, and place on baking sheet. Bake until tender, 30 to 40 minutes. When cool enough to handle, remove skin, and mash flesh with a fork into coarse puree.
- Lower oven temperature to 325 degrees. Butter two 8-by-1 1/2-inch round cake pans, dust with flour, and set aside. In the bowl of an electric mixer fitted with the paddle attachment, beat eggs and sugar together on medium-high speed until light and fluffy, about 5 minutes. Add remaining 1 cup vegetable oil; beat on medium speed until well combined. Add the cooled sweet potatoes; mix until combined.
- Sift together cake flour, baking powder, salt, cinnamon, and nutmeg; mix into sweet potato mixture. Mix in vanilla and brandy until combined. Remove batter from mixer; fold in 1 cup macadamia nuts by hand.
- Evenly distribute cake batter into prepared pans, and transfer to the oven. Bake until a toothpick inserted in center comes out clean, 40 to 45 minutes. Let pans cool on a wire rack 10 minutes. Invert cakes onto rack; cool completely, about 1 1/4 hours.
- Meanwhile, chop white chocolate into small pieces; set aside. Bring 1 cup cream to a boil; pour over chocolate, whisking until chocolate is melted. Chill for 30 to 40 minutes.
- When chocolate mixture has cooled, pour remaining cup cream into an electric mixer; whip on medium until soft peaks form, about 3 minutes. Fold whipped cream into chocolate mixture until fully incorporated.
- Cut each cake layer in half horizontally, creating four layers. Spread 2/3 cup chocolate

frosting on one layer, then stack next layer on top, and frost. Repeat frosting-and-stacking process until each layer is frosted. Spread remaining frosting on sides and top of cake. Arrange remaining 1/2 cup macadamia nuts on top of cake, and serve. Serves 8 to 10. (I had to guess on prep time)

345. White Chocolate Truffle And Chocolate Fudge Layer Cake Recipe

Serving: 12 | Prep: | Cook: 35mins | Ready in:

Ingredients

- **********chocolate stars
- 6 ounces bittersweet (not unsweetened) or semisweet chocolate, chopped
- 1 tablespoon solid vegetable shortening
- Nonstick vegetable oil spray
- **********cake
- 4 ounces unsweetened chocolate, chopped
- 1 3/4 cups all purpose flour
- 1/4 cup unsweetened cocoa powder
- 1 teaspoon baking powder
- 3/4 teaspoon baking soda
- 1/2 teaspoon salt
- 2 cups sugar
- 1/2 cup (1 stick) unsalted butter, room temperature
- 2 teaspoons vanilla extract
- 2 large eggs
- 1 1/2 cups whole milk
- *****Filling and frosting
- 3 cups chilled whipping cream
- 1/4 cup (1/2 stick) unsalted butter, cut into pieces
- 1 pound good-quality white chocolate (such as Lindt or Baker's), finely chopped
- 2 teaspoons vanilla extract
- 1/2 teaspoon almond extract
- 4 tablespoons Amaretto or other almond liqueur

Direction

- **********For chocolate stars:
- Line baking sheet with foil.
- Stir chocolate and shortening in top of double boiler set over simmering water until melted and smooth.
- Pour onto prepared baking sheet, tilting pan to spread chocolate mixture to irregular 14x9-inch rectangle.
- Refrigerate until just firm, about 12 minutes.
- Spray assorted star-shaped cookie cutters with non-stick spray.
- Cut out stars.
- Refrigerate until firm, about 30 minutes.
- Using small offset spatula, carefully transfer stars 1 at a time to another foil-lined baking sheet.
- Refrigerate until ready to use.
- (Can be made 3 days ahead. Cover and keep refrigerated.)
- ****************For cake:
- Preheat oven to 350°F.
- Butter two 9-inch-diameter cake pans with 1 1/2-inch-high sides.
- Line bottoms with parchment paper; butter parchment.
- Stir unsweetened chocolate in heavy medium saucepan over low heat until melted and smooth.
- Cool slightly.
- Sift flour, cocoa powder, baking powder, baking soda, and salt into medium bowl.
- Using electric mixer, beat sugar and butter in large bowl until well blended.
- Beat in lukewarm melted unsweetened chocolate and vanilla.
- Beat in eggs, 1 at a time, blending well after each addition.
- Mix in cocoa powder mixture in 3 additions, alternating with milk in 2 additions.
- Divide batter between prepared pans.
- Bake cakes until tester inserted into center comes out clean, about 35 minutes.
- Cool cakes in pans on racks 10 minutes.
- Run knife around edge of each pan to loosen cakes.

- Turn cakes out onto racks and cool completely.
- Peel off parchment.
- **********For filling and frosting:
- Bring 1 cup cream and butter to simmer in heavy medium saucepan over medium heat, stirring until butter melts.
- Remove from heat. Add white chocolate and stir until smooth.
- Whisk in vanilla.
- Pour 1 1/2 cups white chocolate filling into small bowl; cover and freeze until cold, about 2 hours.
- Let remaining white chocolate mixture in saucepan stand at room temperature until lukewarm, about 20 minutes.
- Using electric mixer, beat remaining 2 cups cream and almond extract in large bowl until peaks form. Working in 3 batches, fold in lukewarm white chocolate mixture.
- Refrigerate whipped cream frosting just until medium peaks hold, folding occasionally, about 3 hours.
- Brush 2 tablespoons amaretto over top of each cake layer.
- Place 1 layer on platter.
- Spread chilled 1 1/2 cups white chocolate filling over.
- Top with second cake layer.
- Spread whipped cream frosting over top and sides of cake.
- Chill until cold and set, about 1 hour.
- (Can be made 1 day ahead. Cover and keep refrigerated.)
- Arrange chocolate stars decoratively atop cake and serve.

346. White Chocolate OPERA Cake Recipe

Serving: 20 | Prep: | Cook: 12mins | Ready in:

Ingredients

- For the joconde:
- 6 large egg whites, at room temperature
- 2 tbsp. (30 grams) granulated sugar
- 2 cups (225 grams) ground blanched almonds
- 2 cups icing sugar, sifted
- 6 large eggs
- ½ cup (70 grams) all-purpose flour
- 3 tbsp. (1½ ounces; 45 grams) unsalted butter, melted and cooled

Direction

- Divide the oven into thirds by positioning a rack in the upper third of the oven and the lower third of the oven.
- Preheat the oven to 425°F. (220°C).
- Line two 12½ x 15½- inch (31 x 39-cm) jelly-roll pans with parchment paper and brush with melted butter.
- In the bowl of a stand mixer fitted with the whisk attachment (or using a handheld mixer), beat the egg whites until they form soft peaks. Add the granulated sugar and beat until the peaks are stiff and glossy. If you do not have another mixer bowl, gently scrape the meringue into another bowl and set aside.
- In another bowl beat the eggs, sugar and almonds on medium speed until light and voluminous, about 3 minutes. Add the flour and beat on low speed until the flour is just combined (be very careful not to over mix here!).
- Using a rubber spatula, gently fold the meringue into the almond mixture and then fold in the melted butter. Divide the batter between the pans and spread it evenly to cover the entire surface of each pan.
- Bake the cake layers until they are lightly browned and just springy to the touch. This could take anywhere from 5 to 9 minutes depending on your oven. Place one jelly-roll pan in the middle of the oven and the second jelly-roll pan in the bottom third of the oven.
- Put the pans on a heatproof counter and run a sharp knife along the edges of the cake to loosen it from the pan. Cover each with a sheet

of parchment or wax paper, turn the pans over, and unmold.
- Carefully peel away the parchment, then turn the parchment over and use it to cover the cakes. Let the cakes cool to room temperature
- For the soaking syrup:
- ½ cup (125 grams) water
- ⅓ cup (65 grams) granulated sugar
- 1 to 2 tbsp. of the flavoring of your choice (i.e., vanilla extract, almond extract, cognac, Limon cello, coconut cream, honey etc.) I used lemon.
- Stir all the syrup ingredients together in the saucepan and bring to a boil. Remove from the heat and let cool to room temperature.
- For the butter cream:
- 1 cup (100 grams) granulated sugar
- ¼ cup (60 grams) water.
- Seeds of one vanilla bean (split a vanilla bean down the middle and scrape out the seeds) or 1 tbsp. pure vanilla extract
- 1 large egg
- 1 large egg yolk
- 1¾ sticks (7 ounces; 200 grams) unsalted butter, at room temperature.
- Flavouring of your choice (a tablespoon of an extract, a few tablespoons of melted white chocolate, citrus zest, etc.) I didn't use any.
- Combine the sugar, water and vanilla bean seeds or extract in a small saucepan and warm over medium heat just until the sugar dissolves. Continue to cook, without stirring, until the syrup reaches 225°F (107°C) on a candy thermometer. Once it reaches that temperature, remove the syrup from the heat. While the syrup is heating, begin whisking the egg and egg yolk at high speed in the bowl of your mixer using the whisk attachment. Whisk them until they are pale and foamy.
- When the sugar syrup reaches the correct temperature and you remove it from the heat, reduce the mixer speed to low speed and begin slowly (very slowly) pouring the syrup down the side of the bowl being very careful not to splatter the syrup into the path of the whisk attachment. Some of the syrup will spin onto the sides of the bowl but don't worry about this and don't try to stir it into the mixture as it will harden!
- Raise the speed to medium-high and continue beating until the eggs are thick and satiny and the mixture is cool to the touch (about 5 minutes or so). While the egg mixture is beating, place the softened butter in a bowl and mash it with a spatula until you have a soft creamy mass. With the mixer on medium speed, begin adding in two-tablespoon chunks. When all the butter has been incorporated, raise the mixer speed to high and beat until the butter cream is thick and shiny. At this point add in your flavoring and beat for an additional minute or so.
- Refrigerate the butter cream, stirring it often, until it's set enough (firm enough) to spread when topped with a layer of cake (about 20 minutes).
- For the white chocolate ganache:
- 7 ounces white chocolate
- 1 cup plus 3 tbsp. heavy cream
- Melt the white chocolate and the 3 tbsp. of heavy cream in a small saucepan. Stir to ensure that it's smooth and that the chocolate is melted. Set aside to cool completely. In the bowl of a stand mixer, whip the remaining 1 cup of heavy cream until soft peaks form. Gently fold the whipped cream into the cooled chocolate to form a mousse. If it's too thin, refrigerate it for a bit until its spread able. If you're not going to use it right away, refrigerate until you're ready to use.
- For the chocolate ganache:
- 8 ounces plain chocolate, chopped
- 1 cup heavy cream
- Heat cream until simmering point and pour over the chopped chocolate. Stir until smooth and cool completely stirring occasionally until thickened.
- To assemble:
- Place the first cake on a serving platter, brush with syrup. Spread half of the butter cream over and then spread the white chocolate ganache carefully. (I only used three quarters of the mixture). Top with the other cake and brush also with syrup. Spread the rest of the

butter cream and then spread the plain chocolate mixture carefully. Chill
- For the glaze:
- 14 ounces white chocolate, coarsely chopped
- ½ cup heavy cream.
- Melt the white chocolate with the heavy cream. Whisk the mixture gently until smooth. Let cool for 10 minutes and then pour over the chilled cake. Using a long metal cake spatula, smooth out into an even layer. Place the cake into the refrigerator for 30 minutes to set.
- For decoration:
- Use melted chocolate to make any decorative pattern of your choice.

347. White Chocolate Mousse Cake 2 Recipe

Serving: 10 | Prep: | Cook: 40mins | Ready in:

Ingredients

- cake ingredients:
- 60 grams plain chocolate, chopped
- 15 grams unsweetened cocoa powder (not Dutch-processed)
- ½ cup boiling water
- 160 grams all purpose flour
- 1 teaspoon baking powder
- 1/2 teaspoon baking soda
- Pinch of salt
- 115 grams unsalted butter, room temperature
- 227grams granulated white sugar
- 2 eggs
- 1 teaspoon pure vanilla extract
- ½ cup milk
- Mousse
- 340 grams good-quality white chocolate (such as Lindt or Baker's), chopped
- 1 1/2 cups chilled whipping cream
- 3 large egg whites
- 12 strawberry halves
- cocoa powder.

Direction

- Cake:
- Preheat oven to 350 degrees. Butter and line with parchment paper, a 23 x 5 cm loose bottomed baking pan. Set aside.
- In a stainless steel or heatproof bowl place the chopped chocolate and cocoa powder. Pour the boiling water over the chocolate and cocoa powder and stir until they have melted. Set aside to cool while you make the batter.
- In a separate bowl, whisk to combine, the flour, baking powder, baking soda, and salt. Set aside.
- In the bowl of your electric mixer, cream the butter. Gradually add the sugar and continue beating until the mixture is fluffy (this will take about 3-5 minutes). Add the eggs, one at a time, mixing well after each addition. Add the vanilla extract and melted chocolate mixture and beat to combine.
- Add the milk and flour mixtures in three additions, beginning and ending with the flour mixture. Beat only until the ingredients are incorporated.
- Pour the batter in the prepared pan and smooth the top. Bake for about 35 - 40 minutes or until a toothpick inserted in the center comes out clean. Remove from oven and place on a wire rack to cool for about 10 minutes.
- When completely cooled, split the cake in half horizontally; place one half in the same baking pan after you have washed it and save the other half for another use. Arrange the
- Strawberry halves in the small empty space between the pan and the cake.
- Mousse:
- Stir white chocolate and 3/4 cup cream in heavy medium saucepan over low heat just until white chocolate is melted. Cool completely.
- Beat remaining 3/4 cup cream in another large bowl until peaks form. Using clean dry beaters beat egg whites in medium bowl until stiff but not dry. Gently fold whites, then whipped cream, into white chocolate mixture. Spoon mousse over cake and chill 3-4

Hours or overnight. Decorate with sifted cocoa powder and one large strawberry.

348. White Chocolate Strawberry Mousse Cake Recipe

Serving: 8 | Prep: | Cook: 30mins | Ready in:

Ingredients

- Sponge cake:
- 5 eggs
- 1 teaspoon vanilla powder
- 150 grams sugar
- 110 grams flour
- 50 grams corn starch
- pinch of salt
- Mousse:
- 2 cups strawberries
- 2 tablespoons fresh lemon juice, divided
- 240 grams white chocolate, finely chopped and MELTED
- 1 1/4 teaspoon unflavored gelatin powder
- 2 cups heavy cream
- 2 tablespoons powdered (confectioner's) sugar
- Garnish:
- 16 strawberry halfs
- whipped cream

Direction

- Cake:
- 1-Preheat oven to 350F, grease a 20cm loose bottom cake pan with butter. Line in parchment paper and grease the paper.
- 2-In the bowl of electric mixer, beat together the eggs, sugar and vanilla powder beginning at low speed and increasing to medium high speed for 10 minutes.
- 3-Sift together the flour, corn starch and salt and fold it in the eggs mixture using a rubber spatula or a large spoon making circular motion from bottom to top. Be patient and make it slowly till all dry mixture is incorporated with the eggs mixture.
- 4- Pour in the pan and bake for 30-40minutes till spongy and a sharp knife inserted in middle comes out clean.
- 5-Take out and cool completely, Using a serrated knife, cut the cake horizontal in half. Put the bottom half back in the pan (after it has been washed) and keep aside. You may cover the other half tightly in the fridge for another use.
- Mousse:
- 1-Put all of the strawberries with 1 tbsp. lemon juice in a blender and mix till puree.
- 2-Put 1/4 cup of cool water into a small bowl. Sprinkle the gelatine powder over the water and let sit for 5 minutes.
- 3-Stir 1/4 cup of the cream and the 2 Tbsp. of powdered sugar in a small saucepan, bring to a simmer over medium heat. Add the gelatine mixture and stir until the gelatine has dissolved. Pour into the bowl of melted chocolate, and stir until smooth.
- Whisk in 3/4 cup of the strawberry puree. Reserve the remaining 1/4 cup of puree. Using an electric mixer, whip the remaining 1 3/4 cup of cream. Beat on medium-high speed until medium peaks form. Whisk one third of the whipped cream into the chocolate mixture.
- 4-Using a large rubber spatula, gently fold the remaining whipped cream into the mixture. Refrigerate for 1 hour.
- 5-Stir the remaining 1 Tbsp. of lemon juice into the reserved sliced berries. Fold the sliced berries into the mousse. Arrange some strawberries halves all around the side of the pan .Spoon mousse over the sponge cake in the pan and level the top. Chill for 4-6 hours.
- 6-Garnish with whipped cream and strawberry halves.

349. White Chocolate Truffle Cake And Mango Pana Cotta Recipe

Serving: 10 | Prep: | Cook: 30mins | Ready in:

Ingredients

- Dacquoise:
- 2 cups toasted hazelnuts
- 1 cup sugar, plus 1/4 cup additional
- 2 tablespoons cornstarch
- 7 medium egg whites
- Pinch of salt
- 2 teaspoons vanilla extract
- 1/4 teaspoon almond extract
- Truffle Topping:
- 1 1/4 cups heavy cream
- 12 ounces white chocolate, broken into pieces
- 1 1/4 cups cream cheese
- 24cm sponge cake layer
- mango pana cotta:
- 2 Cups mango puree
- 2 cups heavy cream
- 3 cups yogurt
- 12 tablespoons sugar
- 2 tsp vanilla essence
- 2 packets unflavored gelatin (2 tsp each)
- 1/4 cup cold water

Direction

- Prepare a silicon baking sheet and draw 2 24cm circle on each. Set aside. Set racks in the lower third of the oven and preheat to 300°F (145°C).
- Place the nuts in a food processor fitted with a metal blade and pulse until coarsely ground. In a bowl, combine the nuts with 1 cup of the sugar and the cornstarch.
- In the bowl of an electric mixer, use the whisk attachment on medium-low speed to whip the egg whites and salt until white and frothy, about 2 minutes. Increase the speed and slowly beat in 1/4 cup of sugar in a stream until the whites form firm peaks. Beat in the extracts. Slowly fold the nut mixture into the whites with a rubber spatula until thoroughly combined. Transfer the mixture to a pastry bag fitted with a 1/2-inch plain round tip and pipe the meringue on the prepared pans into spirals starting at the center of each circle. Bake the dacquoise layers until they're golden and firm, about 90 minutes, rotating the pans halfway through baking. Cool on racks.
- To make the truffle topping, place the cream in a pan and bring to a boil, stirring to prevent it from sticking to the bottom of the pan. Allow to cool slightly, then add the white chocolate pieces, and stir until melted and combined.
- Remove the pan from the heat and stir until almost cool, then stir in the cream cheese (room temperature).
- Mango layer:
- Add the gelatine to cold water and let it soften. Meanwhile whisk together yogurt and mango puree in a bowl till they are combined well together.
- Heat cream in a pot. Add vanilla essence and sugar. Whisk very lightly to mix. When the cream comes to a boil, remove from heat and add softened gelatine.
- Stir well till the entire gelatine is dissolved. Add the cream to the mango yogurt mixture and whisk well.
- Pour in a 20cm glass dish and refrigerate for 3-4 hours.
- Assembly:
- Place the 24cm dacquoise disc into a loose bottom cake ring. Pour 1/3 of the white chocolate mixture over. Top with the sponge cake layer. Pour another 1/3 of the white chocolate mixture. Dip the 20cm mango glass plate in hot water for 30 seconds and flip the panna cotta disc over the white chocolate mousse. Finish with the last 1/3 of the white chocolate mousse. Chill overnight and decorate with cocoa powder hazelnut praline on the sides.

350. Worlds Most Dangerous Chocolate Cake Recipe

Serving: 1 | Prep: | Cook: 3mins | Ready in:

Ingredients

- 1 microwave safe coffee mug (mug, not cup)
- 4 tablespoons all-purpose flour
- 4 tablespoons sugar
- 2 tablespoons baking cocoa
- 1 egg
- 3 tablespoons milk
- 3 tablespoons oil
- 3 tablespoons chocolate chips(optional)
- a small splash of vanilla essence

Direction

- Add dry ingredients to mug, and mix well
- Add the egg and mix thoroughly.
- Pour in the milk and oil and mix well.
- Add the chocolate chips (if using) and vanilla essence, and mix again.
- Put your mug in the microwave and cook for 3 minutes at 1000 watts. The cake will rise over the top of the mug, but don't be alarmed!
- Allow to cool a little, and tip out onto a plate if desired.
- NOTE: It really works!

351. Xtra Moist Chocolate Cake Recipe

Serving: 6 | Prep: | Cook: 35mins |Ready in:

Ingredients

- Cake:
- 500 ml (2 cups)cake flour
- 350 ml (1 1/2 cup)sugar
- pinch of salt
- 125 g (1/2 cup) butter or margarine
- 125 ml (1/2 cup) cocoa powder
- 5 ml (1 teaspoon) baking soda
- 125 ml (1/2 cup) buttermilk
- 2 eggs
- 250 ml (1 cup) water
- Frosting:
- 75 ml (1/4 cup + 1 heaped tablespoon) butter or margarine
- 75 ml (1/4 cup + 1 tablespoon) buttermilk
- 30 ml (2 heaped tablespoons) cocoa powder
- 375 ml (1 1/2 cup) icing sugar
- 5 ml (1 teaspoon)vanilla essence

Direction

- Sift the flour, sugar and salt together.
- Heat up the butter, water, oil and cocoa.
- Let it cool down a bit.
- Mix the buttermilk and baking soda.
- Beat the eggs into the buttermilk mixture.
- Mix the flour and buttermilk mixtures together.
- Bake in a square baking tin at 200 degrees C (390 deg F) for 20 minutes.
- Frosting:
- Heat up the butter, buttermilk and cocoa.
- Bring to the boil.
- Remove from stove.
- Sift in the icing sugar while stirring.
- Stir in the vanilla essence.
- Pour hot sauce over hot cake.
- Let it cool down in the fridge.
- Serve.

352. YIN YANG CHOCOLATE CAKE WITH MARZIPAN DECORATIONS Recipe

Serving: 24 | Prep: | Cook: 60mins |Ready in:

Ingredients

- The basic cake was a 'chocolate Sponge cake'...
- Ingredients for cake:
- eggs - 8
- powdered sugar - 200gms
- flour - 150 gms
- cocoa - 6 tbsps
- cornflour - 4 tbsp
- baking powder - 2 tsps
- salt - 1/2 tsp

- vanilla essence - 2 tsps
- Red food colour - 4-5 drops (optional)
- Filling:
- Cream - 400ml (35% whipping cream)
- Castor sugar - 5-6 tbsps (to taste)
- vanilla extract - 1tsp
- Ganache:
- dark chocolate - 400gms
- Cream - 300ml
- marzipan recipe posted earlier.

Direction

- Method:
- Preheat the oven to 180 degrees C. Line & grease 2 spring form 10" tins. (I made 2 cakes in 2 batches/ 4 eggs each time since I have just 1 tin)
- Sift the flour + cocoa + cornflour + baking powder + salt 3 times.
- Beat eggs & powdered sugar for approx. 10 minutes till mousse like & thick.
- Add vanilla essence & food colour & beat.
- Fold in the flour mix, 1 tbsp. at a time, gently so that the beaten air doesn't escape.
- Turn gently into tins & bake 25-30 minutes till done. Turn out onto racks & cool.
- Cut each cake horizontally to get 4 layers (2 from each cake)
- This was enough for about 25 servings. (You can half the weights; remember to use smaller size tins too.)
- Filling:
- Whip the cream + sugar + extract till the cream is thick & holds shape.
- Sandwich the layers of the sponge with the cream (1/3rd each time).
- Can be done a day in advance. Keep it covered in the fridge.
- Ganache:
- Break the chocolate into pieces & put it in a pan with the cream
- Melt it over low heat, stirring constantly.
- Take off heat. Stir vigorously with spoon. This gives it a gloss.
- Cool. (The ganache will thicken as it cools).
- Assembling etc.:
- Frost the sides of the cake with the ganache. Sprinkle chocolate shavings etc. onto the sides & press gently. (I used a mix of grated Toblerone & chocolate sprinkles)
- Now cover the top of the cake with the remaining ganache. (I reserved some for the 'yin' & a little to glue the marzipan to the sides of the cake)
- Mark an area for the 'yin yang' with a round bowl. Place chocolate flakes around the edges, followed by the marzipan flowers, leaves, bugs etc. (see earlier post for making marzipan)
- Mix a little black food colour into the reserved ganache for the 'yin'.
- Melt some white chocolate with a tsp. of cream to make a white ganache for the 'yang'.
- Fill in the shapes; remember to mark the dots on either side.
- Chill till ready to eat!! Keep out at least an hour before serving.
- This is a luscious, light & chocolicious cake!

353. Yammy Chocolate Marble Cake Recipe

Serving: 16 | Prep: | Cook: 75mins | Ready in:

Ingredients

- 4 oz semisweet chocolate, melted
- 1 teaspoon vanilla extract
- 3 cups all-purpose flour
- 1-1/2 cups sugar
- 2 teaspoons baking powder
- 2 teaspoons baking soda
- 2 teaspoons cinnamon
- 1/2 teaspoon ground ginger
- 1/4 teaspoon ground cloves
- 1/2 teaspoon ground nutmeg
- 2 cups mashed, cold sweet potatoes
- 1 ¼ cups apple butter
- ¼ cup oil
- 4 eggs

Direction

- Preheat oven to 350F.
- Butter and lightly flour a 10-inch tube pan.
- Mix the melted chocolate together with the vanilla.
- Sift together the flour, sugar, baking powder, baking soda, cinnamon, ginger, cloves, and nutmeg. Set aside.
- In a large bowl beat the sweet potatoes, apple butter and oil together.
- Add the eggs one by one, beating until well blended.
- Slowly add the dry ingredients and mix well.
- Place ½ the mixture in another bowl and stir in the chocolate mixture.
- Alternate batters in the tube pan. With a knife cut through the layers and swirl together.
- Bake 1 ¼ hours or until the sides have shrunk away from the pan, and a tester comes out clean.
- Let cool for 10 minutes and remove from the pan and cool on a rack.

354. Yummy Chocolate Cake Recipe

Serving: 16 | Prep: | Cook: 15mins | Ready in:

Ingredients

- 1 pkg(181/4oz) chocolate cake mix
- 1 pkg.(2.1oz) sugar-free instant chocolate pudding mix
- 1 3/4c water
- 3 egg whites
- Frosting:
- 1 1/4c fat-free milk
- 1/4tsp almond extract
- 1 pkg(1.4oz) sugar-free instant chocolate pudding mix
- 1 carton(8oz)frozen reduced-fat whipped topping
- chocolate curls

Direction

- In a large mixing bowl, combine the cake mix, pudding mix, water and egg whites. Beat on low speed for 1 min; beat on medium speed for 2 mins.
- Pour into a 15x10x1" baking pan coated with cooking spray. Bake at 350 for 12-18 mins or till toothpick inserted near center comes out clean Cool on wire rack.
- For frosting, place milk and extract in a large bowl. Sprinkle with a third of the pudding mix; let stand 1 min. Whisk pudding into milk. Repeat twice with remaining pudding mix. Whisk pudding 2 mins. longer. Let stand for 15 minutes. Fold in whipped topping. Frost cake. Garnish with chocolate curls if desired.
- Calories: 197, Fat: 5g, Sat. Fat: 3g. Per slice

355. Zucchini Chocolate Cake Recipe

Serving: 8 | Prep: | Cook: 45mins | Ready in:

Ingredients

- 1/4 cup butter
- 1/2 cup vegetable oil
- 1 3/4 cups sugar
- 2 eggs
- 1 tsp. vanilla
- 1/2 cup buttermilk (or sour milk)
- 2 1/2 cups flour
- 1/4 cup cocoa
- 1/2 tsp. baking powder
- 1 tsp. baking soda
- 1/2 tsp. cinnamon
- 1/2 tsp. cloves
- 2 cups grated zucchini
- 1/4 cup chocolate chips

Direction

- Cream butter, oil, sugar, eggs, vanilla and buttermilk. Sift dry ingredients and add to creamed mixture. Mix in zucchini and chocolate chips. Bake in a greased and floured Bundt pan or a 9"x13" greased pan at 325 F. for 45 minutes. Delicious!

356. Zucchini Fudge Cashew Cake Recipe

Serving: 16 | Prep: | Cook: 2hours | Ready in:

Ingredients

- ½ cup unsweetened apple butter (or Zapple Butter)
- 2 tbsp cashew butter
- ⅓ cup brown sugar
- ¾ cup sugar
- 1 tbsp vanilla
- 3 cups finely shredded zucchini, lightly squeezed (about 1 lb)
- 2 cups GF all-purpose flour (mine was made of chickpea flour, potato starch, tapioca starch, sorghum flour and fava bean flour)
- ½ tsp guar gum
- ½ cup unsweetened cocoa
- 1 tsp baking soda
- ½ tsp salt
- ½ cup chopped cashews

Direction

- Preheat the oven to 350°F and line a 9" pan with parchment
- Mix apple butter, cashew butter, sugars, vanilla and zucchini in a large bowl.
- Add the flour, guar gum, cocoa, baking soda and salt, stirring to combine. Fold in the cashews.
- Bake for 45 minutes. Cool completely in the pan before turning out.

357. Chocolate Covered Cinnamon Apple Cake Recipe

Serving: 12 | Prep: | Cook: 35mins | Ready in:

Ingredients

- 5 eggs
- 200 g sugar
- 1 pkt vanilla sugar
- 1 pinch salt
- 1 tsp cinnamon
- 200 g ground hazelnuts
- 150 g spelt flour
- 2 tsp baking powder
- 250 soft margarine
- 1000 g apples
- 1 squeezed lime
- 200 g dark chocolate
- 100 g butter
- 1 tsp cinnamon
- 2 pkt vanilla sugar

Direction

- Beat eggs until frothy.
- Add sugar, salt, cinnamon and vanilla, and sugar and beat until sugar has dissolved.
- .
- Mix Ground hazelnuts, sifted flour and baking powder, together
- Add the margarine and mix everything together very well
- Cover a baking sheet with baking paper, and distribute the batter.
- .
- Peel apples, remove seeds and cut into thin slices and drizzle with lime juice.
- Spread sliced apples on dough.
- Bake in 160 ° C (325F) for about 35 minutes or apples tender and cake is done
- Melt chocolate with butter and cinnamon
- Spread (or drizzle well) over the cake as desired.
- Let cake cool completely before cutting

358. Chocolate And Apricot Tortilla Cake Recipe

Serving: 6 | Prep: | Cook: | Ready in:

Ingredients

- 7 tortillas
- 1 jar of hazelnut chocolate spread
- 1 can of apricot filling
- 1 pot of custard
- whipped double cream

Direction

- Put the first tortilla onto a plate and cover with chocolate spread.
- Follow with another tortilla and a layer of apricot filling.
- Add another tortilla and a layer of custard.
- Repeat the whole process once ending with a plain tortilla on top.
- Cover the top with cream and chill.

359. Chocolate Bar Cake Recipe

Serving: 8 | Prep: | Cook: 35mins | Ready in:

Ingredients

- 7 eggs
- 200g/ 1 ¾ cups caster sugar
- 150g/ 1 ¼ cups flour
- 50g/ ½ cup cocoa powder
- 50g/ 4 tbsp butter, melted
- Filling:
- 200g/ 7 oz Plain chocolate
- 125g/ ½ cup butter
- 50g/ 4 tbsp icing sugar
- Decoration:
- 75g/ 10tbsp toasted flaked almonds, crushed lightly

Direction

- Grease a deep 23cm/ 9inch square cake pan and line the base with baking parchment.
- Whisk the eggs and sugar in a mixing bowl for 10 minutes, until very light and foamy and the whisk leaves a trail when lifted.
- Sieve the flour and cocoa powder together and fold half into the mixture. Drizzle over the melted butter and fold in the rest of the flour and cocoa. Pour into the prepared pan and bake in a preheated oven 350F, for 30-35 minutes. Leave to cool in the pan
- Slightly and then remove and cool completely on a wire rack.
- To make the filling, melt the butter and chocolate together, then remove from the heat and stir in the icing sugar, leave to cool, and then beat until thick enough to spread.
- Halve the cake lengthways and cut each half into 3 layers. Sandwich the layers with the three-quarters of the chocolate filling. Spread the remainder over the cake and mark a wavy pattern on the top. Press the almonds on the sides.

360. Chocolate Cinnamon Flan Cake Recipe

Serving: 14 | Prep: | Cook: 75mins | Ready in:

Ingredients

- For the caramel sauce:
- 1 cup sugar.
- 1/3 cup butter.
- 3/4 cup whipping cream.
- 3 tbsp hazelnuts
- For the flan:
- 1 can sweeten condensed milk (410grams).
- 1 can evaporate milk (200 grams)
- 11/4 cups heavy cream.
- 5 eggs.
- 1 ½ oz cream cheese cold

- 1 tsp cinnamon
- 2 tbsp cocoa powder
- For the cake:
- 1 box vanilla cake mix.
- Decoration:
- 1 oz white chocolate, melted
- 1 oz plain chocolate, melted

Direction

- Heat the sugar over medium heat till it all dissolve and turn golden color, add the butter in small pieces stirring with a wooden spoon, add the cream in a steady stream so slowly while stirring. Pour the caramel in the pan and keep aside till cooled. Sprinkle with hazelnuts.
- In a mixer, combine all the flan ingredients and keep aside.
- Make the cake batter by following the instructions on the box.
- Pour the cake batter over the caramel sauce in the pan. Using a large spoon, add the flan mixture so slowly on top. Put the pan in a bigger tin and add boiling water to the tin till it comes 2cm of the pan base. Bake for 75minutes till a skewer inserted in the center comes out clean.
- Take out of oven and flip in a glass dish. Serve warm or cold. Can be stored covered in the refrigerator for 3 days.
- When cooled, decorate with hazelnuts, white and plain chocolate.

361. Chocolate Eclair Cake Recipe

Serving: 18 | Prep: | Cook: | Ready in:

Ingredients

- 1 box graham crackers
- 2 small boxes of vanilla instant pudding
- 3 cups cold milk
- 8 ounces Cool Whip
- --
- frosting;
- 4 Tbs. cocoa
- 2 Tbs. vegetable oil
- 2 tsp. vanilla extract
- 3 Tbs. softened butter
- 2 Tbs Karo syrup
- 1 1/2 cups confectioner's sugar
- 3 Tbs. milk

Direction

- Butter a 13" X 9" dish.
- Line bottom with graham crackers.
- mix pudding with milk; add cool whip, mix and spread 1/2 over crackers, place another layer of crackers and spread remainder of pudding mixture over the crackers, place a third layer of crackers.
- Refrigerate for 2 hours.
- >
- >
- Frosting;
- Beat all of the ingredients for frosting until smooth.
- Frost and refrigerate for 24 hour.
- Cut and serve.

362. Gooey Chocolate Cake Recipe

Serving: 58 | Prep: | Cook: 42mins | Ready in:

Ingredients

- 120g dark chocolate, 70% cocoa solids
- 5 eggs, separated
- 200g butter, softened, plus extra for greasing
- 220g caster sugar
- 90g plain flour, sifted, plus extra for dusting
- FOR THE FILLING
- 284ml pot double cream
- 200g pot half-fat crème fraîche

- 2 limes or 1 lemon, grated zest only
- FOR THE GANACHE icing
- 150g dark chocolate
- 142ml pot double cream
- 25g grated chocolate , to serve
- about 100g chocolate shaved into curls, to serve

Direction

- Grease and bottom line a 24cm spring form cake tin. Heat oven to 160C/fan 140C/gas. Melt 120g chocolate in a bowl. Cool for 5 mins, then beat in egg yolks. In a bowl, beat the butter and 100g sugar until soft and creamy. Mix in the melted chocolate and yolks.
- Whisk the egg whites to firm peaks then beat in remaining 120g sugar in three batches and continue whisking until stiff. Beat a third of the meringue into the chocolate mix. Then, gently fold in alternate spoonfuls of the flour and remaining meringue.
- Spoon into the tin, level and bake 40-45 mins until the top forms a light crust. Test the centre with a metal skewer, it should come out clean. Remove, cool 10 mins, before turning out of the tin. When cooled, cut in half carefully as it is fragile, with a large serrated knife.
- To make the filling: in a bowl beat the double cream until thickened, but not stiff. Then mix in the crème fraiche and the zest.
- Spread one half of the cake with all the zesty cream and sandwich together with the other half. Place on a rack with a large plate beneath.
- To make the ganache icing: break up the chocolate into a pan and add the double cream. Melt over the lowest heat and stir until smooth, then cool until the consistency of thick pouring cream. Pour over the cake.
- Let excess icing run onto the plate and spoon it back over to fill any gaps. Spread the icing evenly on the top and around the sides using the back of a spoon or a palette knife. While the icing sets sprinkle the grated chocolate on top and around the sides.
- Make the curls: You will need a large block of chocolate. Ensure the chocolate is at warm room temperature and placed on a worktop. Gordon used a sharp knife to make the curls, but it's easier to draw a swivel vegetable peeler down the side of a thick block of chocolate.
- Place a large ring cutter (about 10cm) in the centre of the cake and fill with the chocolate curls. Carefully remove the ring and let the curls cascade gently out. Serve at room temperature. If chilled ahead the cake should be allowed to come to room temperature before serving.

363. Leebears Quick Chocolate Banana Cake Recipe

Serving: 12 | Prep: | Cook: 35mins | Ready in:

Ingredients

- 1 box chocolate cake mix
- 4 snack size puddings(3.5oz each)ready to eat in plastic cups
- 2 large ripe bananas mashed up
- 2 tsp.cinnamon
- 1 tsp cloves
- 1/4 cup of melted margarine or butter
- 1 tub of chocolate frosting

Direction

- Preheat oven to 350.
- In large bowl combine dry cake mix, cinnamon & cloves - mix well.
- Add all puddings, bananas and melted margarine - mix well.
- Batter will be very thick - like frosting but don't worry.
- Place batter in buttered 9x13 baking pan spread evenly to ends and corners do not leave any gaps.
- Bake for 30 to 35 minutes - check with toothpick should come out clean.
- Let cool for at least 30 minutes - frost and refrigerate or enjoy.

- Refrigerate leftovers.

364. Vanilla Chocolate Pound Cake Recipe

Serving: 10 | Prep: | Cook: 70mins | Ready in:

Ingredients

- vanilla mixture:
- 2 cups plain flour
- 1/2 tsp baking powder
- ½ tsp salt
- 1 cup butter
- 1 2/3 cups granulated sugar
- 4 eggs
- ½ tbsp vanilla
- chocolate mixture:
- 1 3/4 cups plain flour
- ¼ cup cocoa powder
- 1/2 tsp baking powder
- ½ tsp salt
- 1 cup butter
- 1 2/3 cups granulated sugar
- 1 tsp instant coffee powder dissolved in 2 tsp hot water, cooled
- 4 eggs
- ½ tbsp vanilla
- Glaze:
- 8 oz plain chocolate, chopped
- ½ cup heavy cream
- 7 oz white chocolate, chopped
- ½ cup heavy cream

Direction

- Vanilla mixture:
- Preheat oven to 325F (165C). Butter and line the base of two 8 ½ x 4 ½ inch loaf pans.
- Line them with parchment paper and butter the paper. Sift together the flour, baking powder and salt. Beat the butter and sugar together till light and creamy. Break the eggs in a separate bowl and beat lightly, add ¼ cup of the eggs to the butter mixture and beat on medium speed until incorporated. Repeat with the remaining beaten eggs in 3 equal portions. Add vanilla and beat again.
- Add half of the flour mixture and beat in low speed until mixed well, then add the remaining flour and beat until no white streaks are visible.
- Chocolate mixture:
- Sift together the flour, cocoa powder, baking powder and salt. Beat the butter and sugar together till light and creamy. Add the instant coffee. Break the eggs in a separate bowl and beat lightly, add ¼ cup of the eggs to the butter mixture and beat on medium speed until incorporated. Repeat with the remaining beaten eggs in 3 equal portions. Add vanilla and beat again.
- Add half of the flour mixture and beat in low speed until mixed well, then add the remaining flour and beat until no white streaks are visible. Pour the mixtures in the prepared pans beginning with the vanilla mixture and then add a layer of the chocolate mixture. Keep repeating the process until ¾ the loaf pans. Bake for 1 hour and 10 minutes. Let cool in the pans for 30 minutes then invert on a wire rack to cool.
- Make the glaze:
- Heat heavy cream until simmering point and pour over the chopped plain chocolate, stir until smooth and let cool and thickened slightly. Repeat the same with the white chocolate. When cooled and thickened, pour the white chocolate first over the cooled cake then spoon the plain chocolate mixture over the white one and use a fork to a wavy pattern beginning from top to bottom. You want to give the look of wood. Let cool completely until glaze sets.

365. White Chocolate Hazelnut Creamy Cake Recipe

Serving: 10 | Prep: | Cook: 20mins | Ready in:

Ingredients

- 1 20 cm chocolate butter cake (follow my vanilla chocolate pound cake for best results, chocolate batter)
- white chocolate mousse:
- 2 eggs
- ½ tbsp cornstarch
- 2 tbsp sugar
- ¾ cup milk
- ½ tbsp gelatin powder
- 1 ½ tbsp water
- ¾ cup heavy cream
- 3 oz white chocolate
- 4 tbsp hazelnut, chopped
- chocolate glaze:
- 5 oz plain chocolate, chopped
- 1/3 cup heavy cream
- 3 whole hazelnuts
- white chocolate, melted

Direction

- Split the cake in half and set the bottom half in a 20cm cake ring in a serving platter. Keep the other in fridge for another use.
- Separate the eggs. Place the yolks and sugar in a large mixing bowl and whisk until well combined. Place the milk in a pan and heat gently, stirring until almost boiling. Pour the milk on to the egg yolks, whisking.
- Set the bowl over a pan of gently simmering water and cook, stirring until the mixture thickens enough to thinly coat the back of a wooden spoon.
- Sprinkle the gelatine over the water in a small heatproof bowl and leave to go spongy. Place over a pan of hot water and stir until dissolved. Stir into the hot mixture. Leave to cool.
- Whip the cream until just holding its shape. Fold into the egg custard. Melt the white chocolate. Fold into custard. Whisk egg whites until soft peaks and fold into the mixture. Pour over the prepared cake and level the top. Sprinkle chopped hazelnuts over the top Chill until set.
- Make the glaze:
- Heat cream until simmering point and pour over the chopped chocolate. Stir until smooth. Leave to cool and thickens. Pour over the chilled cake and decorate with hazelnuts and white chocolate. Chill again until serving time.

Index

A

Ale 83

Almond 3,6,14,35,132

Apple 3,5,8,37,38,94,188,215

Apricot 8,216

B

Baking 116,168

Banana 3,4,5,8,17,18,19,20,39,60,97,218

Beans 78

Beer 4,49

Berry 69

Blueberry 5,98

Bran 6,94,125,137

Bread 7,168,188

Butter 3,4,5,6,7,10,12,15,19,24,27,29,38,41,42,46,48,59,60,61,65,67,70,73,84,88,96,99,100,105,106,108,109,121,126,130,132,134,138,143,148,155,158,159,160,163,165,167,168,169,172,173,180,181,184,185,186,188,189,190,200,204,205,206,209,214,215,217,219

C

Cake 1,3,4,5,6,7,8,9,10,11,12,14,15,16,17,18,19,20,21,22,23,24,25,26,28,29,30,31,32,33,34,35,36,37,38,39,40,41,42,43,44,45,46,47,48,49,50,51,52,53,54,55,56,57,58,59,60,61,62,63,64,65,66,67,68,69,70,71,72,73,74,75,76,77,78,79,80,81,82,83,84,85,86,87,88,89,90,91,92,93,94,95,96,97,98,99,100,101,102,103,104,105,106,107,108,109,110,111,112,113,114,115,116,117,118,119,120,121,122,123,124,125,126,127,128,129,130,131,132,133,134,135,136,137,138,139,140,141,142,143,144,145,146,147,148,149,150,151,152,153,154,155,156,157,158,159,160,162,163,164,165,166,167,168,169,170,171,172,173,174,175,176,177,178,179,180,181,182,183,184,185,186,187,188,189,191,192,193,194,195,196,197,198,199,200,201,202,203,204,205,206,207,209,210,211,212,213,214,215,216,217,218,219,220

Calvados 38

Caramel 3,4,18,45,46,93,189

Carrot 3,4,29,46,47,61,72,83

Cashew 8,215

Caster sugar 55

Cheese 3,4,5,6,7,32,47,55,82,83,100,105,108,116,147,158,188

Cherry 3,4,5,6,7,32,33,35,49,50,51,52,56,83,99,153,174

Chocolate 1,3,4,5,6,7,8,9,10,11,12,13,14,15,16,17,18,19,20,21,22,23,24,28,29,30,31,32,33,34,35,36,37,38,39,40,41,42,43,44,45,46,47,48,49,50,51,52,53,54,55,56,57,58,59,60,61,62,63,64,65,66,67,68,69,70,71,72,73,74,75,76,77,78,79,80,81,82,83,84,85,86,87,88,89,90,91,92,93,94,95,96,97,98,99,100,101,102,103,104,105,106,107,108,109,110,111,112,113,114,115,116,117,118,119,120,121,122,123,124,125,126,127,128,129,130,131,132,133,134,135,136,137,138,139,140,141,143,144,145,146,147,148,149,150,151,152,153,154,155,156,157,158,159,160,162,163,164,165,166,167,168,169,170,171,172,173,174,175,176,177,178,179,180,181,182,183,184,185,186,187,188,189,191,192,193,194,195,196,197,198,199,200,201,202,203,204,205,206,207,209,210,211,212,213,214,215,216,217,218,219,220

Cider 39

Cinnamon 4,8,82,215,216

Cocoa powder 55,153

Coconut 4,5,7,8,54,100,110,145,170,202

Coffee 3,4,5,6,7,8,19,44,45,55,110,111,128,133,156,195

Cola 7,168

Cream 3,4,5,6,7,8,12,28,34,36,38,41,44,45,47,51,52,53,54,55,56,60,62,63,67,76,80,82,83,84,86,91,102,105,108,109,116,118,119,127,136,138,146,147,152,158,163,169,170,174,177,180,181,186,188,189,202,213,214,220

Custard 13

E

Egg 6,13,14,126,168

F

Fat 168,214

Flour 4,6,7,57,128,129,130,131,132,168,182

Fruit 5,8,85,202

Fudge 4,5,6,7,8,55,58,59,60,74,80,124,134,163,170,200,206,215

G

Gin 83

Gratin 69

H

Hazelnut 4,5,6,8,79,107,139,220

Honey 7,179

I

Ice cream 189

Icing 3,4,29,30,45,59,69,150,151,156,157,200

J

Jus 53,88,90,134,192,201

K

Kirsch 50

L

Liqueur 44,45

M

Macaroon 4,66

Madeira 113

Mango 6,8,151,210,211

Marshmallow 6,129,149

Mascarpone 5,111

Meringue 3,4,11,67,68

Milk 6,42,78,153,154,194

Mint 4,68,69,118,119

Molasses 93

N

Nougat 7,165

Nut 4,6,7,8,74,96,145,149,188,189,196

O

Oatmeal 4,70,71

Oil 20,83,158

Orange 3,4,6,7,36,71,72,83,156,168

P

Pastry 177

Peach 4,73

Pecan 4,7,59,145,170

Peel 49,186,207,215

Pepper 3,5,6,7,32,34,101,124,174,179

Pie 51

Pistachio 4,7,74,175

Polenta 3,4,35,75

Potato 4,7,8,75,189,203,205

Praline 3,4,7,14,76,77,122,175

Prune 4,78

Pulse 107

R

Raspberry 3,4,5,6,7,8,31,33,70,80,97,99,106,130,131,177,194,196,200

Rice 29,142

Ricotta 63,188

Rum 3,4,5,7,23,54,93,123,157

S

Seeds 208

Shin 119

Shortbread 107

Soda 4,83,116

Sponge cake 210,212

Strawberry 5,7,8,32,86,181,187,209,210

Sugar 102,123,153,168

Syrup 5,6,87,88,134,152,157

T

Tea 199

Toffee 5,88

Tofu 83

Truffle 5,7,8,101,102,103,183,198,206,210,211

V

Vegan 3,7,8,14,83,162,199

W

Walnut 5,94,95

Watercress 5,112

White chocolate 205

Y

Yam 8,213

Z

Zest 156,168

Conclusion

Thank you again for downloading this book!

I hope you enjoyed reading about my book!

If you enjoyed this book, please take the time to share your thoughts and post a review on Amazon. It'd be greatly appreciated!

Write me an honest review about the book – I truly value your opinion and thoughts and I will incorporate them into my next book, which is already underway.

Thank you!

If you have any questions, **feel free to contact at:** *author@bisquerecipes.com*

Lori Tyson

bisquerecipes.com

Printed in Great Britain
by Amazon